Work Energy, Power & Gravitation

for JEE Main & Advanced
(Study Package for Physics)

Fully Solved

disha
Nurturing Ambitions

Includes Past
JEE & KVPY Questions

Useful for Class 11,
KVPY & Olympiads

- **Head Office :** B-32, Shivalik Main Road, Malviya Nagar, New Delhi-110017
- **Sales Office :** B-48, Shivalik Main Road, Malviya Nagar, New Delhi-110017
  Tel. : 011-26691021 / 26691713

Page Layout : Prakash Chandra Sahoo

Typeset by Disha DTP Team

Printed at : **Repro Knowledgecast Limited, Thane**

DISHA PUBLICATION

For further information about the books from DISHA,
Log on to **www.dishapublication.com** or email to **info@dishapublication.com**

STUDY PACKAGE IN PHYSICS FOR JEE MAIN & ADVANCED

Booklet No.	Title	Chapter Nos.	Page Nos.
1	Units, Measurements & Motion	Ch 0. Mathematics Used in Physics Ch 1. Units and Measurements Ch 2. Vectors Ch 3. Motion in a Straight Line Ch 4. Motion in a Plane	1-202
2	Laws of Motion and Circular Motion	Ch 5. Laws of Motion and Equilibrium Ch 6. Circular Motion	203-318
3	Work Energy, Power & Gravitation	Ch 7. Work, Energy and Power Ch 8. Collisions and Centre of Mass Ch 9. Gravitation	319-480
4	Rotational Motion	Ch 1. Rotational Mechanics	1-120
5	Properties of Matter & SHM	Ch 2. Properties of Matter Ch 3. Fluid Mechanics Ch 4. Simple Harmonic Motion	121-364
6	Heat & Thermodynamics	Ch 5. Thermometry, Expansion & Calorimetry Ch 6. Kinetic Theory of Gases Ch 7. Laws of Thermodynamics Ch 8. Heat Transfer	365-570
7	Waves	Ch 9. Wave – I Ch 10. Wave –II	571-698
8	Electrostatics	Ch 0. Mathematics Used in Physics Ch 1. Electrostatics Ch 2. Capacitance & Capacitors	1-216
9	Current Electricity	Ch 3. DC and DC circuits Ch 4. Thermal and Chemical effects of Current"	217-338
10	Magnetism, EMI & AC	Ch 5. Magnetic Force on Moving Charges & Conductor Ch 6. Magnetic Effects of Current Ch 7. Permanent Magnet & Magnetic Properties of Substance Ch 8. Electromagnetic Induction Ch 9. AC and EM Waves	339-618
11	Ray & Wave Optics	Ch 1. Reflection of Light Ch 2. Refraction and Dispersion Ch 3. Refraction at Spherical Surface, Lenses and Photometry Ch 4. Wave optics	1-244
12	Modern Physics	Ch 5. Electron, Photon, Atoms, Photoelectric Effect and X-rays Ch 6. Nuclear Physics Ch 7. Electronics & Communication	245-384

Contents

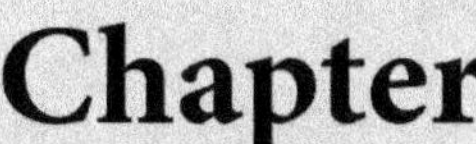

Chapter

7

Work, Energy and Power (319 -364)

Chapter contents

James Joule

James Joule (1818-1889) was the first person to show that a certain amount of mechanical work, such as turning a handle, produces a certain quantity of heat. In other words, mechanical work and heat are two different forms of the same thing energy. Joule's investigation of heat led to a new branch of science called thermodynamics, which shows how energy is converted from one form to another. ....

DEFINITIONS, EXPLANATIONS AND DERIVATIONS

7.1 WORK DONE BY CONSTANT FORCE

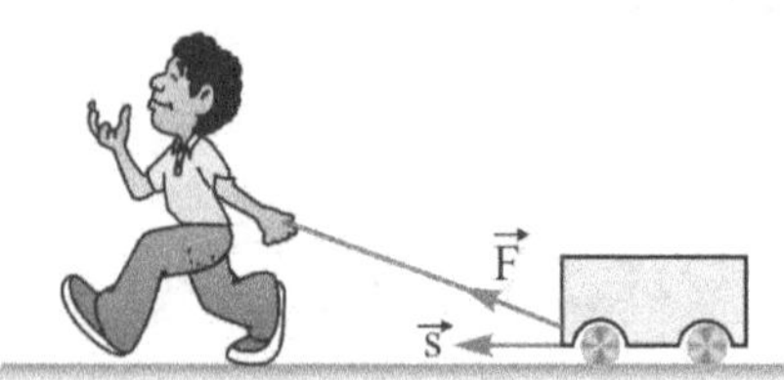

A child pulling the cart

Figure. 7.1

Consider a cart which is being pulled by applying a constant force as shown in *fig.* 7.2. Here force is along the string while cart is moving horizontally. The displacement of the cart is not in the direction of the applied force.

Suppose a constant force $\vec{F}$, makes an angle θ with the displacement. The work done by the force W, when its point of application undergoes a displacement $\vec{s}$, is defined as the product of the component of force in the direction of displacement and the displacement. Thus workdone

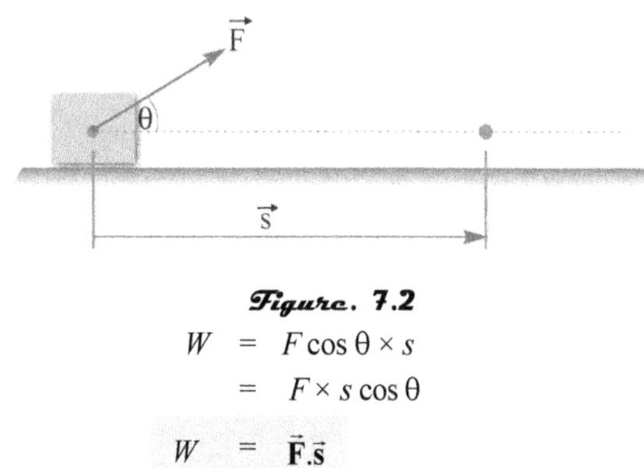

Figure. 7.2

$$W = F\cos\theta \times s$$
$$= F \times s\cos\theta$$

or $$W = \vec{F}.\vec{s}$$

Work done in different situations

Although work done is a scalar quantity but its value may be positive, negative or zero.

Positive work : Work done by the force will be positive for $\theta < 90°$. In practice there are numerous examples of positive work. When a body, falls under gravity ($\theta = 0°$); the work done by gravity is positive.

Here work done $= F_g s \cos 0 = F_g s$.

Figure. 7.3   *Figure. 7.4*

Negative work : Work done by a force will be negative for $\theta > 90°$. When a body is thrown up, the work done by gravity on the body is negative. Here work done $W = F_g s \cos 180° = -F_g s$.

Zero work done : Work done by force is zero if either $\theta = 90°$ or $\vec{s} = 0$. The work done by centripetal force in uniform circular motion, $W = Fs\cos 90° = 0$.

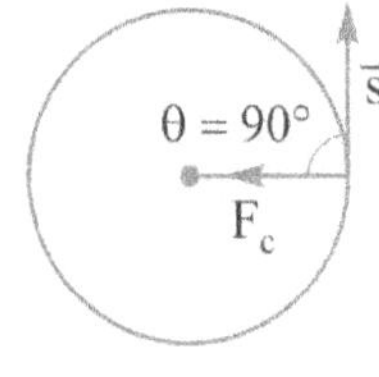

Figure. 7.5

Work done by friction

Friction can does positive, negative or zero work.

(i) **Work done by kinetic friction:** The force of kinetic friction acts opposite to the displacement of the block, so

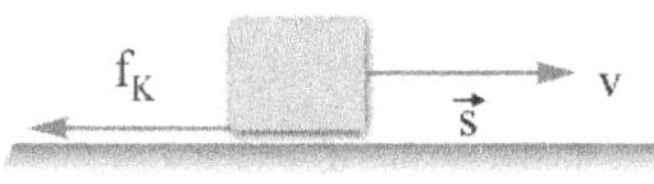

Figure. 7.6

$$W = f_k s \cos 180°$$
$$= -f_k s$$

(ii) **Work done by static friction:** The force of friction on the upper block is in the direction of displacement, so

$$W = f_s s \cos 0°$$
$$= +f_s s$$

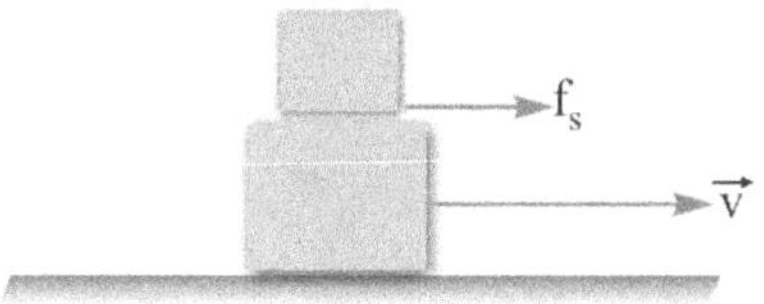

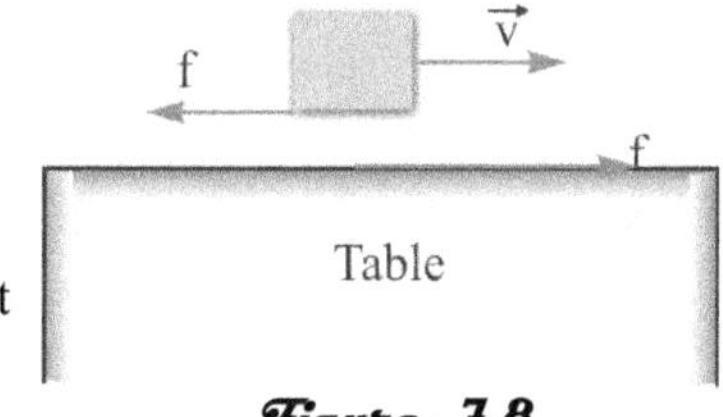
Figure. 7.7

(iii) **Work done by friction on the table is zero:** As table is not displaced by frictional force, so work done

$$W = F \times 0$$
$$= 0.$$

More about work done

(i) If force displaces the particle from its initial position $\vec{r}_i$ to final position $\vec{r}_f$, then displacement vector

$$\vec{s} = \vec{r}_f - \vec{r}_i.$$

∴ Work done, $$W = \vec{F}.\vec{s}$$

or $$W = \vec{F}.(\vec{r}_f - \vec{r}_i)$$

Figure. 7.8

(ii) In terms of rectangular components, the force and displacement vectors can be written as;

$$\vec{F} = F_x\hat{i} + F_y\hat{j} + F_z\hat{k}$$

and $$\vec{s} = x\hat{i} + y\hat{j} + z\hat{k}.$$

∴ Work done $$W = \vec{F}.\vec{s}$$

$$= (F_x\hat{i} + F_y\hat{j} + F_z\hat{k}).(x\hat{i} + y\hat{j} + z\hat{k})$$

or $$W = F_x x + F_y y + F_z z .$$

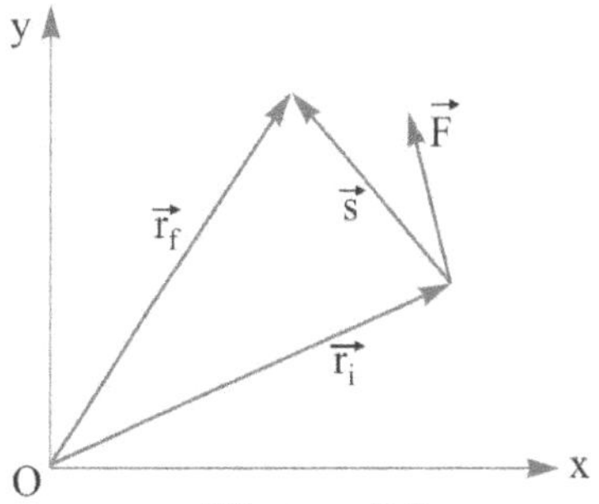

Figure. 7.9

7.2 WORK DONE BY VARIABLE FORCE

Let us calculate the work done when body moves from initial position s_i to final position s_f under the variable force $\vec{F}$ (see *fig.* 7.10). The displacement can be divided into a large number of small displacement Δs. During small displacement Δs, the force F can be assumed constant. Then work done in small displacement Δs.

$$\Delta W = F\Delta s = \text{area of the shaded strip}$$

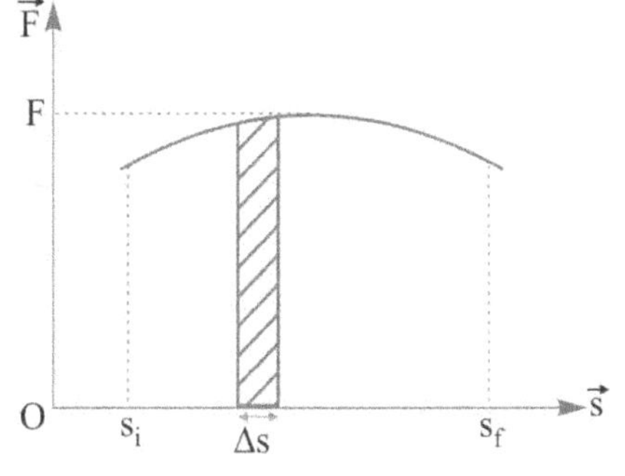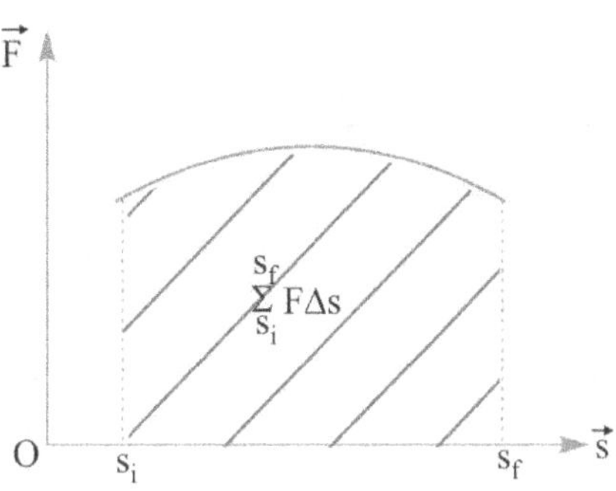
Figure. 7.10

Total work done, $$W = \Sigma(\Delta W)$$

$$= \sum_{s_i}^{s_f} F\Delta s$$

$$= \text{Area of shaded graph between } s_i \text{ and } s_f$$

We can take $\Delta s \rightarrow 0$, then

$$W = \lim_{\Delta s \rightarrow 0} \sum_{s_i}^{s_f} F\,\Delta s$$

or

$$W = \int_{s_i}^{s_f} F\,ds$$

Note :

When force varies in magnitude and direction both, work done

$$W = \int_{s_f}^{s_f} F\,ds\,\cos\theta$$

or

$$W = \int_{s_i}^{s_f} \vec{F}.d\vec{s}\,.$$

If

$$\vec{F} = F_x\,\hat{\mathbf{i}} + F_y\,\hat{\mathbf{j}} + F_z\,\hat{\mathbf{k}}$$

and

$$d\vec{s} = dx\,\hat{\mathbf{i}} + dy\,\hat{\mathbf{j}} + dz\,\hat{\mathbf{k}}\,,\text{ then}$$

$$W = \int (F_x\hat{\mathbf{i}} + F_y\hat{\mathbf{j}} + F_z\hat{\mathbf{k}}).(dx\hat{\mathbf{i}} + dy\hat{\mathbf{j}} + dz\hat{\mathbf{k}})$$

or

$$W = \int_{x_i}^{x_f} F_x\,dx + \int_{y_i}^{y_f} F_y\,dy + \int_{z_i}^{z_f} F_z\,dz\,.$$

Work done by spring

Consider a spring of force constant k. The force $\vec{F}$, exerted on the spring is proportional to the displacement $\vec{x}$ of the free end from its position when the spring is in the relaxed state. The force F is given by

$$\vec{F} = k\,\vec{x}\ \text{(Hooke's law)}\,.$$

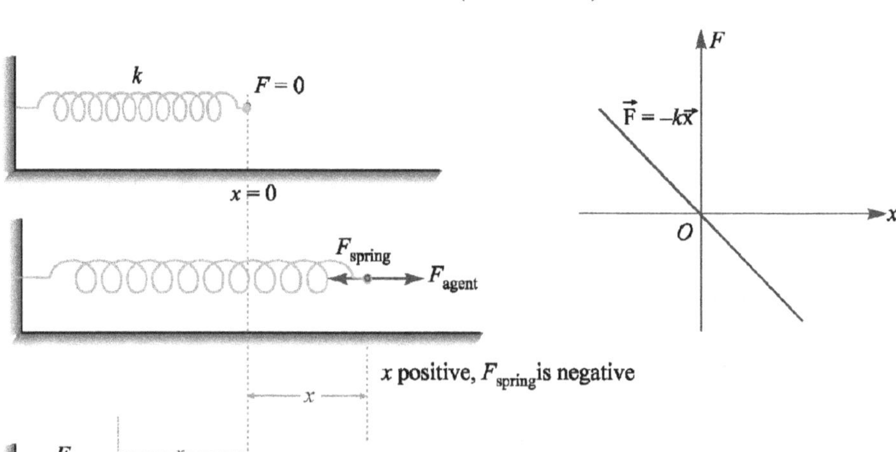

Figure. 7.11

Let the agent displaces the free end of the spring from its initial position x_i to a final position x_f, he does work on the spring and spring does opposite work on the agent.

The work done by the spring on the agent

$$W_{spring} = \int_{x_i}^{x_f} F\,dx = \int_{x_i}^{x_f} (-kx)\,dx = \left(-\frac{1}{2}k\right)\Big|x^2\Big|_{x_i}^{x_f}$$

$$= -\frac{1}{2}k(x_f^2 - x_i^2).$$

If $\qquad x_i = 0$ and $x_f = x$, then

$$W_{spring} = -\frac{1}{2}kx^2$$

Thus work done by the agent on the spring

$$W_{agent} = +\frac{1}{2}kx^2.$$

Note:

Work done by the spring is always $(-1/2\ kx^2)$; spring is either in extension or in compression.

7.3 KINETIC ENERGY

The energy possessed by a body by virtue of its motion is called its **kinetic energy.**

Consider a body of mass m which initially is at rest. A constant force $\vec{F}$ is applied on the body which produces a displacement $d\vec{s}$ in its direction. The work done by the force on the body is

$$W = \int F\,ds$$

$$= \int (ma)\,ds$$

$$= \int m\left(\frac{dv}{dt}\right)ds = \int m\left(\frac{ds}{dt}\right)dv$$

$$= \int_0^v mv\,dv = \frac{1}{2}mv^2. \qquad \left(\because \frac{ds}{dt} = v\right)$$

This work done appears as the kinetic energy (K) of the body. Thus kinetic energy

$$K = \frac{1}{2}mv^2.$$

As. $\qquad p = mv$

$\therefore \qquad K = \frac{p^2}{2m}$ or $p = \sqrt{2mK}.$

7.4 Work-energy theorem

Consider a body which is subjected to a system of forces (of any kind) $\vec{F}_1, \vec{F}_2, \ldots\ldots$. Let their resultant be $\vec{F}_{net}$ along the direction shown in *figure* 7.12.

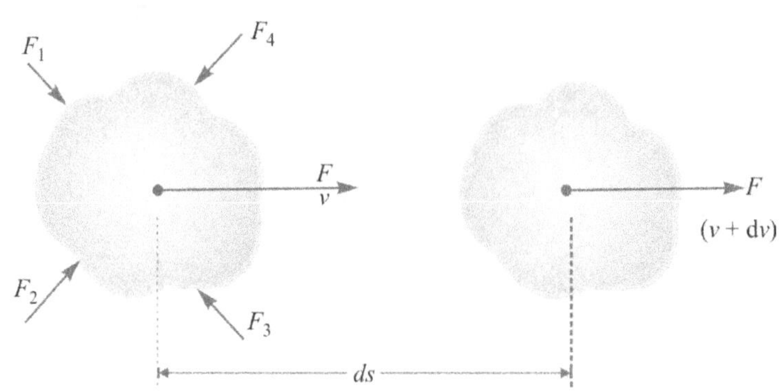

𝓕𝒾𝑔𝓊𝓇𝑒. 7.12

Suppose the velocity of body changes by dv after travelling a distance ds. By Newton's second law of motion, we have

$$F_{net} = ma$$

Multiplying both sides of above equation by *ds*, we have

$$F_{net}\,ds = ma\,ds$$

or

$$dW_{net\ force} = m\frac{dv}{dt}\,ds$$

or

$$dW_{net\ force} = m\left(\frac{ds}{dt}\right)dv$$

or

$$dW_{net\ force} = mv\,dv$$

Integrating both sides of above equation, we get

$$\int dW_{net\ force} = \int_{v_i}^{v_f} mv\,dv$$

or

$$W_{net\ force} = \frac{1}{2}m\left|v^2\right|_{v_i}^{v_f}$$

or

$$W_{net\ force} = \frac{1}{2}mv_f^2 - \frac{1}{2}mv_i^2$$

or

$$W_{net\ force} = K_f - K_i = \Delta K.E.$$

Thus work done by net force is equal to the change in kinetic energy of the body. This is called **work-energy theorem**.

Note:

1. The work-energy theorem is not independent of Newton's second law. It may be viewed as scalar form of second law.
2. Work-energy theorem holds in all types of frames; inertial or non-inertial. In non-inertial frame we have to include the pseudo force in the calculation of the net force.
3. Work-energy theorem is very useful in solving the problems where variable forces are involved. Because in using this theorem we need only initial and final velocities.

Work done by internal forces : Internal work

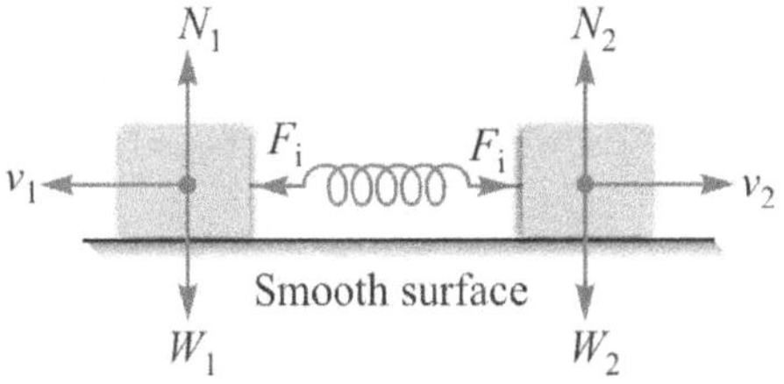

Let us consider a compressed spring is put in between two blocks and then placed on smooth surface. The blocks start moving away from each other. The forces acting on the blocks are; their weights W_1 and W_2, the upward reactions N_1 and N_2 exerted by the ground and internal force F_i.

The work done by N_1, N_2, W_1 and W_2 are zero because they are perpendicular to the displacements of the blocks. But the kinetic energy of the blocks will increase. Here work, being zero, is not equal to the increase in kinetic energy of the system. Here the new situation arises that the different parts of the system can move in relation to each other and thus can do work on each other, even in the absence of any interaction with externally applied forces. Such work is called **internal work**. Although internal forces play no role in accelerating the composite system, but their points of application can move so that work is done; thus the kinetic energy of blocks change even though the external forces do no work. Thus we have

$$W_{internal} = \Delta K.E.$$

When both external and internal forces act on the system, we can write

$$W_{external} + W_{internal} = \Delta K.E.$$

Work done by pseudo force

Consider a block A placed on block B, which is accelerating towards right with respect to ground. Let the velocity of block A changes from v_i to v_f. In accelerating frame, the forces on the block A are ; its weight, (W) acts vertically downward, normal reaction (N) vertically upward, frictional force (f_s) towards right and pseudo force towards left. The work done by W and N are zero because they act perpendicular to the displacement of the block A. Thus in this frame, we have

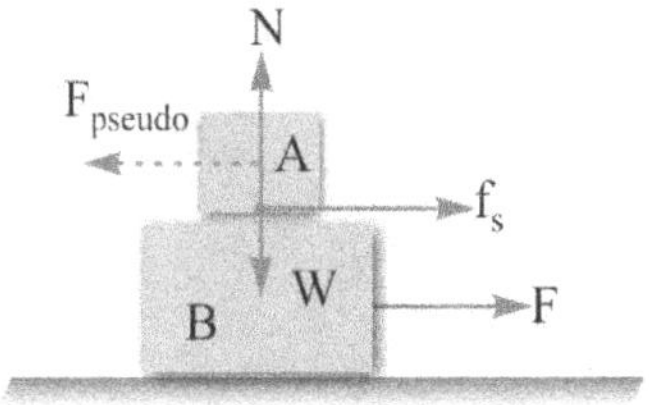

$$W_{friction} + W_{pseudo} = \Delta K.E.$$

If block A is at rest with respect to block B, then ΔK.E. = 0 and therefore

$$W_{pseudo} = -W_{friction}$$

Now it is more useful to write the work-energy theorem in non-inertial frame as;

$$W_{external} + W_{internal} + W_{pseudo} + W_{other} = \Delta K.E.$$

Conservative and non-conservative forces

If work done by the force in displacing a particle does not depend on path followed by the particle and depends only on ends points, the force is said to be **conservative**. *Examples; gravitational force, electrostatic force and elastic force.*

If work done by a force in displacing a particle depends on path, the force is said to be non-conservative or dissipative forces. *Examples; frictional force, viscous force.*

Note:

For two bodies, we can write, $\vec{F}_{12} + \vec{F}_{21} = 0.$

But the sum of the work done by the two forces need not always cancel, i.e., $W_{12} + W_{21} = 0$. However it may be true.

Work – energy theorem can also be written as ;

$$W_c + W_{nc} + W_{other} = \Delta K.E.$$

7.5 POTENTIAL ENERGY

The energy associated due to interaction between the particles of same body or between particles of different bodies is called **potential energy**. The following are the cases of potential energy :

- Energy due to interaction between particles of same body is called *self energy or internal potential energy* U_i.

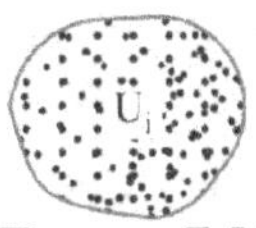

Figure. 7.15

- Energy due to interaction between particles of different bodies is called *external potential energy U_e* or simply potential energy.

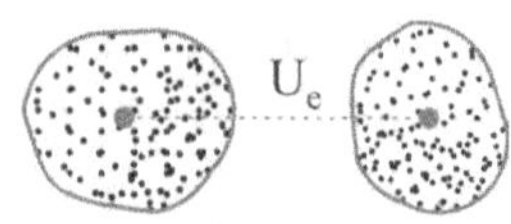

Figure. 7.16

- System of bodies possess, internal as well as external potential energy. Thus for the system of bodies, the total energy $U = U_i + U_e$.

Potential energy in relation to conservative force

The potential energy is the energy associated with the configuration of a system in which conservative force acts.

Let us consider a body-earth system in which body falls from some height. The work done by the gravity (conservative force) is positive. The body will achieve the state of lower potential energy. Thus we can say that work done by conservative force is equal to the decrease in potential energy of the system. Therefore,

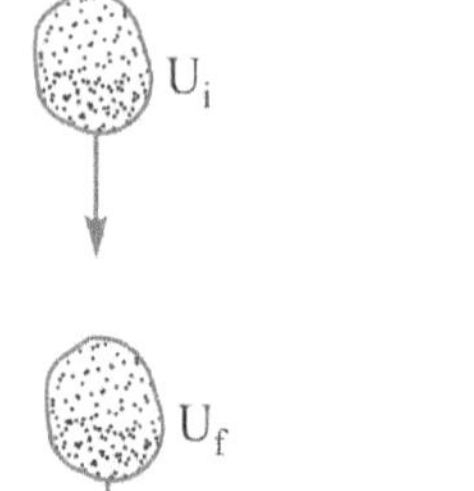

Figure. 7.17

$$W_c = -\Delta U. \qquad \text{...(i)}$$

Let Δx be the displacement in the direction of conservative force F_c, the work done for small displacement $\Delta W = F_c \Delta x$. From equation (i), we get

$$F_c \Delta x = -\Delta U$$

$$\Rightarrow \quad F_c = -\frac{\Delta U}{\Delta x}. \quad \text{For} \quad \Delta x \to 0,\ F_c = \frac{-dU}{dx}$$

For the *three dimensional force system,* we have

$$F_x = -\frac{\partial U}{\partial x},\ F_y = -\frac{\partial U}{\partial y}\ and\ F_z = -\frac{\partial U}{\partial z}.$$

The resultant force,

$$\vec{F} = -\left[\frac{\partial U}{\partial x}\hat{i} + \frac{\partial U}{\partial y}\hat{j} + \frac{\partial U}{\partial z}\hat{k}\right] ....(ii)$$

Here symbol ∂ uses for *partial differentiation.*

7.6 MECHANICAL ENERGY

The sum of the kinetic energy and potential energy of the body is called ***mechanical energy***. Thus

$$M.E. = K.E. + P.E.$$

$$\text{or} \qquad E = K + U .$$

Principle of conservation of mechanical energy

We know the work -energy theorem;

$$W_c + W_{nc} + W_{other} = \Delta K.E.$$

$$\text{Also} \qquad W_c = -\Delta P.E.$$

$$\therefore \quad -\Delta P.E. + W_{nc} + W_{other} = \Delta K.E.$$

$$\text{or} \qquad W_{nc} + W_{other} = \Delta K.E. + \Delta P.E.$$

$$\text{or} \qquad W_{nc} + W_{other} = \Delta M.E.$$

If only conservative forces act on the body, then we have, $W_{nc} = 0$ and $W_{other} = 0$

$$\therefore \qquad 0 = \Delta M.E.$$

$$\text{or} \qquad M.E. = \text{Constant.}$$

Note:

(1) When work done by conservative force is positive, the potential energy of body decreases.

(2) Work done by a body against friction results in a loss of its kinetic energy.

Determining the potential energy

Suppose that a force $\vec{F}$, *either weight or a spring force*, acts on a particle and does an amount of work W, then

$$W = -\Delta U. \qquad \ldots (i)$$

For one-dimensional force from (i), we have

$$\int_{x_0}^{x} F dx = -[U(x) - U(x_0)]$$

or $\qquad U(x) - U(x_0) = -\int_{x_0}^{x} F dx \qquad \ldots (ii)$

where x_0 is an arbitrary reference configuration, and $U(x_0)$ is the corresponding potential energy of the system, which is usually set equal to zero. Thus we can write equation (ii) as;

$$U(x) = -\int_{x_0}^{x} F dx, \quad \text{where } U(x_0) = 0. \qquad \ldots (iii)$$

Gravitational potential energy

Consider a particle moving up or down along a vertical y-axis close to earth's surface, acted on only by the gravitational force. That force is $F(y) = -mg$, where minus indicates that the force is downward. The gravitational potential energy

$$U(y) = -\int_{0}^{y=h} F dy$$

$$= -\int_{0}^{y=h} (-mg) dy$$

or $\qquad U_g = mgh$

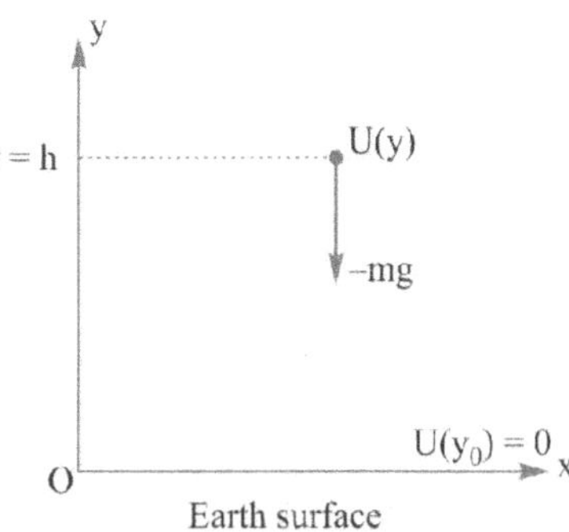

Figure. 7.18

Elastic potential energy (Internal energy)

Let us choose the reference configuration (x) of a spring, (x_0) to be its relaxed state. Thus $U(x_0) = 0$. The elastic potential energy of the spring

$$U_{el} = -\int_{0}^{x} F dx$$

$$= -\int_{0}^{x} (-kx) dx$$

or $\qquad U_{el} = \dfrac{1}{2} kx^2.$

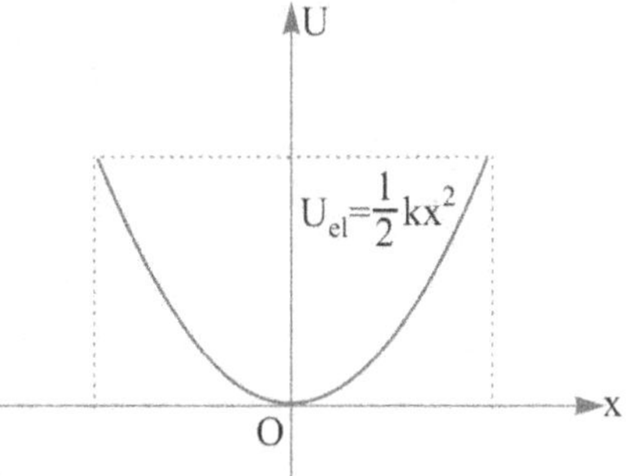

Figure. 7.19

> *Note:*
> Potential energy depends on the reference level chosen, but difference of potential energy does not depend on the reference level.

7.7 PRINCIPLE OF CONSERVATION OF ENERGY

In numerous examples we have seen that one form of energy is converting into another form, yet its total amount remains constant. This is the principle of conservation of energy which can be stated as; **The total energy of isolated system remains constant.**

7.8 EINSTEIN'S MASS-ENERGY EQUIVALENCE

In 1905, Albert Einstein discovered that mass can be converted into energy. He showed that mass and energy are equivalent and are related as; $E = mc^2$, where c is the speed of light in vacuum which is approximately 3×10^8 m/s.

FORMULAE USED

1. Work done by constant force, $W = \vec{F}.\vec{s} = Fs\cos\theta$
   For $\theta = 0$, $W = Fs$.

2. Work done by variable force, $W = \int_{s_1}^{s_2} \vec{F}.d\vec{s}$

   For $\theta = 0$, $\qquad\qquad W = \int_{s_1}^{s_2} Fds$

3. Work done by graph : W = area under the force-displacement graph between s_1 and s_2.

4. Work done by spring :
   Work done in stretching or compressing the spring
   $$W = \frac{1}{2}kx^2.$$
   Work done by the spring on the agent
   $$W = -\frac{1}{2}kx^2.$$

5. Kinetic energy, $K = \frac{1}{2}mv^2 = \frac{P^2}{2m}$.

6. Work-energy theorem : $W_{\text{net force}} = K_f - K_i$

7. Potential energy : Potential energy in relatioin to conservative force,
   $$W_c = -\Delta U$$
   and conservative force, $F_c = -\dfrac{\Delta U}{\Delta s}$.

8. Mechanical energy = kinetic energy + potential energy
   or $\qquad\qquad\qquad E = K + U$
   If system is acted by conservative forces only, then
   $\qquad\qquad\qquad$ M.E. = constant

9. Gravitational potential energy, $U = mgh$.

10. Elastic potential energy, $U = \frac{1}{2}kx^2$.

Problem-solving strategy : Work and kinetic, potential energy

Identify the relevant concept : In the problems, involving speeds of the body at different positions, work-energy theorem is extremely useful. In case if only conservative forces are acting on the body, then we can use conservation of mechanical energy.

Set up the problem :

1. Choose the initial and final positions of the body, and draw FBD, showing all the forces acting on the body.

2. List the known and unknown quantities. The unknowns may be the body's displacement or any force or initial and find speeds.

Execute the solution :

1. Use work-energy theorem,
   $$W_{\text{all forces}} = K_f - K_i$$

2. If only conservative forces are acting, then we can use
   $$[K_i + U_i] = [K_f + U_f]$$
   Finally, solve the equations to get the unknowns.

EXAMPLES BASED ON WORK, KINETIC AND POTENTIAL ENERGY

Example 1. A body constrained to move along the z–axis of a coordinate system is subjected to a constant force $\vec{F} = (-\hat{i} + 2\hat{j} + 3\hat{k})\,\text{N}$ where $\hat{i}, \hat{j}$ & $\hat{k}$ are unit vector along the x, y & z– axis respectively. What is the work done by this force in moving the body over a distance of 4m along the z-axis?

[NCERT]

Sol. $\vec{F} = (-\hat{i} + 2\hat{j} + 3\hat{k})N$ and $\vec{s} = 4\hat{k}$ m

Work done

$$W = \vec{F}.\vec{s} = (-\hat{i} + 2\hat{j} + 3\hat{k}).(4\hat{k}) = 12\,J \cdot$$

Example 2.

Figure. 7.20

In *figure* 7.20 (a) the man walks 2 m carrying a mass of 15 kg on his hands. In figure (b), he walks the same distance pulling the rope behind him. The rope goes over a pulley and mass of 15 kg hangs at its other end. In which case is the work done greater?   [NCERT]

Sol.

(a)   Work done by the man against gravity is zero. Because displacement of block is perpendicular to the force applied (N) by him on the block.

(b)   Work has to be done against gravity ; $W = T s = mg \times 2 = 2\,mg$ J. In addition to this, work is to be done against friction while moving a distance of 2 m. Thus the work done in case (b) is greater than in case (a).

Example 3. A person is holding a bucket by applying a force of 10 N. He moves a horizontal distance of 10 m and then climbs up a vertical distance of 10 m. Find the total work done by him. [NCERT]

Sol. For his horizontal motion

$$W_H = F s_H \cos 90° = 0.$$

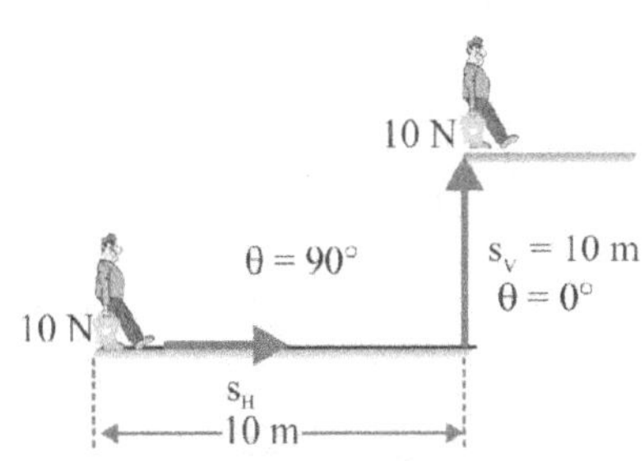

Figure. 7.21

For his vertical motion

$$W_v = F s_v \cos 0°$$
$$= 10 \times 10 \times 1 = 100 \text{ J}.$$

Thus total work done $= W_H + W_v$
$$= 100 \text{ J} \qquad\qquad Ans.$$

Example 4. A body moves from point A to B under the action of a force, varying in magnitude as shown in *figure* 7.22. Obtain the work done. Force is expressed in newton and displacement in metre.

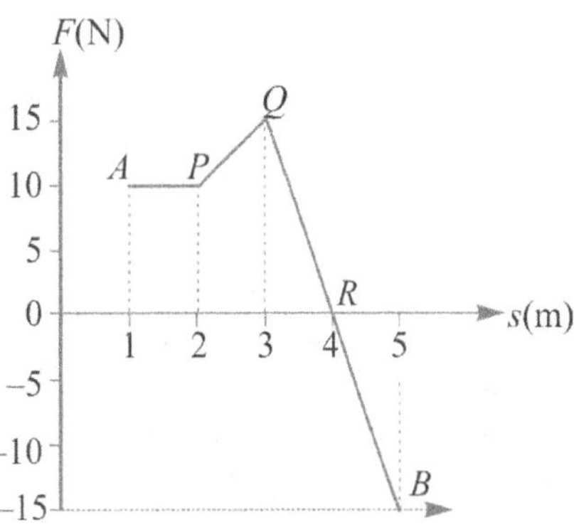

Figure. 7.22

Sol. Work done = Area under F-s graph

or $$W_{AB} = W_{AP} + W_{PQ} + W_{QR} + W_{RB}$$

$$= 10 \times 1 + \frac{1}{2}(10+15) \times 1 + \frac{1}{2}$$
$$\times 1 \times 15 - \frac{1}{2} \times 1 \times 15$$
$$= 22.5 \text{ J.} \qquad\qquad Ans.$$

Example 5. Under the action of force, 2 kg body moves such that its position x as a function of time t is given by $x = \dfrac{t^3}{3}$, x is in metre and t in second. Calculate the work done by the force in the first 2 second.

Sol. Method -I

Given that $$x = \frac{t^3}{3}$$

$\therefore$ Velocity $$v = \frac{dx}{dt} = t^2$$

$\Rightarrow$ $$dx = t^2 dt$$

Acceleration $$a = \frac{dv}{dt} = 2t$$

$\therefore$ Force $$F = ma$$
$$= 2(2t) = 4t$$

Work done by the force

$$W = \int F dx$$

$$= \int_0^2 4t(t^2 dt)$$

$$= 4 \int_0^2 t^3 dt$$

$$= 4 \left| \frac{t^4}{4} \right|_0^2$$

$$= \frac{4}{4}(2^4 - 0^4)$$

$$= 16 \text{ J} \cdot \qquad\qquad Ans.$$

Method -II By work - energy theorem

Given $\quad x = t^3/3$

$\therefore$ Velocity $\quad v = \dfrac{dx}{dt} = t^2$

At $t = 0$, $\quad v_i = 0^2 = 0$

At $t = 2$, $\quad v_f = 2^2 = 4$ m/s

Work done $\quad W = \dfrac{1}{2}m(v_f^2 - v_i^2)$

$$= \dfrac{1}{2} \times 2 \times (4^2 - 0)$$

$$= 16 \text{ J}. \qquad \qquad \textit{Ans.}$$

Example 6. An object of mass 5 kg falls from rest through a vertical distance of 20 m and reaches with a velocity of 10 m/s. How much work is done by push of air on the object? ($g = 9.8$ m/s^2)

Sol. The forces acting on the object are:

(i) Weight of the object mg downward

(ii) Push of air upward let F

Work done by gravity

$$W_g = mg \times 20 = 20\, mg$$

Let work done by push of air be W_F, then by work-energy theorem,

$$W_g + W_F = \Delta \text{K.E.}$$

or $\quad 20\, mg + W_F = \dfrac{1}{2}m(10^2 - 0^2)$

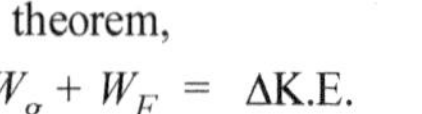

Figure. 7.23

$$\Rightarrow \qquad W_F = \dfrac{1}{2}m \times 10^2 - 20mg$$

$$= 50 \times 5 - 20 \times 5 \times 9.8 = -730 \text{ J}. \textit{ Ans.}$$

Example 7. Given below (*figure 7.24*) are examples of some potential energy functions in one dimension. The total energy of the particle is indicated by a cross on the ordinate axis. In each case, specify the regions, if any, in which the particle cannot be found for the given energy. Also, indicate the minimum total energy the particle must have in each case. Think of simple physical contexts for which these potential energy shapes are relevant.

[NCERT]

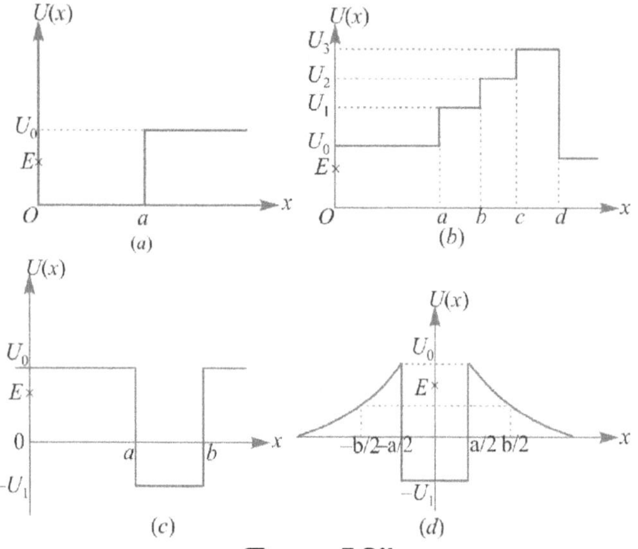

Figure. 7.24

Sol. Total mechanical energy

$$E = K + U$$

$\therefore \qquad K = E - U$

As kinetic energy K is always positive, so particle can exist for U value less than E.

(a) For $x > a$, $U > E$

$\Rightarrow K$ becomes negative, hence particle cannot exist in the region $x > a$.

(b) For any value of x, $U > E$, $\therefore$ the particle cannot exist.

(c) In a region $x < a$ and $x > b$, the value $U > E$,

$\therefore K$ is negative. The particle cannot be found in these regions.

(d) In the region $-b/2 < x < -a/2$, $U > E$, hence particle cannot be found into the region. For $a/2 < x < b/2$, $U \leq E$. Hence particle may be found twice

Example 8. A rod of mass m and length *l* is held vertical. Find its gravitational potential energy with respect to zero potential energy at its lower end.

Sol. Choose a small element of length dy, its mass

$$dm = \dfrac{m}{\ell}dy .$$

The potential energy of the element

$$dU = (dm)gy.$$

The potential energy of the entire rod

$$U = \int_0^\ell (dm)g\, y$$

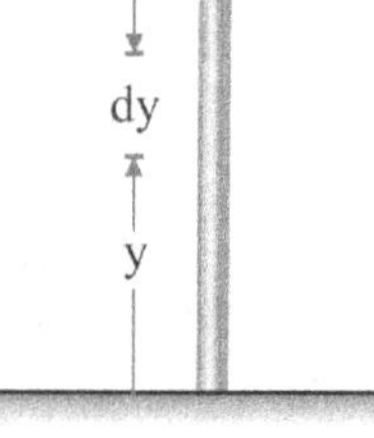

Figure. 7.25

$$= \dfrac{m}{\ell}g\int_0^\ell y\,dy = \dfrac{m}{\ell}g\left|\dfrac{y^2}{2}\right|_0^\ell = \dfrac{mg\ell}{2} .$$

The gravitational potential energy of an object of uniform size and density can be simply calculated as; $U = mg \times$ height of centre of gravity from the reference level.

Example 9. A uniform chain of length *l* and mass *m* overhangs a smooth table with its two third part lying on the table. Find the kinetic energy of the chain as it completely slip of the table.

Sol.

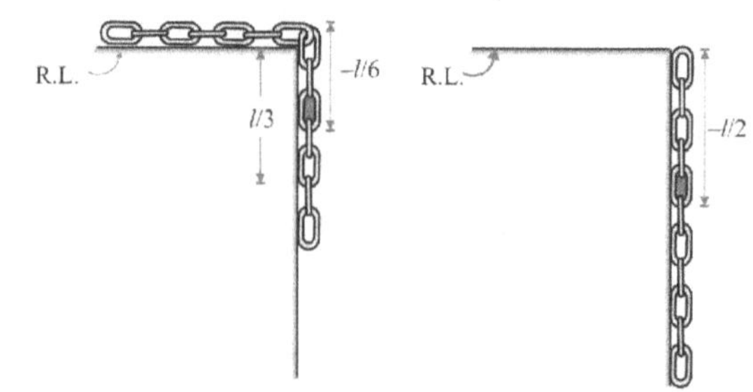

Figure. 7.26

With respect to the top of the table, the initial potential energy of the chain

U_i = P.E. of the chain lying on the table + P. E. of the over hanging part of the chain

$$= \dfrac{2m}{3}g \times 0 + (m/3)g \times (-\ell/6) = -\dfrac{mg\ell}{18} .$$

P.E. of chain at the instant of slip

$$U_f = 0 + mg(-\ell/2) = -\frac{mg\ell}{2}.$$

Since only gravity is acting on the chain, therefore we have

$$-\Delta U = \Delta K$$

or
$$\Delta K = -(U_f - U_i)$$

$$= -\left[\frac{-mg\ell}{2} - \left(\frac{-mg\ell}{18}\right)\right] = \frac{4}{9}mg\ell$$

Since
$$K_i = 0$$

$$\therefore \qquad K_f = \frac{4}{9}mg\ell. \qquad\qquad \textit{Ans.}$$

Example 10. **The potential energy of a diatomic molecule is given by**

$$U = \frac{A}{r^{12}} - \frac{B}{r^6}$$

where r is the separation between the atoms that make up the molecule and A and B are positive constants. This potential energy is due to the force that binds the atoms together.

(a) **Find the equilibrium separation, that is , the distance between the atoms at which force on each atom is zero. Is the force repulsive (the atoms are pushed apart) or attractive (they are pulled together) if their separation is**

(b) **smaller and**

(c) **larger than the equilibrium separation?**

Sol.

(a) The force is radial i.e. along the line joining the atoms. Which can be obtained as

$$F = \frac{-dU}{dr} = \frac{12A}{r^{13}} - \frac{6B}{r^7}. \qquad\qquad ...(i)$$

At the equilibrium separation r_0, $F = 0$

or
$$\frac{12A}{r^{13}} - \frac{6B}{r^7} = 0$$

$$r = r_0 = 1.12\,(A/B)^{1/6}.$$

(b) Differentiating (i) w.r.t. r, we have

$$\frac{dF}{dr} = -\frac{12 \times 13A}{r^{14}} + \frac{7 \times 6B}{r^8} \qquad\qquad ...\,(ii)$$

Substituting the value of r_0, we get

$$dF/dr = -15\,A^{-4/3}B^{7/3}$$

The derivative is negative so the force is positive if r is slightly less than r_0. *Ans.*

(c) If r is slightly greater than r_0 the force is negative, indicating force of attraction.

Example 11. **In *figure* 7.27, a block slides along a track from one level to a higher level by moving through an intermediate valley. The track is frictionless until the block reaches the higher**

level. **There is a frictional force stops the block in a distance d. The block's initial speed v_0 is 6.0 m/s; the height difference h is 1.1 m; and the coefficient of kinetic friction μ is 0.60. Find d.**

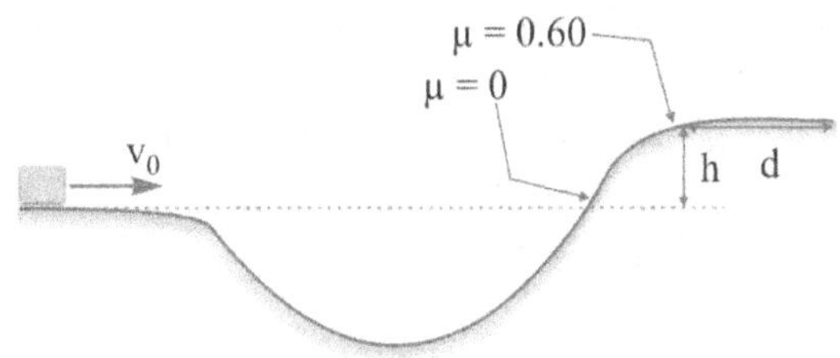

Figure. 7.27

Sol. Loss in kinetic energy = gain in potential energy + work done against friction

or
$$\frac{1}{2}mv_0^2 = mgh + F_1 \times d$$

or
$$\frac{1}{2}mv_0^2 = mgh + \mu mg \times d$$

Substituting $\qquad h = 1.1$ m and $\mu = 0.60$, we get

$$d = 1.2 \text{ m.} \qquad\qquad \textit{Ans.}$$

Example 12. **In *fig.* 7.28, what constant force P is required to bring the 50 kg body, which starts from rest, to a velocity of 10 m/s in 7 m? Neglect friction.**

Sol. Work done by force P in displacing the block by 7m

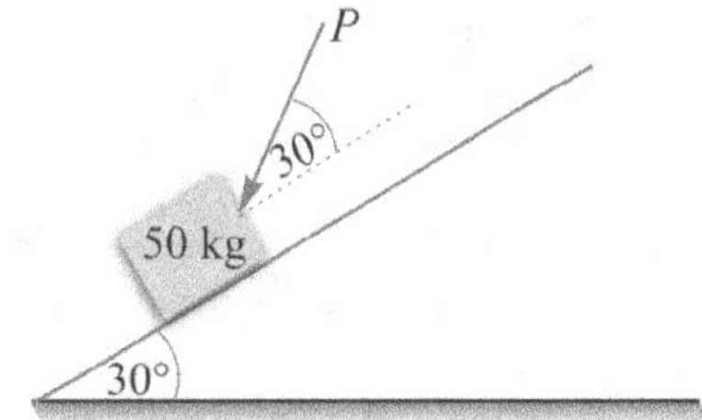

Figure. 7.28

$$W_1 = Fs\cos\theta$$

$$= P \times 7 \times \cos 30° = \frac{7\sqrt{3}}{2}P \text{ J}.$$

$$W_2 = mgh = 50 \times 9.8 \times 7\sin 30° = 1715.$$

Using work-energy theorem, $W = \Delta K.E.$

or
$$W_1 + W_2 = \frac{1}{2}m(v_f^2 - v_i^2)$$

or
$$\frac{7\sqrt{3}}{2}P + 1715 = \frac{1}{2} \times 50 \times (10^2 - 0^2)$$

or
$$6.06\,P + 1715 = 2500$$

$$\therefore \qquad P = 129.5 \text{ N.} \qquad\qquad \textit{Ans.}$$

Example 13. A person trying to lose weight lifts a 10 kg mass, to a height of 0.5 m each time for 1000 times. Assume that PE lost each time she lowers the mass is dissipated

[NCERT]

(a) How much work does she do against the gravitational force?

(b) Fat supplies 3.8×10^7 J of energy/kg which is converted to mechanical energy with a 20% efficiency rate. How much fat will the dieter use up?

Sol. (a) $m = 10$kg, h = 0.5 m, $n = 1000$

Work done against the gravitational force

$= n$ (mg$h$)

$= 1000 \times 10 \times 9.8 \times 0.5 = 49000$ J.

(b)   Mechanical energy supplied by 1 kg of fat

with 20% efficiency $= 3.8 \times 10^7 \times \dfrac{20}{100}$

$= 0.76 \times 10^7$ J

or 0.76×10^7 J energy is supplied by

$= 1$ kg fat.

$\therefore$ Fat used up by dieter in the exercise

$= \dfrac{1}{0.76 \times 10^7} \times 49000 = 6.45 \times 10^{-3}$ kg

---

In Chapter Exercise 7.1

1. You drop a 2.00 kg textbook to a friend who stands on a ground 10.0 m below the textbook without stretched hands 1.50 m above the ground (see figure).

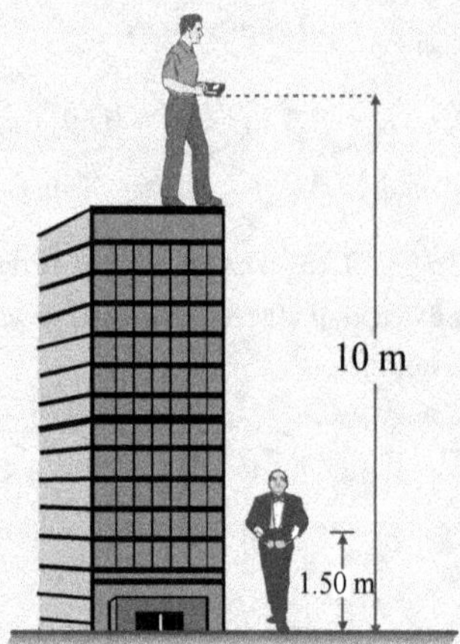

(a) How much work W is done on the textbook by the gravitational force as it drops to your friend's hands?

(b) What is the change ΔU in the gravitational potential energy of the textbook-earth system during the drop? If the gravitational potential energy U of that system is taken to be zero at ground level, what is U when the testbook

(c) is released and (d) reaches the hands ?
Now take U to be 100 J at ground level and again find (e) W, (f) ΔU (g) U at the release point, and (h) U at the hands. (Take $g = 10$ m/s^2)

Ans. (a) 170 J   (b) $\Delta U = -170$ J   (c) 200 J
      (d) 30 J   (e) 170 J   (f) $\Delta U = -170$ J
      (g) 300 J   (h) 130 J.

2. Figure shows a ball with mass m=1kg attached to the end of a thin rod with length 1m and negligible mass. The other end of the rod is pivoted so that the ball can move in a vertical circle. The rod is held in the horizontal position as shown and then given enough of a downward push to cause the ball to swing down and around and just reach the vertically upward position, with zero speed there. How much work is done on the ball by the gravitational force from the initial point to (a) the lowest point, (b) the highest point, and (c) the point on the right at which the ball is level with the initial point ? If the gravitational potential energy of the ball-earth system is taken to be zero at the initial point, what is the value when ball reaches (d) the lowest point, (e) the highest point, and (f) the point on the right that is level with the initial point ? (g) suppose the rod is pushed harder so that the ball passed through the highest point with non zero speed. Would the change in the gravitational potential energy from the lowest point to the highest point then be greater, less or the same ? ($g = 10$ m/s^2)

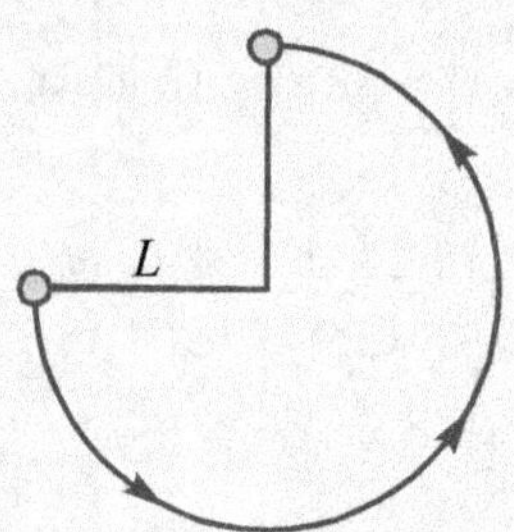

Ans. (a) $mgL = 10$ J   (b) $-mgL = -10$ J
     (c) 0   (d) $-mgL = -10$ J
     (e) $mgL = 10$ J   (f) 0
     (g) same.

3. Figure shows a frictionless roller coaster of mass m tops the first hill with speed v_0. How much work does the gravitational force do on it from that point to (a) point A (b) point B (c) the speed at point C.

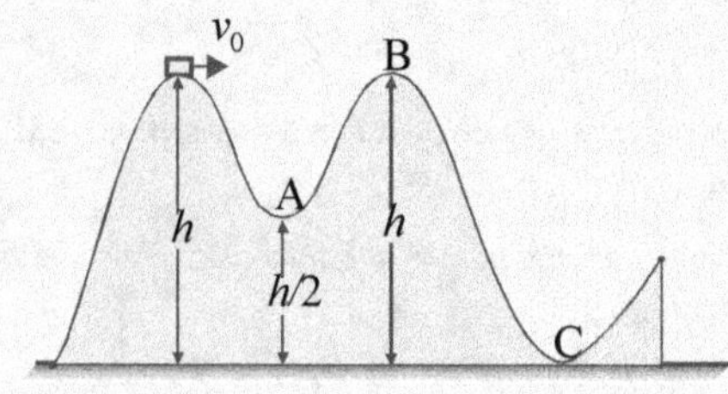

Ans. (a) $\dfrac{mgh}{2}$ (b) **zero**   (c) $\sqrt{v_0^2 + 2gh}$

4. A unidirectional force acting on a particle of mass 16 kg is plotted in figure. What is the velocity of the particle at 40 s ? Initially the particle is at rest. *Ans.* **55.78 m/s**

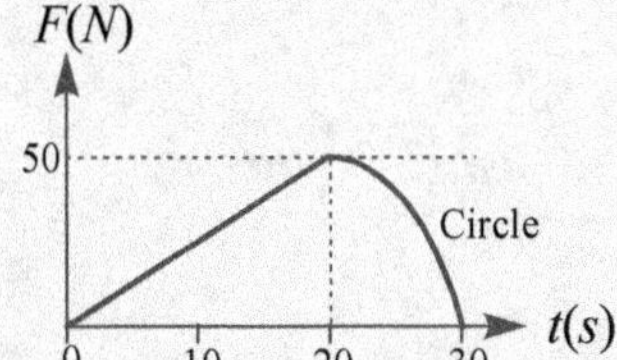

5. A body weighing 300 N is pushed up a 30^0 plane by a 400 N force acting parallel to the plane. If the initial velocity of the body is 1.5 m/s and coefficient of kinetic friction is $\mu = 0.2$, what velocity will the body have after moving 6 m ?

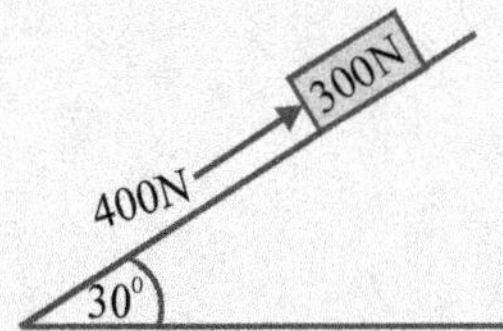

Ans. v = **8.94 m/s**

6. In what distance will body A of figure attain a velocity of 3 m/s, starting from rest ? Take $\mu = 0.2$. Pulleys are frictionless and massless.

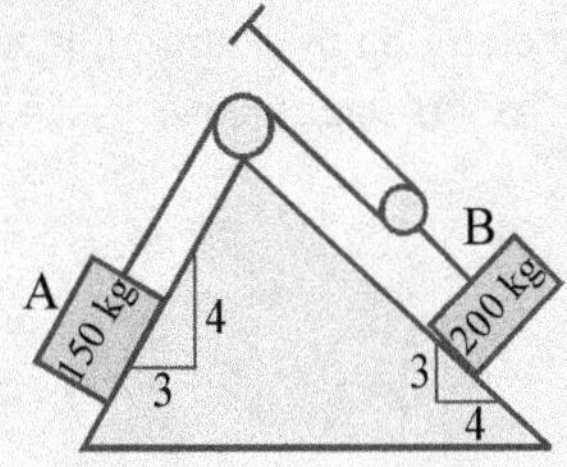

Ans. s = **3.529 m**

7. A string with one end fixed on a rigid wall, passing over a fixed frictionless pulley at a distance of 2 m from the wall, has a point mass 2 kg attached to it at a distance of 1 m from the wall. A mass m = 0.5 kg attached to the free end is held at rest so that the string is horizontal between the wall and the pulley and vertical beyond the pulley. What will be the speed with which the mass M will hit when the mass m is released ?

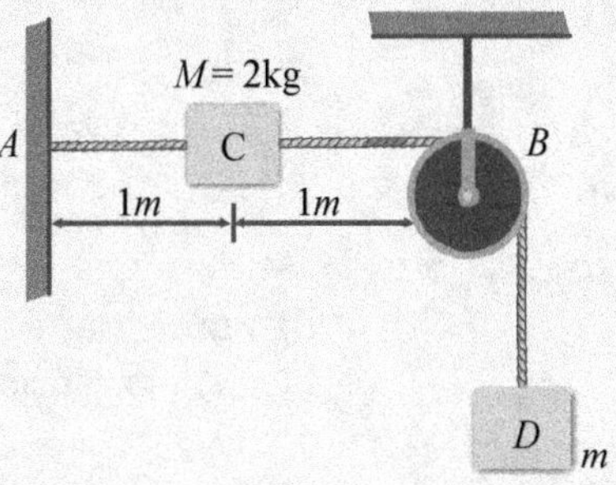

Ans. **3.36 m/s**

8. A 100000 kg engine is moving a slope of gradient 5° at a speed of 100 m/hr. The coefficient of friction between the engine and the rails is 0.1. If the engine has an efficiency of 4% for converting heat into work, find the amount of coal, the engine has to burn up in one hour (Burning of 1 kg of coal yields 50000 joules).

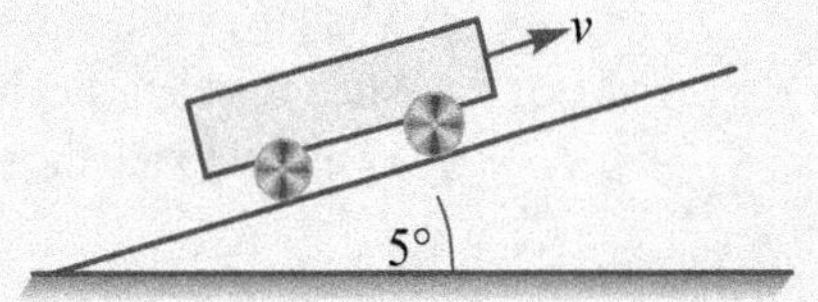

Ans. **9.154 × 10^3 kg**

7.9 POWER

Work done per unit time is called *power*. If an agent does work ΔW in small time Δt, then average power delivered is given by

$$P_{av} = \frac{\Delta W}{\Delta t}.$$

Instantaneous power

It is defined as the limiting value of average power as the time interval approaches zero. Thus

$$P = \lim_{\Delta t \to 0} \frac{\Delta W}{\Delta t}$$

or

$$P = \frac{dW}{dt}.$$

The work done by a constant force F is $W = \vec{\mathbf{F}}.\vec{\mathbf{s}}$

$\therefore$

$$P = \frac{d(\vec{\mathbf{F}}.\vec{\mathbf{s}})}{dt}$$

$$= \vec{\mathbf{F}}.\frac{d\vec{\mathbf{s}}}{dt}$$

or

$$P = \vec{\mathbf{F}}.\vec{\mathbf{v}} = Fv\cos\theta$$

If $\theta = 0°$, $P = Fv$

The SI unit of power is J/s. 1 J/s = 1 W .

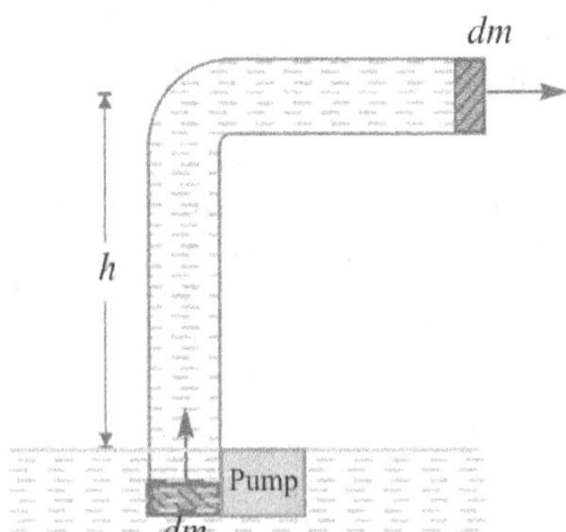

Figure. 7.29

Power of pump to left the water from the well

Let us consider a pump lifting water from h meter deep well and delivering at the rate of (dm/dt) with a velocity of v. Suppose dm amount of water is delivered in time dt. The work done

$$dW = (dm)gh + \frac{1}{2}(dm)v^2$$

$\therefore$ Power delivered

$$P = \frac{dW}{dt} = \left(\frac{dm}{dt}\right)\left[gh + \frac{v^2}{2}\right].$$

Special cases:

1. Power of pump required to just lift the water, $v = 0$,

$$\therefore \qquad P = \left(\frac{dm}{dt}\right)gh.$$

2. If efficiency of pump is η, then

$$\eta = \frac{P_{out}}{P_{in}}.$$

Gradual and sudden loading of a spring

Consider a spring of force constant k hanging from the ceiling. Now a small block of mass m is attached to its lower end and allowed to move slowly without acceleration by putting finger below the block. When block reaches its lowest position, remove the finger. At this stage the block is in static equilibrium. Let extension in the spring is y_0. By Hooke's law, we have

$$mg = ky_0 \Rightarrow y_0 = \frac{mg}{k}.$$

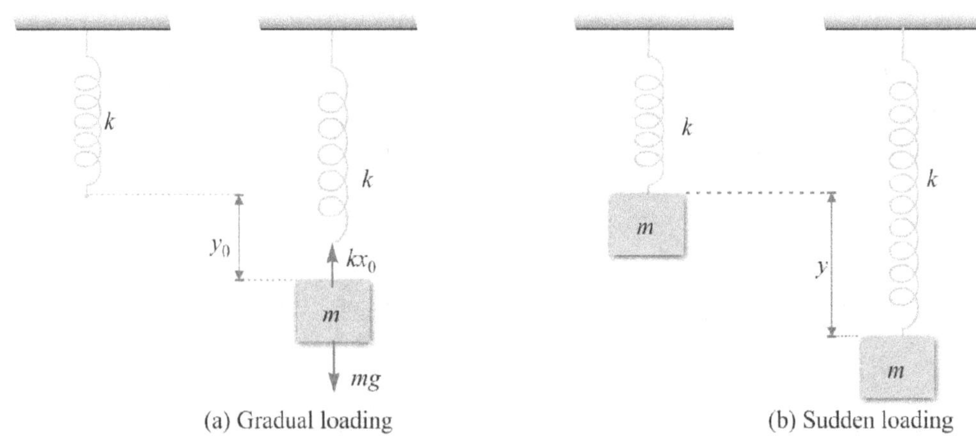

Figure. 7.30

Now the block is attached to lower end of the spring and left to fall freely. The block starts oscillating about mean position. Here the block is not in static equilibrium at its lowest position. Let the maximum extension of the spring is y. At the lowest position of the block $ky > mg$. By conservation of mechanical energy, we have

$$mgy = \frac{1}{2}ky^2$$

$$y = \frac{2mg}{k} = 2y_0.$$

Types of equilibrium

For the equilibrium of any body, the net force on it must be zero. That is $\vec{F}_{net} = 0$. For the equilibrium of body under conservative forces, we have

$$\left[F_c\right]_{net} = \frac{-dU}{dx} = 0$$

or

$$\frac{dU}{dx} = 0.$$

There are three types of equilibrium:

(i) Stable equilibrium :

When a particle is displaced slightly from its initial position, the force acting on it bring the particle back to initial position, it is called *stable equilibrium*.

A body placed at the bottom of bowl is in stable equilibrium. For stable equilibrium, we have

(a) $\dfrac{dU}{dx} = 0$,   (b) $\dfrac{d^2U}{dx^2} = +\text{ve}$,

(c) P.E. is minimum,

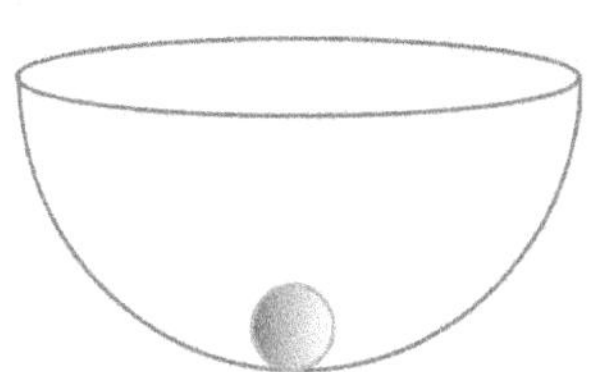

Figure. 7.31

(ii) Unstable equilibrium :

When a particle is displaced slightly from its initial position, the force acting on it tries to displace the particle further away from initial position, it is called *unstable equilibrium*.

A body on the top of the bowl is in unstable equilibrium. For *unstable equilibrium*, we have

(a) $\dfrac{dU}{dx} = 0$,   (b) $\dfrac{d^2U}{dx^2} = -\text{ve}$,

(c) P.E. is maximum.

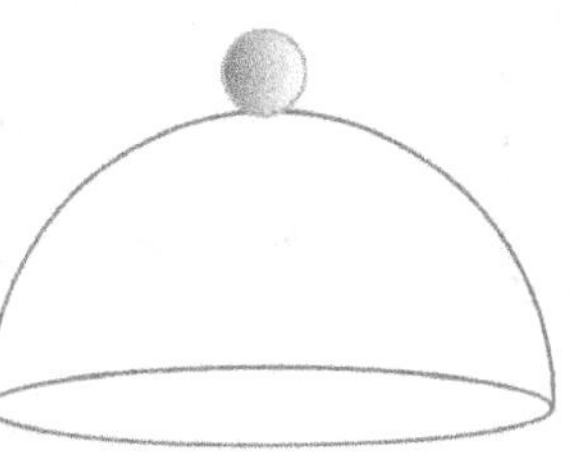

Figure. 7.32

(iii) Neutral equilibrium :

When a particle is slightly displaced from its initial position, if it continues to be in the displaced position, it is said to be in neutral equilibrium.

A body placed on horizontal sruface is in neutral equilibrium. For *neutral equilibrium*, we have

(a) $\dfrac{dU}{dx} = 0$,   (b) $\dfrac{d^2U}{dx^2} = 0$,

(c) P.E. remains constant.

Potential energy and equilibrium :

In *fig.* 7.34

At A; $\dfrac{dU}{dx} = 0$ and $\dfrac{d^2U}{dx^2} = +\text{ve}$

Thus at A the particle is in stable equilibrium.

At B; $\dfrac{dU}{dx} = 0$ and $\dfrac{d^2U}{dx^2} = -\text{ve}$.

Thus at B, particle is in unstable equilibrium.

Figure. 7.33

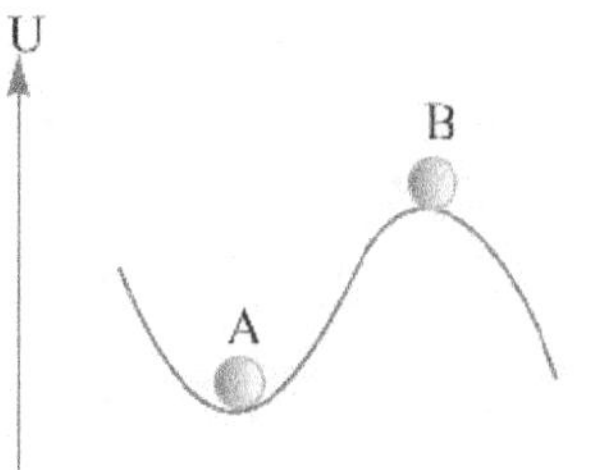

Figure. 7.34

FORMULAE USED

1. Average power, $P_{av} = \dfrac{\Delta W}{\Delta t}$

2. Instantaneous power, $P = \vec{F}.\vec{v} = Fv\cos\theta$
    For $\theta = 0$; $P = Fv$.

3. Efficiency, $\eta = \dfrac{\text{output}}{\text{input}}$.

EXAMPLES BASED ON POWER

Example 14. A machine gun fires 60 bullets per minute with a velocity of 700 m/s. If each bullet has a mass of 50 g, find the power developed by the gun

Sol.

Mass of bullets $\quad M = \dfrac{60 \times 50}{1000} = 3$ kg

Power $\quad\quad P = \dfrac{W}{t} = \dfrac{\frac{1}{2} M v^2}{t}$

$$= \dfrac{\frac{1}{2} \times 3 \times (700)^2}{60} = 12250 \text{ W} \quad\quad \textit{Ans.}$$

Example 15. A 90 kg man runs up an escalator while it is not in operation in 10 s (see *fig.* 7.35). What is the average power developed by the man. Suppose next that the escalator is running so that the escalator steps move at a speed of 0.6m/s. What is then the power developed by the man as seen by the ground reference if he moves at the same speed relative to the escalator steps as he did when the escalator is not in operator?

Sol.

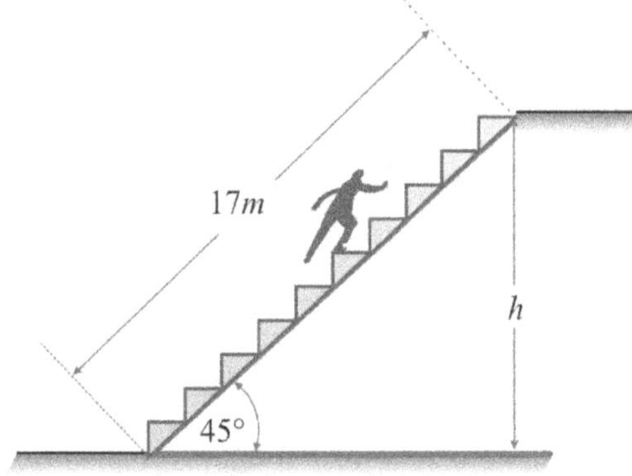

Figure. **7.35**

Work done by the man in climbing the escalator

$$W = mgh$$
$$= 90 \times 9.8 \times 17 \sin 45° = 10611 J$$

With the escalator stationary, man takes 10s to climb up therefore, average power

$$P = \dfrac{W}{t} = \dfrac{10611}{10} = 1061.1 \text{ W.} \quad\quad \textit{Ans.}$$

Speed of the man when escalator is stationary

$$v = \dfrac{17}{10} = 1.7 \text{m/s}.$$

In the second case the speed of the man relative to the moving escalator is also 1.70 m/s.

His speed relative to ground = 0.6 + 1.7 = 2.3 m/s.

Accordingly the time taken by man is climbing

$$= \dfrac{17}{2.3} = 7.4 s$$

The power developed by the man as seen from the ground reference is then, on the average:

$$\Rightarrow \quad\quad \text{Power} = \dfrac{W}{t} = \dfrac{10611}{7.4} = 1434 \text{ W.} \quad\quad \textit{Ans.}$$

Example 16. A body is initially at rest. It undergoes one dimensional motion with constant acceleration. The power delivered to it at time t is proportional to what ?   [NCERT]

Sol. $v = u + at = 0 + at = at$

Power , $P = F \times v = ma \times at = ma^2 t$

$\because$ m and a are constants, $P \propto t \therefore$ Ans

Example 17. A body is moving unidirectionally under the influence of a source of constant power. Find displacement in terms of time.

Sol. Power, $\quad\quad\quad P = Fv$

$$= m\left(v\dfrac{dv}{ds}\right)v$$

or $\quad\quad v^2 dv = \dfrac{P}{m} ds$

On integrating both sides, we get

$$\dfrac{v^3}{3} = \dfrac{P}{m} s$$

or $\quad\quad v = \left[\dfrac{3P}{m}\right]^{1/3} s^{1/3}$

or $\quad\quad \dfrac{ds}{dt} = \left[\dfrac{3P}{m}\right]^{\frac{1}{3}} s^{1/3}$

or $\quad\quad s^{-1/3}\, ds = \left[\dfrac{3P}{m}\right]^{\frac{1}{3}} dt$

Again on integrating, we get

$$\dfrac{s^{2/3}}{2/3} = \left[\dfrac{3P}{m}\right]^{1/3} t \Rightarrow s \propto t^{3/2}.$$

Example 18. The blades of a windmill sweep out a circle of area A   [NCERT]

(a) If the wind flows at a velocity v perpendicular to the circle, what is the mass of air passing through it in time t?

(b) What is KE of the air?

(c) Assume that the wind mill converts 25% of the wind's energy into electrical energy and that A= 30 m², v = 36 km/h and the density of air is 1.2 kg/m³. What is the electrical power produced?

Given that circular area swept by the blades of windmill = A

velocity of wind = v

Sol. Let, ρ be the density of air, then distance covered by wind in time 't' is = vt.

(a) Vol. of wind flowing/s = Av,

Mass of wind flowing/s = $Av\rho$

(b) Mass of wind flowing in t sec $= Av\rho t$

$$\text{KE of air} = \frac{1}{2}mv^2$$

$$= \frac{1}{2}(Av\rho t)v^2 = \frac{1}{2}Av^3\rho t$$

(c) Electrical energy produced

$$= \frac{25}{100}\times KE \text{ of air} = \frac{1}{4}\times\frac{1}{2}Av^3\rho t = \frac{1}{8}Av^3\rho t$$

$$\left[\text{Given that efficiency} = \frac{\text{output power}}{\text{Input power}}\right]$$

$$\therefore \quad \text{Power} = \frac{\text{energy}}{\text{time}} = \frac{\frac{1}{8}Av^3\rho t}{t} = \frac{1}{8}Av^3\rho$$

$$= \frac{1}{8}\times 30\times 10^3\times 1.2 = 4500 \text{ W} = 4.5 \; k\text{W} \textbf{ Ans.}$$

Example 19. A family uses 8 kW of power. Direct solar energy is incident on the horizontal surface at an average rate of 200 W per square meter. If 20% of this energy can be converted to useful electrical energy, how large an area is needed to supply 8 kW? **[NCERT]**

Sol. Let A → area of the surface in square metre.

1 m² receives power = 200 W

∴ Useful electrical energy produced

$$= \frac{20}{100}(200) = 40 \text{ W}$$

40 W power is produced by an area of 1m²

⇒   8 kW power will be produced by an area

$$= \frac{1}{40}\times 8000 = 200 \,\text{m}^2 \quad \textbf{Ans.}$$

In Chapter Exercise 7.2

1. Water falling from a 100 m high fall is to be used for generating electric energy. If 1.8×10^5 kg of water falls per hour and half the gravitational potential energy can be converted into electric energy, how many 100 W lamps can be lit ? *Ans.* **245.**

2. A truck can move up a road having a grade of 1 m rise in every 50 m with a speed of 24 km/h, the resisting force is equal to $\frac{1}{25}$ weight of the truck. How fast will the same truck move down the hill with the same power ?

    [Integer]   *Ans.* **72 km/h**

3. A tram car weighs 120 kN, the tractive resistance on the level being 5 N/kN, what power will be required to propel the car at a uniform speed of 20 kmph ?
    (1) On level surface
    (2) Up an incline of 1 is 300 and
    (3) Down an inclination of 1 in 300 ?
    Take efficiency of motor as 80 %.
    Ans. **(1) 4.17 kW   (2) 6.94 kW   (3) 1.39 kW**

4. A body of mass m is thrown at an angle α to the horizontal with the initial velocity v_0. Find the mean power developed by gravity over the whole time of motion of the body, and the instantaneous power of gravity as a function of time.
    Ans. $< P > = 0$, $P = mg\,(gt - v_0\sin\alpha)$

5. A light inextensible string that goes over a smooth fixed pulley as shown in the figure connects two blocks of masses 0.36 kg and 0.72 kg. Taking $g = 10 \text{ m/s}^2$, find the work done **(in joules)** by the string on the block of mass 0.36 kg during the first second after the system is released from rest.
    [Integer] [IIT 2009]
    Ans. **8**

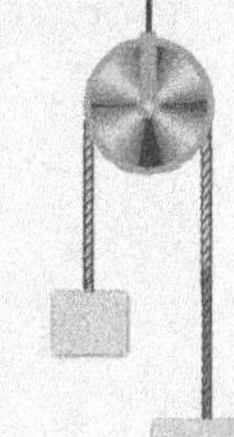

EXAMPLES FOR JEE-(MAIN AND ADVANCED)

Example 1. A force $\vec{F} = -k(y\hat{i} + x\hat{j})$, where k is a positive constant, acts on a particle moving in the xy – plane. Starting from the origin, the particle is taken along the positive x-axis to a point $(a, 0)$ and then parallel to the positive y-axis to a point (a, a). Calculate the total work done by the force on the particle.

Sol. Displacement vector,

$$d\vec{s} = dx\hat{i} + dy\hat{j}$$

Given $\qquad \vec{F} = -k(y\hat{i} + x\hat{j})$.

∴ Work done $\quad W = \int\vec{F}.d\vec{s} = \int -k(y\hat{i} + x\hat{j}).(dx\hat{i} + dy\hat{j})$

$$= -k\int_{(0,0)}^{(a,a)} (ydx + xdy) = -k\int_{(0,0)}^{(a,a)} d(xy)$$

$$= -k\left|(xy)\right|_{0,0}^{a,a} = -k(a\times a) = -ka^2. \quad \textbf{Ans.}$$

Example 2. A particle of mass 0.5 kg travels in a straight line with velocity $v = ax^{3/2}$, where $a = 5 \text{ m}^{-1/2}\text{s}^{-1}$. What is the work done by the net force during its displacement from $x = 0$ to $x = 2$m?

Sol. Given, $\qquad v = ax^{3/2}$

Acceleration, $\qquad a = \dfrac{dv}{dt} = \dfrac{d(ax^{3/2})}{dt}$

$$= \frac{3}{2}ax^{1/2}\left(\frac{dx}{dt}\right) = \frac{3}{2}ax^{1/2}(v)$$

$$= \frac{3}{2}ax^{1/2}\left(ax^{3/2}\right)$$

$$= \frac{3}{2}a^2x^2 .$$

Force, $\qquad F = ma$

$$= \frac{3}{2} ma^2 x^2$$

Work done, $\qquad W = \int_0^2 F dx$

$$= \frac{3}{2} ma^2 \int_0^2 x^2 dx$$

$$= \frac{3}{2} ma^2 \left| \frac{x^3}{3} \right|_0^2$$

$$= \frac{3 \times 0.5 \times 5^2}{2 \times 3} [2^3 - 0^3]$$

$$= 50 \text{ J.} \qquad\qquad \textbf{\textit{Ans.}}$$

Example 3. A locomotive of mass m starts moving so that its velocity varies according to the law $v = \alpha \sqrt{s}$, where a is a constant and s is the distance covered. Find the total work done by all the forces acting on the locomotive during first t second after the beginning of motion.

Sol.

Given, velocity $\qquad v = \alpha s^{1/2}$

Acceleration, $\qquad a = \dfrac{dv}{dt} = \dfrac{d}{dt}(\alpha s^{1/2})$

$$= \frac{1}{2} \alpha s^{-1/2} \left(\frac{ds}{dt} \right)$$

$$= \frac{1}{2} \alpha s^{-1/2} v$$

$$= \frac{1}{2} \alpha s^{-1/2} \left(\alpha s^{1/2} \right)$$

$$= \frac{\alpha^2}{2}$$

Now force, $\qquad F = ma$

$$= \frac{m\alpha^2}{2}.$$

Distance covered by locomotive in first t second

$$s = ut + \frac{1}{2} at^2$$

$$= 0 + \frac{1}{2} \left(\frac{\alpha^2}{2} \right) t^2$$

$$= \frac{\alpha^2 t^2}{4}.$$

Work done, $\qquad W = Fs$

$$= \frac{m\alpha^2}{2} \times \frac{\alpha^2 t^2}{4}$$

$$= \frac{m\alpha^4 t^2}{8}. \qquad\qquad \textbf{\textit{Ans.}}$$

Example 4. A block of mass $m = 1$ kg moving on a horizontal surface with speed $v_i = 2$ m/s enters a rough patch ranging from $x = 0.10$ m to $x = 2.01$ m. The retarding force F_r on the block in this range is inversely proportional to x over this range.

$$F_r = \frac{-k}{x} \qquad 0.1 < x < 2.01 \text{ m}$$

$$= 0 \qquad \text{for } x < 0.1 \text{ m and } x > 2.01 \text{ m}$$

where $k = 0.5$ J. What is the final kinetic energy and speed v_f of the block as it crosses this patch?

Sol. By work-energy theorem, we have

$$W = k_f - k_i$$

$$\therefore \qquad k_f = k_i + W$$

$$= k_i + \int F dx$$

$$= \frac{1}{2} mv_i^2 + \int_{0.1}^{2.01} \left(\frac{-k}{x} \right) dx$$

$$= \frac{1}{2} \times 1 \times 2^2 - k \left| \ln x \right|_{0.1}^{2.01}$$

$$= 2 - 0.5 \left| \ln \frac{2.01}{0.1} \right| = 2 - 0.5 \ln 20.1$$

$$= 0.5 \text{ J.}$$

Now $\qquad k_f = \dfrac{1}{2} mv_f^2 = 0.5$

$$\therefore \qquad v_f = \sqrt{\frac{2 \times 0.5}{1}} = 1 \text{ m/s}. \qquad \textbf{\textit{Ans.}}$$

Example 5. The potential energy of a 2 kg particle free to move along the x-axis is given by

$$U(x) = \left[\frac{x}{b} \right]^4 - 5 \left[\frac{x}{b} \right]^2 \text{ J}$$

where $b = 1$ m. Plot this potential energy, identifying the extremum points. Identify the regions where particle may be found and its maximum speed. Given that the total mechanical energy is (i) 36 J; (ii) −4 J.

Sol. Given $\qquad U(x) = \left[\dfrac{x}{b} \right]^4 - 5 \left[\dfrac{x}{b} \right]^2$

For $\qquad b = 1, U = x^4 - 5x^2 \qquad\qquad …(i)$

and $\qquad \dfrac{dU}{dx} = 4x^3 - 10x \qquad\qquad …(ii)$

For extremum points

$$\frac{dU}{dx} = 0$$

or $\qquad 4x^3 - 10x = 0$

or $\qquad 2x(2x^2 - 5) = 0$

$\therefore \; x = 0, \pm \sqrt{\dfrac{5}{2}}$ are the extremum points

$x(m)$	0	± 1	$\pm\sqrt{5/2}$	± 2	± 3
$U(J)$	0	-4	-6.25	-4	$+36$

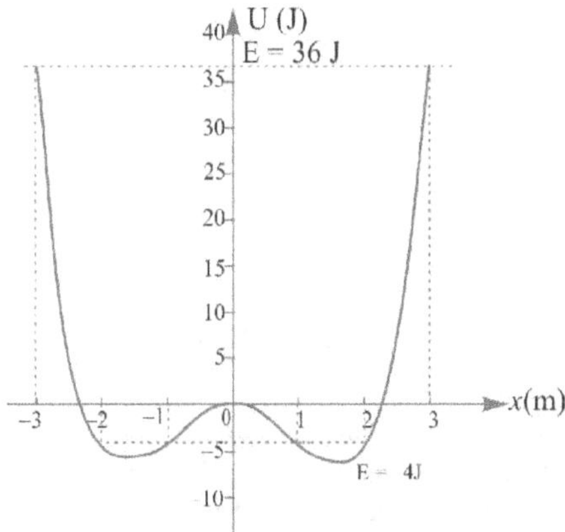

Variation of U with x

Figure. **7.36**

Thus in a region $-3 < x < 3$, we have

$$U_{\min} = -6.25 \text{ J and } U_{\max} = 36 \text{ J}$$

(i) Here $E = K + U = 36$ J

The particle is in the region $-3 < x < 3$

At $x = 0, U = 0,$

$\therefore \quad K + 0 = 36$

$\Rightarrow \quad K = 36$ J

At $x = \pm\sqrt{5/2}, U_{\min} = -6.25$ J

$\therefore \quad K + (-6.25) = 36$

$\Rightarrow \quad K = 36 + 6.25$

$\quad = 42.25$ J

or $\quad \dfrac{1}{2}mv_{\max}^2 = 42.25$ J

or $\quad v_{\max} = \sqrt{\dfrac{2 \times 42.25}{2}} = 6.5$ m/s .

(ii) Here $E = K + U = -4$ J

The particle is in the region $-2 < x < -1$ and $1 < x < 2$

$$x = \pm\dfrac{\sqrt{5}}{2}, U_{\min} = -6.25 \text{ J}$$

$\therefore \quad K + (-6.25) = -4$

$\Rightarrow \quad K = 2.25$ J

or $\quad \dfrac{1}{2}mv_{\max}^2 = 2.25$ J

$$v_{\max} = \sqrt{\dfrac{2 \times 2.25}{2}} = 1.5 \text{ m/s} . \qquad \textbf{\textit{Ans.}}$$

Example 6. A chain of length l and mass m lies on the surface of a smooth hemisphere of radius $R > l$ with one end tied to the top of the hemisphere. Find the gravitational potential energy of the chain.

Sol. Choose a small element of chain of width $d\theta$ at an angle θ from the vertical.

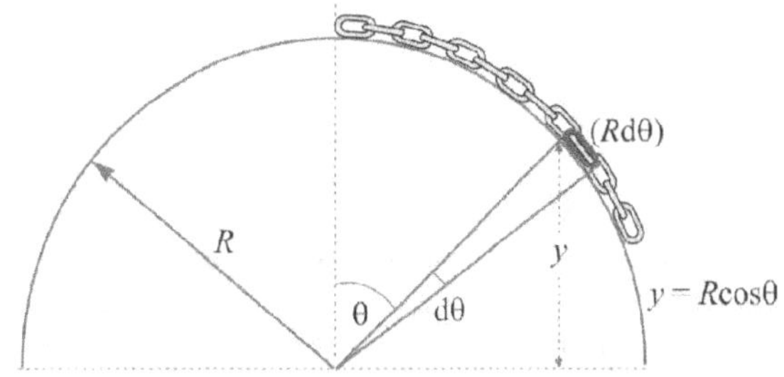

Figure. **7.37**

The mass of the element

$$dm = \left(\dfrac{m}{\ell} R d\theta\right)$$

The gravitational potential energy of the element $dU = (dm)gy$. Thus the gravitational potential energy of whole chain

$$U = \int (dm)gy$$

$$= \int_0^{(\ell/R)} \left(\dfrac{m}{\ell} R d\theta\right) g (R\cos\theta)$$

$$= \dfrac{mR^2 g}{\ell} \int_0^{(\ell/R)} \cos\theta\, d\theta$$

$$= \dfrac{mgR^2}{\ell} |\sin\theta|_0^{\ell/R}$$

$$= \dfrac{mgR^2}{\ell} \sin(\ell/R) . \qquad \textbf{\textit{Ans.}}$$

Example 7. A smooth light horizontal rod AB can rotate about a vertical axis passing through its end A. The rod is fitted with a small sleeve of mass m attached to the end A by weightless spring of length l_0 and stiffness k. What work must be performed to slowly gets this system going and reaching the angular velocity ω?

Sol. Let x be the stretching in the spring. Then spring force will be kx which counter balance by the centrifugal force $m\omega^2 (l_0 + x)$ acting on the sleeve. Therefore we have

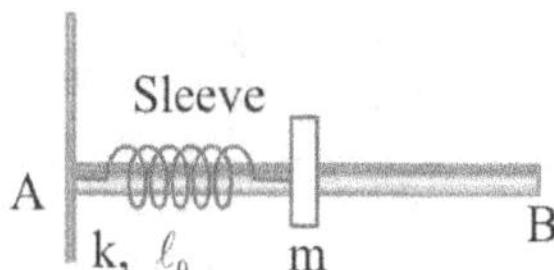

Figure. **7.38**

$$kx = m\omega^2 (l_0 + x)$$

$$\therefore \quad x = m\omega^2 l_0 /(k - m\omega^2). \qquad \text{... (i)}$$

Now from the work-energy theorem

Work done = K.E. gained by the sleeve + energy stored in the spring in stretching it by x.

or $$W = \dfrac{1}{2}m\omega^2 (l_0 + x) + \dfrac{1}{2}kx^2 \qquad \text{...(ii)}$$

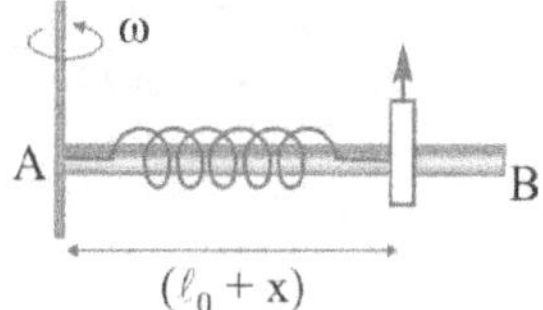

Figure. **7.39**

Solving equations (i) and (ii), we get

$$W = \frac{k\ell_0{}^2\eta(1+\eta)}{2(1-\eta)^2},$$

where $\eta = m\omega^2/k$. **Ans.**

Example 8. Two bars of masses m_1 and m_2 connected by a non-deformed light spring rest on a horizontal plane. The coefficient of friction between the bars and the surface is equal to μ. What minimum constant force has to be applied in the horizontal direction to the bar of mass m_1 in order to shift the other bar?

Sol. The bar 2 will be shifted if spring exerts a force which equal to the frictional force on this. If spring compresses by x, then we have $kx = \mu m_2 g \quad \Rightarrow x = \mu m_2 g/k$.

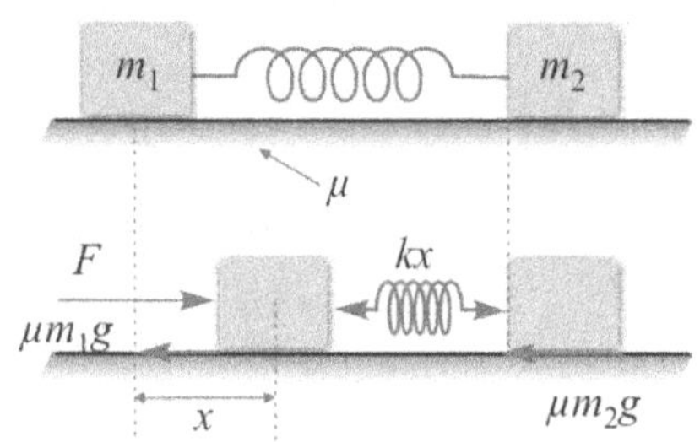

Figure. 7.40

This compression in the spring will occur when m_1 shifts horizontally by the same amount (x).

To do this, the work is to be done in compressing the spring and against the frictional force for displacement x

$$\therefore \qquad Fx = (\mu m_1 g)x + \frac{1}{2}kx^2$$

Substituting the value of x, we get

$$F = \mu g(m_1 + m_2/2). \qquad \textbf{Ans.}$$

Example 9. A small disc A slides down with initial velocity equal to zero from the top of a smooth hill of the height H having a horizontal portion as shown in *fig.* 7.41. What must be the height of the horizontal portion h to ensure the maximum distance s covered by the disc? What is equal to?

Sol. In order to get velocity at point B, applying the law of conservation of energy

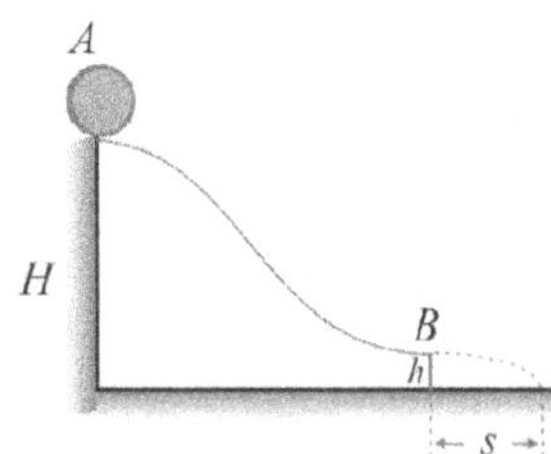

Figure. 7.41

Loss in P.E. at B = Gain in K.E. at B

i.e., $\qquad mg(H - h) = \frac{1}{2}mv^2$

or $\qquad v = \sqrt{2g(H - h)}$. $\qquad$ ... (i)

Let disc takes time t in falling vertical height h,

$$h = \frac{1}{2}gt^2 \Rightarrow t = \sqrt{(2h/g)}$$

Now

$$s = v \times t = \sqrt{2g(H-h)} \times \sqrt{(2h/g)}$$

$$= \sqrt{4h(H-h)} \qquad \text{... (ii)}$$

For maximum s, $\quad ds/dh = 0$

After solving , we get

$$h = H/2$$

Substituting this value in equation in (i), we get

$$s = H. \qquad \textbf{Ans.}$$

Example 10. A small body A starts sliding from the height h down an inclined groove passing into a half-circle of radius $h/2$ *fig.* 7.42. Assuming the friction to be negligible, find the velocity of the body at the highest point of its trajectory (after breaking off the groove).

Sol. From the geometry of the figure, we have

$$BD = \frac{h}{2}(1+\cos\theta) .$$

At the point C, $mg\cos\alpha - N = mv_c{}^2/R$, where $R = h/2$.

When the body is on the point of breaking off the groove, normal reaction at this point becomes zero. i.e., $N = 0$.

$$\therefore \qquad mg\cos\alpha = \frac{mv_c{}^2}{(h/2)}$$

or $\qquad v_c = \sqrt{\frac{gh\cos\alpha}{2}}$. $\qquad$ ...(i)

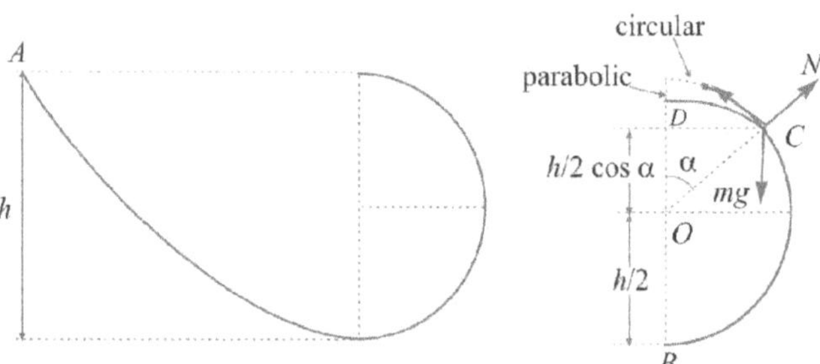

Figure. 7.42

Applying conservation of energy at this point

$$mgh = mg\frac{h}{2}(1+\cos\alpha) + \frac{1}{2}mv_c^2 \qquad \text{... (ii)}$$

Solving equations (i) and (ii), we get

$$\cos\alpha = 2/3$$

and $\qquad v_c = \sqrt{(gh/3)}$.

After breaking off the groove the body will move like a projectile making an angle α with the horizontal. Therefore at the highest point of trajectory, the horizontal component of velocity will be $= v_c \cos\alpha$.

or $\qquad v_h = (2/3)\sqrt{(gh/3)}$. $\qquad$ **Ans.**

Example 11. A mass m falls from a height h on to the end of a platform as shown in the *fig.* 7.43. The spring is initially unstretched and the mass of the platform can be neglected. Assuming that there is no loss of energy, calculate the elongation of the spring.

Sol. Let y be the elongation in the spring.

The height up to which mass falls before striking the platform is $(h + x)$, where x will be $(a/b)y$.

From the conservation of the energy, we have

Fall in P.E. of the mass = Energy stored in the spring;

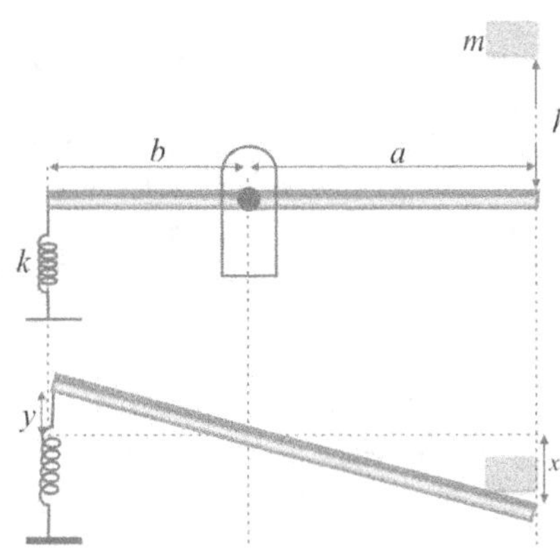

Figure. 7.43

or $$mg(h + x) = \frac{1}{2}ky^2$$

or $$mgh + mg(a/b)y = \frac{1}{2}ky^2$$

or $$\frac{1}{2}ky^2 - \frac{mgay}{b} - mgh = 0$$

Solving above equation, we get

$$y = \frac{(mga/b) \pm \sqrt{(amg/b)^2 + 4(k/2)(mgh)}}{2(k/2)}$$

The quantity in under radical sign is > 1, and elongation must be positive. Therefore,

$$y = \frac{(mga/b) + \sqrt{(amg/b)^2 + 4(k/2)(mgh)}}{k}$$

Ans.

Example 12. A body A is released from rest on a vertical circular path as shown in *fig.* 7.44. If there is a constant resistance force of 1 N along the path, what is the speed of the body when it reaches B? The mass of the body is 0.5 kg and the radius r of the path is 1.6 m.

Sol. Arc distance $AB = r\theta = 1.6 \times \dfrac{\pi}{6}$ m

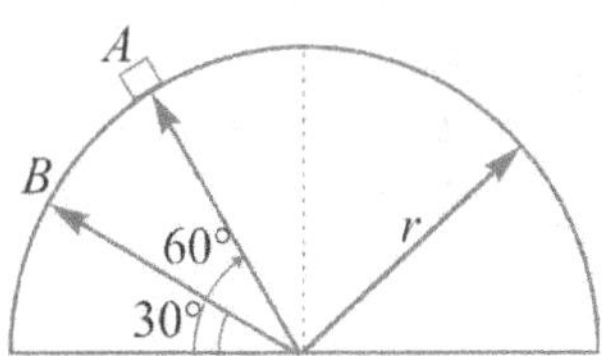

Figure. 7.44

The work done by resistance force from A to B,

$$W_1 = -fs = (-1) \times 1.6 \times \frac{\pi}{6}\text{ J} = \frac{-1.6\pi}{6}\text{ J}$$

Work done by gravity

$$\begin{aligned}W_2 &= mgh \\ &= mgr\,(\cos30° - \cos60°) \\ &= 0.5 \times 9.8 \times 1.6\,(\cos30° - \cos60°) = 2.87\text{ J}.\end{aligned}$$

Now by work-energy theorem

$$W = \Delta\text{K.E.} \quad \text{or} \quad W_1 + W_2 = \Delta\text{K.E.}$$

or $$-\frac{1.6\pi}{6} + 2.87 = \frac{1}{2}m(v^2 - 0^2)$$

or $$\frac{1}{2}mv^2 = 2.87 - 0.83 = 2.04$$

$$\therefore \quad v = \sqrt{\frac{2 \times 2.04}{m}} = \sqrt{\frac{2 \times 2.04}{0.5}}$$

$$= 2.86 \text{ m/s}. \qquad\qquad \textit{Ans.}$$

Example 13. A railroad car travelling 32 km/s runs into a stop at a railroad terminal (see *fig.* 7.45). A vehicle having a mass of 1800 kg is held by a linear - restoring system that has an equivalent spring constant of 20,000 N/m. If the railroad car is assumed to stop suddenly and wheels on the vehicle are free to turns, what is the maximum force developed by the equivalent sloping system? Neglect friction and the inertia of the wheels.

Sol. The velocity of the vehicle

$$= 32 \text{ km/h} = 32 \times \frac{5}{18} = \frac{80}{9} \text{ m/s}.$$

Let the spring gets compressed by x, by the vehicle after railroad car stops. Then

by conservation of mechanical energy

$$\frac{1}{2}kx^2 = \frac{1}{2}mv^2$$

Figure. 7.45

$$x = \sqrt{\frac{mv^2}{k}}.$$

The force in the spring corresponding to the compression of the spring x

$$F = kx = k\sqrt{\frac{mv^2}{k}} = v\sqrt{mk}$$

$$= \frac{80}{9}\sqrt{1800 \times 20000} = \frac{80}{9} \times 6 \times 10^3$$

$$= \frac{160}{3} \times 10^3 = 53.33 \times 10^3 \text{ N} \qquad \textit{Ans.}$$

Example 14. **A smooth rubber cord of length ℓ whose coefficient of elasticity is k is suspended by one end from the point O. The other end is fitted with a catch B. A small sleeve of mass m starts from the point O. Neglecting the masses of the thread and the catch, find the maximum elongation of the cord.**

Sol. Let y be the elongation of the thread.

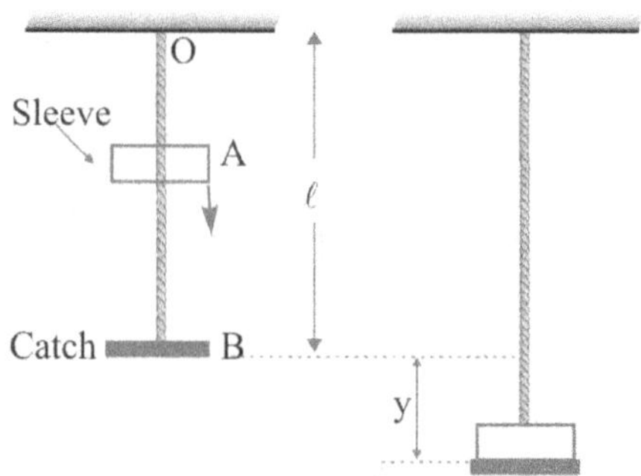

Figure. 7.46

From the energy conservation;

decrease in P.E. of the sleeve in falling total distance $(\ell + y)$ = elastic P.E. stored in the rubber cord in stretching y

i.e.
$$mg(\ell + y) = \frac{1}{2}ky^2$$

or
$$\frac{1}{2}ky^2 - mgy - mg\ell = 0$$

$\therefore$
$$y = \frac{mg \pm \sqrt{(mg)^2 + 4(k/2).mg\ell}}{2.(k/2)}$$

or
$$y = (mg/k)[1 \pm \sqrt{1 + 2k\ell/mg}].$$

As the quantity under the radical sign is > 1 and elongation is a positive quantity, therefore

$$y = (mg/k)[1 + \sqrt{1 + 2k\ell/mg}]. \qquad \textbf{Ans.}$$

Example 15. **A chain of mass $m = 0.80$ kg and length $\ell = 1.5$ rests on a rough-surfaced table so that one of its ends hangs over the edge. The chain starts sliding off the table all by itself provided the over hanging part equals $\ell = 1/3$ of the chain length. What will be the total work performed by the friction forces acting on the chain by the moment it slides completely off the table?**

Sol. Let λ be the mass per unit length of the chain.

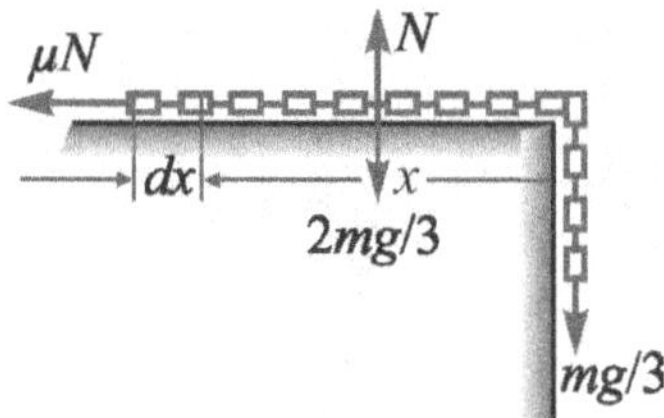

Figure. 7.47

Force of gravity acting on the hanging part causes the tension in the chain which will equal to the frictional force on the chain lying on the table.

i.e. $mg/3 = \mu N$, where $N = 2\,mg/3$

which gives $\mu = 1/2$.

Work done in sliding through a small distance dx supposing that x length is on the table

$$dW = -f\,dx = -(\mu N)dx = -\mu\,(\lambda x\,g)dx$$

$\therefore$
$$W = -\int_{0}^{2\ell/3} \mu(\lambda xg)dx$$

$\Rightarrow$
$$W = -\frac{\mu\lambda g}{2}\Big[x^2\Big]_0^{2\ell/3} = \frac{-mg\ell}{9}$$

$$= -1.306 \text{ J}. \qquad \textbf{Ans.}$$

Example 16. **A 0.50 kg block slides from the point A as shown in *fig.* 7.48 on horizontal track with an initial speed of 3.0 m/s towards a weightless horizontal spring of length 1 m and force constant $k = 2$ N/m. The part AB of the track is frictionless and the part BC has a coefficient of static and kinetic friction as 0.22 and 0.2 respectively. If the distances AB and BD are 2 m and 2.14 m respectively, find the total distance through which the block moves before it comes to rest completely.**

Sol. The track AB is frictionless, the block moves through this distance without any change in K.E. When the block enters the track BC, having coefficient of friction 0.2, its K.E. is lost in doing work against friction.

Initial K.E. of block $= \frac{1}{2}mv^2 = \frac{1}{2} \times 0.5 \times 3^2 = 2.25$ J.

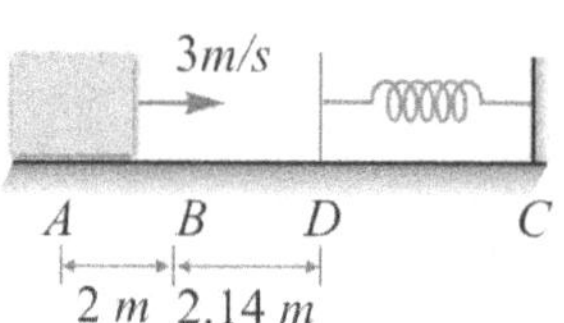

Figure. 7.48

Work done against friction over the distance

$$BD = \mu_k N \times s = \mu_k mg \times s$$
$$= 0.2 \times 0.5 \times 10 \times 2.14 = 2.14 \text{ J}$$

This work done is less than the initial K.E. of the block, so the block moves further and compresses the spring by a distance x (say).

Then according to the law of conservation of energy;

Initial K.E. of the block = Work done against friction + P.E. stored in the spring

$$\frac{1}{2}mv^2 = \mu_k mg(BD + x) + \frac{1}{2}kx^2$$

or
$$2.25 = 0.2 \times 0.5 \times 10 \times (2.14 + x) + \frac{1}{2}.2.x^2$$

$$x^2 + x = 0.11$$

which gives $x = 0.10$ m   or -1.1 m.

As x can not be negative, therefore $x = 0.10$ m.

After moving through distance x, the block comes to rest. Now the compressed spring exerts a force $F = 2 \times 0.1 = 0.2$ N on the block which is less than the limiting frictional force $(= \mu_s\, mg = 0.22 \times 0.5 \times 10 = 1.1$ N). Therefore the block does not move.

The total distance moved by the block

$$= AB + BD + x$$
$$= 2 + 2.14 + 0.1 = 4.24 \text{ m} \qquad \textbf{Ans.}$$

Example 17. *AB is a quarter of a smooth circular track of radius 4 m as shown in the fig. 7.49. A particle P of mass 5 kg moves along the track from A to B under the action of following forces;*

(i) A force F_1 directed always towards point B, its magnitude is constant and equals 4 N.

(ii) A force F_2 is directed along the instantaneous tangent to the circular track, its magnitude is $(20 - s)$N where s is the distance travelled in metre.

(iii) A horizontal force F_3 of magnitude 25 N.

If the particle starts with speed of 10 m/s, what is speed at point B.

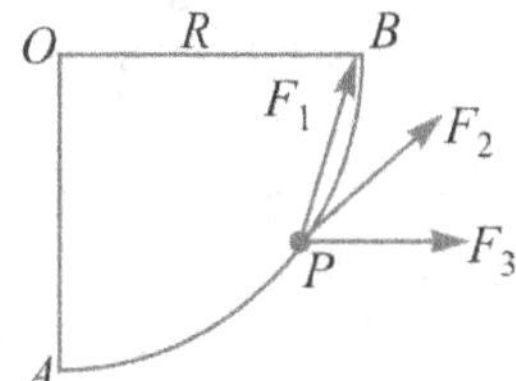

Figure. 7.49

Sol.

(i) Let the particle be at point P at any instant of time t. The particle moves from position P to Q in small time dt. The direction of force F_1 on P will be in direction PB. It is clear from the figure that the angle between $\vec{F}$ and $\vec{s}$ changes from θ to 0.

Also,

$$2\theta = \frac{\pi}{2} \quad \therefore \quad \theta = \frac{\pi}{4}.$$

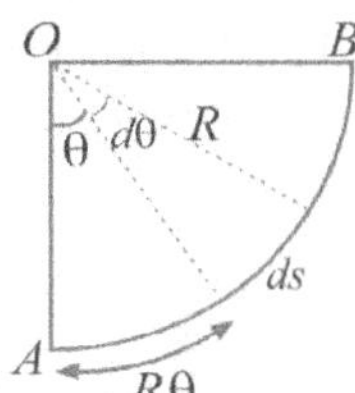

Figure. 7.50

Therefore

$$dW_1 = F_1 . ds = F_1 \cos \theta\, R\, d\theta.$$
$$= F_1 \cos \theta\, R\, (d\theta)$$
$$= 4 \cos \theta \times 4 \times d\theta = 16 \cos \theta\, d\theta$$

The total work done as the particle moves from A to B

$$W_1 = \int_0^{\pi/4} 16 \cos\theta\, d\theta = 11.32 \text{ J} \qquad \textit{Ans.}$$

(ii) Work done by force F_2

$$dW_2 = F_2 . ds = F_2\, ds \cos\theta = F_2\, ds$$

(Since F_2 always acts along the tangent $\therefore \theta = 0°$)

$$= (20 - s) \times R\, d\theta = (20 - R\theta) \times R\, d\theta$$
$$(R = 4 \text{ m})$$

$$\therefore \qquad W_2 = \int_0^{\pi/4} (20 - R\theta) \times R\, d\theta\,.$$

$$= \int_0^{\pi/4} (80 - 16\theta)\, d\theta = 248.67 \text{ J} \qquad \textit{Ans.}$$

(iii) Work done by force F_3, which is always horizontal :

Work done $\quad W_3 = F_3 \times$ displacement in the direction of force
$$= 25 \times 4 = 100 \text{ J}$$

The work done against gravity

$$W_4 = -5 \times 9.8 \times 4 = -196 \text{ J.}$$
$$\text{(Since vertical displacement } R = 4 \text{ m)}$$

Total work done

$$W = W_1 + W_2 + W_3 + W_4$$
$$= 11.32 + 248.67 + 100 - 196 = 163.99 \text{ J.}$$

Let v_A and v_B be the velocity of the particle at A and B respectively, then

$$\frac{1}{2}mv_B^2 - \frac{1}{2}mv_A^2 = W$$

$$\frac{1}{2} \times 5 \times v_B^2 - \frac{1}{2} \times 5 \times (10)^2 = 163.99$$

$$v_B = 12.85 \text{ m/s} \qquad \textit{Ans.}$$

MCQ Type 1 — Exercise 7.1

Work, Kinetic and Potential Energy

1. Choose the correct alternative among the following:
   (a) When a conservative force does positive work on a body, the potential energy of the body increases.
   (b) Work done by a body against friction always results in a loss of its kinetic energy.
   (c) The rate of change of total momentum of a many particle system is proportional to the sum of the internal forces on the system.
   (d) In an elastic collision kinetic energy of the colliding bodies before collision is equal to kinetic energy during collision

2. A force $\vec{F} = 6\vec{i} + 2\vec{j} + 3\vec{k}$ acts on a particle and produces a displacement of $\vec{s} = 2\vec{i} - 3\vec{j} - x\vec{k}$. If the work done is zero, the value of x is :
   (a) 2
   (b) 1 / 2
   (c) 6
   (d) 3

3. A force $\vec{F} = (5\hat{i} + 3\hat{j})$ newton is applied over a particle which displaces it from its origin to the point $\vec{r} = (2\hat{i} - 1\hat{j})$ meter. The work done on the particle is:
   (a) – 7 joule
   (b) + 13 joule
   (c) + 7 joule
   (d) + 11 joule

4. If W_1, W_2 and W_3 represent the work done in moving a particle from A to B along three different paths 1, 2, 3 respectively (as shown) in the gravitational field of a point mass m, find the correct relation between W_1, W_2 and W_3 :

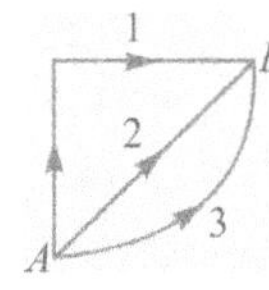

   (a) $W_1 > W_2 > W_3$
   (b) $W_1 = W_2 = W_3$
   (c) $W_1 < W_2 < W_3$
   (d) $W_2 > W_1 > W_3$

5. A spring of spring constant k is stretched by a length x from its natural length and released. What about its potential energy :
   (a) remain stored in spring in any form
   (b) converted into heat
   (c) transfer to air molecules
   (d) none of the above

6. A bullet is fired from a rifle. If the rifle recoils freely, then the kinetic energy of the rifle is
   (a) less than that of the bullet
   (b) more than that of the bullet
   (c) same as that of the bullet
   (d) equal or less than that of the bullet

7. A light and a heavy body have equal momenta. Which one has greater $K.E.$
   (a) the light body
   (b) the heavy body
   (c) the $K.E.$ are equal
   (d) data is incomplete

8. If the $K.E.$ of a body is increased by 300%, its momentum will increase by
   (a) 100%
   (b) 150%
   (c) $\sqrt{300}\%$
   (d) 175%

9. A body of mass 0.5 kg travels in a straight line with velocity $v = 5x^{3/2}$. The work done by the net force during the displacement from $x = 0$ to $x = 2$m is
   (a) 25 J
   (b) 50 J
   (c) 75 J
   (d) 100 J

10. Figure gives the acceleration of a, 2.0 kg body as it moves from res along x-axis while a variable force acts on it from $x = 0$ m rest to $x = 9$ m. The work done by the force on the body when it reaches $x = 7$m is given by

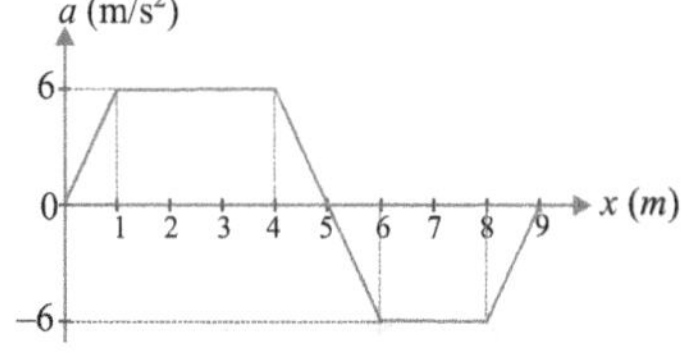

   (a) 30 J
   (b) 42 J
   (c) 45 J
   (d) 21 J

11. The graph of kinetic energy (K) of a body versus velocity (v) is represented as:

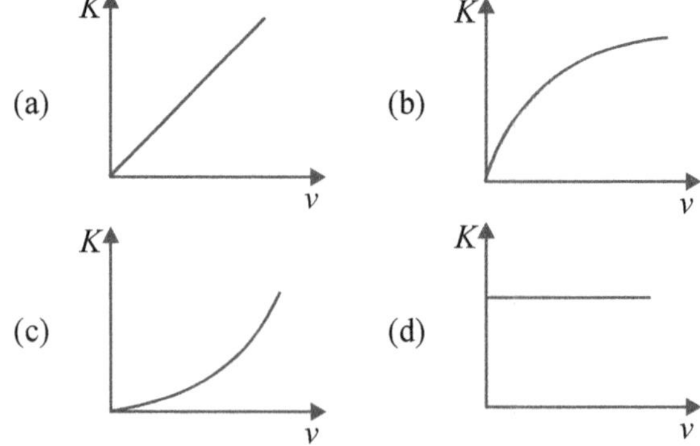

| Answer | 1 | (b) | 2 | (a) | 3 | (c) | 4 | (b) | 5 | (c) | 6 | (a) |
| Key | 7 | (a) | 8 | (a) | 9 | (b) | 10 | (a) | 11 | (c) | | |

12. The potential energy of a book placed in almirah is 15 J w.r.t. ground. One person *A* says that the potential energy of a book kept in an almirah is 20 J and the other person *B* says it is 25 J :

(a) person *A* is correct
(b) person *B* is correct
(c) both are wrong
(d) both are correct

13. Starting from rest a 10 kg object is acted upon by only one force as shown in figure. The total workdone by the force is :

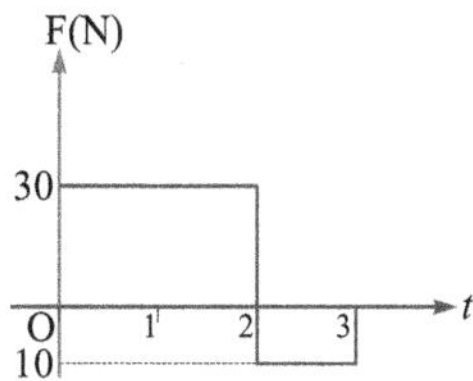

(a) 20 J
(b) 125 J
(c) 245 J
(d) 490 J

14. The only force acting on a 2 kg body as it moves along the positive *x* axis has component $F_x = -6x$ N, where *x* is in metre. The velocity of the body at $x = 3$m is 8 m/s. The velocity of the body at $x = 4$ m is :

(a) 10 m/s
(b) 9 m/s
(c) 7.4 m/s
(d) 6.6 m/s

15. Figure shows three forces applied to a trunk that moves leftward by 3 m over a smooth floor. The force magnitudes are $F_1 = 5$N, $F_2 = 9$N, and $F_3 = 3$N. The net work done on the trunk by the three forces

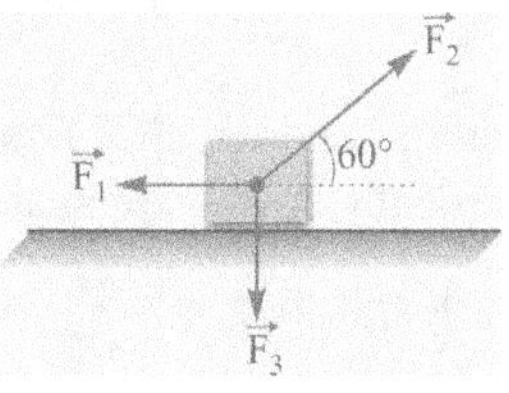

(a) 1.50 J
(b) 2.40 J
(c) 3.00 J
(d) 6.00 J

16. The figure gives the potential energy function $U(x)$ for a system in which a particle is in one-dimensional motion. In which region the magnitude of the force on the particle is greatest :

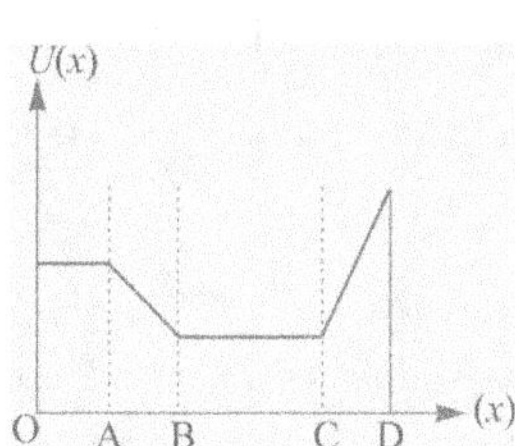

(a) *OA*
(b) *AB*
(c) *BC*
(d) *CD*

17. A pendulum bob has a speed of 3 m/s at its lowest position. The pendulum is 0.5 m long. The speed of the bob, when the length makes an angle of 60° with the vertical, will be $(g = 10 \text{ m/s}^2)$

(a) 3 m/s
(b) $\dfrac{1}{3}$ m/s
(c) $\dfrac{1}{2}$ m/s
(d) 2 m/s

18. A toy gun has a spring of force constant *k*. After charging the spring by compressing it through a distance *x*, the toy releases off shot of mass *m* vertically upwards. Then the shot will travel a vertical height of

(a) $\dfrac{2mg}{kx}$
(b) $\dfrac{kx^2}{mg}$
(c) $\dfrac{kx}{mg}$
(d) $\dfrac{kx^2}{2mg}$

19. A bolt of mass 0.3 kg falls from the ceiling of an elevator moving down with a uniform speed of 7 m/s. It hits the floor of the elevator (length of the elevator = 3 m) and does not rebound. The heat produced is $(g = 10 \text{ m/s}^2)$

(a) 9 J
(b) 9.73 J
(c) 12.12 J
(d) 15 J

20. The block of mass m is pulling, vertically up with constant speed, by applying force *P*. The free end of the string is pulled by *l* meter, the increase in potential energy of the block is :

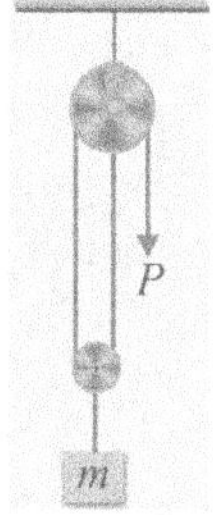

(a) $\dfrac{mgl}{2}$
(b) mgl
(c) $2\,mgl$
(d) $\dfrac{mgl}{4}$

21. The potential energy of a particle in a force field is

$$U = \dfrac{A}{r^2} - \dfrac{B}{r},$$ where *A* and *B* are positive constants and *r*

is the distance of particle from the centre of the field. For stable equilibrium, the distance of the particle is

(a) *B/A*
(b) -600 J
(c) *2A/B*
(d) *A/B*

Answer	12	(d)	13	(b)	14	(d)	15	(a)	16	(d)
Key	17	(d)	18	(d)	19	(a)	20	(a)	21	(c)

22. A block of mass M is hanging over a smooth and light pulley through a light string. The other end of the string is pulled by a constant force F. The kinetic energy of the block increases by 20 J in 1 s :

(a) the tension of the string is Mg

(b) the tension in the string is F.

(c) the work done by the tension on the block is 20 J in the above 1 s.

(d) the work done by the force of gravity is -20 J in the above 1 s.

23. An open knife edge of mass M is dropped from a height h on a wooden floor. If the blade penetrates s into the wood, the average resistance offered by the wood to the blade is:

(a) Mg

(b) $\dfrac{Mg}{2}\left(1+\dfrac{h}{s}\right)$

(c) $Mg\left(1+\dfrac{h}{s}\right)$

(d) $Mg\left(1+\dfrac{h}{s}\right)^2$

24. A force acts on a 30 g particle in such a way that the position of the particle as a function of time is given by $x = 3t - 4t^2 + t^3$, where x is in metres and t is in seconds. The work done during the first 4 seconds is

(a) 5.28 J

(b) 450 J

(c) 490 J

(d) 530 J

25. If we throw a body upwards with velocity of 4 m/s, at what height does its kinetic energy reduce to half of the initial value (Taking g = 10 m / s^2)

(a) 4 m

(b) 2 m

(c) 1 m

(d) 0.4 m

26. A particle of mass 100g is thrown vertically upwards with a speed of 5m/s. The work done by the force of gravity during the time the particle goes up is

(a) -1.25 J

(b) 5.17 kJ

(c) 0.5 j

(d) -0.5 J

27. Two bodies A and B have masses 20 kg and 5 kg respectively. Each one is acted upon by a force of 4 kg wt. If they acquire the same kinetic energy in times t_A and t_B, then the ratio $\dfrac{t_A}{t_B}$ is

(a) $\dfrac{1}{2}$

(b) 2

(c) $\dfrac{2}{5}$

(d) $\dfrac{5}{6}$

28. A spherical ball of mass 20 kg is stationary at the top of a hill of height 100 m. It slides down a smooth surface to the ground, then climbs up another hill of height 30 m and finally slides down to a horizontal base at a height of 20 m above the ground. The velocity attained by the ball is

(a) 10 m/s

(b) $10\sqrt{30}$ m/s

(c) 40 m/s

(d) 20 m/s

29. An object of mass m is tied to string of length L and a variable horizontal force is applied on it which starts at zero and gradually increases (it is pulled extremely slowly so that equilibrium exists at all times) until the string makes an angle θ with the vertical. Work done by the force F is :

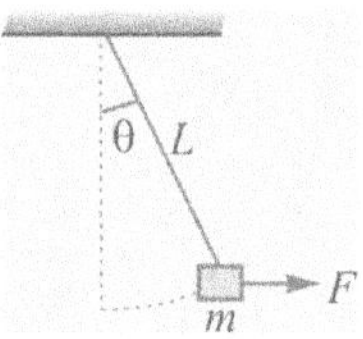

(a) $mgL\,(1 - \cos\theta)$

(b) $mg\,L\,(1 - \sin\theta)$

(c) $mg\,L$

(d) $mg\,L\,(1 + \tan\theta)$

30. Two blocks, each of mass m moving with speed v, collide with the spring of force constant k as shown in figure. The maximum compression of the spring is :

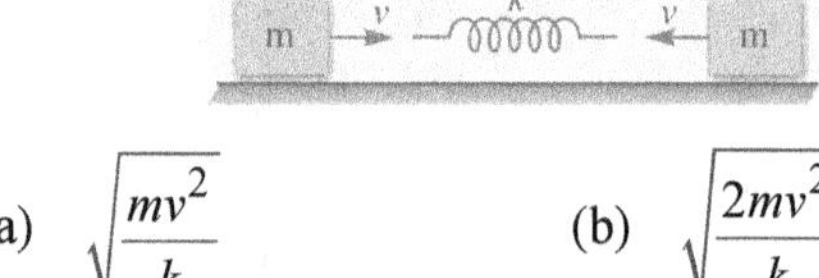

(a) $\sqrt{\dfrac{mv^2}{k}}$

(b) $\sqrt{\dfrac{2mv^2}{k}}$

(c) $\sqrt{\dfrac{mv^2}{2k}}$

(d) zero

31. A spring of mass M and length L (stiffness constant k) is compressed vertically downward against the floor so that its compressed length becomes $\dfrac{L}{2}$. On releasing it, the work done by it on the floor is :

(a) $\dfrac{1}{2}kL^2$

(b) $\dfrac{1}{2}k\left(\dfrac{L}{2}\right)^2$

(c) zero

(d) kL^2

32. Calculate the work done, if a wire is loaded by 'Mg' weight and the increase in length is 'l' :

(a) Mgl

(b) $\dfrac{Mgl}{2}$

(c) $2\,Mg\,l$

(d) zero

33. Two masses m_1 and m_2 $(m_1 < m_2)$ are positioned as shown in figure, m_1 being on the ground and m_2 at a height h above the ground. When m_2 is released, the speed at which it hits the ground will be

Answer	22	(b)	23	(c)	24	(a)	25	(d)	26	(a)	27	(b)
Key	28	(c)	29	(a)	30	(b)	31	(c)	32	(b)		

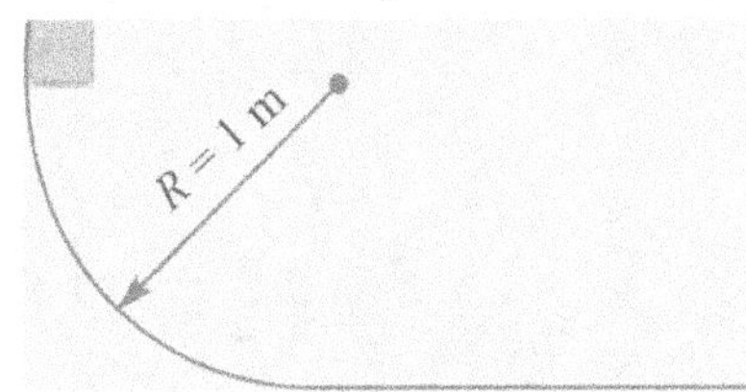

(a) $\sqrt{\dfrac{2ghm_1}{m_2}}$

(b) $\sqrt{\dfrac{2gh(m_1 - m_2)}{(m_1 + m_2)}}$

(c) $\sqrt{\dfrac{2gh(m_1 + m_2)}{(m_1 - m_2)}}$

(d) $\sqrt{\dfrac{2gh(m_2 - m_1)}{(m_1 + m_2)}}$

34. A 60 g bullet is fired through a stack of fibre board sheets 200 mm thick. If the bullet approaches the stack with a velocity of 600 m/s, and emerges out with a velocity of 300 m/s, the average resistance offered to the bullet is :

(a) 40.5 kN   (b) 2 k N

(c) 20.25 kN   (d) 10 kN

35. A block of mass of 1 kg slides down a curved track that is one quadrant of a circle of radius 1 m. Its speed at the bottom is 2 m/s. The work done by the frictional force is :

(a) 8 J   (b) -8 J

(c) 4 J   (d) -4 J

Power

36. The force required to tow a boat at constant velocity is proportional to the speed. If a speed of 4 km/h requires 7.5 kW, then a speed of 12 km/h requires nearly

(a) 68 kW   (b) 72 kW

(c) 15 kW   (d) 22.5 kW

37. A body of density 'D' and volume 'V' is lifted through height 'h' in a liquid of density 'd' ($<D$). The increase in potential energy of the body is:

(a) $V(D - d)\, hg$ (b) $VDgh$

(c) $Vdgh$ (d) $V(D + d)\, gh$

38. A force of $2\hat{i} + 3\hat{j} + 4\hat{k}$ N acts on a body for 4 second, produces a displacement of $(3\hat{i} + 4\hat{j} + 5\hat{k})m$. The power used is

(a) $9.5\ W$ (b) $7.5\ W$

(c) $6.5\ W$ (d) $4.5\ W$

39. Power of a water pump is 2 kW. If $g = 10$ m/s^2, the amount of water it can raise in one minute to a height of 10 m is

(a) 2000 litre   (b) 1000 litre

(c) 100 litre   (d) 1200 litre

40. A car of mass m starts from rest and accelerates so that the instaneous power delivered to the car has a constant magnitude P_0, the instantaneous velocity of the car is proportional to

(a) t^2 (b) $t^{1/2}$

(c) $t^{-1/2}$ (d) $\dfrac{t}{\sqrt{m}}$

41. An elevator of total mass (elevator + passenger) 1800 kg is moving up with a constant speed of 2 m/s. A frictional of 4000 N opposes its motion. Determine the approximate power delivered by the motor to the elevator ($g = 10$ m/s^2) **[NTSE -2005]**

(a) 59 hp   (b) 22 hp

(c) 34 hp   (d) 44 hp

42. A car of mass m is driven with acceleration a along a straight level road against a constant external resistive force R. When the velocity of the car is v, the rate at which the engine of the car is doing work will be

(a) Rv (b) mav

(c) $(R + ma)v$ (d) $(ma - R)v$

43. Water falls from a height of 60 m at the rate of 15 kg/s to operate a turbine. The losses due to frictional forces are 10% of energy. How much power is generated by the turbine ($g = 10$ m/s^2)

(a) 12.3 kW   (b) 7.0 kW

(c) 8.1 kW   (d) 10.2 kW

44. For the arrangement of pulleys shown in figure, the effort (P) required to raise the given load (W). Assume efficiency of the system as 80%:

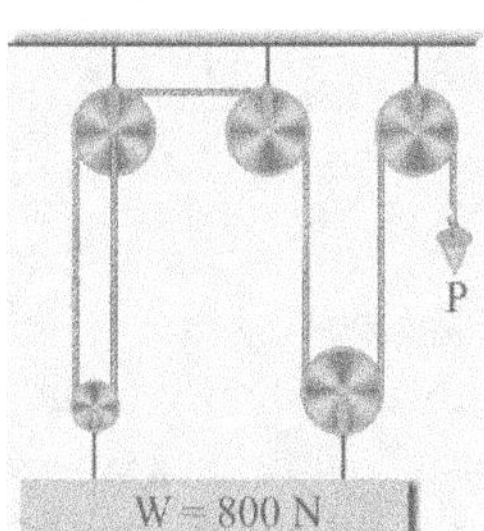

(a) 200 N   (b) 250 N

(c) 500 N   (d) 1000 N

Answer	33	(d)	34	(a)	35	(b)	36	(a)	37	(a)	38	(a)
Key	39	(d)	40	(b)	41	(d)	42	(c)	43	(c)	44	(b)

Work, Kinetic Energy, Potential Energy

1. At $t = 0$ a 1.0 kg ball is thrown from the top of a tall tower with velocity $\vec{v} = \left(8\hat{i} + 9\hat{j}\right)$ m/s. The change in the potential energy of the ball-earth system between $t = 0$ to $t = 5$ s : $(g = 10$ m/s$^2)$

(a) 800 J
(b) 1536 J
(c) 2100 J
(d) none of these

2. A particle in a conservative force field has a potential energy given by $U = \left(\dfrac{20xy}{z}\right)$. The force exerted on it is

(a) $\left(\dfrac{20y}{z}\right)\hat{i} + \left(\dfrac{20x}{z}\right)\hat{j} + \left(\dfrac{20xy}{z^2}\right)\hat{k}$

(b) $-\left(\dfrac{20y}{z}\right)\hat{i} - \left(\dfrac{20x}{z}\right)\hat{j} + \left(\dfrac{20xy}{z^2}\right)\hat{k}$

(c) $-\left(\dfrac{20y}{z}\right)\hat{i} - \left(\dfrac{20x}{z}\right)\hat{j} - \left(\dfrac{20xy}{z^2}\right)\hat{k}$

(d) $\left(\dfrac{20y}{z}\right)\hat{i} + \left(\dfrac{20x}{z}\right)\hat{j} - \left(\dfrac{20xy}{z^2}\right)\hat{k}$

3. A block of mass 10 kg is moving in x-direction with a constant speed of 10 m/s. It is subjected to a retarding force $F = -0.1\,x$ J/m during its travel from $x = 20$ m to $x = 30$ m. Its final kinetic energy will be :

(a) 475 J
(b) 450 J
(c) 275 J
(d) 250 J

4. Two springs A and B are identical but A is harder than $B(k_A > k_B)$. Let W_A and W_B represent the work done when the springs are stretched through the same distance and W'_A and W'_B are the work done when these are stretched by equal forces, then which of the following is true

(a) $W_A > W_B$ and $W'_A = W'_B$
(b) $W_A > W_B$ and $W'_A < W'_B$
(c) $W_A > W_B$ and $W'_A > W'_B$
(d) $W_A < W_B$ and $W'_A < W'_B$

5. The blades of a windmill sweap out a circle of area A. If the wind of density ρ flows at a velocity v perpendicular to the circle, then the kinetic energy of the air is

(a) $Av^2\rho t$
(b) $Av^3\rho t^2$
(c) $\dfrac{1}{2}Av^3\rho t$
(d) $\dfrac{Av^3\rho t}{2}$

6. A chain of length ℓ and mass m lies on the surface of a smooth hemisphere of radius $R > l$ with one end tied to the top of the hemisphere. Gravitational potential energy of the chain with reference level of the top of the hemisphere is :

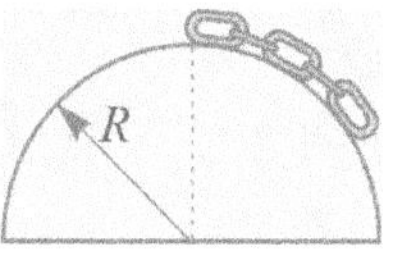

(a) $mg\,R$
(b) $\dfrac{mR^2 g}{l}$
(c) $mg\,R\sin\dfrac{l}{R}$
(d) $\dfrac{mR^2 g}{l}\left[\sin\dfrac{l}{R} - \dfrac{l}{R}\right]$

7. A point particle of mas 0.5 kg is moving along the x-axis under a force described by the potential energy U shown below. It is projected towards the right from the origin with a speed v.

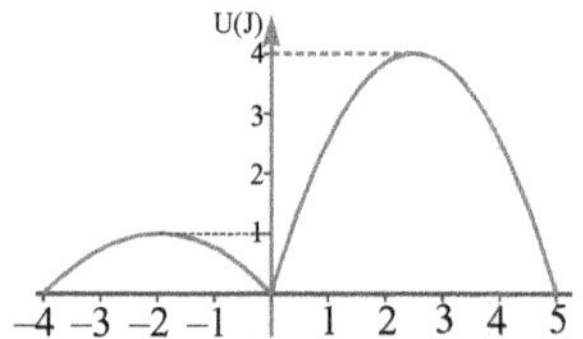

What is the minimum value of v for which the particle will escape infinitely far away from the origin : **[KVPY -2013]**

(a) $2\sqrt{2}$ m/s
(b) 2 m/s
(c) 4 m/s
(d) the particle will never escape

8. A variable force P is maintained tangent to a frictionless cylindrical surface of radius a as shown in figure. By slowly varying this force, a block of weight W is moved and the spring to which it is stretched from position 1 to position 2. The work done by the force P is :

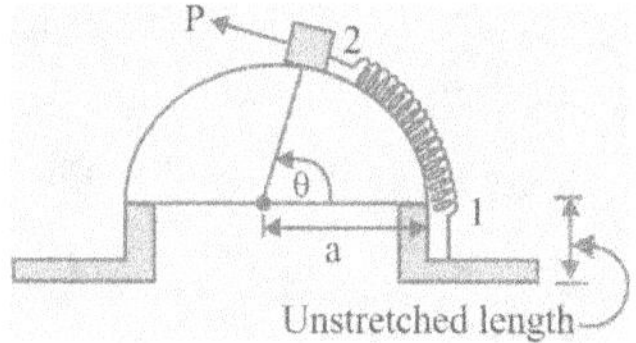

(a) $W\,a\sin\theta$
(b) $\dfrac{1}{2}ka^2\,\theta^2$
(c) $W\,a\sin\theta + k\,a^2\,\theta^2$
(d) $W\,a\sin\theta + \dfrac{1}{2}k\,a^2\,\theta^2$

Answer	1	(a)	2	(b)	3	(a)	4	(b)	5	(c)
Key	6	(d)	7	(d)	8	(d)				

9. A locomotive of mass m starts moving so that its velocity varies according to law $v = a\sqrt{s}$, where a is a constant, and s is the distance covered. The total work done performed by all the forces which are acting on the locomotive during first t seconds after the beginning of motion is :

   (a) ma^2t

   (b) $\dfrac{Ma^4t}{2}$

   (c) $\dfrac{Ma^4t^2}{8}$

   (d) none of these

10. A load hangs from a travelling crane, moving horizontally with velocity v. If the load is not to swing more than $4\,m$ horizontally, when the crane is stopped suddenly, what is the maximum allowable speed of the crane?

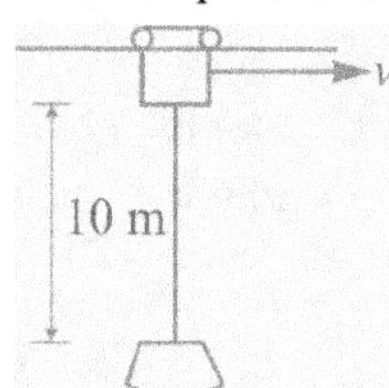

   (a) 4.05 m/s

   (b) 4.00 m/s

   (c) 3.00 m/s

   (d) 3.50 m/s

11. A meter stick, pivoted about horizontal axis through its centre, has a body of mass 2 kg attached to one end and a body of mass 1 kg attached to the other end. The system released from rest with the stick horizontal, the velocity of either mass as the stick swing through vertical position :

   (a) 2.2 m/s

   (b) 1.8 m/s

   (c) 1.5 m/s

   (d) 0.75 m/s

12. A block of mass m is released from rest at point 'A'. The compression in spring when the speed of the block is maximum:

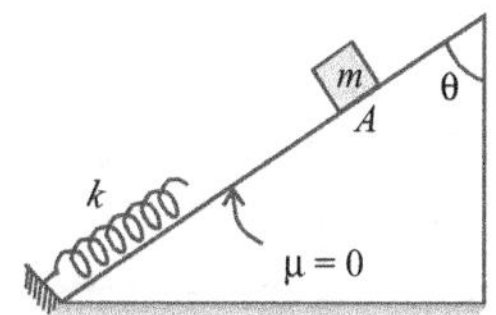

   (a) $\dfrac{mg\sin\theta}{k}$

   (b) $\dfrac{2mg\sin\theta}{k}$

   (c) $\dfrac{mg\cos\theta}{k}$

   (d) $\dfrac{mg}{k}$

13. A 10 kg block is pulled in the vertical plane along a frictionless surface in the form of an arc of a circle of radius 10 m. The applied force is of 200 N as shown in figure. If the block had started from rest at A, the velocity at B would be :

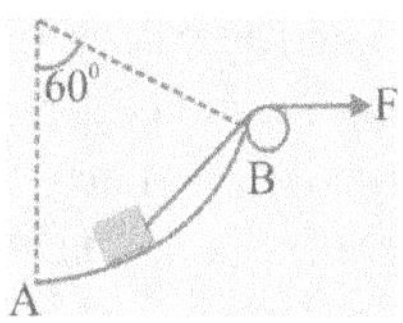

   (a) 1.7 m/s

   (b) 17 m/s

   (c) 27 m/s

   (d) 34 m/s

14. System shown in the figure is released from rest when spring is unstretched. Pulley and spring are massless and friction is absent everywhere. The speed of 5 kg block when 2 kg block leaves the contact with ground is: (Take force constant of spring $k = 40$ N/m and $g = 10$ m/s^2)

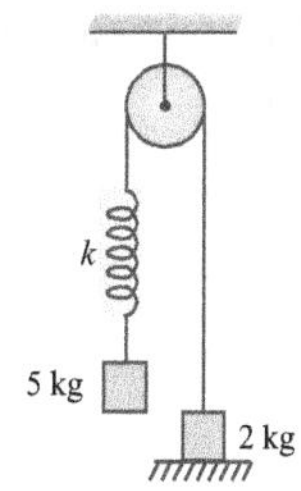

   (a) $\sqrt{2}$ m/s

   (b) $2\sqrt{2}$ m/s

   (c) 2 m/s

   (d) $4\sqrt{2}$ m/s

15. A vertical spring with force constant k is fixed on a table. A ball of mass m at a height h above the free upper end of the spring falls vertically on the spring so that the spring is compressed by a distance d. The net work done in the process is

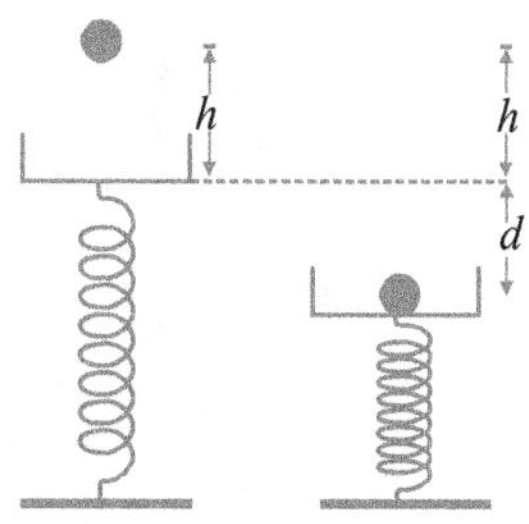

   (a) $mg(h+d) + \dfrac{1}{2}kd^2$

   (b) $mg(h+d) - \dfrac{1}{2}kd^2$

   (c) $mg(h-d) - \dfrac{1}{2}kd^2$

   (d) $mg(h-d) + \dfrac{1}{2}kd^2$

16. A block of mass 5 kg is suspended from the end of a vertical spring which is stretched by 10 cm under the load of the block. The block is given a sharp impulse from below so that it esquires an upward speed of 2m/s. The block will rise to a height ($g = 10 m/s^2$)

   (a) 0.10 m

   (b) 0.20 m

   (c) 0.25 m

   (d) none of these

Answer	9	(c)	10	(a)	11	(b)	12	(c)	13	(b)
Key	14	(b)	15	(b)	16	(b)				

17. Two identical cylindrical vessels with their bases at same level each contains a liquid of density ρ. The height of the liquid in one vessel is h_1 and that in the other vessel is h_2. The area of either base is A. The work done by gravity in equalizing the levels when the two vessels are connected, is

(a) $(h_1 - h_2)g\rho$

(b) $(h_1 - h_2)gA\rho$

(c) $\dfrac{1}{2}(h_1 - h_2)^2 gA\rho$

(d) $\dfrac{1}{4}(h_1 - h_2)^2 gA\rho$

18. A block of 60 kg is released from rest when comparison in the spring is 2m (normal length of spring is 8 m). Surface AB is smooth while surface BC is rough. Block travels x distance on rough surface before coming to complete rest. The value of x is : (g = 10 m/s^2)

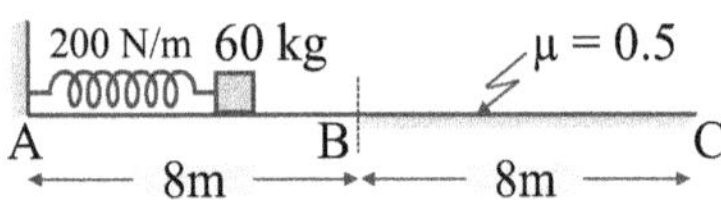

(a)   1 m

(b)   2 m

(c)   3 m

(d)   zero

19. In the figure shown PRQ is a curved vertical wall with rough inner surface with the floor is smooth. The radius of the curved wall is r and its length is quarter of a circle. A particle of mass m is projected on the floor at P, grazing the rough wall as shown , with an initial velocity v_0. The velocity of the particle at Q will be

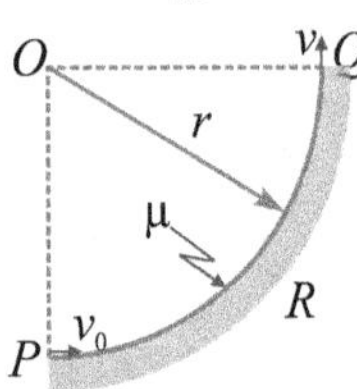

(a) $v = v_0 e^{-\mu\pi}$

(b) $v = v_0 e^{\frac{-\mu\pi}{r}}$

(c) $v = v_0 e^{\mu\pi}$

(d) $v = 0$

20. An object of mass m is travelling on a horizontal surface. There is a coefficient of kinetic friction μ between the object and the surface. The object has speed v when it reaches at $x = 0$ and later encounters a spring. The object compresses the spring, stops and then recoils and travel in opposite direction. When object reaches $x = 0$ on its return trip, it stops. From this information the spring constant k is

(a) $\dfrac{2\mu^2 mg^2}{v^2}$

(b) $\dfrac{4\mu^2 mg^2}{v^2}$

(c) $\dfrac{3\mu^2 mg^2}{v^2}$

(d) $\dfrac{16\mu^2 mg^2}{v^2}$

Power

21. An engine is hauling a train of mass M kg on a level track at a constant speed v m/s. The resistance due to friction is f N/kg. What extra power must the engine develop to maintain the speed up a gradient of h in s :

(a) $\dfrac{Mghv}{s}$

(b) $\dfrac{Mghs}{v}$

(c) $Mghvs$

(d) zero

22. From an automatic gun a man fires 360 bullet per minute with a speed of 360 km/hour. If each weight 20 g, the power of the gun is

(a)   600 W

(b)   300 W

(c)   150 W

(d)   75 W

23. A particle A of mass 10/7 kg is moving in the positive direction of x. Its initial position is $x = 0$ & initial velocity is 1 m/s. The velocity at $x = 10$ is: (use the graph given)

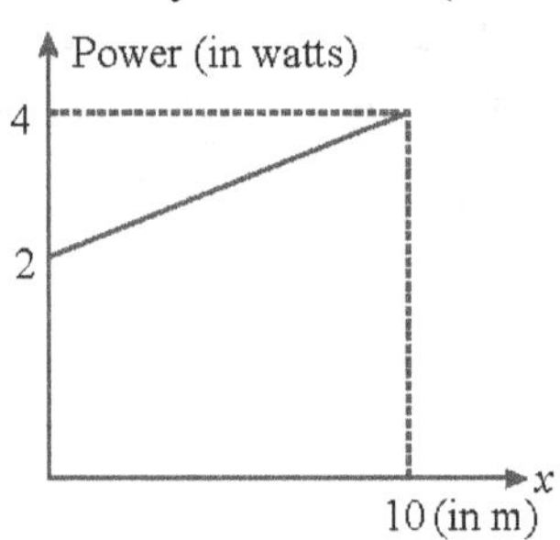

(a)   4 m/s

(b)   2 m/s

(c) $3\sqrt{2}$ m/s

(d)   100/3 m/s

24. A wind powered generator converts wind energy into electrical energy. Assume that the generator converts a fixed fraction of wind energy intercepted by its blades into electrical energy. For wind speed v, the electrical power output will be proportional to

(a) v

(b) v^2

(c) v^3

(d) v^4

Answer	17	(d)	18	(a)	19	(b)	20	(b)
Key	21	(a)	22	(a)	23	(a)	24	(c)

 Mechanics   **MCQ Type 2**   Exercise 7.2

Multiple Options Correct

1. No work is done by a force on an object if
   (a) the force is always perpendicular to its velocity
   (b) the force is always perpendicular to its acceleration
   (c) the object is stationary but the point of application of the force moves on the object
   (d) all the above

2. If a particle under the action a force F has potential energy U, then in equilibrium :
   (a) $F = 0$ and $U = 0$ (b) $F \neq 0$ but $U = 0$
   (c) $F = 0$ but $U \neq 0$ (d) $F \neq 0$ and $U \neq 0$

3. A ball of mass m is attached to the lower end of a light vertical spring of force constant k. The upper end of the spring is fixed. The ball is released from rest with the spring at its normal (unstretched) length, and comes to rest again after descending through a distance x :
   (a) $x = \dfrac{mg}{k}$

   (b) $x = \dfrac{2mg}{k}$

   (c) the ball will have no acceleration at the position where it has descended through $\dfrac{x}{2}$
   (d) the ball will have an upward acceleration equal to g at its lowermost position.

4. Consider two observes moving with respect to each other along a straight line. They observe a block moving a distance x on a rough surface. The following quantities will be different for two observes
   (a) kinetic energy of the block
   (b) work done by friction
   (c) acceleration of the block
   (d) force acting on the boc

5. A particle of mass $m = 1$ kg lying on x-axis experiences a force given by law $F = x(3x - 2)$ newton, where x is the x-coordinate of the particle in meters.
   The points on x-axis where the particle is in equilibrium are
   (a) $x = 0$ (b) $x = 1/3$
   (c) $x = 2/3$ (d) $x = 1$

6. A chain of mass m and length l rests on a rough - surfaced table so that one of its ends hangs over the edge. The chain starts sliding off the table all by itself provided the over hanging part equal to $\dfrac{1}{3}$ of the chain length. then :
   (a) coefficient of friction between table and chain is $\dfrac{1}{2}$

   (b) coefficient of friction between table and chain is $\dfrac{2}{3}$

   (c) the work done by the frictional forces acting on the table to completely sliding off the chain is $\dfrac{2}{3}\,mg\,l$

   (d) the work done by the frictional forces acting on the table to completely sliding off the chain is $\left[\dfrac{-mg\ell}{9}\right]$.

7. The potential energy of a particle of mass 5 kg, moving in the xy plane, is given by $U = -7x + 24y$, x and y being in metre. Initially (t = 0) the particle is at the origin and has velocity $\mathbf{u} = 14.4\,\hat{\mathbf{i}} + 4.2\,\hat{\mathbf{j}}$ m/s. Then
   (a) the speed of the particle at $t = 4$s is 25 m/s
   (b) the acceleration of the particle is 5 m/s^2
   (c) the direction of acceleration of the particle is perpendicular to its direction of motion initially
   (d) the direction of acceleration of the particle is along the direction of motion initially.

8. A simple pendulum consists of a point mass m attached to a light in extensible string of length L. The pendulum is given as initial angular displacement of $60°$ from the mean position and released from rest. During the period it moves from 60^0 to $30°$.
   (a) work done by gravity is $\dfrac{mgL(\sqrt{3}-1)}{4}$

   (b) work done by the string tension is $\dfrac{mgL(\sqrt{3}-1)}{4}$

   (c) work done by gravity is $\dfrac{mgL(\sqrt{3}-1)}{2}$

   (d) total work done by gravity and the string tension is $\dfrac{mgL(\sqrt{3}-1)}{2}$

9. A particle moves in one dimension in a conservative force field. The potential energy is depicted in the graph below. If the particle starts to move rest from the point A, then :
   [NSE -2013]

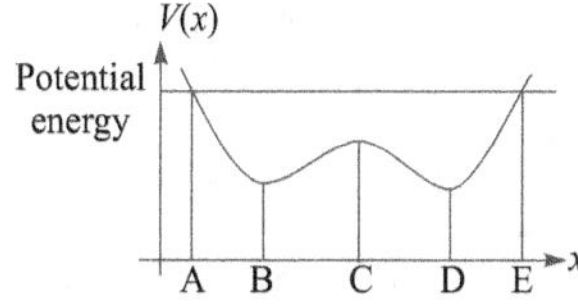

   (a) the speed is zero at the point A and E.
   (b) the acceleration vanishes at the point A, B, C, D, E
   (c) the acceleration vanishes at the points B, C, D
   (d) the speed is maximum at the point D.

Answer	1	(a,c)	2	(a, c)	3	(b, c, d)	4	(a, b)	5	(a, c)
Key	6	(a, d)	7	(a, b, c, d)	8	(c, d)	9	(a, c)		

10. Consider three fixed surfaces shown in the figure. Three blocks each of mass m are released from rest from top of the three surfaces. All blocks reach ground with same speed. Length of path travelled by blocks is same for second and third surface if coefficient of friction of three surfaces are μ_1, μ_2 and μ_3 respectively, then

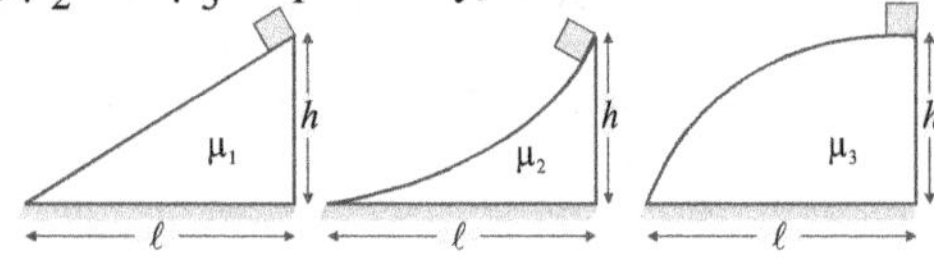

(a) $\mu_1 = \mu_2$ (b) $\mu_1 > \mu_2$

(c) $\mu_2 = \mu_3$ (d) $\mu_2 < \mu_3$

11. Two blocks of masses m and $2m$ are connected by a compressed spring with a string as shown in figure. The spring has an initial compression of $x = 1$ m. The force constant $k = 6$ N/m. Whole system is moving towards right with speed 1 m/s. Now if the spring is cut, then (Take $m = 1$ kg and no friction anywhere)

(a) when m is having maximum speed, the energy stored in the spring will be 6 J.

(b) the minimum speed attained by $2m$ is zero.

(c) when m is having maximum speed, the energy stored in the spring will be 3 J.

(d) The maximum speed attained by m is 3 m/s.

Answer Key	10	(b, d)	11	(b, d)		

Mechanics   # Reasoning Type Questions   Exercise 7.3

Read the two statements carefully to mark the correct option out of the options given below:

(a)   **Statement - 1** is true, **Statement - 2** is true; **Statement - 2** is correct explanation for **Statement - 1**.

(b)   **Statement -1** is true, **Statement - 2** is true; **Statement - 2** is not correct explanation for **Statement - 1**.

(c)   **Statement - 1** is true, **Statement - 2** is false.

(d)   **Statement - 1** is false, **Statement - 2** is true

1.   **Statement - 1** Work done by friction on a body sliding down an inclined plane is positive.
Statement - 2 Work done is greater than zero, if angle between force and displacement is acute.

2.   **Statement - 1**
The rate of change of total momentum of a many particle system is proportional to the sum of the internal forces of the system.
Statement - 2 Internal forces can change the kinetic energy but not the momentum of the system.

3.   **Statement - 1**
The linear momentum of body increases by 50%, the corresponding increase in kinetic energy is 100 %.

Statement - 2 Kinetic energy, $K = \dfrac{p^2}{2m}$ then it may be written as $\dfrac{\Delta K}{K} = 2\dfrac{\Delta P}{P}$.

4.   **Statement - 1** If the velocity of a body is doubled and stopping force remains same then stopping distance becomes 2 times.

Statement - 1 Kinetic energy of the body $K = \dfrac{1}{2}mv^2$.

5.   **Statement - 1**
A force applied on the body always does work on the body.
Statement - 2
If a force applied on a body displaces the body along the direction of force work done will be maximum.

6.   **Statement - 1**
No work is done on a revolving electron around the nucleus of an atom.
Statement - 2 Work done is centripetal force is always zero.

7.   **Statement - 1**
When a body moves vertically upward, work done by gravitational force is negative.
Statement - 2
According to conservation of mechanical energy, $\Delta K + \Delta U = 0$.

8.   **Statement - 1**
A man rowing a boat upstream is at rest with respect to the bank. He is doing no external work.
Statement - 2 Work done by constant force, $W = F s \cos \theta$.

9.   **Statement - 1**
When a machine gun fires n bullets per second each with kinetic energy K, the power of a gun is $P = nK$
Statement - 2 Power P = work done / time

10.   **Statement - 1**
A block of mass m starts moving on a rough horizontal surface with a velocity v. It stops due to friction between the block and the surface after moving through a certain distance. The surface is now tilted to an angle 30° with the horizontal and the same block is made to go up on the surface with the same initial velocity v. The decrease in the mechanical energy in the second situation is smaller than that in the first situation.
Statement - 2
The coefficient of friction between the block and the surface decreases with the increase in the angle of inclination.

11.   **Statement - 1:** A work done by friction is always negative.
Statement - 2: Frictional force acts on a body its $K.E.$ may decrease.

12.   **Statement - 1:** The work done in moving a body over a closed loop is zero for every force in nature.
Statement - 2: Work done depends on nature of force.

Answer	1	(d)	2	(d)	3	(d)	4	(d)	5	(d)	6	(a)
Key	7	(b)	8	(a)	9	(a)	10	(c)	11	(d)	12	(b)

Mechanics | **Passage & Matrix** | **Exercise 7.4**

PASSAGES

Passage for (Questions 1 & 2) :

A block of mass M is suspended through a vertical spring of force constant k. A mud piece of mass M is dropped on the block from a height $2\,h$. The mud piece sticks to the block after the impact.

1. Kinetic energy of the block + mud just after impact is :
  - (a) $Mg\,h$
  - (b) $2\,Mg\,h$
  - (c) $4\,Mg\,h$
  - (d) $8\,Mg\,h$

2. The maximum extension of the spring is :

  - (a) $\dfrac{2Mg}{k}$

  - (b) $\dfrac{2Mg+\sqrt{4M^2g^2+2Mgkh}}{k}$

  - (c) $\dfrac{Mg+\sqrt{2M^2g^2+2Mgkh}}{2k}$

  - (d) none

Passage for (Questions. 3 & 4) :

A heavy particle is suspended by a string of length l. The particle is given a horizontal velocity v_0. The string becomes stack at an angle θ and the particle proceeds on a parabola as shown in figure :

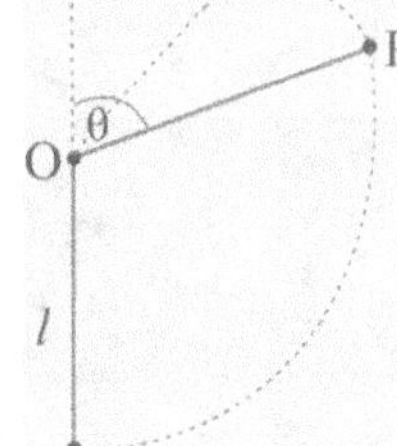

3. The value of θ is :
  - (a) $45°$
  - (b) $\cos^{-1}(\sqrt{2})$
  - (c) $\tan^{-1}(\sqrt{2})$
  - (d) $\sin^{-1}(\sqrt{2})$

4. If the particle passes through the point of suspension, then the value of v_0 is :
  - (a) $\sqrt{2}\,gl$
  - (b) $\sqrt{gl}(\sqrt{3}+1)$
  - (c) $3\sqrt{2}\,gl$
  - (d) $\sqrt{gl}(2+\sqrt{3})^{1/2}$

Passage for (Questions 5 & 6) :

A ball with mass m is attached to the end of a rod of mass M and length l. The other end of the rod is pivoted so that the ball can move in a vertical circle. The rod is held in the horizontal position shown in figure and then given just enough a downward push so that the ball swings down and around and just reaches the vertical upward position, having zero speed there.

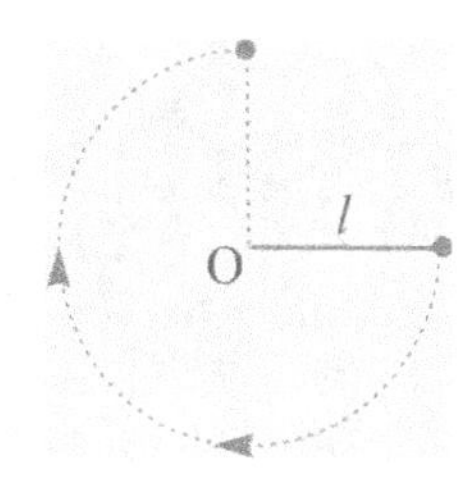

5. The change in potential energy of the system (ball + rod) :
  - (a) $mg\,l$
  - (b) $(M+m)\,gl$
  - (c) $\left(\dfrac{M}{2}+m\right)gl$
  - (d) $\dfrac{(M+m)}{2}\,gl$

6. The initial speed was given to the ball :
  - (a) $\sqrt{\dfrac{Mgl+2mgl}{m}}$
  - (b) $\sqrt{2gl}$
  - (c) $\sqrt{\dfrac{2Mgl+mgl}{m}}$
  - (d) none

Passage for (Questions 7 to 9) :

A block of mass m is kept over another block of mass $2m$ and the system rests on a horizontal surface as shown in figure. A constant horizontal force F acting on the lower block produces an acceleration $\left(\dfrac{F}{6m}\right)$ in the system, the two blocks always move together.

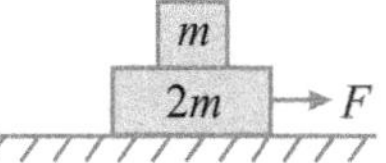

7. The coefficient of kinetic friction between bigger block and horizontal surface is
  - (a) $\dfrac{F}{3mg}$
  - (b) $\dfrac{F}{g}$
  - (c) $\dfrac{F}{6mg}$
  - (d) $\dfrac{3mg}{F}$

8. The frictional force acting on the smaller blcok is
  - (a) $\dfrac{F}{6}$
  - (b) $\dfrac{F}{3}$
  - (c) $\dfrac{F}{4}$
  - (d) $\dfrac{F}{2}$

9. The work done by frictional force on the smaller block by the bigger block during a displacement 1 m is
  - (a) $\dfrac{F}{6}$
  - (b) $\dfrac{F}{3}$
  - (c) $\dfrac{F}{4}$
  - (d) $\dfrac{F}{2}$

Passage for (Questions 10 & 11) :

A small block of mass 1 kg is released from rest at the top of a rough track. The track is a circular arc of radius 40 m. The block slides along the track without toppling and a frictional force acts on it in the direction opposite to the instantaneous velocity. The work done in overcoming the friction up to the point Q, as shown in the figure below, is 150 J.
(Take the acceleration due to gravity, $g = 10$ ms^{-2})

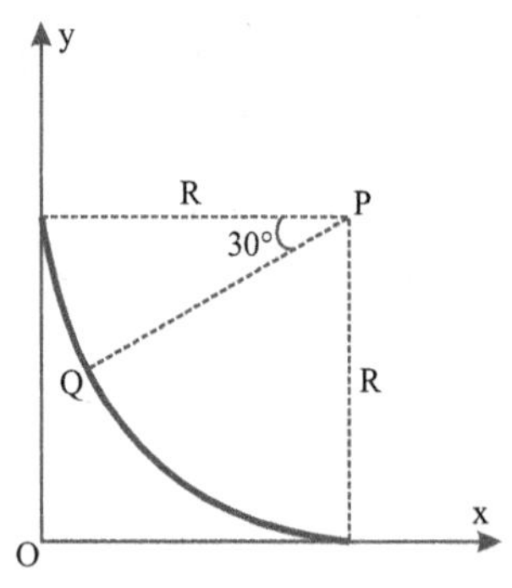

10. The magnitude of the normal reaction that acts on the block at the point Q is

(a) 7.5 N   (b) 8.6 N

(c) 11.5 N   (d) 22.5 N

11. The speed of the block when it reaches the point Q is

(a) 5 ms^{-1} (b) 10 ms^{-1}

(c) $10\sqrt{3}$ ms^{-1} (d) 20 ms^{-1}

(JEE Adv. 2013)

MATRIX MATCHING

12. Column I represents work done by forces and column II represents change in kinetic energy Δk, change in potential energy ΔU, change in mechanical energy ΔE. Then match the two column:

Column I

A. Work done by conservative force

B. Work done by non-conservative force

C. Work done by internal force

D. Work done by external force

Column II (magnitude only)

(p) ΔK

(q) ΔU

(r) ΔE

13. An automobile of mass m accelerates, starting from rest, while the engine supplied constant power P. Match the following columns:

Column I

A. Acceleration at time t

B. Velocity at time t

C. Position at time t

Column II

(p) $(2pt/m)^{\frac{1}{2}}$

(q) $(8p/9m)^{\frac{1}{2}} t^{3/2}$

(r) $\left(\dfrac{P}{2mt}\right)^{\frac{1}{2}}$

Answer Key	1	(a)	2	(b)	3	(c)	4	(d)	5	(c)	6	(a)
	7	(c)	8	(a)	9	(a)	10	(a)	11	(a)		
	12	A → p, q; B → p, q; C → p, q; D → p, r					13	A → r; B → p; C → q				

Mechanics   # Best of JEE-(Main & Advanced)   Exercise 7.5

JEE- (Main)

1. A particle moves in a straight line with retardation proportional to its displacement. Its loss of kinetic energy for any displacement x is proportional to   **[AIEEE 2004]**

(a) x^2 (b) e^x

(c) x (d) $\log_e x$

2. The block of mass M moving on the frictionless horizontal surface collides with the spring of spring constant k and compresses it by length L. The maximum momentum of the block after collision is :   **[AIEEE 2005]**

(a) $\dfrac{ML^2}{k}$ (b) zero

(c) $\dfrac{kL^2}{2M}$ (d) $\sqrt{MkL}$

3. A body of mass m accelerates uniformly from rest to velocity v_1 in time t_1. The instantaneous power delivered to the body is :   **[AIEEE 2005]**

(a) $mv_1^2 t_1/t^2$ (b) $mv_1^2 t_1^2/t$

(c) $mv_1^2 t/t_1^2$ (d) $mv_1^2 t^2/t_1^3$

4. A mass of M kg is suspended by a weightless string. The horizontal force that is required to displace it until the string makes an angle of $45°$ with the initial vertical direction is :   **[AIEEE 2006]**

(a) $Mg(\sqrt{2}-1)$ (b) $Mg(\sqrt{2}+1)$

(c) $Mg\sqrt{2}$ (d) $\dfrac{Mg}{\sqrt{2}}$

5. The potential energy of 1 kg particle free to move along the x-axis is given by $U(x) = \left(\dfrac{x^4}{4} - \dfrac{x^2}{2}\right)$ J . The total mechanical energy of the particle is 2 J then, the maximum speed in (m/s) is :   **[AIEEE 2006]**

(a) 2

(b) $\dfrac{3}{\sqrt{2}}$

(c) $\sqrt{2}$

(d) $\dfrac{1}{\sqrt{2}}$

6. The potential energy between two atoms in a molecule is given by $U(x) = \dfrac{a}{x^{12}} - \dfrac{b}{x^6}$; where a and b are positive constants and x is the distance between the atoms. The atom is in stable equilibrium when :   **[AIEEE 2010]**

(a) $x = \sqrt[3]{\dfrac{11a}{5b}}$

(b) $x = \sqrt{\dfrac{a}{2b}}$

(c) $x = 0$

(d) $x = \sqrt[6]{\dfrac{2a}{b}}$

13. When a rubber-band is stretched by a distance x, it exerts restoring force of magnitude $F = ax + bx^2$ where a and b are constants. The work done in stretching the unstretched rubber-band by L is: **[JEE-Main 2014]**

(a) $aL^2 + bL^3$

(b) $\dfrac{1}{2}\left(aL^2 + bL^3\right)$

(c) $\dfrac{aL^2}{2} + \dfrac{bL^3}{3}$

(d) $\dfrac{1}{2}\left(\dfrac{aL^2}{2} + \dfrac{bL^3}{3}\right)$

JEE- (Advanced)

8. A particle is placed at the origin and a force $F = kx$ is acting on it (where k is positive constant). If $U(0) = 0$, the graph of $U(x)$ versus x will be (where U is the potential energy function) :   **[IIT-JEE 2004]**

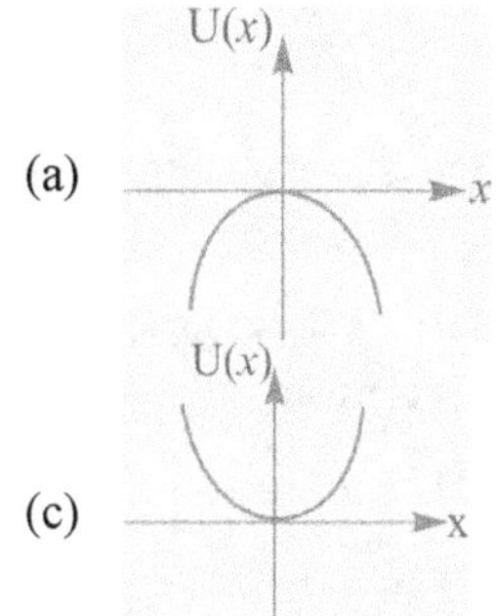

(a)

(b)

(c)

(d)

9. A block B is attached to two unstretched springs S_1 and S_2 with spring constants k and $4k$, respectively (see figure I). The other ends are attached to identical supports M_1 and M_2 not attached to the walls. The springs and supports have negligible mass. There is no friction anywhere. The block B is displaced towards wall 1 by small distance x (figure II) and released. The block returns and moved a maximum distance y towards wall 2. Displacements x and y are measured with respect to the equilibrium position of the block B. The ratio $\dfrac{y}{x}$ is :   **[IIT-JEE 2008]**

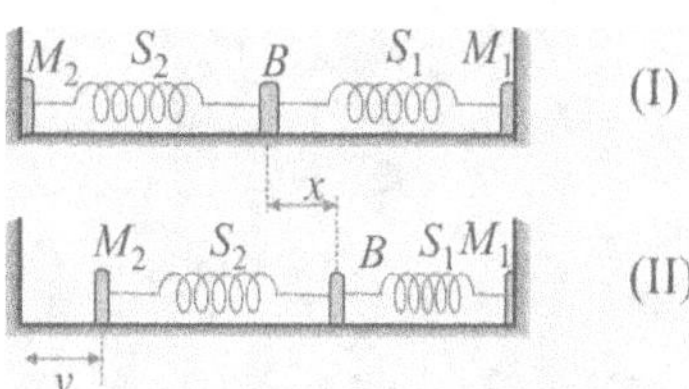

(a) 4

(b) 2

(c) $\dfrac{1}{2}$

(d) $\dfrac{1}{4}$

10. A ball moves over a fixed track as shown in the figure. From A to B the ball rolls without slipping. Surface BC is frictionless K_A, K_B and K_C are kinetic energies of the ball at A, B and C respectively. Then :   **[IIT-JEE 2009]**

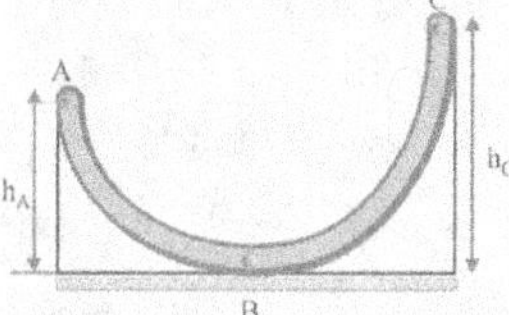

(a) $h_A > h_C$; $K_B > K_C$

(b) $h_A > h_C$; $K_C > K_A$

(c) $h_A = h_C$; $K_B = K_C$

(d) $h_A < h_C$; $K_B > K_C$

11. A block of mass 2 kg is free to move along the x-axis. It is at rest and from t = 0 onwards it is subjected to a time-dependent force $F(t)$ in the x direction. The force $F(t)$ varies with t as shown in the figure. The kinetic energy of the block after 4.5 seconds is   **[IIT-JEE 2010]**

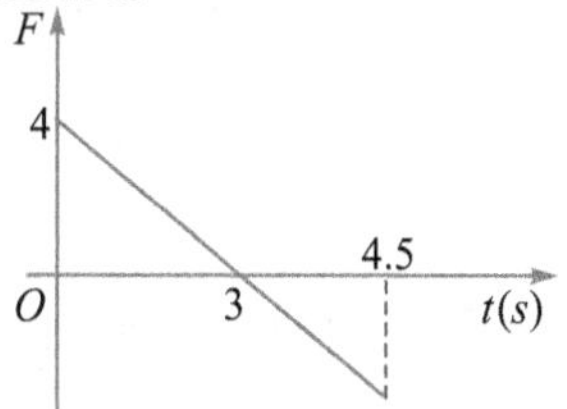

(a) 4.50 J

(b) 7.50 J

(c) 5.06 J

(d) 14.06 J

12. At time $t = 0$ s, particle starts moving along the x-axis. If its kinetic energy increases uniformly with time t, the net force acting on it must be proportional to   **[IIT-JEE 2011]**

(a) $\sqrt{t}$

(b) constant

(c) t

(d) $\dfrac{1}{\sqrt{t}}$

13. The work done on a particle of mass m by a force,

$$K\left[\dfrac{x}{(x^2 + y^2)^{3/2}}\hat{i} + \dfrac{y}{(x^2 + y^2)^{3/2}}\hat{j}\right]$$

(K being a constant of appropriate dimensions), when the particle is taken from the point $(a, 0)$ to the point $(0, a)$ along a circular path of radius a about the origin in the $x - y$ plane is   **[JEE Adv. 2013]**

(a) $\dfrac{2K\pi}{a}$

(b) $\dfrac{K\pi}{a}$

(c) $\dfrac{K\pi}{2a}$

(d) 0

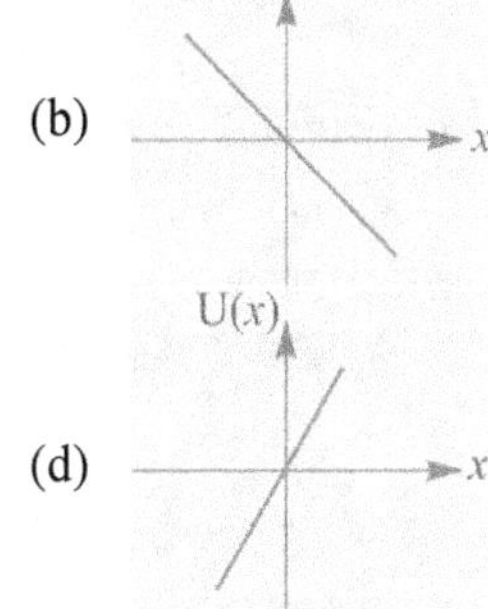

Answer	1	(a)	2	(d)	3	(c)	4	(a)	5	(b)	6	(d)	7	(c)
Key	8	(a)	9	(c)	10	(a, b)	11	(c)	12	(d)	13	(d)		

Hints & Solutions

In Chapter Exercise -7.1

1. (a) Work done by gravitational force
$$W = mgh = 2 \times 10 \times 8.5 = 170 \text{ J}$$

(b) The change in potential energy
$$\Delta U = -W = -170 \text{ J}$$

(c) $$U_i = mgh_i = 2 \times 10 \times 10 = 200 \text{ J}$$

(d) $$U_f = mgh_f = 2 \times 10 \times 1.5 = 30 \text{ J}$$

(e) Work done, $$W = mgh = 2 \times 10 \times 8.5 = 170 \text{ J}$$

(f) $$\Delta U = -170 \text{ J}$$

(g) $$U_i = 100 + mgh_i = 300 \text{ J}$$

(h) $$U_f = 100 + mgh_f = 130 \text{ J}$$

2. (a) The work done from initial to lowest point,
$$W = [\text{gravitational force}] \times [\text{displacement}] = mgL.$$

(b) Upto highest point, $W = mg(-L) = -mgL$

Do the next parts similarly.

3. (a) Work done by gravitational force
$$W = [\text{gravitational force}] \times [\text{displacement in its direction}]$$
$$= mg \times \frac{h}{2} = \frac{mgh}{2} \qquad \textbf{\textit{Ans.}}$$

(b) $W = mg \times 0 = 0$ **_Ans._**

(c) By conservation of mechanical energy, we have
$$\frac{1}{2}mv_0{}^2 + mgh = \frac{1}{2}mv^2$$
$$\therefore \qquad v = \sqrt{v_0{}^2 + 2gh} \qquad \textbf{\textit{Ans.}}$$

4. Force acts for 30 s, so impulse of force in this duration = area of $F-t$ graph

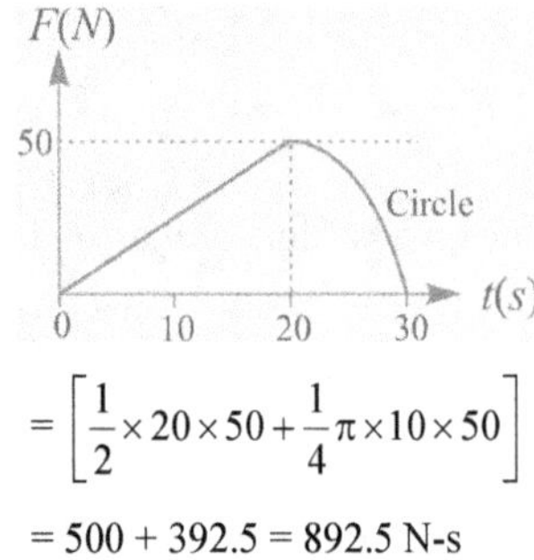

$$= \left[\frac{1}{2} \times 20 \times 50 + \frac{1}{4}\pi \times 10 \times 50\right]$$
$$= 500 + 392.5 = 892.5 \text{ N-s}$$

Let v be the velocity of the particle after 30 s, then
$$\vec{J} = m(\vec{v_f} - \vec{v_i}) \text{ or } 892.5 = 16\,(v - 0)$$
or $v = \textbf{55.78 m/s}$ *Ans*

As no force acts after 30s, so speed of the particle remains constant thereafter. Therefore speed of particle at 40 s will be 55.78 m/s.

5. By work-energy theorem, we can write
$$W_{\text{friction}} + W_{\text{external force}} + W_{\text{gravity}} = \Delta K$$

$$-fs + 400 \times s - 300 \times s \sin 30° = \frac{1}{2}m\left(v^2 - 1.5^2\right)$$

$$0.2 \times 300 \cos 30° \times 6 + 400 \times 6 - 300 \times 6 \sin 30°$$
$$= \frac{1}{2} \times 30 \times \left(v^2 - 1.5^2\right)$$

After solving, we get $v = 8.94$ m/s   **_Ans._**

6. If a is the acceleration of the block A, then acceleration of block B will be $a/2$. Thus
$$150g\sin\theta_1 - (T + \mu \times 150g\cos\theta_1) = 150\,a \qquad ...(i)$$
and $$T' = 2T$$
$$T' - (200g\sin\theta_2 + \mu \times 200g\cos\theta_2) = 200\,a \qquad ...(ii)$$
The velocity of the block A,
$$v^2 = 0 + 2as$$

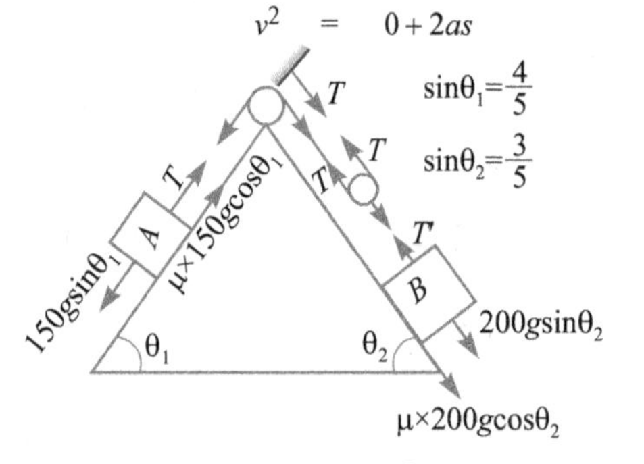

$$\therefore \qquad s = \frac{v^2}{2a} \qquad ...(iii)$$

After substituting the known values and simplifying, we get
$$s = 3.529 \text{ m} \qquad \textbf{\textit{Ans.}}$$

7. Suppose block D will rise to height h when block C hits the wall. As total length of the string is constant, so
$$1 + 1 + y + h = 1 + \sqrt{2^2 + 1^2} + y$$
$$\therefore \qquad h = \left(\sqrt{5} - 1\right)\text{m}$$

If v is the velocity of the block C, then its component along BC will be $v\cos\theta$. Thus upward velocity of block D will be $v\cos\theta$, where $\cos\theta = 2/\sqrt{5}$.

Now by conservation of mechanical energy, we have

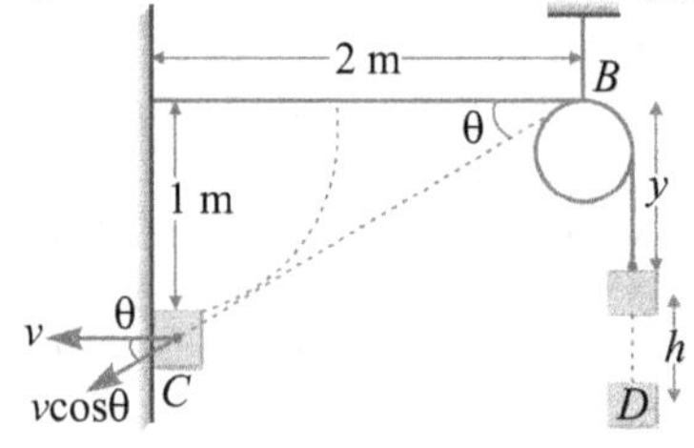

$$Mg \times 1 = mgh + \frac{1}{2}Mv^2 + \frac{1}{2}m(v\cos\theta)^2$$

After substituting the values and solving, we get
$$v = 3.36 \text{ m/s} \qquad \textbf{\textit{Ans.}}$$

8. The force needed to move the engine with constant speed

$$F = mg\sin\theta + \mu mg\cos\theta$$
$$= 100000\times 9.8\times 0.087 + 0.1\times 100000\times 9.8\times 0.99$$
$$= 182887\ \text{N}$$

The energy needed

$$E = Fvt$$
$$= 182887\times 100\times 1$$
$$= 18288700\ \text{J}$$

The amount of coal needed with the engine efficiency 4%,

$$m = \frac{E}{\eta\times 50000}$$
$$= \frac{18288700}{0.04\times 50000} = 9.15\times 10^3\,\text{kg}$$

Ans.

In Chapter Exercise -7.2

1. The power generated $= \eta\left[\dfrac{mgh}{t}\right]$

$$= 0.50\left[\frac{1.8\times 10^5\times 9.8\times 100}{3600}\right]$$
$$= 2.45\times 10^4\,\text{W}$$

The number of 100 W bulb can be lit from this power

$$= \frac{2.45\times 10^4}{100} = 245$$

Ans.

2. Given, $\sin\theta = \dfrac{1}{50}$

The force needed to move the truck up the plane

$$F_1 = W\sin\theta + \frac{W}{25} = \frac{W}{50} + \frac{W}{25} = \frac{3W}{50}$$

When truck moves down the plane, force needed

$$F_2 = \frac{W}{25} - W\sin\theta = \frac{W}{25} - \frac{W}{50} = \frac{W}{50}$$

If v_2 is the speed of truck down the plane, then for same power,

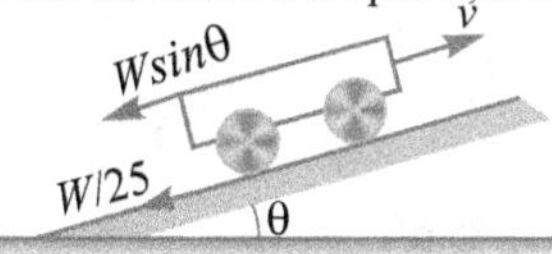

$$F_1 v_1 = F_2 v_2$$
$$\therefore\quad v_2 = 3v_1 = 3\times 24 = 72\ \text{km/h}$$

Ans.

3. (1) The tractive resistance $F_1 = 5\times 120 = 600\ \text{N}$

The power required P_1

$$= \frac{F_1 v}{\eta} = \frac{600\times\left(20\times\dfrac{5}{18}\right)}{0.80}$$
$$= 4170\ \text{W}$$

Ans.

(2) Force needed $F_2 = 600 + Mg\sin\theta$

$$= 600 + \left(120\times 10^3\right)\times\frac{1}{300}$$
$$= 1000\ \text{N}$$

Power needed P_2

$$= \frac{F_2 v}{\eta} = \frac{1000\times\left(20\times\dfrac{5}{18}\right)}{0.80}$$
$$= 6940\ \text{W}$$

Ans.

(3) Force needed $F_3 = 600 - 400 = 200\ \text{N}$

Power needed P_3

$$= \frac{F_3\times v}{\eta} = \frac{200\times\left(20\times\dfrac{5}{18}\right)}{0.80}$$
$$= 1390\ \text{W}$$

Ans.

4. The velocity of mass m at any instant

$$\vec{\mathbf{v}} = v_0\cos\alpha\,\hat{\mathbf{i}} + \left(v_0\sin\alpha - gt\right)\hat{\mathbf{j}}$$

and $\vec{\mathbf{F}} = mg\left(-\hat{\mathbf{j}}\right).$

The instantaneous power

$$P = \vec{\mathbf{F}}\cdot\vec{\mathbf{v}} = mg\left(gt - v_0\sin\alpha\right)$$

The average power

$$P_{av} = \frac{1}{T}\int_0^T P\,dt = 0$$

Ans.

5. Given $m = 0.36$ kg, $M = 0.72$ kg. The figure shows the forces on m and M. When the system is released, let the acceleration be a. Then

$$T - mg = ma$$
$$Mg - T = Ma$$
$$\therefore\quad a = \frac{(M-m)g}{M+m} = g/3$$

and $T = 4\,mg/3$

For block m :

$u = 0$, $a = g/3$, $t = 1$, $s = ?$

$$s = ut + \frac{1}{2}at^2 = 0 + \frac{1}{2}\times\frac{g}{3}\times 1^2 = g/6$$

$\therefore$ Work done by the string on m is

$$\vec{T}.\vec{s} = Ts = 4\frac{mg}{3}\times\frac{g}{6} = \frac{4\times 0.36\times 10\times 10}{3\times 6} = 8\text{J}$$

---

1. (b)

2. (a) $\vec{F}\cdot\vec{s} = 0$

or $(6\hat{i} + 2\hat{j} + 3\hat{k}).(2\hat{i} - 3\hat{j} - x\hat{k}) = 0$

or $6\times 2 - 2\times 3 - 3x = 0$

$\therefore\qquad x = 2$

3. (c) $W = \vec{F}.(\vec{r}_f - \vec{r}_i) = (5\hat{i} + 3\hat{j}).(2\hat{i} - \hat{j})$

$= 5\times 2 - 3\times 1 = 7\,\text{J}$

4. (b) Work done does not depend on path and so $W_1 = W_2 = W_3$

5. (c) Potential energy of the spring will transfer to the kinetic energy of air molecules.

6. (a)
$$0 = P_{bullet} + P_{rifle}$$
$$\therefore \quad P_{rifle} = -P_{bullet}$$

As $K = \dfrac{p^2}{2m}$, $\therefore K_{rifle}$ will be less than K_{bullet}

7. (a) As $K = \dfrac{P^2}{2m}$; $K \propto \dfrac{1}{m}$.

8. (a) $P = \sqrt{2mK}$, and $P' = \sqrt{2m(K+3K)} = 2P$

$$\therefore \quad \frac{P'-P}{P} \times 100 = \frac{2P-P}{P} \times 100 = 100\%$$

9. (b) At $x = 0$, $v_i = 5(0)^{3/2} = 0$

and $x = 2\ m$, $v_f = 5(2)^{3/2} = 5\sqrt{8}$ m/s

$W = \Delta K$

$$= \frac{1}{2} m \left(v_f^2 - v_i^2 \right)$$

$$= \frac{1}{2} \times 0.5 \left[\left(5\sqrt{8} \right)^2 - 0^2 \right]$$

$$= 50 \text{ J}$$

10. (a) W = area of $\vec{F} - x$

$$= m \left[\text{area of } \vec{a} - x \right]$$

$$= 2 \left[\frac{1}{2}(5+3) \times 6 - \frac{1}{2}(2+1) \times 6 \right] = 30 \text{ J}$$

11. (c) We known that $K = \dfrac{1}{2} mv^2$

$\Rightarrow$ It represent a parabola about y-axis.

12. (d) As potential energy depends on reference level, so it may be 20 J or 25 J, both are correct.

13. (b) $J = P - P_i$

or $30 \times 2 - 10 \times 1 = P - 0 \Rightarrow P = 50$ N-s

Now $\qquad W = K = \dfrac{P^2}{2m} = \dfrac{50^2}{2 \times 10} = 125 \text{ J}$

14. (d) $\qquad\qquad W = K_f - K_i$

or $\qquad \displaystyle\int_3^4 (-6x)\,dx = \dfrac{1}{2} \times 2(v_f^2 - 8^2)$

or $\qquad \left| \dfrac{-6x^2}{2} \right|_3^4 = v_f^2 - 64$

or $\quad -3\,|\,4^2 - 3^2\,| = v_f^2 - 64$

$\therefore \qquad\qquad v_f = 6.6$ m/s

15. (a) $\vec{F} = -5\hat{i} + 9\cos 60°\hat{i} + 9\sin 60°\hat{j} - 3\hat{j}$

$$= -5\hat{i} + \frac{9}{2}\hat{i} + \frac{9\sqrt{3}}{2}\hat{j} - 3\hat{j}$$

$$= -\frac{\hat{i}}{2} + \left(\frac{9\sqrt{3}}{2} - 3 \right)\hat{j}$$

$\vec{s} = -3\hat{i}$.

$$W = \vec{F}.\vec{s} = \left[-\frac{\hat{i}}{2} + \left(\frac{9\sqrt{3}}{2} - 3 \right)\hat{j} \right].(-3\hat{i})$$

$$= 1.5 \text{ J}.$$

16. (d) $|F| = \dfrac{dU}{dx}$, which is greatest in the reagion CD.

17. (d) $\dfrac{1}{2} mv^2 + mgh = \dfrac{1}{2} m(3)^2$

or $\dfrac{v^2}{2} + g \times 0.5(1 - \cos 60°) = \dfrac{9}{2}$

$\therefore v = 2$ m/s

18. (d) $\dfrac{1}{2} kx^2 = mgh$

or $h = \dfrac{kx^2}{2mg}$

19. (a) Heat produced = loss in P.E.

$= mgh$

$= 0.3 \times 10 \times 3 = 9$ J

20. (a) In the device when free end of the string is pulled by ℓ, the block will rise by $\ell/2$. So increase in potential energy $U = mg\ell/2$.

21. (c) $F = -\dfrac{dU}{dr} = 0$

22. (b) The tension in the string, $T = F$.

Also $W_{gravity} + W_{tension} = \Delta K$

$\therefore \qquad W_{tension} = \Delta K - W_{gravity}$

23. (c) $\qquad Mg(h+s) = Fs$

$\therefore \qquad\qquad F = Mg\left(1 + \dfrac{h}{s} \right)$.

24. (a) $v = \dfrac{dx}{dt} = \dfrac{d(3t - 4t^2 + t^3)}{dt} = 3 - 8t + 3t^2$

$t = 0$, $\qquad 3$ m/s

$t = 4$, $v_f = 3 - 8 \times 4 + 3 \times 4^2 = 19$ m/s

Now, $\qquad W = \dfrac{1}{2} m(v_f^2 - v_i^2)$

$$= \frac{1}{2} \times 30 \times 10^{-3}[19^2 - 3^2] = 5.28 \ J.$$

25. (d) $\qquad \dfrac{1}{2} m \times 4^2 = mgh + \dfrac{\dfrac{1}{2} m(4)^2}{2}$

$\therefore \qquad\qquad h = 0.4$ m

26. (a) $\qquad W = \dfrac{1}{2} m(v_f^2 - v_i^2)$

$$= \frac{1}{2} \times 100 \times 10^{-3}(0^2 - 5^2)$$

$$= -1.25 \ J.$$

27. (b) $a_A = \dfrac{40}{20} = 2\,\text{m/s}^2$ and $a_B = \dfrac{40}{5} = 8\,\text{m/s}^2$

$\therefore \quad v_A = 2t_A$ and $v_B = 8t_B$

Now $\dfrac{1}{2} \times 20 \times (2t_A)^2 = \dfrac{1}{2} \times 5 \times (8t_B)^2$

$\therefore \dfrac{t_A}{t_B} = 2$

28. (c) $mg(100 - 20) = \dfrac{1}{2}mv^2$

$\therefore \quad v = 40\ \text{m/s}$

29. (a) $W_F + W_g = \Delta K = 0$

$\therefore \qquad W_F = -W_g$

$= -\,mg \times (-y)$

$= mgL(1 - \cos\theta)$

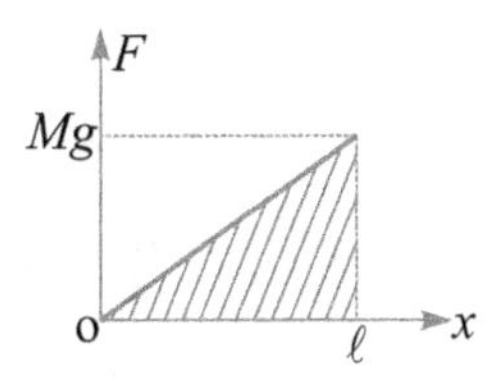

30. (b) $\dfrac{1}{2}kx^2 = 2 \times \dfrac{1}{2}mv^2$

$\therefore \qquad x = \sqrt{\dfrac{2mv^2}{k}}$

31. (c) The displacement produced by spring of the floor is $= 0$, and so $W = 0$.

32. (b) $W = \dfrac{Mg \times \ell}{2} = \dfrac{Mg\ell}{2}.$

33. (d) $m_2 gh = m_1 gh + \dfrac{1}{2}(m_1 + m_2)v^2$

$\therefore\ v = \sqrt{\dfrac{2gh(m_2 - m_1)}{m_1 + m_2}}$

34. (a) $Fx = \dfrac{1}{2}m(v_f^2 - v_i^2)$

or $F \times 200 \times 10^{-3} = \dfrac{1}{2} \times 60 \times 10^{-3}(300^2 - 600^2)$

$\therefore \qquad F = 40.5 \times 10^3\ \text{N}$

35. (b) $mgh + W_f = \dfrac{1}{2}mv_f^2 - 0$

or $1 \times 10 \times 1 + W_f = \dfrac{1}{2} \times 1 \times 2^2 - 0$

$\therefore \qquad W_f = -8\ \text{J}$

36. (a) $F = kv$ and $P = Fv = (kv) \times v = kv^2$

$\therefore \dfrac{P_1}{P_2} = \dfrac{v_1^2}{v_2^2} \ \Rightarrow\ P_2 = \left(\dfrac{12}{4}\right)^2 \times 7.5 = 67.5\ kW$

37. (a) $\Delta U = -W_{conservative\ force}$

$= -[-VDgh - Vdgh]$

$= V(D - d)gh$

38. (a) $W = \vec{F}.\vec{s} = (2\hat{i} + 3\hat{j} + 4\hat{k}).(3\hat{i} + 4\hat{j} + 5\hat{k})$

$= 2 \times 3 + 3 \times 4 + 4 \times 5 = 38\ \text{J}$

$P = \dfrac{W}{t} = \dfrac{38}{4} = 9.5\,W.$

39 (d) $P = \dfrac{mgh}{t}$

$\therefore \qquad m = \dfrac{Pt}{gh} = \dfrac{2 \times 10^3 \times 60}{10 \times 10} = 1200\ \text{kg}$

40. (b) $P_0 = (ma)v = \left(\dfrac{mdv}{dt}\right)v$

$\int v(dv) = \dfrac{P_0}{m}\int dt \ \Rightarrow\ v \propto t^{1/2}$

41. (d) $P = Fv = (1800\ g + 4000) \times 2 = 44000\ \text{W}.$

42. (c) If F is the force exerted by the engine of the car, then

$F - R = ma,$

$\therefore \qquad F = (R + ma)$

The power $P = Fv = (R + ma)v\,.$

43. (c) Power $= 0.9\left(\dfrac{m}{t}gh\right)$

$= 0.9 \times 15 \times 10 \times 60 = 8100\text{W}$

44. (b) $4P = 800,$

$\therefore \qquad P = 200\ \text{N}$

Now $0.80 = \dfrac{P_{out}}{P_{in}}$

$\therefore \qquad P_{in} = \dfrac{P_{out}}{0.8} = \dfrac{200}{0.8} = 250\ \text{N}.$

Exercise 7.1 Level -2

1. (a) $v_i = (8\hat{i} + 9\hat{j})\,\text{m/s}$

and $\vec{v}_f = 8\hat{i} + (9 - g \times 5)\hat{j} = (8\hat{i} - 41\hat{j})\text{m/s}$

So $v_i = \sqrt{8^2 + 9^2} = \sqrt{147}$

and $v_f = \sqrt{8^2 + 41^2} = \sqrt{1745}$

$\Delta U = -\Delta K = \dfrac{1}{2} \times 1 \times [145 - 1745]$

$= -800\ \text{J}.$

2. (b) Given, $U = 20xyz^{-1}$

$F_x = -\dfrac{\partial U}{\partial x} = -\dfrac{20y}{z}$

$$F_y = -\frac{\partial U}{\partial y} = -\frac{20x}{z}$$

and $\quad F_z = -\frac{\partial U}{\partial z} = \frac{20xy}{z^2}$

$\therefore \qquad \vec{F} = F_x\hat{i} + F_y\hat{j} + F_z\hat{k}$

$$= \left(\frac{-20y}{z}\right)\hat{i} - \left(\frac{20x}{z}\right)\hat{j} + \frac{20xy}{z^2}\hat{k}$$

3.   (a) $\qquad\qquad W = K_f - K_i$

or $\quad \displaystyle\int_{20}^{30} -0.1x\,dx = K_f - \frac{1}{2}\times 10\times 10^2$

or $\quad -0.1\left.\frac{x^2}{2}\right|_{20}^{30} = K_f - 500$

$\therefore \qquad\qquad K_f = 475\ \text{J}.$

4.   (b) $\quad W_A = \dfrac{1}{2}k_A x^2$ and $W_B = \dfrac{1}{2}k_B x^2$

As $k_A > k_B$, and so $W_A > W_B$,

Also $\qquad\qquad W = \dfrac{1}{2}kx^2 = \dfrac{F^2}{2k}$

As $k_A > k_B$, $\therefore W_A' < W_B'$.

5.   (c)

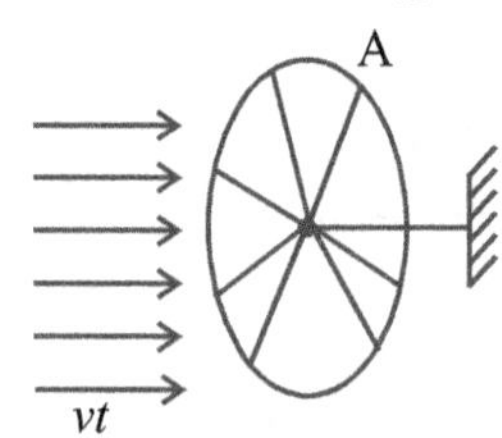

The volume of air sweaps in time $t = Avt$

Mass of air sweaps, $m = \rho V$

$\qquad\qquad\qquad\qquad = \rho\,Avt$

Kinetic energy, $\quad K = \dfrac{1}{2}mv^2$

$\qquad\qquad\qquad = \dfrac{1}{2}(\rho Avt)v^2$

$\qquad\qquad\qquad = \dfrac{1}{2}\rho Av^3 t$

6.   (d) $\quad dU = (dm)g(-y)$

$\qquad = -\dfrac{m}{\ell}(Rd\theta)gR(1-\cos\theta)$

$\qquad = -\dfrac{mgR^2}{\ell}(1-\cos\theta)$

$\therefore \quad U = \displaystyle\int_{0}^{\theta=\frac{\ell}{R}} dU = -\frac{mgR^2}{\ell}\int_{0}^{\ell/R}(1-\cos\theta)d\theta$

$$= -\frac{mgR^2}{\ell}(\theta - \sin\theta)_{0}^{\ell/R}$$

$$= \frac{mgR^2}{\ell}\left(\sin\frac{\ell}{R} - \frac{\ell}{R}\right).$$

7.   (d) $\quad K_{min} + U_{min} = 0$

$\qquad \dfrac{1}{2}\times 0.5\times v^2 = 1$

$\qquad \therefore v = 2$ m/s

8.   (d) $\qquad\qquad W = mgh + \dfrac{1}{2}kx^2$

$\qquad\qquad\qquad = mg(a\sin\theta) + \dfrac{1}{2}k(a\theta)^2$

$\qquad\qquad\qquad = Wa\sin\theta + \dfrac{1}{2}ka^2\theta^2.$

9.   (c) See examples

10.   (a)

$y = 10 - \sqrt{10^2 - 4^2} = 0.84\,m$

Thus $\qquad \dfrac{1}{2}mv^2 = mgy$

or $\qquad\qquad v = \sqrt{2gy} = \sqrt{2\times 9.8\times 0.84}$

$\qquad\qquad\qquad = 4.05$ m/s.

11.   (b) $\quad 0 = -2g\times 0.5 + 1\times g\times 0.5$

$\qquad + \dfrac{1}{2}\times 2\times v^2 + \dfrac{1}{2}\times 1\times v^2$

$\qquad \therefore v = 1.8$ m/s

12.   (c) The maximum speed of the block is at the mean position and so

$$x = \frac{mg\cos\theta}{k}.$$

13.   (b) $\quad W_{gravity} + W_F = \Delta K$

$-10\times g(10 - 10\cos 60°) + 200\times 10\sin 60°$

$\qquad\qquad\qquad = \dfrac{1}{2}\times 10\times v_f^2 - 0$

$\therefore \qquad\qquad v_f = 17$ m/s

14.   (b) If x is the extension in the spring, then

$\qquad\qquad\qquad kx = 2g$

or $\qquad x = \dfrac{2g}{k} = \dfrac{2\times 10}{40} = 0.5$ m

By conservation of energy, we have

$5\,g\times 0.5 = \dfrac{1}{2}\times 40\times 0.5^2 + \dfrac{1}{2}5\times v^2$

$\therefore \quad v = 2\sqrt{2}$ m/s

15. (b)
$$W_{net} = W_{gravity} + W_{spring}$$
$$= mg(h+d) - \frac{1}{2}kx^2.$$

16. (b)

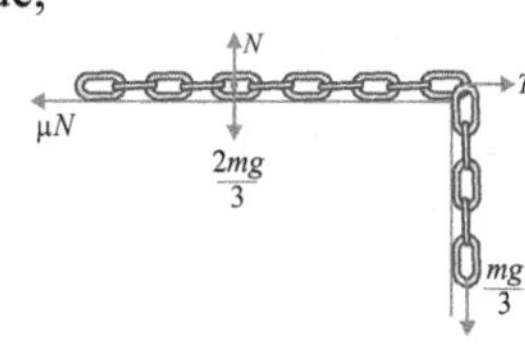

$$\frac{1}{2}m(2)^2 + \frac{1}{2}k(0.1)^2 = mgh + \frac{1}{2}k(h-0.1)^2$$

After solving, we get $h = 0.2$ m

17. (d) $U = \dfrac{mgh}{2} = \dfrac{\rho(Ah)gh}{2} = \dfrac{\rho gAh^2}{2}$

$\therefore U_i = \dfrac{\rho gAh_1^2}{2} + \dfrac{\rho gAh_2^2}{2}$

$U_f = 2 \times \dfrac{\rho gAh^2}{2}, \; h = \dfrac{h_1+h_2}{2}$

$W = U_f - U_i = \dfrac{1}{4}(h_1-h_2)^2 gA\rho.$

18. (a) $\dfrac{1}{2} \times 200 \times 2^2 = 0.5 \times (60 \times 10)x + \dfrac{1}{2}200x^2$

$\therefore x = 1$ m

19. (b)
$$m(a) = \frac{-\mu mv^2}{r}$$

or $\qquad mv\dfrac{dv}{ds} = \dfrac{-\mu mv^2}{r}$

or $\qquad \displaystyle\int_{v_0}^{v} \frac{dv}{v} = \int_{0}^{\pi/2} \frac{-(rd\theta)}{r}$

$\therefore \qquad v = v_0 e^{\frac{-\pi\mu}{r}}$

20. (b) $\dfrac{1}{2}mv^2 = (\mu mg)x$ and $\dfrac{1}{2}kx^2 = \dfrac{1}{2}mv^2$

on solving, we get $k = \dfrac{4m\mu^2 g^2}{v^2}$.

21. (a) Extra power, $P = mg\sin\theta \times v$

$$= Mg \times \frac{h}{s} \times v = \frac{Mghv}{s}.$$

22. (a) $P = \dfrac{\dfrac{1}{2}mv^2}{t} = \dfrac{\dfrac{1}{2} \times (20 \times 10^{-3} \times 360) \times \left(360 \times \dfrac{5}{18}\right)^2}{60}$

$\quad = 600$ W.

23. (a) Area under P-x graphs $= \displaystyle\int p\,dx = \int \left(m\frac{dv}{dt}\right)vdx$

$= \displaystyle\int_{1}^{v} mv^2 dv = \left[\frac{mv^3}{3}\right]_{1}^{v} = \frac{10}{7 \times 3}(v^3 - 1)$

From graph : area $= \dfrac{1}{2}(2+4) \times 10 = 30$

$\therefore \dfrac{10}{7 \times 3}(v^3 - 1) = 30 \quad \therefore v = 4$ m/s

24. (c) We have got, $P = \dfrac{1}{2}\rho Av^3 t$

$\therefore \quad P \propto v^3$

EXERCISE 7.2

1. (a, c) If $\theta = 90°$, $W = Fs\cos 90° = 0$.

or, if $s = 0$, $W = F \times 0 = 0$

2. (a, c) For the equilibrium, F = 0. The U may be zero or not, it depends on type of equilibrium.

3. (b, c, d) $\dfrac{1}{2}kx^2 = mgx$, $\therefore \; x = \dfrac{2mg}{k}$

At $\dfrac{x}{2}$, force in the spring, $F = k\dfrac{x}{2} = k\dfrac{mg}{k} = mg$,

so, net force on the block is zero. Also at extreme position the block has net upward force and so net upward acceleration.

4. (a, b) According to principle of invariance, acceleration and force will remain same in different inertia frames.

5. (a, c) For equilibrium, $F = 0$,

or $x(3x - 2) = 0$, $\therefore \; x = 0, \dfrac{2}{3}$.

6. (a, d) To slide,

$\mu N = T = mg/3$

or $\quad \mu\left(\dfrac{2mg}{3}\right) = \dfrac{mg}{3} \Rightarrow \mu = \dfrac{1}{2}$

$W = \displaystyle\int_{2\ell/3}^{0} f\,dx = \int_{2\ell/3}^{0} \mu N\,dx = \int_{2\ell/3}^{0} \left(\mu\frac{m}{\ell}xg\right)dx$

$= \dfrac{\mu mg}{\ell}\left|\dfrac{x^2}{2}\right|_{2\ell/3}^{0} = -\dfrac{\mu mg}{2\ell} \times \dfrac{4\ell^2}{9} = \dfrac{-\dfrac{1}{2}mg\ell \times 4}{2 \times 9} = \dfrac{-mg\ell}{9}$

7. (a, b, c, d)

8. (c, d) $W_{gravity} = mgy = mgL(\cos 30° - \cos 60°)$

$$= \frac{mgL}{2}(\sqrt{3}-1).$$

$$W_{Tension} = 0.$$

9. (a, c) $K_A + U_A = K_E + U_E$

As $U_A = U_E$ and $K_A = 0$, $\therefore K_E = 0$

$$F = \frac{-dU}{dx} = 0$$

Slope is zero at points B, C and D.

10. (b, d) $mgh - \mu\,mg\cos\theta = \frac{1}{2}mv^2$

As h and v are same for all and so $\mu\cos\theta$ also must be same. Here θ is the inclination angle of the slope.

11. (b, d) $\frac{1}{2}k(1)^2 = \frac{1}{2}\times 1\times v_1^2 + \frac{1}{2}\times 2\times v_2^2$

and $1 \times v_1 = 2\,v_2$

$\therefore v_1 = 1$ m/s (left) and 2 m/s (right)

Therefore velocity of m becomes $2 + 1 = 3$ m/s

and that of $2m$ becomes $= 1 - 1 = 0$

1. (d)   Work done by friction on inclined plane will be negative

$W = Fs\cos\theta = +ve$, if $\theta < 90°$.

2. (d)   Explained in the theory.

3. (d) $K = \dfrac{P^2}{2m}$, and $K' = \dfrac{(1.5P)^2}{2m} = 2.25\dfrac{P}{2m} = 2.25K$

$\therefore \dfrac{\Delta K}{K}\times 100 = \dfrac{2.25K - K}{K}\times 100 = 125\%$

If change in P is small enough, then statement -2 is correct.

4. (d)   Stopping distance, $s = \dfrac{v^2}{2a}$, $\therefore$ stopping distance becomes four times when v is doubled.

5. (d)   Work done may be zero, even F is not zero.

$W = Fs\cos 0° = Fs$ (maximum).

6. (a)   Revolving electron experiences centripetal force, which makes 90° with displacement vector ans so $W = 0$.

7. (b) $W = Fs\cos 180° = -mgs$.

8. (a)   In this case, $s = 0$, and so $W = 0$.

9. (a)   Power $= \dfrac{W}{t} = \dfrac{K}{1/n} = nK$

10. (c) In first case the total mechanical energy of the block will convert into heat energy by friction. But in second case some part of it will change into potential energy and rest will convert into heat energy.

11. (d) Static friction does positive work.

12. (b) In close loop, $s = 0$, and so $W = Fs = 0$.

Passage for (Questions 1 & 2)

1. (a)   Velocity of mud piece before impact

$$v = \sqrt{2g(2h)} = 2\sqrt{gh}$$

Now $M \times 2\sqrt{gh} + 0 = (M+m)v'$

$$\therefore \quad v = \sqrt{gh}$$

Kinetic energy of the system,

$$K = \frac{1}{2}(M+M)v'^2$$

$$= \frac{1}{2}\times 2M + gh = Mgh.$$

2. (b)   If x is the extension of the spring, then

$$\frac{1}{2}(2M)v'^2 = \frac{1}{2}kx^2 - (2M)gx$$

or $Mgh = \dfrac{1}{2}kx^2 - (2Mgx)$

$$\therefore \quad x = \left[\frac{2Mg + \sqrt{4M^2g^2 + 2Mghk}}{k}\right]$$

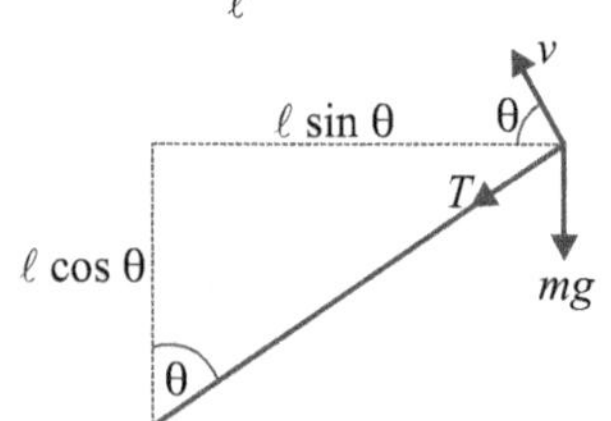

Passage for (Questions 3 & 4)

3. (c)   4. (d)

If v is the speed of the particle at P, then

$$v^2 = v_0^2 - 2g(\ell + \ell\cos\theta) \dots \text{(i)}$$

Now $T + mg\cos\theta = \dfrac{mv^2}{\ell}$

As $T = 0$, and so

$$mg\cos\theta = \frac{mv^2}{\ell} \qquad \dots \text{(ii)}$$

After solving above equations, we get

$$\tan\theta = \sqrt{2},$$

and $v_0 = \sqrt{g\ell}(2+\sqrt{3})^{1/2}.$

Passage for (Questions 5 & 6)

5. (c) By conservation of mechanical energy, we have

$$\Delta U = U_f - U_i$$

$$= \left(Mg\frac{\ell}{2} + mg\ell \right) - 0$$

$$= \left(\frac{M}{2} + m \right) g\ell$$

6. (a)

$$\frac{1}{2}mv^2 = Mg\frac{\ell}{2} + mg\ell$$

$$\therefore \quad v = \sqrt{\frac{Mg\ell + 2mg\ell}{m}}.$$

7. (c) $F - f_k = (3m) \times \dfrac{F}{6m}$ or $f_k = F/2$

$$\therefore \mu_k = \frac{f_k}{N} = \frac{F/2}{3mg} = \frac{F}{6mg}$$

8. (a) Frictional force on the smaller block

$$f = ma = m \times \frac{F}{6m} = \frac{F}{6}$$

9. (a)

$$W = F \times s = \frac{F}{6} \times 1 = F/6$$

10. (a)

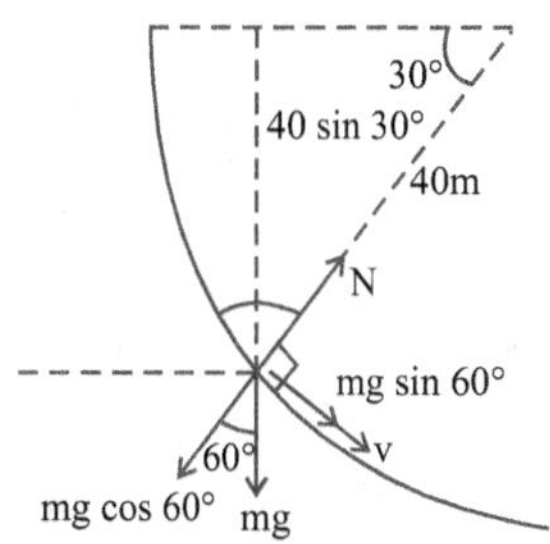

$$N - mg \cos 60° = \frac{mv^2}{r}$$

$$\therefore \quad N = mg \cos 60° + \frac{mv^2}{r} \qquad \text{...(1)}$$

Loss in P.E. = mg × 40 sin 30° = 200 J

Work done in over coming friction = 150 J

$\therefore$ K.E. possessed by the particle = 50 J

$$\therefore \quad \frac{1}{2}mv^2 = 50J$$

$$\therefore \quad mv^2 = 100 \text{ J} \qquad \text{...(2)}$$

From (1) and (2), N $= 1 \times 10 \times \dfrac{1}{2} + \dfrac{100}{40}$

$$= 5 + 2.5 = 7.5 \text{ N}$$

(a) is the correct option.

11. (b) From (2), $mv^2 = 100$

$\therefore v = 10 \text{ ms}^{-1}$

(b) is the correct option.

12. A → p, q; B → p, q; C → p, q; D → p, r

13. A → r; B → p; C → q

1. (a)

$$-\frac{dv}{dt} = kx$$

or

$$v\frac{dv}{dx} = -kx$$

or

$$\int_{v_i}^{v_f} v\,dv = -k\int_0^x x\,dx$$

or

$$\frac{1}{2}[v_f^2 - v_i^2] = -\frac{kx^2}{2}$$

or

$$\frac{1}{2}m(v_f^2 - v_i^2) = -\frac{mkx^2}{2}$$

Thus loss in K.E. $\propto x^2$

2. (d)

$$\frac{1}{2}Mv^2 = \frac{1}{2}kL^2$$

$$\therefore \quad v = \sqrt{\frac{kL^2}{M}}$$

Momentum, $P = Mv = M\sqrt{\dfrac{k}{M}}L = \sqrt{kM}\,L$

3. (c) $a = \dfrac{v_1}{t_1}, \therefore F = ma = \dfrac{mv_1}{t_1}$; $s = \dfrac{1}{2}at^2 = \dfrac{1}{2}\left(\dfrac{v_1}{t_1}\right)t^2$

$$W = Fs = \frac{mv_1}{t_1} \times \frac{1}{2}\left(\frac{v_1}{t_1}\right)t^2 = \frac{mv_1^2 t^2}{2t_1^2}$$

$$P = \frac{dW}{dt} = \frac{mv_1^2 t}{t_1^2}$$

4. (a) By using work - energy theorem, $W_{all} = \Delta K$, we have Work done by F + work done by $Mg = 0$

$$F(AB) - Mg(AC) = 0$$

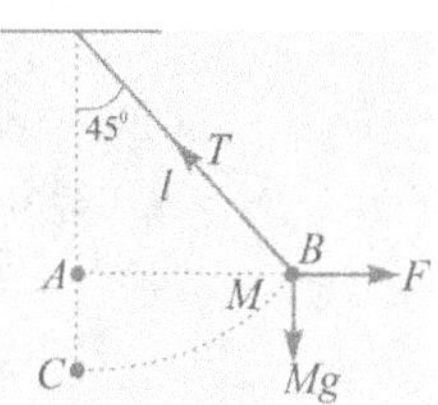

$$F = Mg\left(\frac{AC}{AB}\right) = \left[\frac{l - l/\sqrt{2}}{l/\sqrt{2}}\right]$$

$$= Mg(\sqrt{2} - 1).$$

5. (b) $U + K = 2$

For maximum K, U should be minimum, and so

$$\frac{dU}{dx} = 0 \text{, or } \frac{d}{dx}\left(\frac{x^4}{4} - \frac{x^2}{2}\right) = 0$$

or $\qquad x = 0, \pm 1$

$$U_{min} = \frac{(1)^4}{4} - \frac{(1)^2}{2} = -\frac{1}{4} J$$

$$\therefore -\frac{1}{4} + \frac{1}{2} \times 1 \times v_{max}^2 = 2$$

or $\qquad v_{min} = \dfrac{3}{\sqrt{2}}$ m/s .

6.   **(d)**   For stable equilibrium, $F = 0$ or $\dfrac{dU}{dx} = 0$

$$\text{or } \frac{d}{dx}\left[\frac{a}{x^{12}} - \frac{b}{x^6} \right] = 0$$

$$\text{or } -12ax^{-13} - (-6bx^{-7}) = 0$$

$$\therefore \qquad x = \sqrt[6]{\frac{2a}{b}}$$

7.   **(c)**   Work done in stretching the rubber-band by a distance dx is

$$dW = F\, dx = (ax + bx^2)dx$$

Integrating both sides,

$$W = \int_0^L ax\,dx + \int_0^L bx^2\,dx = \frac{aL^2}{2} + \frac{bL^3}{3}$$

8.   **(a)** $U = -\int_0^x F\,dx = -\int_0^x kx\,dx = -\dfrac{1}{2}kx^2 .$

It is correctly drawn in (a)

9.   **(c)** $\dfrac{1}{2}kx^2 = \dfrac{1}{2}(4k)y^2 ,\qquad \therefore \dfrac{y}{x} = \dfrac{1}{2}$

10.   **(a, b)** $\qquad K + U = $ constant

$\qquad\qquad\quad$ or $\qquad K_A + U_A = K_C + U_C$

If $h_A > h_C$, then $U_A > U_C$ and so $K_A < K_C$.

$U_B < U_C$ and so $K_B > K_C$.

11.   **(c)**   Area under $F-t$ graph gives the impulse or the change in the linear momentum of the body. As the initial velocity (and therefore the initial linear momentum) of the body is zero, the area under $F-t$ graph gives the final linear momentum of the body.

Area of $\Delta\, AOB$

$$= \frac{1}{2} \times 3 \times 4 = 6\,\text{N-s}$$

Also $\dfrac{OA}{OB} = \dfrac{CD}{CB}$

$$\Rightarrow \frac{4}{3} = \frac{CD}{1.5}\,f$$

$\Rightarrow CD = 2$

$$\therefore \text{Area of } \Delta BCD = -\left[\frac{1}{2} \times 1.5 \times 2\right] = -1.5\,N\text{-}s$$

$\therefore$ The final linear momentum $= 6 - 1.5 = 4.5$ N-s

$$\therefore \text{Kinetic energy of the block} = \frac{p^2}{2m} = \frac{(4.5)^2}{2 \times 2} = 5.06\,\text{J}$$

12.   **(d)** $K = ct$

Momentum, $P = \sqrt{2mK}$

$$= \sqrt{2mct} = c't^{1/2}$$

$$\therefore \text{Force,} \quad F = \frac{dp}{dt}$$

$$= c'\frac{d}{dt}t^{1/2}$$

$$= c'\frac{1}{2}t^{-1/2}$$

13.   **(d)**   Let us consider a point on the circle

The equation of circle is $x^2 + y^2 = a^2$

The force is

$$\vec{F} = K\left[\frac{x\hat{i}}{(x^2 + y^2)^{3/2}} + \frac{y\hat{j}}{(x^2 + y^2)^{3/2}} \right]$$

$$\vec{F} = K\left[\frac{x\hat{i}}{(a^2)^{3/2}} + \frac{y\hat{j}}{(a^2)^{3/2}} \right]$$

$$\vec{F} = \frac{K}{a^3}\left[x\hat{i} + y\hat{j} \right]$$

The force acts radially outwards as shown in the figure and the displacement is tangential to the circular path. Therefore the angle between the force and displacement is $90°$ and $W = 0$

option (d) is correct.

Collisions & Centre of Mass

(365 - 422)

Chapter contents

Hermann Helmholtz

Hermann Helmholtz (1821-1894) developed the law of conservation of energy. He says that energy is never created or destroyed. It is simply changed from one form to another. Helmholtz studied various form of energy, including the newly discovered radio waves. He was also a mathematician and medical researcher....

Definitions, Explanations and Derivations

8.1 INTRODUCTION

Collision is the interaction between two or more bodies for a short time interval.

Let us consider two bodies of masses m_1 and m_2 moving along the same line with velocities u_1 and u_2 ($u_1 > u_2$) as shown in *figure* 8.1. Suppose they remain in contact for time interval Δt. After collision let their velocities become v_1 and v_2 respectively. The mutual force of interaction during collision, is shown in the figure.

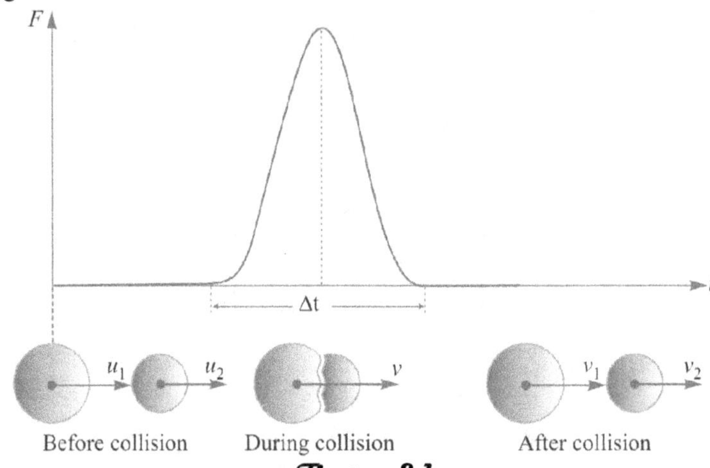

Before collision   During collision   After collision

Figure. **8.1**

During collision

During collision, the interactive forces are very large and the magnitude of the interactive forces are often unknown. Therefore Newton's second law can not be used during collision. During collision bodies in contact get deformed, and some part of their kinetic energy will store in elastic potential energy, andbBoth the bodies have same velocity. The stored potential energy come back into kinetic energy and bodies will separate after collision. After collision bodys will get new velocities

Thus during collision:

(i)   The colliding bodies have same velocity.

(ii)   Kinetic energy does not remain conserved.

(iii)   The elastic potential energy during collision = decrease in kinetic energy

$$= \left[\frac{1}{2}m_1 u_1^2 + \frac{1}{2}m_2 u_2^2\right] - \left[\frac{1}{2}(m_1 + m_2)v^2\right].$$

Conservation of momentum

During collision bodies exert mutual repulsive forces on each other. Let the change in momentum of bodies are $\Delta \vec{P}_1$ and $\Delta \vec{P}_2$, then we have

$$\Delta \vec{P}_1 = \vec{F}_{12}\Delta t$$

and
$$\Delta \vec{P}_2 = \vec{F}_{21}\Delta t.$$

According to Newton's third law

$$\vec{F}_{12} = -\vec{F}_{21}$$

or
$$\vec{F}_{12}\Delta t = -\vec{F}_{21}\Delta t$$

or
$$\vec{F}_{12}\Delta t + \vec{F}_{21}\Delta t = 0$$

or
$$\Delta \vec{P}_1 + \Delta \vec{P}_2 = 0$$

or
$$\Delta(\vec{P}_1 + \vec{P}_2) = 0$$

or
$$\vec{P}_1 + \vec{P}_2 = \text{constant.}$$

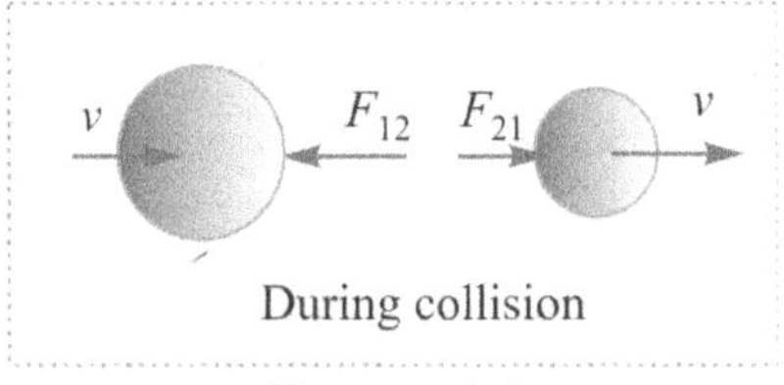

During collision

Figure. **8.2**

Thus during collision the linear momentum of the colliding bodies together remains constant, even though the forces vary in a complex manner. Thus we can say that momentum of the system (colliding bodies) remains constant in each type of collision.

8.2 Types of collision

1. **Elastic collision :** If there is no loss of kinetic energy of the system during collision, it is called an elastic collision. In this type of collision:

    (i)   The momentum of the system remains conserved.

    (ii) The kinetic energy of the system before collision is equal to the kinetic energy after collision.

    (iii) Forces involved during collision are conservative in nature.

2. **Inelastic collision :** If there is a loss of kinetic energy during collision, it is called an inelastic collision. In this type of collision:

    (i)   The momentum remains conserved.

    (ii) The kinetic energy after collision will be less than then kinetic energy before collision.

    (iii) Some or all the forces involved during collision are non-conservative.

    (iv) A part of mechanical energy is converted into heat, light and sound.

If colliding bodies stick together and move as a single body after collision, then the collision is said to be *perfectly inelastic collision.* In such collision, momentum of the system remains conserved, but the loss of kinetic energy is maximum. Ex. A bullet fired into a wooden block and remains embedded in it.

8.3 Analysis of 1-D or head-on elastic collision

If colliding bodies before and after collision remain in the same line, the collision is said to be head-on collision. This will happen when bodies move along the line joining their geometric centres.

Consider two bodies of masses m_1 and m_2 moving with velocities $\vec{u}_1$ and $\vec{u}_2\,(\vec{u}_1 > \vec{u}_2)$ along the same straight line. Let after collision their velocities become $\vec{v}_1$ and $\vec{v}_2$ in the same initial direction. Then

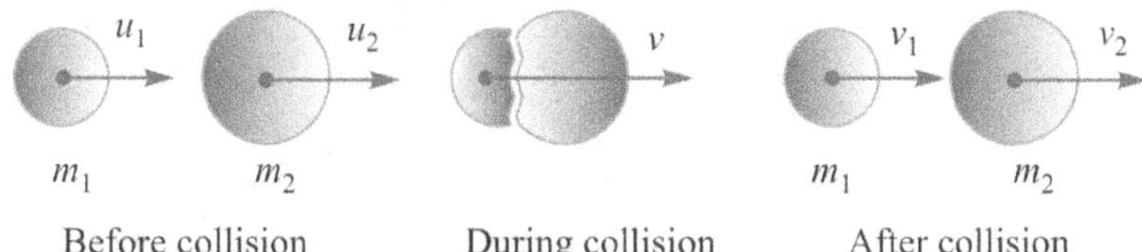

Before collision   During collision   After collision

Figure. 8.3

according to conservation of linear momentum, we have

$$m_1\vec{u}_1 + m_2\vec{u}_2 \;=\; m_1\vec{v}_1 + m_2\vec{v}_2.$$

Since all the colliding bodies before and after collision remain in the same line, so we can drop the vector signs from them. Thus we can write

$$m_1u_1 + m_2u_2 \;=\; m_1v_1 + m_2v_2 \qquad \ldots(i)$$

or $$m_1(u_1 - v_1) \;=\; m_2(v_2 - u_2) \qquad \ldots(ii)$$

As kinetic energy before collision = kinetic energy after collision

$$\therefore \qquad \frac{1}{2}m_1u_1^2 + \frac{1}{2}m_2u_2^2 \;=\; \frac{1}{2}m_1v_1^2 + \frac{1}{2}m_2v_2^2 \qquad \ldots(iii)$$

or $$m_1(u_1^2 - v_1^2) \;=\; m_2(v_2^2 - u_2^2)$$

or $$m_1(u_1 + v_1)(u_1 - v_1) \;=\; m_2(v_2 + u_2)(v_2 - u_2) \qquad \ldots(iv)$$

Dividing equation (iv) by (ii), we get

$$u_1 + v_1 \;=\; v_2 + u_2$$

or $$u_1 - u_2 \;=\; v_2 - v_1. \qquad \ldots(v)$$

Thus velocity of m_1 w.r.t. m_2 before collision = velocity of m_2 w.r.t. m_1 after collision.

or $\qquad$ velocity of approach $\;=\;$ velocity of separation

Also we have,

$$v_1 = \left(\frac{m_1 - m_2}{m_1 + m_2}\right)u_1 + \left(\frac{2m_2}{m_1 + m_2}\right)u_2 \quad \text{...(vi)}$$

and

$$v_2 = \left(\frac{m_2 - m_1}{m_1 + m_2}\right)u_2 + \left(\frac{2m_1}{m_1 + m_2}\right)u_1. \quad \text{...(vii)}$$

Special cases :

(i) When colliding bodies are of equal masses, let $m_1 = m_2 = m$. From equation (vi) and (vii), we get
$$v_1 = u_2 \text{ and } v_2 = u_1$$
Hence when two bodies of equal masses collide elastically, their velocities get exchanged.

(ii) If $m_1 = m_2 = m$ and $u_2 = 0$, then
$$v_1 = 0 \text{ and } v_2 = u_1.$$

(iii) When a light body collides with a massive stationary body. Here $m_1 \ll m_2$ and $u_2 = 0$
$$\therefore \qquad v_1 = -u_1 \text{ and } v_2 \simeq 0.$$
Hence when a light body collides with a massive stationary body, the light body rebounds after the collision with an equal speed while the massive body remains at rest.

(iv) When a massive body collides with a light body at rest. Here $m_1 \gg m_2$ and $u_2 = 0$
$$\therefore \qquad v_1 = u_1 \text{ and } v_2 = 2u.$$

Transfer of kinetic energy during collision: Kinetic energy transferred from projectile to the target
$$\Delta K = \text{decrease in K.E. of projectile}$$

$$= \frac{1}{2}m_1 u_1^2 - \frac{1}{2}m_1 v_1^2.$$

Fractional decrease in K.E.

$$\frac{\Delta K}{K} = \frac{\frac{1}{2}m_1 u_1^2 - \frac{1}{2}m_1 v_1^2}{\frac{1}{2}m_1 u_1^2}$$

or

$$\frac{\Delta K}{K} = 1 - \left(\frac{v_1}{u_1}\right)^2. \qquad \text{...(viii)}$$

8.4 PERFECTLY INELASTIC COLLISION IN 1-D

Consider two bodies of masses m_1 and m_2 moving with velocities u_1 and u_2 along a straight line. They make perfectly inelastic collision. Let after collision, their common velocity becomes v, then by conservation of momentum, we have
$$m_1 u_1 + m_2 u_2 = (m_1 + m_2)v$$

$$\therefore \qquad v = \left[\frac{m_1 u_1 + m_2 u_2}{m_1 + m_2}\right].$$

The loss of K.E. in collision

$$\Delta K = \left(\frac{1}{2}m_1 u_1^2 + \frac{1}{2}m_2 u_2^2\right) - \frac{1}{2}(m_1 + m_2)v^2$$

$$= \left(\frac{1}{2}m_1 u_1^2 + \frac{1}{2}m_2 u_2^2\right) - \frac{1}{2}(m_1 + m_2)\left(\frac{m_1 u_1 + m_2 u_2}{m_1 + m_2}\right)^2$$

$$= \frac{1}{2}\left(\frac{m_1 m_2}{m_1 + m_2}\right)(u_1 - u_2)^2.$$

The loss of K.E.. will appear as heat and sound.

PERFECTLY INELASTIC COLLISION 1D

General analysis of 1-D collision

Newton's experimental law : Coefficient of restitution
It is defined as;

$$e = \frac{\text{velocity of separation}}{\text{velocity of approach}}$$

$$= \frac{v_2 - v_1}{u_1 - u_2}$$

or $\qquad e = -\left[\frac{v_2 - v_1}{u_2 - u_1}\right] = -\left[\frac{v_1 - v_2}{u_1 - u_2}\right].$

The value of e depends on materials of colliding bodies. The value of e can be $e \leq 1$.
(i)   For perfectly elastic collision, $e = 1$.
(ii) For perfectly inelastic collision, $e = 0$.

Note :

The coefficient of restitution is a 1–D concept. Thus in problem involving oblique collision, 'e' is defined only along the line of collision. In the absence of tangential forces the collision in the perpendicular direction is taken as elastic.

Consider two bodies of masses m_1 and m_2 moving with velocities u_1 and u_2 along a line. Let the coefficient of restitution between the bodies is e. After collision their velocities become v_1 and v_2 respectively. Then we have,

$$m_1 u_1 + m_2 u_2 = m_1 v_1 + m_2 v_2 \qquad \ldots (i)$$

and $\qquad e = -\dfrac{v_1 - v_2}{u_1 - u_2}. \qquad \ldots (ii)$

Solving equations (i) and (ii), we get

$$v_1 = \left(\frac{m_1 - em_2}{m_1 + m_2}\right)u_1 + \left(\frac{(1+e)m_2}{m_1 + m_2}\right)u_2 \quad \ldots (iii)$$

and $\qquad v_2 = \left(\dfrac{m_2 - em_1}{m_1 + m_2}\right)u_2 + \left(\dfrac{(1+e)m_1}{m_1 + m_2}\right)u_1 \quad \ldots (iv)$

Special case
If $m_1 = m_2 = m$ and $u_1 = u, u_2 = 0$, then

$$mu = mv_1 + mv_2$$

and $\qquad e = -\dfrac{v_1 - v_2}{u - 0}$

After solving above equations, we get

$$v_1 = \frac{u}{2}(1-e)$$

$$v_2 = \frac{u}{2}(1+e)$$

$\therefore \qquad \dfrac{v_1}{v_2} = \dfrac{1-e}{1+e}.$

FORMULAE USED

1. For one-dimensional elastic collision

$$m_1 u_1 + m_2 u_2 = m_1 v_1 + m_2 v_2 \qquad \ldots\ldots\ldots (i)$$

$$\frac{1}{2} m_1 u_1^2 + \frac{1}{2} m_2 u_2^2 = \frac{1}{2} m_1 v_1^2 + \frac{1}{2} m_2 v_2^2 \qquad \ldots\ldots\ldots (ii)$$

2. Coefficient of restitution, $e = -\left[\dfrac{v_1 - v_2}{u_1 - u_2}\right],\ 0 \le e \le 1$.

   For perfectly elastic collision, $e = 1$. For perfectly inelastic collision, $e = 0$.

3. For a ball rebounding from wall or floor after n^{th} collision $v_n = e^n u$.

4. During collision, energy stored in the colliding bodies

$$= \left[\frac{1}{2} m_1 u_1^2 + \frac{1}{2} m_2 u_2^2\right] - \left[\frac{1}{2}(m_1 + m_2)v^2\right]$$

   Here v is the velocity of bodies during collision.

5. In completely inelastic collision, common velocity of bodies together, $\vec{v}$ can be obtained

$$m_1 \vec{u}_1 + m_2 \vec{u}_2 = (m_1 + m_2)\vec{v}.$$

6. Loss in K.E.,

$$= \left(\frac{1}{2} m_1 u_1^2 + \frac{1}{2} m_2 u_2^2\right) - \left(\frac{1}{2} m_1 + m_2\right) v^2$$

$$= \frac{1}{2}\left[\frac{m_1 m_2}{m_1 + m_2}\right](u_1 - u_2)^2$$

7. When a steady stream of bodies, each of mass m and speed v collide with a fixed body, the average force on fixed body

$$F = n\frac{\Delta P}{\Delta t} = nm\left(\frac{\Delta v}{\Delta t}\right).$$

Problem-solving strategy : Conservation of momentum/collision

Identify the Relevant Concept : First you see, whether net force on system is zero. It might be zero in any specific direction. Then conservation of momentum can be used in that direction only

Set up the problem :

1. Treat each body as a particle. Draw "before" and "after" sketches. After choosing the positive direction of motion, give sign to the all known variables and no sign to unknown variable(s).

2. Identify the unknown(s) from target variables(s).

Execute the solution as follows :

1. If collision is perfectly elastic, then any two of the following equations can be used :

$$m_1 u_1 + m_2 u_2 \ = \ m_1 v_1 + m_2 v_2 \qquad \ldots\ldots\ldots (i)$$

$$\frac{1}{2} m_1 u_1^2 + \frac{1}{2} m_2 u_2^2 \ = \ \frac{1}{2} m_1 v_1^2 + \frac{1}{2} m_2 v_2^2 \qquad \ldots\ldots\ldots (ii)$$

$$1 \ = \ -\left[\frac{v_1 - v_2}{u_1 - u_2}\right] \qquad \ldots\ldots\ldots (iii)$$

2. If collision is inelastic, then any of the following two equations may be used :

$$m_1 u_1 + m_2 u_2 \ = \ m_1 v_1 + m_2 v_2 \qquad \ldots\ldots\ldots (i)$$

and
$$e \ = \ -\left[\frac{v_1 - v_2}{u_1 - u_2}\right] \qquad \ldots\ldots\ldots (ii)$$

   Solve the equations to get the unknown (target variables).

EXAMPLES BASED ON ONE-DIMENSIONAL COLLISION

Example 1. A 8 kg ball moving with velocity 4 m/s collides with a 2 kg ball moving with a velocity 8 m/s in opposite direction. If the collision be perfectly elastic, what are the velocities of balls after the collision.

Sol. By conservation of momentum

$$8 \times 4 - 2 \times 8 = 8 v_1 + 2v_2 \qquad \dots \text{(i)}$$

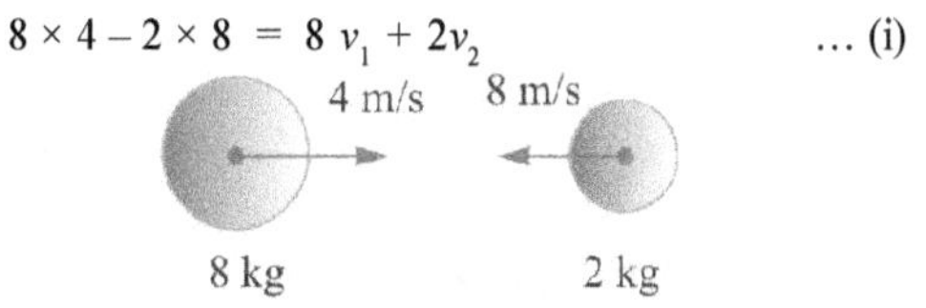

Figure. 8.4

As collision is elastic, so we have

$$\frac{1}{2} \times 8 \times 4^2 + \frac{1}{2} \times 2 \times 8^2 = \frac{1}{2} \times 8 \times v_1^2 + \frac{1}{2} \times 2 \times v_2^2 \qquad \dots \text{(ii)}$$

Solving equations (i) and (ii), we get

$$v_1 = -\frac{4}{5} \text{ m/s}$$

$$\text{or} \qquad v_2 = \frac{56}{5} \text{ m/s}. \qquad \textit{Ans.}$$

Example 2. Two identical balls marked 2 and 3, in contact with each other and at rest on a horizontal smooth surface, are hit head-on by another identical ball marked 1 moving initially with speed v as shown in the *figure* 8.5. If collision is elastic. Then which of the case (s) are possible? **[NCERT]**

Sol.

Before collision

After collision

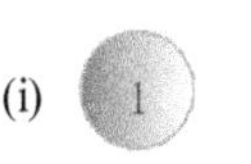
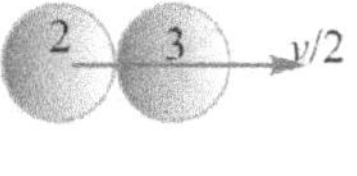

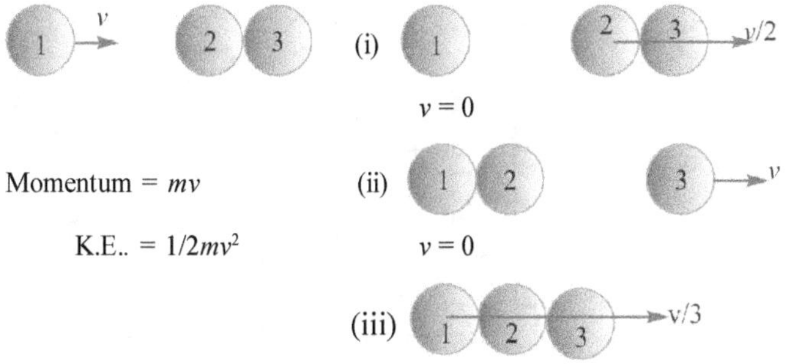

(i) $v = 0$

Momentum = mv

(ii)  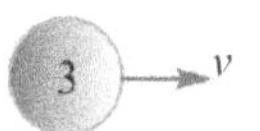

$v = 0$

K.E.. = $1/2 mv^2$

(iii) 

Figure. 8.5

Since collision is elastic, the kinetic energy and momentum before and after collision remain constant.

Case (i) momentum $= 2m \times \dfrac{v}{2} = mv$

$$K.E. = \frac{1}{2}(2m)\left(\frac{v}{2}\right)^2 = \frac{1}{4}mv^2.$$

Case (ii) momentum $= mv$

$$K.E. = \frac{1}{2}mv^2.$$

Case (iii) momentum $= 3 m \times v/3 = mv$

$$K.E. = \frac{1}{2}(3m)\left(\frac{v}{3}\right)^2 = \frac{1}{6}mv^2.$$

Therefore only case (ii) is the possible one.

Example 3. A gun is mounted on a railroad car. The mass of the car, the gun, the shell and the operator is 50m where m is the mass of one shell. If the muzzle velocity of the shells is 200 m/s, what is the recoil speed of the car after the second shot? Neglect friction.

Sol. Let v_1 is the velocity of car after firing 1st shot. By conservation of momentum, we have

$$0 = (49\,m)v_1 + m \times 200$$

$$\text{or} \qquad v_1 = \frac{200}{49} \text{ m/s}.$$

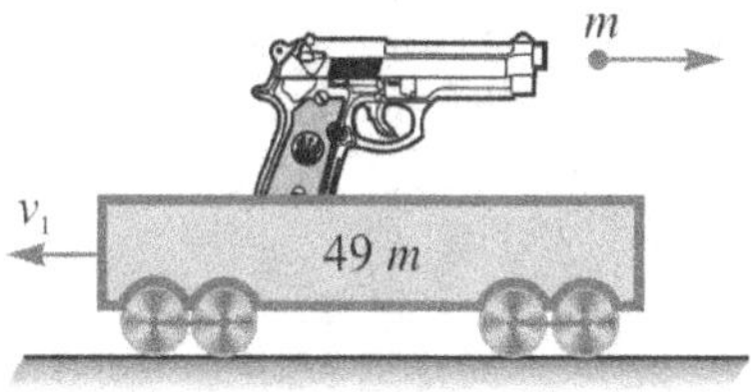

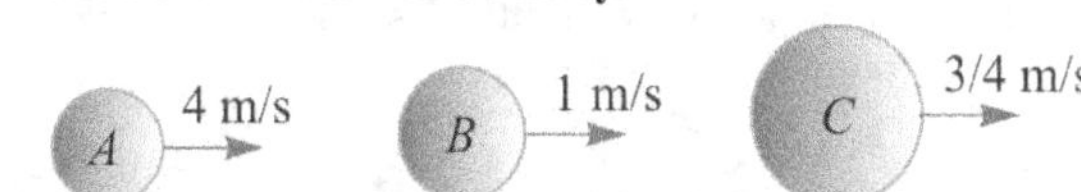

Figure. 8.6

After firing 1st shot, let velocity of shell w.r.t. ground is v_{shell}, then

$$v_{\text{shell}} - v_{\text{gun}} = 200$$

$$\therefore \quad v_{\text{shell}} = 200 + v_{\text{gun}} = 200 - v_1$$

$$= 200 - \frac{200}{49} = 200 \times \frac{48}{49}$$

Now by conservation of momentum, we have

$$-(49\,m) \times \frac{200}{49} = 48mv_2 + m \times \left(200 \times \frac{48}{49}\right)$$

After solving, we get $v_2 = -200\left(\dfrac{1}{48} + \dfrac{1}{49}\right)$ m/s. *Ans.*

Example 4. Three balls A, B and C of masses 2 kg, 4 kg, and 8 kg respectively move along the same straight line and in the same direction, with velocities 4 m/s, 1m/s, and 3/4 m/s. If A collides with B and subsequently B collides with C show that the balls A and B will be brought to rest by the collision which will take place. Take the coefficient of restitution as unity.

Figure. 8.7

Sol. First consider the collisions of balls A and B. Let v_1 and v_2 be the velocities of the balls A and B after collision, then
Momentum before collision = Momentum after collision

$$\text{or} \qquad 2 \times 4 + 4 \times 1 = 2 v_1 + 4 v_2 \qquad \dots \text{(i)}$$

$$\text{and} \qquad 1 = -\frac{(v_1 - v_2)}{(4 - 1)}. \qquad \dots \text{(ii)}$$

Solving above equations, we get

$$v_1 = 0 \text{ and } v_2 = 3 \text{ m/s}.$$

Hence after collisions the ball A is rest, while the ball B will move with a velocity of 3 m/s.
Now consider the collision of the balls B and C.
Let v'_2 and v_3 be the velocities of the balls B and C after collision, then

$$4 \times 3 + 8 \times 3/4 = 4v'_2 + 8 v_3 \qquad \dots \text{(iii)}$$

$$\text{and} \qquad 1 = -\frac{(v_2' - v_3)}{3 - \dfrac{3}{4}} \qquad \dots \text{(iv)}$$

Solving above equations, we get

$$v'_2 = 0 \text{ and } v_3 = 9/4 \text{ m/s}$$

Hence the ball B after collision with the ball C will be brought to rest.

Example 5. A block of mass 2.0 kg is moving on a frictionless horizontal surface with a velocity of 1.0 m/s towards another block of equal mass kept at rest (see *figure* 8.8). The spring constant of the spring fixed at one end is 100 N/m. Find the maximum compression of the spring.

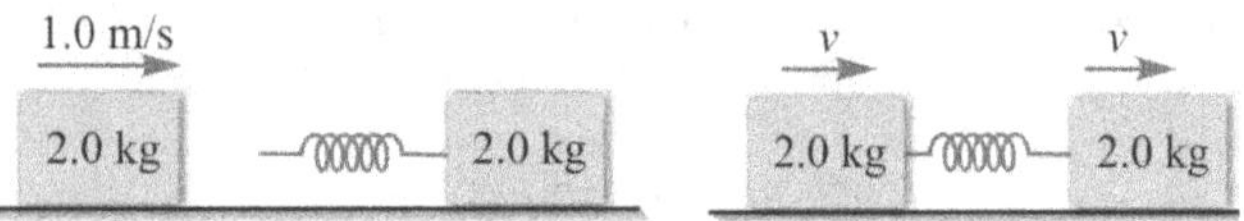

Figure. 8.8

Sol. Maximum compression will occur when their velocities become equal (i.e. approach velocity becomes zero). Let the velocity of each block at this instant is v. Then by conservation of momentum, we have

$$2 \times 1 + 0 = 2v + 2v$$

$$\therefore \qquad v = \frac{1}{2}\text{m/s}.$$

Now by conservation of mechanical energy, we have

$$\frac{1}{2} \times 2 \times 1^2 + 0 = \frac{1}{2} \times 2 \times v^2 + \frac{1}{2} \times 2 \times v^2 + \frac{1}{2} \times 100 \times x_{max}^2$$

where x_{max} is the maximum compression of the spring.

As
$$v = \frac{1}{2}\text{m/s}$$

$$\therefore \qquad \frac{1}{2} \times 2 \times 1^2 = \frac{1}{2} \times 2 \times \left(\frac{1}{2}\right)^2 + \frac{1}{2} \times 2 \times \left(\frac{1}{2}\right)^2$$

$$+ \frac{1}{2} \times 100 \times x_{max}^2$$

After solving, we get

$$x_{max} = 0.1 \text{ m}. \qquad\qquad Ans.$$

Example 6. A ball moving with a velocity v strikes a wall moving towards the ball with a velocity u. An elastic impact occurs. Determine the velocity of ball after the impact. What is the cause of change in kinetic energy of the ball? Consider the mass of the wall to be infinitely great.

Sol.

Figure. 8.9

Velocity of ball w.r.t. wall before collision $= v - (-u) = v + u$.
After collision the velocity of ball w.r.t. wall will be $= -(v + u)$.
Velocity of ball relative to ground $= -(v + u) - u = -(v + 2u)$.
The change in kinetic energy

$$\frac{1}{2}m(v + 2u)^2 - \frac{1}{2}mv^2 = 2mu(u + v)$$

Reaction force from wall

$$F = \frac{\Delta P}{\Delta t} = \frac{m[-(v + 2u) - v]}{\Delta t}$$

or
$$F = -\frac{2m(v + u)}{\Delta t},$$

where Δt is the duration of collision.
Work done of this force

$$W = Fs = \frac{2m(v + u)}{\Delta t} \times u\Delta t = 2m(v + u)u.$$

Thus, we can say that K.E. of ball changes due to workdone by the wall.

In Chapter Exercise 8.1

1. A particle of mass 0.1kg moving at an initial speed u collides with another identieal stationary particle. The total kinetic energy becomes 0.2 J. After the collision u are $2x$ m/s and $\sqrt{2}y$ m/s respectively, then find the value of x and y.   *Ans.* $x = 1$, $y = 2$

2. A ball of mass 1 kg falls onto a floor. The collisions between ball and floor one perfectly elastic. The average force exerted by the ball on the floor during a long time interval is $5x$ newton. Find the value of x.   [Integer]
     Ans. $x = 2$

3. A 1 kg bullet moving directly upward at 200 m/s strikes and passes through the centre of mass of a 5kg block initially at rest. The bullet emerges from the block moving directly upward at 100 m/s. The block rises to $10x$ m. Find the value of x. ($g = 10$ m/s^2)   [Integer]

     Ans.. $x = 2$

4. The 1 kg sphere shown is figure in released from rest when $\theta = 90^0$. The coefficient of restitution between the sphere and the block is 0.70. If the coefficient of friction between the block and the horizontal surface is 0.3, determine how far the block will move after the impact?

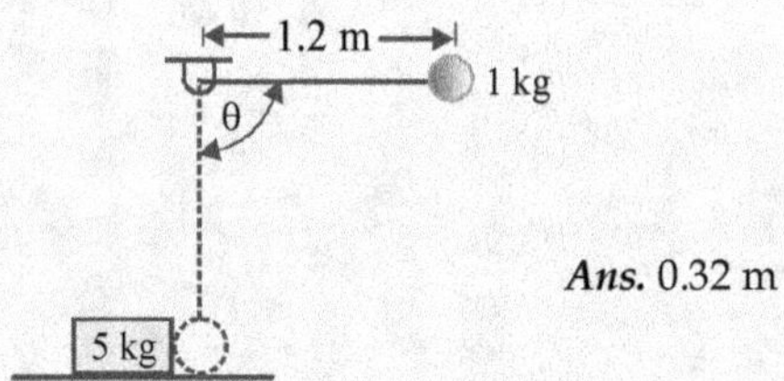

     Ans. 0.32 m

5. A particle of mass 1.0 g moving with velocity $\vec{v_1} = 3.0\,\hat{i} - 2.0\,\hat{j}$ experiences a perfectly inelastic collision with another particle of mass 2.0 g and velocity $\vec{v_2} = 4.0\,\hat{j} - 6.0\,\hat{k}$. Find the velocity of the formed particle (both the vector $\vec{v}$ and its modulus), if the components of the vectors v_1 and v_2 are given in the SI units.

     Ans. $\vec{v} = 1.0\,\hat{i} + 2.0\,\hat{j} - 4.0\,k$, $v = 4.6$ m/s.

6. A particle of mass m_1 experienced a perfectly elastic collision with a stationary particle of mass m_2. What fraction of the kinetic energy does the striking particle lose, if
   (a) it recoils at right angles to its original motion direction;
   (b) the collision is a head-on one ?

     Ans. (a) $\eta = \dfrac{2m_1}{(m_1 + m_2)}$; (b) $\eta = \dfrac{4m_1 m_2}{(m_1 + m_2)^2}$.

7. A ball of mass m is projected with speed u into barrel of spring gun of mass M initially at rest on a frictionless surface. The mass m sticks in the barrel at the point of maximum compression of the spring. What fraction of the initial energy of the ball is stored in the spring? Neglect friction.

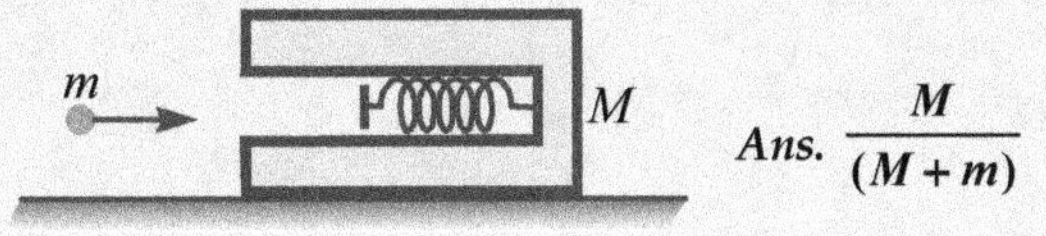

Ans. $\dfrac{M}{(M+m)}$

8. Two blocks of masses $m_1 = 2$ kg and $m_2 = 5$ kg are moving in the same direction along a frictionless surface with speeds 10 m/s and 3 m/s respectively, m_2 being ahead of m_1. An ideal spring with $k = 1120$ N/m is attached to back side of m_2. Find the maximum compression of the spring when the blocks collide.

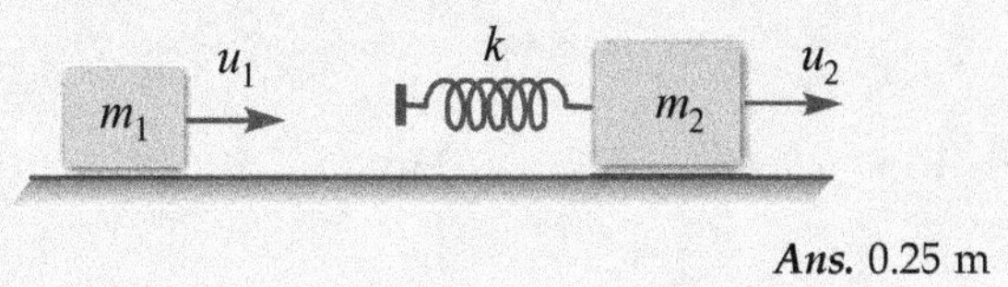

Ans. 0.25 m

8.5 ELASTIC OBLIQUE COLLISION

When line joining the geometric centres of the colliding bodies is different from the line of motion; this results *oblique collision*.

Consider a body of mass m_1 moving along x-axis with a velocity u_1 makes elastic oblique collision with another body of mass m_2, initially at rest. Let after collision their velocities become v_1 and v_2, making angles θ_1 and θ_2 with the x-axis.

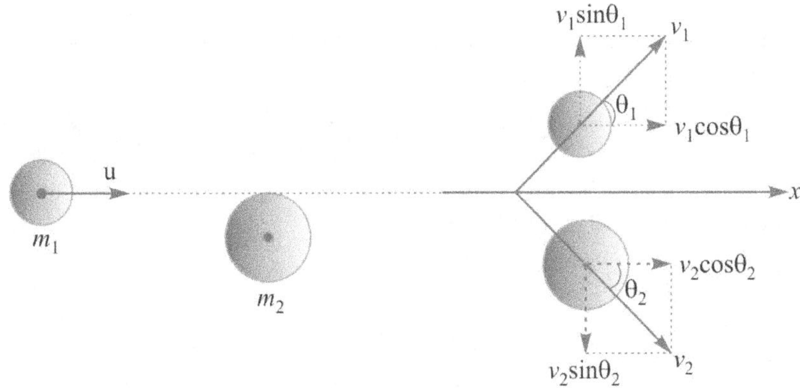

Figure. 8.10

Using principle of conservation of momentum;

(i) along x-axis,

$$m_1 u + 0 \;=\; m_1 v_1 \cos\theta_1 + m_2 v_2 \cos\theta_2 \qquad \dots \text{(i)}$$

(ii) along y-axis,

$$0 + 0 \;=\; m_1 v_1 \sin\theta_1 - m_2 v_2 \sin\theta_2 \qquad \dots \text{(ii)}$$

As the collision is elastic, so we have

$$\frac{1}{2} m_1 u^2 + 0 \;=\; \frac{1}{2} m_1 v_1^2 + \frac{1}{2} m_2 v_2^2 \qquad \dots \text{(iii)}$$

Here we have three equations, but *four unknowns*. To get all unknowns, some experimental data is to be provided. Assuming $\theta_1 + \theta_2 = \theta$, called deflection angle, and solving above equations, we get

$$\sin\theta \;=\; \frac{m_1}{m_2}. \qquad \text{Here } m_1 \leq m_2. \qquad \dots \text{(iv)}$$

Special cases :

Method I :

(i) Glancing collision

Here $\theta_1 \simeq 90°$ and $\theta_2 \simeq 0°$

Figure. 8.11

From equations (i) and (ii), we get

$$v_1 = u \text{ and } v_2 = 0,$$

$\therefore$ K.E. of the body $m_2 = \dfrac{1}{2}m_2 v_2^2 = 0$

(ii)   If $m_1 = m_2 = m$, then from equation (iv), we get

$$\sin\theta = 1,$$

or $\theta = \theta_1 + \theta_2 = 90°.$

Method II :

$$m\vec{u} = m\vec{v}_1 + m\vec{v}_2$$

or $\vec{u} = \vec{v}_1 + \vec{v}_2$

or $\vec{u}.\vec{u} = (\vec{v}_1 + \vec{v}_2).(\vec{v}_1 + \vec{v}_2)$

or $u^2 = v_1^2 + v_2^2 + 2\vec{v}_1.\vec{v}_2$

As $v_1^2 + v_2^2 = u^2$, thus we have

$$\vec{v}_1.\vec{v}_2 = 0$$

That is $\theta = \theta_1 + \theta_2 = 90°.$

Hence if two identical bodies make elastic oblique collision, they will move *perpendicular* to each other after collision.

FORMULAE USED

1.   When two bodies, one body initially at rest of masses ($m_1 < m_2$), make elastic oblique collision, the angle of deflection ($\theta = \theta_1 + \theta_2$) if given by,

$$\sin\theta = \frac{m_1}{m_2}.$$

2.   For $m_1 = m_2$, $\theta = 90°.$

EXAMPLES BASED ON TWO-DIMENSIONAL COLLISION

Example 7. A bomb explodes in air when it has a horizontal speed of v. It breaks into two identical pieces of equal mass. If one goes vertically up at a speed of $4v$, find the velocity of other immediately after the explosion.

Sol. Momentum of bomb before explosion

$$\vec{P} = mv\hat{i}.$$

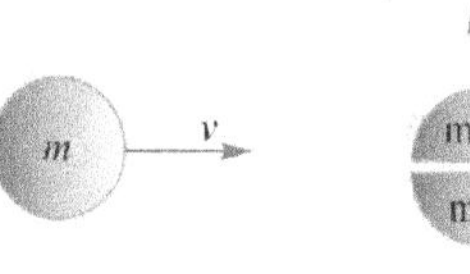

Figure. 8.12

Using conservation of momentum

$$\vec{P} = \vec{P}_1 + \vec{P}_2$$

$\therefore$ $\vec{P}_2 = \vec{P} - \vec{P}_1$

where $\vec{P}_1 = \dfrac{m}{2} \times 4v\hat{j}$

$\therefore$ $\vec{P}_2 = mv\hat{i} - 2mv\hat{j}$

or $\dfrac{m}{2}\vec{v}_2 = mv\hat{i} - 2mv\hat{j}$

or $\vec{v}_2 = 2v\hat{i} - 4v\hat{j}.$ ***Ans.***

Example 8. A ball strikes a wall at an angle α with the horizontal. It rebounds at an angle θ with the horizontal. Calculate the coefficient of restitution between the ball and wall.

Sol. Since the line of collision is AB, therefore the velocity of the ball along a line parallel (normal to AB) to wall does not change.

$\therefore$ $u\sin\alpha = v\sin\theta$ ... (i)

and $e = -\dfrac{(-v\cos\theta - 0)}{(u\cos\alpha - 0)}$ ... (ii)

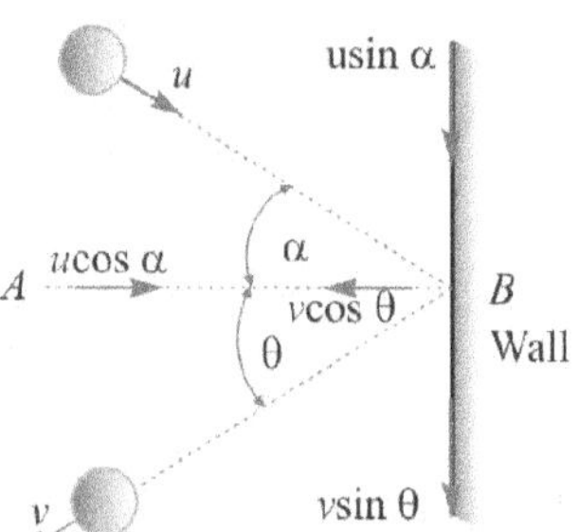

Figure. 8.13

where u and v are the velocities of the ball before and after collision. The velocity of the wall before and after collision practically be zero. Solving above equations, we get

$$e = \tan\alpha / \tan\theta.$$ ***Ans.***

Example 9. A spherical ball A of mass m is released from rest on a smooth bowl 0.2 m high. The sphere slides down and collide elastically with another sphere B of mass $m/4$ placed on the bottom of the bowl. If the ball B has to just reach the top and escape the bowl, calculate from where A should be released?

Sol. Let ball A be released from height h.

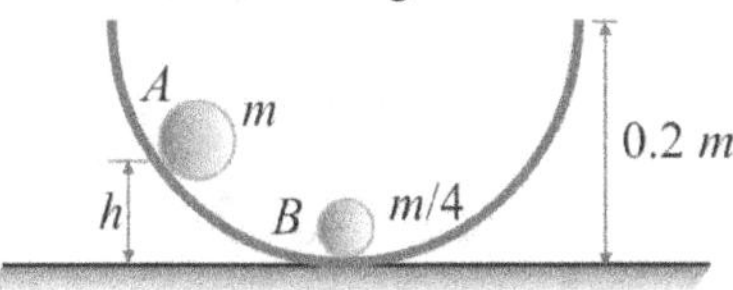

Figure. 8.14

Let v be the velocity of ball B just after collision, then

$$\frac{1}{2}(m/4)v^2 = (m/4)g \times 0.2$$

which gives

$$v = \sqrt{(0.2g \times 2)} = 2\text{m/s}$$

Now elastic collision between ball A and ball B

$$mv_1 + 0 = mv'_1 + (m/4) \times 2 \qquad \ldots \text{(i)}$$

where v_1 and v'_1 be the velocities of the ball A before and after collision.

Also

$$1 = -\frac{(v'_1 - 2)}{(v_1 - 0)}. \qquad \ldots \text{(ii)}$$

Solving above equations, we get $v_1 = 1.25$ m/s

Now

$$\frac{1}{2}mv_1^2 = mgh$$

which after solving gives

$$h = 0.078 \text{ m.} \qquad\qquad \textit{Ans.}$$

Example 10. A small particle travelling with a velocity v collides elastically with a spherical body of equal mass and radius r initially kept at rest. The centre of the spherical body is located at a distance $(\rho < r)$ away from the direction of motion of the particle. Find the final velocity of the particle.

Sol. During collision :

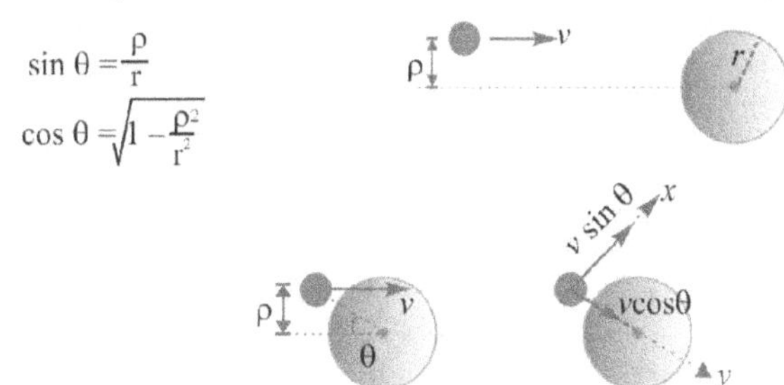

Figure. 8.15

Using conservation of momentum along y-axis, we get

$$m(v \cos \theta) + 0 = mv_1 + mv_2 \qquad \ldots \text{(i)}$$

and

$$\frac{1}{2}m(v\cos\theta)^2 + 0 = \frac{1}{2}mv_1^2 + \frac{1}{2}mv_2^2 \qquad \ldots \text{(ii)}$$

After solving above equations we get

$$v_1 = 0 \text{ and } v_2 = v \cos \theta$$

$$= \frac{v\sqrt{r^2 - \rho^2}}{r}$$

The resultant velocity of the particle will be $v\sin\theta$ along x-axis (see figure)

In Chapter Exercise 8.2

1. A body of weight P slides without friction down an inclined board into a cart standing at rest. What velocity v will be imparted to the cart when the body drops on it? The weight of the cart is Q, the initial height of the body above the level of the cart is h and the angle at which the board is inclined to the horizontal is α (figure). The cart moves without friction.

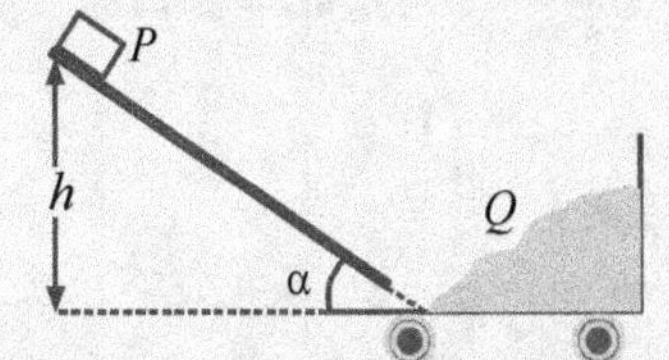

$$\textbf{Ans.} \quad v = \frac{P\sqrt{2gh}\cos\alpha}{(P+Q)}$$

2. A ball dropped on to a smooth horizontal floor and bounces as shown in figure. Drive expression for coefficient of restitution in terms of
    (a) two successive heights,
    (b) two successive ranges. Also determine the time of flight in n^{th} bounce.

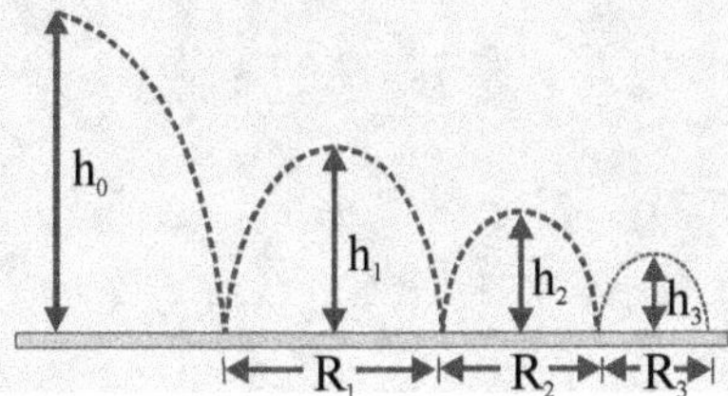

$$\textbf{Ans. (a) } e = \sqrt{\frac{h_n}{h_{n-1}}} \text{ (b) } e = \frac{R_n}{R_{n-1}}, \ t = 2\sqrt{\frac{2h_n}{g}}$$

3. A particle of mass m having collided with a stationary particle of mass M deviated by an angle $\frac{\pi}{2}$ whereas the particle M recoiled at an angle $\theta = 30°$ to the direction of the initial motion of the particle m. How much (in percent) and in what way has the kinetic energy of this system changed after the collision , if $\frac{M}{m} = 5.0$?

$$\textbf{Ans.} \quad \frac{\Delta K}{K} \times 100 = \left(1 + \frac{m}{M}\right)\tan^2\theta + \frac{m}{M} - 1 = -40\%.$$

4. A horizontally flying bullet of mass m gets stuck in a body of mass M suspended by two identical threads of length ℓ shown in the figure. As a result, the threads swerve through an angle θ. Assuming m << M, find

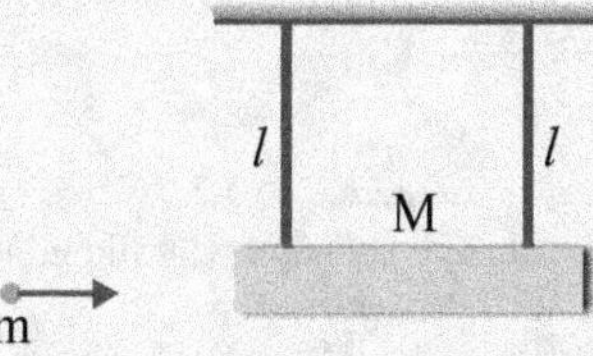

(a) the velocity of the bullet before striking the body;
    (b) the fraction of the bullet's initial kinetic energy that turned into heat.

$$\textbf{Ans. (a) } v \approx \left(\frac{2M}{m}\right)\sqrt{g\ell}\sin\left(\frac{\theta}{2}\right); \text{ (b) } \eta \approx 1 - \frac{m}{M}.$$

EXAMPLES FOR JEE-(MAIN AND ADVANCED)

Example 1. Two blocks A and B of mass m and $2m$ respectively are connected by a spring of force constant k. The masses are moving to the right with uniform velocity v each, the heavier mass, leading the lighter one. The spring is of natural length in the motion. Block B collides head on with a third block C of mass m, at rest, the collision being completely inelastic. Determine the velocity of blocks at the instant of maximum compression of the spring.

Sol.

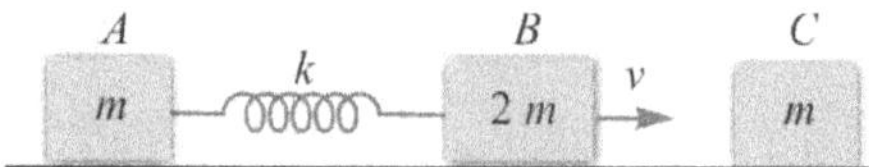

Figure. 8.16

Collision between blocks B and C
$$2mv = (2m + m)v'$$
$$\Rightarrow \qquad v' = \frac{2v}{3}.$$

After the collision the blocks move as shown in *fig.* 8.17.

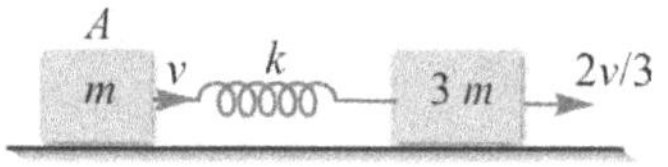

Figure. 8.17

When both the blocks will get equal velocity the spring will have maximum compression. Let velocity be v_0.
Using principle of conservation of momentum, we have

$$mv + 3m \times \frac{2v}{3} = mv_0 + 3mv_0$$

After solving, we get

$$v_0 = \frac{3v}{4}. \qquad\qquad \textbf{Ans.}$$

Example 2. Consider a ball falling from some height h. Let e be the coefficient of restitution between the ball and the ground and ball rebounds again and again, then find
(i) velocity after n^{th} collision
(ii) height attained after n^{th} collision
(iii) total distance travelled by ball before stop
(iv) total time of motion.
Sol.

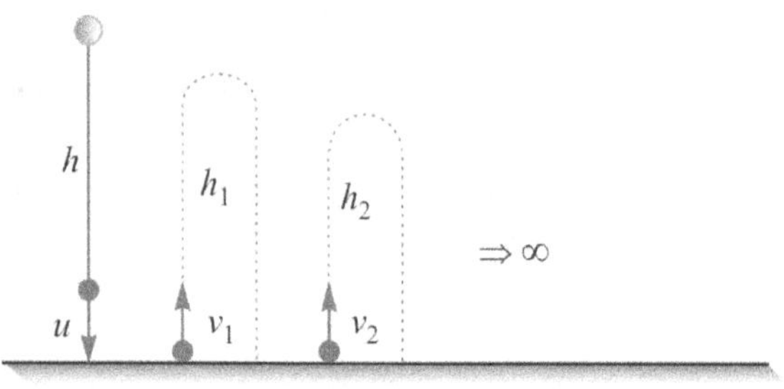

Ground

Figure. 8.18

Velocity of the ball just before collision with the ground
$$u = \sqrt{2gh}.$$

(a) After first collision

$$e = -\frac{v_1 - v_2}{u_1 - u_2}$$

here suffix 1 is for ball and 2 is for ground (earth).

Earth on being very massive in comparison to ball,
$$u_2 = 0 \text{ and } v_2 = 0.$$

$$\therefore \qquad e = -\frac{v_1 - 0}{u - 0} \Rightarrow v_1 = -eu = -e\sqrt{2gh}.$$

Minus sign indicates that after collision the direction of velocity becomes opposite.
Now height attained after first collision

$$mgh_1 = \frac{1}{2}mv_1^2$$

$$\Rightarrow \qquad h_1 = \frac{v_1^2}{2g} = \frac{(e\sqrt{2gh})^2}{2g} = e^2 h$$

(b) Before second collision, velocity of the ball is $v_1 = e\sqrt{2gh}$

$\therefore$ The velocity after second collision
$$v_2 = -ev_1$$
$$= -e(-e\sqrt{2gh}) = +e^2\sqrt{2gh}.$$

The height attained after second collision,

$$mgh_2 = \frac{1}{2}mv_2^2 = \frac{1}{2}m(e^2\sqrt{2gh})^2$$

$$\Rightarrow \qquad h_2 = e^4 h.$$

After n^{th} collision :

(i) $\qquad v_n = e^n\sqrt{2gh}$

(ii) $\qquad h_n = e^{2n}h.$

(iii) Theoretically ball will make infinite collision with the ground. Thus the total distance travelled till last

$$L = h + 2[h_1 + h_2 + h_3 + \dots \infty]$$
$$= h + 2[e^2 h + e^4 h + e^6 h + \dots \infty]$$
$$= h + 2e^2 h[1 + e^2 + e^4 + \dots \infty]$$

or $\qquad L = \left(\frac{1+e^2}{1-e^2}\right)h.$

(iv) Total time of motion $\quad T = t + 2(t_1 + t_2 + \dots \infty)$

$$= \sqrt{\frac{2h}{g}} + 2\left[\sqrt{\frac{2h_1}{g}} + \sqrt{\frac{2h_2}{g}} + \sqrt{\frac{2h_3}{g}} + \dots \infty\right]$$

$$= \sqrt{\frac{2h}{g}} + 2\sqrt{\frac{2}{g}}\left[\sqrt{h_1} + \sqrt{h_2} + \sqrt{h_3} + \dots \infty\right]$$

$$= \sqrt{\frac{2h}{g}} + 2\sqrt{\frac{2}{g}}\left[\sqrt{e^2 h} + \sqrt{e^4 h} + \sqrt{e^6 h} + \dots \infty\right]$$

$$= \sqrt{\frac{2h}{g}} + 2\sqrt{\frac{2h}{g}}\left[e + e^2 + e^3 + \dots \infty\right]$$

or $\qquad T = \left(\frac{1+e}{1-e}\right)\sqrt{\frac{2h}{g}}.$

Example 3. Two identical balls in contact on a table are in equilibrium. A third ball collides them simultaneously symmetrically and remains at rest after impact. Calculate coefficient of restitution between the balls.

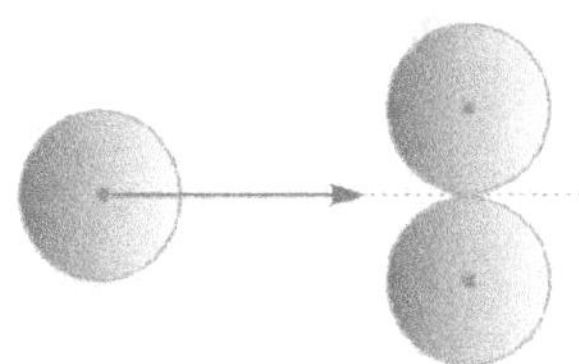

Figure. 8.19

Sol.

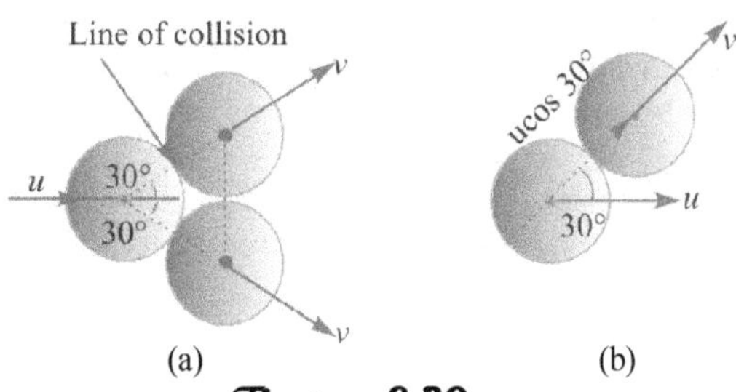

Figure. 8.20

Using conservation of momentum in the direction of motion of colliding ball

$$mu = mv\cos 30° + mv\cos 30°$$

or

$$u = \sqrt{3}v.$$

Coefficient of restitution

$$e = -\left(\frac{v_1 - v_2}{u_1 - u_2}\right),$$

where velocities of balls are along the line of collision.

$$\therefore \qquad e = -\frac{(0 - v)}{(u\cos 30° - 0)}$$

$$= \frac{v}{u\cos 30°} = \frac{v}{\sqrt{3}v \times \frac{\sqrt{3}}{2}} = \frac{2}{3}. \qquad Ans.$$

Example 4. A small sphere of mass m = 1kg moving with a velocity $(4\hat{i} - \hat{j})$ m/s. It hits a fixed smooth floor and rebounds with velocity $(\hat{i} + 3\hat{j})$ m/s. The coefficient of restitution between the sphere and the floor is $e = \dfrac{9}{x}$. Find the value of x. [Integer]

Sol. The impulse

$$\vec{J} = m(\vec{v}_f - \vec{v}_i)$$

$$= \left[(\hat{i} + 3\hat{j}) - (4\hat{i} - \hat{j})\right]$$

$$= -3\hat{i} + 4\hat{j}$$

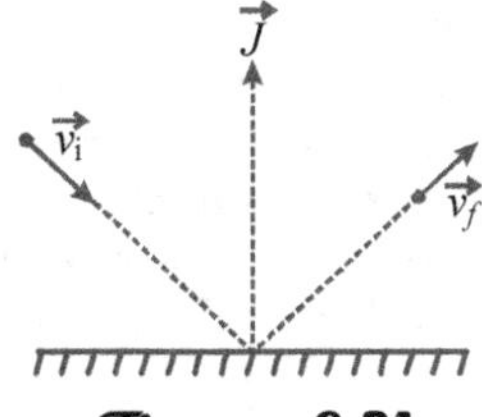

Figure. 8.21

The component of $(4\hat{i} - \hat{j})$ along $(-3\hat{i} + 4\hat{j})$ is

$$= \frac{[(4\hat{i} - \hat{j}).(-3\hat{i} + 4\hat{j})]\,(-3\hat{i} + 4\hat{j})}{(\sqrt{3^2 + 4^2})^2}$$

$$= \frac{-16}{25}(-3\hat{j} + 4\hat{j})$$

or speed, $\qquad u_1 = \dfrac{16}{25} \times 5 = \dfrac{16}{5}$ m/s

Component of $(\hat{i} + 3\hat{j})$ along $(-3\hat{i} + 4\hat{j})$ is

$$= [(\hat{i} + 3\hat{j}).(-3\hat{i} + 4\hat{j})]\frac{(-3\hat{i} + 4\hat{j})}{(\sqrt{(3^2 + 4^2)})^2}$$

$$= \frac{9}{25}(-3\hat{i} + 4\hat{j})$$

or speed $\qquad v_1 = \dfrac{9 \times 5}{25} = \dfrac{9}{5}$ m/s.

If u_2 and v_2 are the speed of floor before and after collision, then

$$e = -\left[\frac{v_2 - v_1}{u_2 - u_1}\right]$$

$$= -\left[\frac{0 - (-9/5)}{0 - 16/5}\right]$$

$$= \frac{9}{16}.$$

Thus, x = 16

Example 5. A shell of mass $(m_1 + m_2)$ is fined with a given velocity in a given direction. At the highest point of its path, the shell explodes into two fragments of mass m_1, and m_2. The explosion produces an additional kinetic energy E and the fragments separate in a horizontal direction. Find the horizontal distance on the ground at which they hit the ground, if vertical component of velocity is v_0.

Sol. Time taken by the shell to reach the highest point $\quad T = \dfrac{v_0}{g}$.

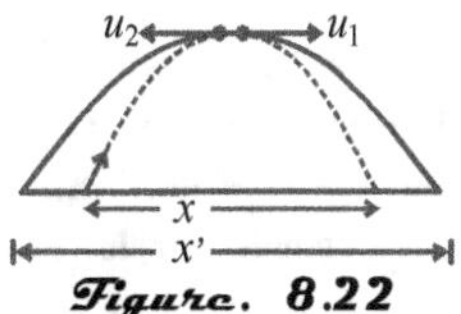

Figure. 8.22

The fragments m_1 and m_2 take the same time T to reach the ground. In this durations the horizontal component of relative speed of the fragments is $(v_1 + v_2)$, so

$$x' = (v_1 + v_2)\, T = (u_1 + u_2)\frac{v_0}{g}. \qquad ...(i)$$

If u is the speed of shell before explosion, then

$$(m_1 + m_2)\, u = m_1 u_1 - m_2 u_2 \qquad ...(ii)$$

and $\quad \dfrac{1}{2}(m_1 + m_2)u^2 + E = \dfrac{1}{2}m_1 u_1^2 + \dfrac{1}{2}m_2 u_2^2 \qquad ...(iii)$

After solving above equations, we get

$$x' = \frac{v_0}{g}\sqrt{2E\left(\frac{1}{m_1} + \frac{1}{m_2}\right)}.$$

The collision will take place along normal direction. In the tangential direction no force acts and the velocity does not change in this direction.

Example 6. **Two identical buggies 1 and 2 with one man in each move without friction due to inertia along the parallel rails towards each other. When the buggies get opposite each other, the men exchange their places by jumping in the direction perpendicular to the motion direction. As a consequence, buggy 1 stops and buggy 2 keeps moving in the same direction, with its velocity becoming equal to v. Find the initial velocities of the buggies v_1 and v_2 if the mass of each buggy (without a man) equals M and the mass of each man m.**

Sol.

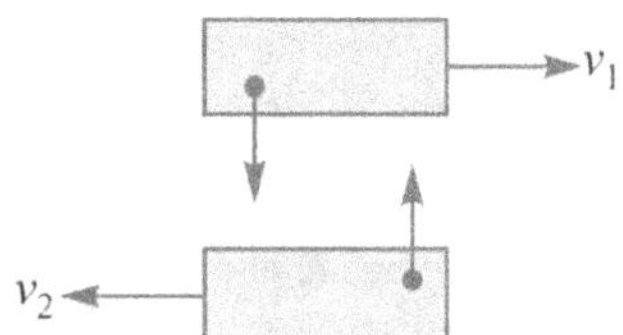

Figure. 8.23

Let v_1 and v_2 be the initial velocities of the buggies. The direction of v_1 taken as positive and that of v_2 taken as negative.

The momentum of the man in the buggy 2 will be mv_2 in the direction of the motion of the buggy 2. When he jumps into buggy 1 perpendicular to its motion, as the buggy stops, its momentum becomes zero

$$Mv_1 - mv_2 = 0. \qquad \ldots (i)$$

Man in buggy 1 jumps into buggy 2 perpendicular to its direction, then

$$Mv_2 - mv_1 = (M + m)v \qquad \ldots (ii)$$

Solving equations (i) and (ii), we get

$$v_1 = -\frac{mv}{(M-m)}$$

and $$v_2 = \frac{Mv}{(M-m)}. \qquad \textbf{\textit{Ans.}}$$

Example 7. **Two identical buggies move one after the other due to inertia (without friction) with the same velocity v_0. A man of mass m rides the rear buggy. At a certain moment the man jumps into the front buggy with a velocity u relative to his buggy. Knowing that the mass of each buggy is equal to M, find the velocities with which the buggies will move after that.**

Sol. Initially rear buggy + man were moving with velocity v_0. After the man jump into the front buggy, let the velocity of the rear buggy becomes v_{rear}. Since the velocity of the man relative to rear buggy is u, it follows that

$$\vec{u} = \vec{v}_{man} - \vec{v}_{rear}$$

where $\vec{v}_{man}$ is the velocity of the man with respect to the ground.

Thus $$v_{man} = u + v_{rear}.$$

Applying momentum conservation for the rear buggy, we have

$$(M + m)v_0 = Mv_{rear} + m(u + v_{rear})$$

or $$v_{rear} = v_0 - \frac{mu}{(M+m)}. \qquad \ldots (i)$$

When the man jumps into the front buggy, let the velocity of this buggy becomes v_{front}. For the two buggies system from momentum conservation, we have

$$Mv_0 + (M + m)v_0 = Mv_{rear} + (M + m)v_{front} \qquad \ldots (ii)$$

Upon substituting the value of v_{rear} in equation (ii), we get

$$v_{front} = v_0 + \frac{mMu}{(M+m)^2}. \qquad \textbf{\textit{Ans.}}$$

Example 8. **A ball moving translationally collides elastically with another stationary ball of the same mass. At the moment of impact the angle between the straight line passing through the centres of the balls and the direction of the initial motion of the striking ball is equal to $\alpha = 45°$. Assuming the balls to be smooth, find the fraction η of the kinetic energy of the striking ball that turned into potential energy at the moment of the maximum deformation.**

Sol. Let the velocity of the colliding ball be u. Applying the law of conservation of momentum along x-axis, we have

$$mu \cos \alpha + 0 = mv_{1x} + mv_{2x}$$

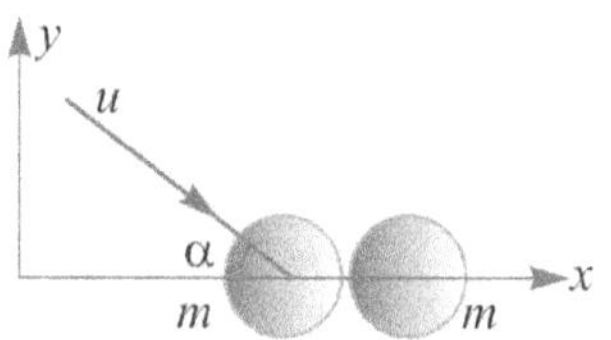

Figure. 8.24

At the maximum deformation

$$v_{1x} = v_{2x}$$

$$\therefore \quad u \cos \alpha + 0 = v_{1x} + v_{2x} = 2v_{1x}$$

or $$v_{1x} = \frac{u \cos \alpha}{2}$$

Initial K.E. of the system

$$= \frac{1}{2}mu^2 + 0 = \frac{1}{2}mu^2$$

Final K.E. of the system

$$= \frac{1}{2}mv_{1x}^2 + \frac{1}{2}mv_{2x}^2$$

$$= 2 \cdot \frac{1}{2}mv_{1x}^2 = \frac{mu^2 \cos^2 \alpha}{4}$$

Now $$\eta = \frac{\text{Final K.E.}}{\text{Initial K.E.}} = \frac{\left[\dfrac{mu^2 \cos^2 \alpha}{4}\right]}{\dfrac{1}{2}mu^2}$$

$$= \frac{\cos^2 45°}{2} = 0.25 \qquad \textbf{\textit{Ans.}}$$

Example 9. **Three identical discs A, B and C as shown in the figure rest on a smooth horizontal plane. The disc A is set in motion with velocity v after which it experiences an elastic collision simultaneously with the discs B and C. The distance between the centres of the latter discs prior to the collision is η times greater than the diameter of each disc. Find the velocity of disc A after the collision. At what value of η will the disc A recoil after the collision; stop, move on?**

Sol. From the figure

$$\cos\theta \;=\; \frac{\eta d/2}{d} = \eta/2$$

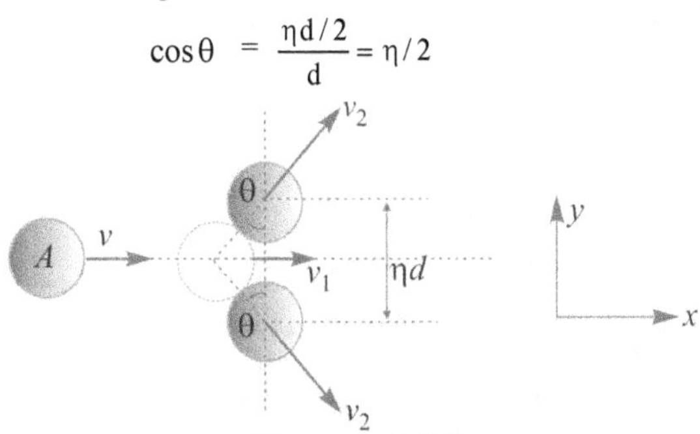

Figure. **8.25**

Applying the law of conservation of momentum along x-axis, we have

$$mv + 0 \;=\; mv_1 + 2\,mv_2\sin\theta \qquad \dots \text{(i)}$$

where v_1 and v_2 are the velocities of the discs after collision.
From Newton's law of collision,

$$e \;=\; \frac{-(v_1\sin\theta - v_2)}{v\sin\theta}$$

For perfectly elastic collision $e = 1$

$$\therefore \qquad 1 \;=\; \frac{-(v_1\sin\theta - v_2)}{v\sin\theta} \qquad \dots \text{(ii)}$$

Solving above equations, we get

$$v_1 \;=\; \frac{v(1-2\sin^2\theta)}{(1+2\sin^2\theta)} \qquad \dots \text{(iii)}$$

After substituting value of $\cos\theta$ in equation (iii), we get

$$v_1 \;=\; \frac{v(\eta^2-2)}{(6-\eta^2)}$$

Disc A will stop after collision, $v_1 = 0$

$$\text{or} \qquad \frac{v(\eta^2-2)}{(6-\eta^2)} = 0$$

$$\text{or} \qquad \eta = \sqrt{2}$$

For recoil, v_1 should be negative or less than 0

$$\text{or} \qquad v_1 < 0$$

$$\therefore \qquad \eta = \sqrt{2}$$

For move in its direction of initial motion $v_1 > 0$

$$\text{or} \qquad \eta = \sqrt{2} \qquad\qquad \textit{Ans.}$$

Example 10. A block of mass $m_1 = 150$ kg is at rest on a very long frictionless table, one end which is terminated in a wall. Another block of mass m_2 is placed between the first block and the wall, and set in motion towards m_1 with constant speed u_2. Assume that all collisions are perfectly elastic, find the value of m_2 for which both the blocks move with the same velocity after m_2 once with m_1 and once with the wall. The wall has effectively infinite mass.

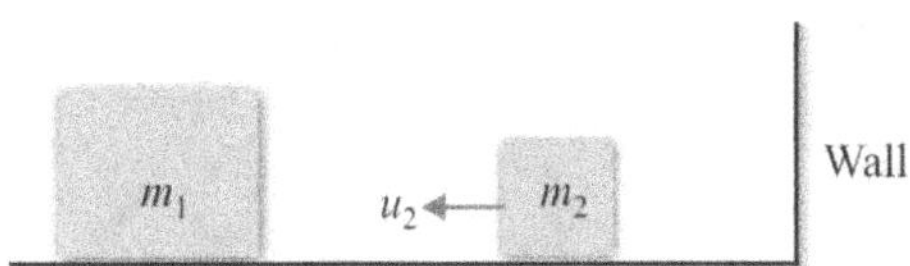

Figure. **8.26**

Sol. Let v_1 and v_2 be the velocities of the blocks towards left just after collision. Applying momentum conservation, we have

$$0 + m_2u_2 \;=\; m_1v_1 + m_2v_2 \qquad \dots \text{(i)}$$

$$\text{and} \qquad 1 \;=\; -\frac{(v_1-v_2)}{(0-u_2)}. \qquad \dots \text{(ii)}$$

Solving above equations, we have

$$v_1 \;=\; \frac{2m_2u_2}{m_1+m_2}$$

$$\text{and} \qquad v_2 \;=\; -\frac{(m_1-m_2)u_2}{m_1+m_2}$$

The –ve sign with v_2 indicates that block of mass m_2 moves towards right (or wall). It rebounds elastically from the wall with same velocity (v_2). According to the given condition both the blocks start moving with the same velocity

$$\text{i.e.} \qquad v_1 = v_2$$

$$\text{or} \qquad \frac{2m_2u_2}{m_1+m_2} = \frac{(m_1-m_2)u_2}{m_1+m_2}$$

which after solving gives $m_2 = m_1/3 = 150/3 = 50$ kg.   *Ans.*

Example 11. *A small sphere of mass 10 g is attached to a point of a smooth vertical wall by a light string of length 1 m. The sphere is pulled out in a vertical plane perpendicular to the wall so that the string makes an angle of 60° with the wall and is then released. It is found that after the first rebound the string makes a maximum angle of 30° with the wall. Calculate the coefficient of restitution and the loss of K.E. due to impact. If all the energy converted into heat, find the heat produced by the impact.*

Sol. Let v_1 is the velocity of the sphere just before the collision with the wall, then

$$mgh \;=\; \frac{1}{2}mv_1^2, \quad \text{where } h = (1-1\cos 60°) = \frac{1}{2}$$

$$\therefore \qquad v_1 \;=\; \sqrt{g}\,.$$

If v_2 is the velocity of the sphere after collision with the wall, then

$$\frac{1}{2}mv_2^2 \;=\; mg(1-\cos 30°)$$

$$\text{or} \qquad v_2 \;=\; \sqrt{g(2-\sqrt{3})}\,.$$

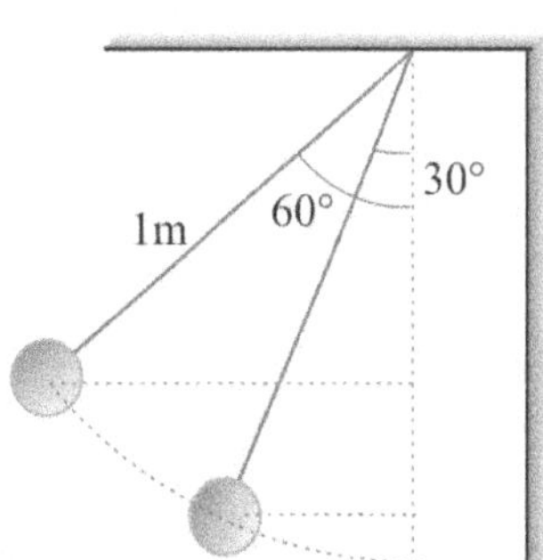

Figure. **8.27**

Now according to the Newton's experimental law

$$e \;=\; -\frac{(v_2-0)}{(v_1-0)}$$

$$=\; \frac{\sqrt{g(2-\sqrt{3})}}{\sqrt{g}} = 0.518\,.$$

Loss of K.E.

$$=\; \frac{1}{2}mv_1^2 - \frac{1}{2}mv_2^2$$

$$=\; \frac{1}{2}\times 0.01\times g - \frac{1}{2}\times 0.01\times g(2-\sqrt{3})$$

$$=\; 0.036 \text{ J} \qquad\qquad \textit{Ans.}$$

In Chapter Exercise 8.3

1. Three objects A, B and C are kept in a straight line on a frictionless horizontal surface. These have masses m, $2m$ and m, respectively. The object A moves towards B with a speed 9 m/s and makes an elastic collision with it. There after, B makes completely inelastic collision with C. All motions occur on the same straight line. Find the final speed (**in m/s**) of the object C.

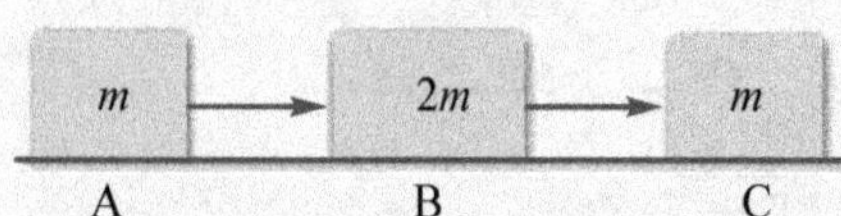

Ans. **4**   [IIT 2009]

2.   A block of mass 0.18 kg is attached to a spring of force-constant 2 N/m. The coefficient of friction between the block and the floor is 0.1. Initially the block is at rest and the spring is un-stretched. An impulse is given to the block as shown in the figure. The block slides a distance of 0.06 m and comes to rest for the first time. The initial velocity of the block in m/s is V = N/10. Then N is   [IIT 2011]

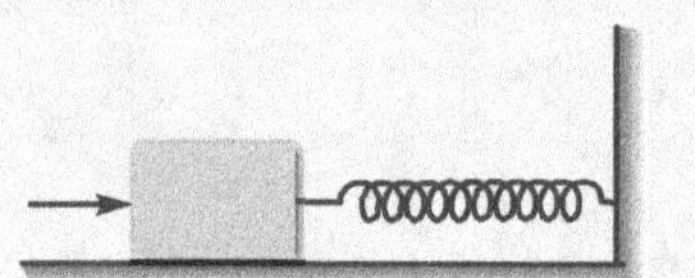

Ans. **4**

3. A particle of mass 0.2 kg is moving in one dimension under a force that delivers a constant power 0.5 W to the particle. If the initial speed (in ms^{-1}) of the particle is zero, the speed (in ms^{-1}) after 5 s is   *Ans.* **5**   [JEE Adv. 2013]

4. A bob of mass m, suspended by a string of length l_1, is given a minimum velocity required to complete a full circle in the vertical plane. At the highest point, it collides elastically with another bob of mass m suspended by a string of length l_2, which is initially at rest. Both the strings are mass-less and inextensible. If the second bob, after collision acquires the minimum speed required to complete a full circle in the vertical plane, the ratio $\dfrac{l_1}{l_2}$ is

Ans. **5**   [JEE Adv. 2013]

CENTRE OF MASS

8.6 NEWTON'S SECOND LAW FOR SYSTEM OF PARTICLES

Consider a system consisting of two particles of masses m_1 and m_2. They are acted by external forces $\vec{F}_1^{\,ext}$ and $\vec{F}_2^{\,ext}$ respectively in addition to internal forces between them as shown in *figure* 8.28. Let at any instant their positions are $\vec{r_1}$ and $\vec{r_2}$ respectively. Their accelerations are defined as;

$$\vec{a_1} = \frac{d^2 \vec{r_1}}{dt^2} \text{ and } \vec{a_2} = \frac{d^2 \vec{r_2}}{dt^2}.$$

Figure. 8.28

According to Newton's second law of motion, we have

$$\vec{F}_{12} + \vec{F}_1^{\,ext} = m_1 \vec{a}_1 \qquad \text{(i)}$$

and

$$\vec{F}_{21} + \vec{F}_2^{\,ext} = m_2 \vec{a}_2 . \qquad \text{...(ii)}$$

Adding equations (i) and (ii), we get

$$(\vec{F}_{12} + \vec{F}_{21}) + (\vec{F}_1^{\,ext} + \vec{F}_2^{\,ext}) = m_1 \vec{a}_1 + m_2 \vec{a}_2 .$$

By Newton's third law, we know that

$$\vec{F}_{12} = -\vec{F}_{21}$$

$$\therefore \qquad \vec{F}_1^{\,ext} + \vec{F}_2^{\,ext} = m_1 \vec{a}_1 + m_2 \vec{a}_2$$

or

$$\vec{F}_{net}^{\,ext} = m_1 \vec{a}_1 + m_2 \vec{a}_2 . \qquad \text{...(iii)}$$

Suppose the total mass of the system is M. Then

$$m_1 + m_2 = M.$$

Thus we can write the Newton's second law for total mass of the system as;

$$\vec{F}_{net}^{\,ext} = M\vec{a} . \qquad \text{...(iv)}$$

Now from equation (iii) and (iv), we get

$$\vec{a} = \frac{m_1\vec{a}_1 + m_2\vec{a}_2}{M}.$$

Which defined the acceleration of total mass of the system which is called **acceleration of centre of mass** of system. Thus we can write

$$\vec{a}_{cm} = \frac{m_1\vec{a}_1 + m_2\vec{a}_2}{m_1 + m_2}. \qquad ...(1)$$

Equation (1) can be written as

$$\frac{d^2\vec{r}_{cm}}{dt^2} = \frac{m_1\dfrac{d^2\vec{r}_1}{dt^2} + m_2\dfrac{d^2\vec{r}_2}{dt^2}}{m_1 + m_2}$$

$$= \frac{d^2}{dt^2}\left[\frac{m_1\vec{r}_1 + m_2\vec{r}_2}{m_1 + m_2}\right]$$

or
$$\vec{r}_{cm} = \frac{m_1\vec{r}_1 + m_2\vec{r}_2}{m_1 + m_2}. \qquad ...(2)$$

Equation (2) defined the position of centre of mass at which total mass $(m_1 + m_2)$ is supposed to be concentrated.

Similarly velocity of centre of mass can be defined as;

$$\vec{v}_{cm} = \frac{d\vec{r}_{cm}}{dt} = \frac{m_1\vec{v}_1 + m_2\vec{v}_2}{m_1 + m_2} \qquad ...(3)$$

8.7 Centre of mass of n - particle system

Consider a system of n particles of masses $m_1, m_2 \,....., m_n$ and position vectors $\vec{r}_1, \vec{r}_2,.... \vec{r}_n$ re origin O as shown in *figure* 8.29. The centre of mass of the system can be defined as

$$\vec{r}_{cm} = \frac{m_1\vec{r}_1 + m_2\vec{r}_2 + ... + m_n\vec{r}_n}{m_1 + m_2 + ... + m_n}$$

or
$$\vec{r}_{cm} = \frac{1}{M}\sum_{i=1}^{n} m_i\vec{r}_i \quad ; M = m_1 + m_2 + ... + m_n$$

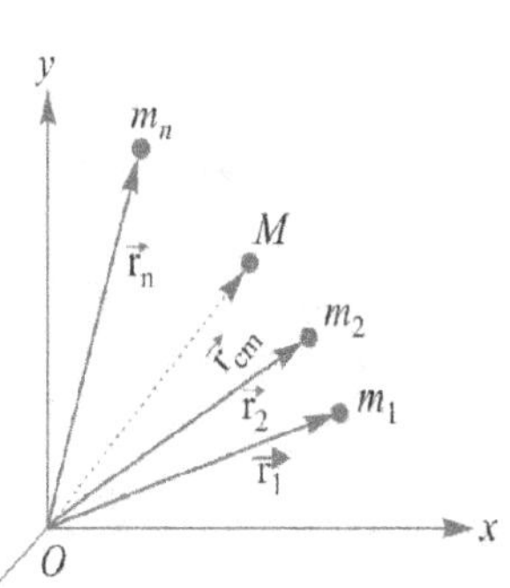

Figure. **8.29**

Cartesian coordinates of centre of mass

If x_{cm}, y_{cm} and z_{cm} are the Cartesian coordinates of the centre of mass of the system, then

$$x_{cm} = \left[\frac{m_1x_1 + m_2x_2 + ... + m_nx_n}{m_1 + m_2 + ... + m_n}\right] = \frac{\sum mx}{M}$$

$$y_{cm} = \left[\frac{m_1y_1 + m_2y_2 + ... + m_ny_n}{m_1 + m_2 + ... + m_n}\right] = \frac{\sum my}{M}$$

and
$$y_{cm} = \left[\frac{m_1z_1 + m_2z_2 + ... + m_nz_n}{m_1 + m_2 + ... + m_n}\right] = \frac{\sum mz}{M}$$

Similarly for n-particle system, we can write

$$\vec{v}_{cm} = \left[\frac{m_1\vec{v}_1 + m_1\vec{v}_2 + ... + m_n\vec{v}_n}{m_1 + m_2 + ... + m_n}\right] = \frac{\vec{P}_{net}}{M}$$

8.8 CENTRE OF MASS OF A RIGID BODY

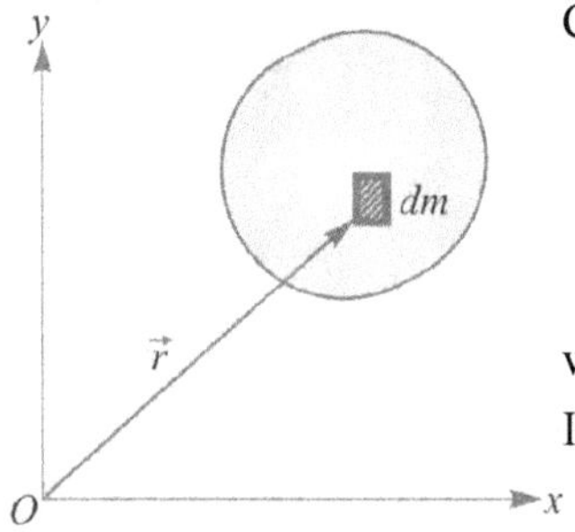

Centre of mass $\vec{r}_{cm}$ of a rigid body can be defined as;

$$\vec{r}_{cm} = \frac{\int dm\,\vec{r}}{\int dm} = \frac{1}{M}\int dm\,\vec{r}$$

where M, is the total mass of the body.

In Cartesian coordinate system we have

$$x_{cm} = \frac{\int dm\,x}{\int dm}, \quad y_{cm} = \frac{\int dm\,y}{\int dm} \quad \text{and} \quad z_{cm} = \frac{\int dm\,z}{\int dm}.$$

Also

$$\vec{r}_{cm} = x_{cm}\hat{i} + y_{cm}\hat{j} + z_{cm}\hat{k}.$$

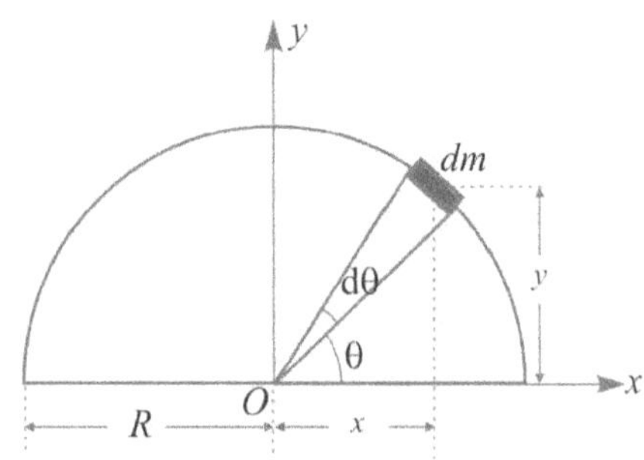
Figure. 8.30

Centre of mass of semicircular wire

Let M be the mass and r be the radius of semicircular wire. Take the origin at the centre of the wire. Choose a small element of angular width $d\theta$ at an angular position θ as shown in *figure* 8.31. The mass of the element

$$dm = \left(\frac{m}{\pi}\right)d\theta.$$

Its centre of mass from origin is at $x = R\cos\theta$ and $y = R\sin\theta$. The centre of mass of whole wire can be defined as;

Figure. 8.31

$$x_{cm} = \frac{\int\limits_{0}^{\pi} dm\,x}{\int\limits_{0}^{\pi} dm} = \frac{\int\limits_{0}^{\pi}\left(\frac{m}{\pi}d\theta\right)R\cos\theta}{\int\limits_{0}^{\pi}\left(\frac{m}{\pi}d\theta\right)}$$

$$= \frac{|\sin\theta\,|_{0}^{\pi}}{|\theta\,|_{0}^{\pi}} = 0$$

and

$$y_{cm} = \frac{\int\limits_{0}^{\pi} dm\,y}{\int\limits_{0}^{\pi} dm} = \frac{\int\limits_{0}^{\pi}\left(\frac{m}{\pi}d\theta\right)R\sin\theta}{\int\limits_{0}^{\pi}\left(\frac{m}{\pi}d\theta\right)}$$

$$= \frac{R\,|-\cos\theta\,|_{0}^{\pi}}{|\theta\,|_{0}^{\pi}} = \frac{2R}{\pi}.$$

Thus the centre of mass coordinates of a *semicircular wire* are $\left(0, \dfrac{2R}{\pi}\right)$.

Centre of mass of semicircular plate

Let M be the mass and R be the radius of the plate. Choose an element of thickness dr at a distance r all over the semicircular plate. The mass of the element

$$dm = \frac{M}{\left(\dfrac{\pi R^2}{2}\right)} \times (2\pi r\, dr) = \frac{2M}{\pi R^2}(2\pi r dr).$$

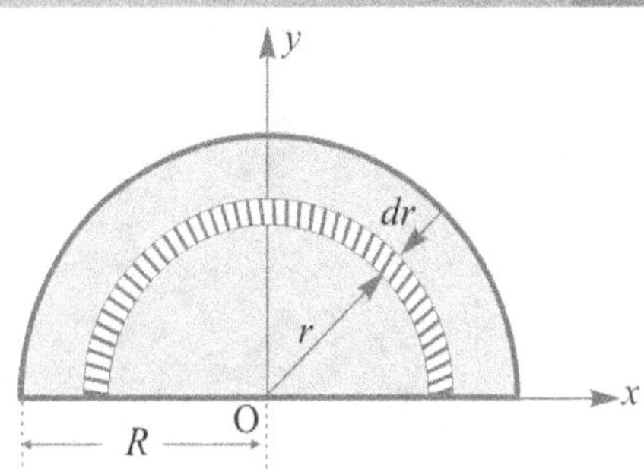

Figure. 8.32

Because of symmetric distribution of mass of plate about y-axis, its x coordinate of c.m. will be zero. The y coordinate of c.m. of plate is given by

$$y_{cm} = \frac{\displaystyle\int_0^R dm\, y}{\displaystyle\int_0^R dm} \; ; \qquad \text{where } y = \frac{2r}{\pi}$$

$$= \frac{\left(\dfrac{2M}{\pi R^2}\right)\displaystyle\int_0^R (2\pi r dr)\dfrac{2r}{\pi}}{\dfrac{2M}{\pi R^2}\displaystyle\int_0^R 2\pi r dr}$$

$$= \frac{2\displaystyle\int_0^R r^2 dr}{\displaystyle\int_0^R r dr} = \frac{2|\,r^3/3\,|_0^R}{|\,r^2/2\,|_0^R} = \frac{4R}{3\pi}.$$

Thus the centre of mass coordinates of a *semicircular* plate are $\left(0, \dfrac{4R}{3\pi}\right)$.

Centre of mass of a hemisphere

Let M be the mass and R be the radius of the hemisphere. Choose an element in the form of disc of thickness dy at a distance y from the origin. The radius of the disc $x^2 = (R^2 - y^2)$

The mass of the element
$$= \left[\frac{M}{\dfrac{2}{3}\pi R^3}\right] \times (\pi x^2)dy$$

$$= \left[\frac{3M}{2\pi R^3}\right] \times \pi (R^2 - y^2)dy.$$

The centre of mass of the hemisphere can be defined as

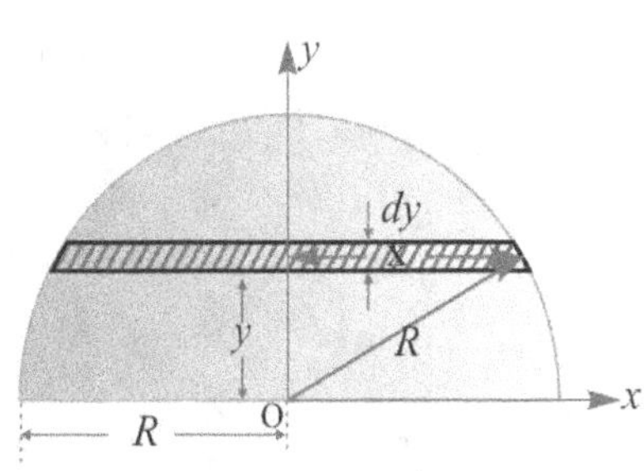

Figure. 8.33

$$y_{cm} = \frac{1}{M}\int_0^R dm\, y$$

$$= \frac{1}{M}\int_0^R \left(\frac{3M}{2\pi R^3}\right)\pi(R^2 - y^2)dy \times y$$

$$= \frac{3}{2R^3}\int_0^R (R^2 y - y^3)dy$$

$$= \frac{3}{2R^3}\int_0^R \left[\frac{R^2 y^2}{2} - \frac{y^4}{4}\right]_0^R = \frac{3R}{8}.$$

Thus the centre of mass coordinates of a *hemisphere* are $\left(0, \dfrac{3R}{8}\right)$.

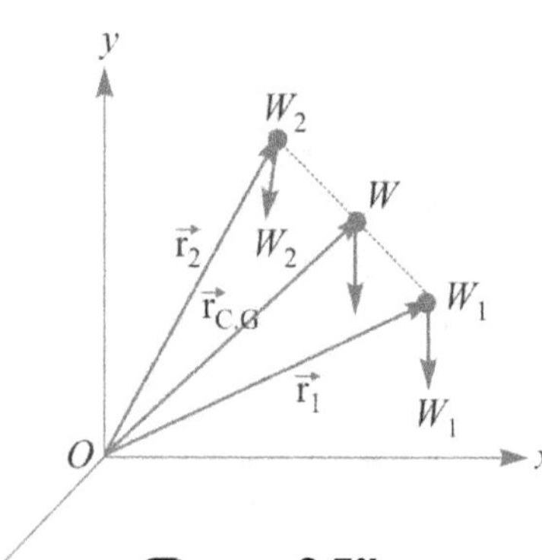

Figure. 8.34

8.9 CENTRE OF GRAVITY

Centre of gravity is the point at which whole weight of the system is supposed to act. Consider a system of two particles of weight W_1 and W_2. Their centre of gravity can be defined as;

$$\vec{r}_{C.G.} = \frac{W_1\vec{r_1} + W_2\vec{r_2}}{W_1 + W_2} = \frac{m_1g_1\vec{r_1} + m_2g_2\vec{r_2}}{m_1g_1 + m_2g_2}.$$

If value of gravity is same every where, then

$$g_1 = g_2, \text{ we have}$$

$$\vec{r}_{C.G.} = \frac{m_1\vec{r_1} + m_2\vec{r_2}}{m_1 + m_2} = \vec{r}_{C.M.}$$

Thus, if 'g' is same everywhere, then centre of gravity and centre of mass lie at the same point. Therefore for practical objects, centre of mass and centre of gravity are not differentiable.

8.10 CENTROID

It is the point at which whole area is supposed to concentrated. It can be defined as;

$$\vec{r}_{centroid} = \frac{A_1\vec{r_1} + A_2\vec{r_2}}{A_1 + A_2}$$

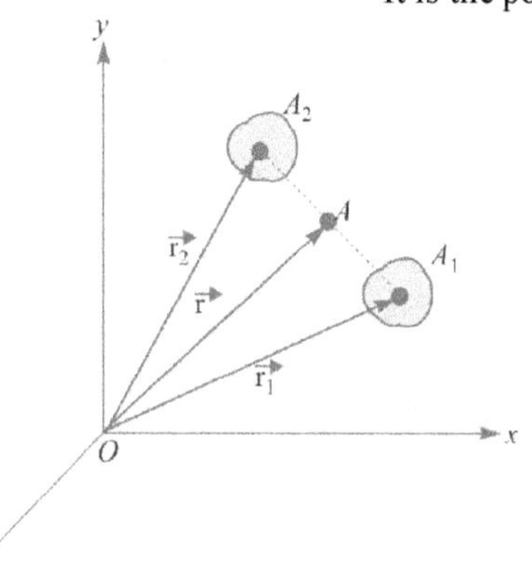

Figure. 8.35

Centroid of a triangle

Consider a triangle of width b and height h as shown in *figure* 8.35 Let us locate its centroid from the base. Choose an element of width b_1 and thickness dy at a distance y from the base. Since $\triangle ABC$ and A_1BC_1 are similar triangles, we can write;

$$\frac{b_1}{b} = \frac{h-y}{h} \text{ or } b_1 = \left(\frac{h-y}{h}\right)b$$

$\therefore$ Area of the element

$$dA = b_1 dy = \left(\frac{h-y}{h}\right)bdy$$

Area of the triangle $\qquad A = \frac{1}{2}bh.$

The centroid of the triangle can be defined as;

$$\bar{y} = \frac{\displaystyle\int_0^h (dA)y}{A} = \frac{\displaystyle\int_0^h \left[\frac{(h-y)}{h}bdy\right]y}{\left(\frac{bh}{2}\right)}$$

$$= \frac{2}{h^2}\int_0^h \left[hy - y^2\right]dy = \frac{2}{h^2}\left|\frac{hy^2}{2} - \frac{y^3}{3}\right|_0^h$$

$$= \frac{h}{3}.$$

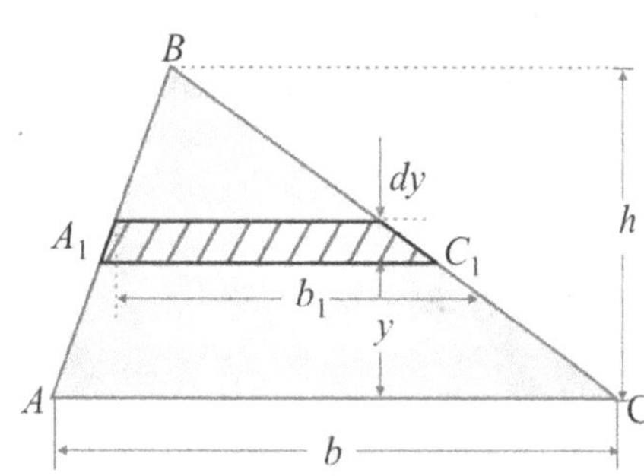

Figure. 8.36

Thus the centroid of triangle of any shape from its base will be $\left(\dfrac{1}{3}\right)$ *times the height of the triangle.*

Centre of mass of right circular cone

Consider a cone of height h. Let M be the mass and R be the radius of its base. Choose an elemental disc of radius x and thickness dy at a height y from the base.

In similar triangles $A'O'C$ and AOC, we have

$$\frac{x}{h-y} = \frac{R}{h} \Rightarrow x = \left(\frac{h-y}{h}\right)R$$

The mass of the element $\qquad dm \;=\; \left(\dfrac{M}{\dfrac{\pi}{3}R^2 h}\right) \times \pi x^2 \, dy.$

The centre of mass of the cone can be defined as

$$
\begin{aligned}
y_{cm} &= \frac{1}{M}\int_0^h (dm)\,y = \frac{1}{M}\int_0^h \left(\frac{M}{\dfrac{\pi}{3}R^2 h}\right)\pi x^2 \, dy \times y \\[2mm]
&= \frac{3}{h}\int_0^h \left(\frac{h-y}{h}\right)^2 y\,dy \\[2mm]
&= \frac{3}{h^3}\int_0^h (h^2 + y^2 - 2yh)\,y\,dy \\[2mm]
&= \frac{3}{h^3}\int_0^h (h^2 y + y^3 - 2y^2 h)\,dy \\[2mm]
&= \frac{3}{h^3}\int_0^h \left[\frac{h^2 y^2}{2} + \frac{y^4}{4} - \frac{2y^3}{3}h\right]_0^h = \frac{h}{4}.
\end{aligned}
$$

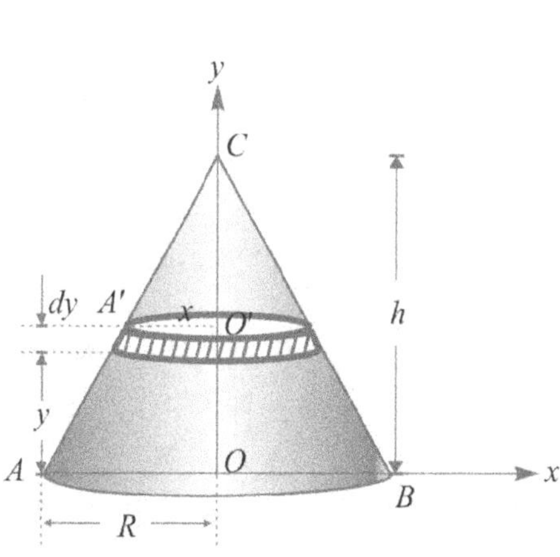

Figure. 8.37

Thus the centre of mass of cone is at a *height* $\dfrac{h}{4}$ *from the base*.

Centre of mass of some common bodies

1. $y_{cm} = \dfrac{h}{3}$

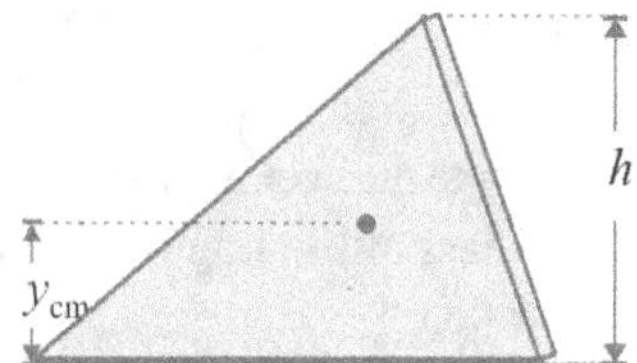

Triangular plate

Figure. 8.38

2. $y_{cm} = \dfrac{h}{4}$

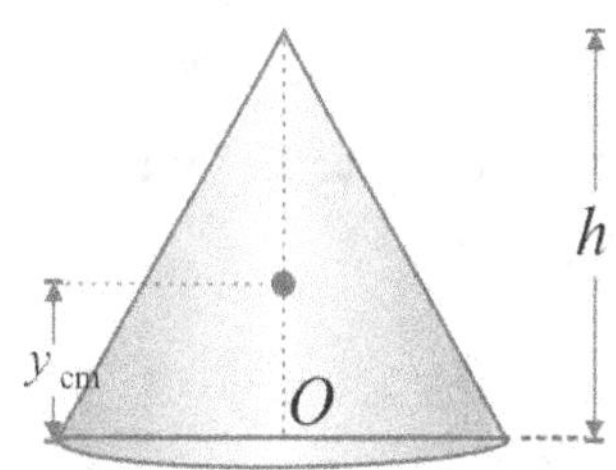

Right circular cone

Figure. 8.39

3. $y_{cm} = \dfrac{4R}{3\pi}$

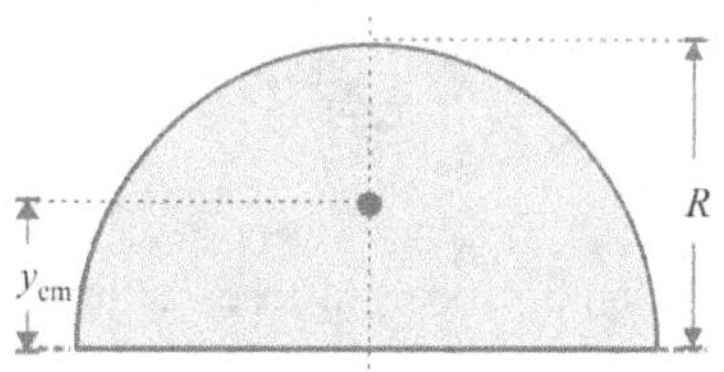

Semicircular plate

Figure. 8.40

4. $y_{cm} = \dfrac{2R}{\pi}$

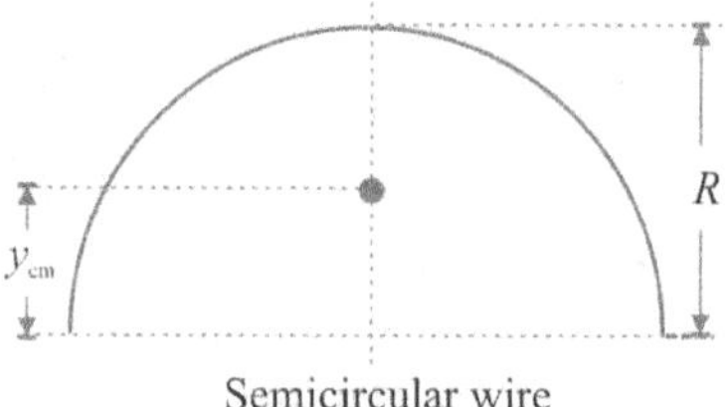

Semicircular wire

Figure. 8.41

5. $y_{cm} = \dfrac{3R}{8}$

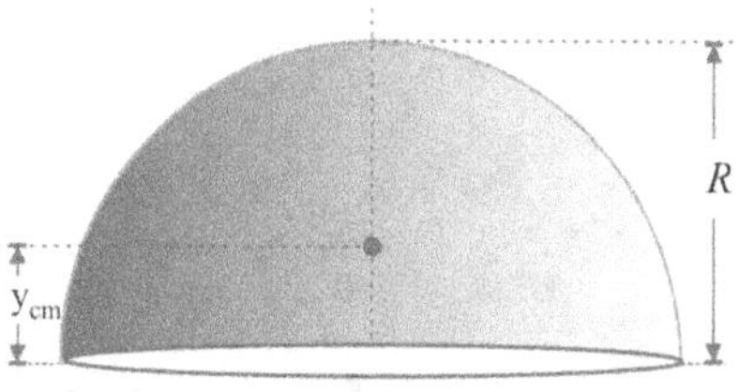

Hemi - sphere

Figure. 8.42

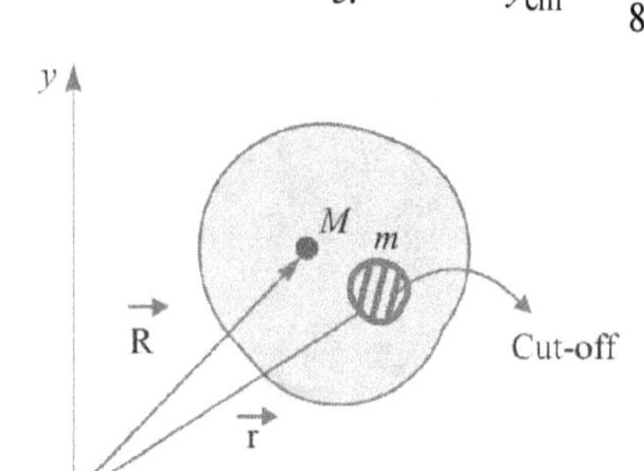

Figure. 8.43

Centre of mass of residual body

Consider a body of mass M, let its C.M. is $\vec{R}$ with respect to the origin of the coordinate system. Now mass m is cut off from the body at the position $\vec{r}$, then the C.M. of the residual body can be defined as;

$$\vec{r}_{cm} = \frac{M\vec{R} - m\vec{r}}{M - m}.$$

If mass m is added into the body then C.M. of resulting body can be defined as;

$$\vec{r}_{cm} = \frac{M\vec{R} + m\vec{r}}{M + m}.$$

Motion of C.M. of a bomb exploding in air

Suppose a bomb is projected at some angle with the ground, it is moving on a parabolic path. Suddenly it explodes in flight and splits into number of fragments. Since the explosion is caused due to internal forces only, so the centre of mass of the fragments all together will continue to move on the same parabolic path as before explosion.

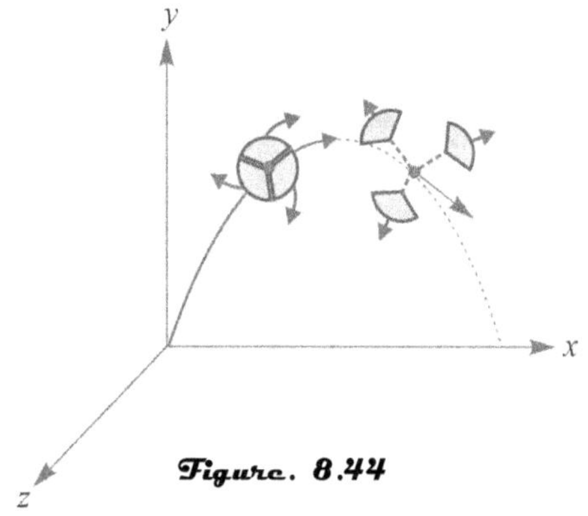

Shift in position of centre of mass

Consider a system of two particles, their C.M. is defined as;

$$\vec{r}_{cm} = \frac{m_1\vec{r_1} + m_2\vec{r_2}}{m_1 + m_2}. \qquad \ldots(i)$$

If $\Delta\vec{r_1}$ and $\Delta\vec{r_2}$ be the shift in positions of the particles, then shift in position of C.M. of the system is,

$$\Delta\vec{r}_{cm} = \frac{m_1\Delta\vec{r_1} + m_2\Delta\vec{r_2}}{m_1 + m_2} \qquad \ldots(ii)$$

Thus if $\vec{F}_{external} = 0$, then

$$\Delta\vec{r}_{cm} = \frac{m_1\Delta\vec{r_1} + m_2\Delta\vec{r_2}}{m_1 + m_2} = 0$$

Figure. 8.44

or $m_1\Delta\vec{r_1} + m_2\Delta\vec{r_2} = 0$

Note: If there is no net external force acting on the system, and the particles move due to internal forces, then

$\vec{F}_{external} = 0$, so $\Delta\vec{r}_{cm} = 0$ and $\vec{P}$ is constant, so $\vec{v}_{cm}$ is constant and $\vec{a}_{cm}$ is zero.

8.11 TILTING OF A BODY

Consider a rectangular block of weight W placed on a rough horizontal surface (μ). It is acted by a pushing force F. If line of action of force F is above the centre of gravity, then block experiences a force and a torque. Accordingly block may slide or lift about the edge. The block has.

(i)   Force F in addition to weight W, normal reaction N and frictional force μN.

(ii) If F acts at a height h from the base, then its torque about P,

$$\tau = F h.$$

(iii) Restoring torque due to W about P

$$\tau_{\text{rest}} = W \times \frac{a}{2} \; ;$$

where a is the length of the block.

For the equilibrium of the block, we have

$$F = \mu N \text{ and } N = W$$

$$\therefore \qquad F = \mu W \qquad \qquad \ldots(i)$$

and

$$Fh = W \, a/2 \qquad \qquad \ldots(ii)$$

From equations (i) and (ii), we have

$$\mu = \frac{a}{2h}.$$

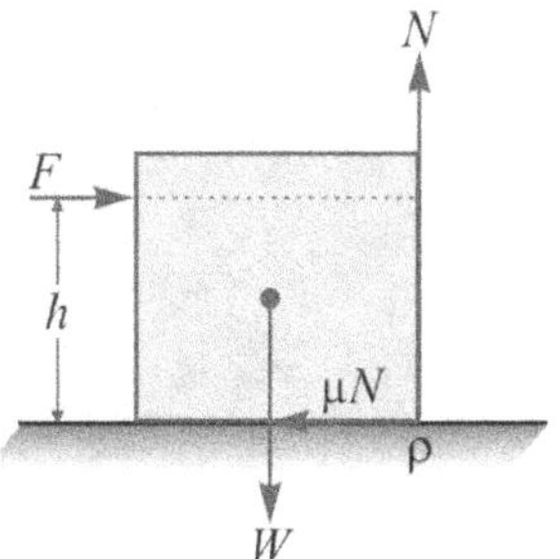

Figure. 8.45

Thus;

(i)   *If $\mu < \dfrac{a}{2h}$, block will slide.*

(ii) *If $\mu > \dfrac{a}{2h}$, block will tilt about the edge.*

FORMULAE USED

1.   The centre of mass of a system of discrete particles in cartesian coordinates is given by

$$x_{\text{cm}} = \frac{1}{M} \sum_{i=1}^{n} m_i x_i \,,$$

$$y_{\text{cm}} = \frac{1}{M} \sum_{i=1}^{n} m_i y_i$$

$$z_{\text{cm}} = \frac{1}{M} \sum_{i=1}^{n} m_i z_i$$

2.   In polar coordinates system

$$\vec{r}_{cm} = \frac{1}{M} \sum m_i \vec{r}_i$$

3.   Centre of mass of a rigid body,

$$\vec{r}_{cm} = \frac{1}{M} \int \vec{r}\,(\text{dm})$$

4.   Shift in position of CM is given by

$$\Delta \vec{r}_{cm} = \left[\frac{m_1 \Delta \vec{r}_1 + m_2 \Delta \vec{r}_2}{m_1 + m_2} \right]$$

5.   If not net external force acts on the system $\Delta \vec{r}_{cm} = 0$

$$\therefore \qquad m_1 \Delta \vec{r}_1 + m_2 \Delta \vec{r}_2 = 0.$$

6.   Velocity of centre of mass

$$\vec{v}_{cm} = \frac{m_1\vec{v}_1 + m_2\vec{v}_2}{m_1 + m_2}$$

For $\overrightarrow{F_{ext}} = 0$, $m_1\vec{v}_1 + m_2\vec{v}_2 = 0$

7.   Acceleration of centre of mass

$$\vec{a}_{cm} = \frac{m_1\vec{a}_1 + m_2\vec{a}_2}{m_1 + m_2}.$$

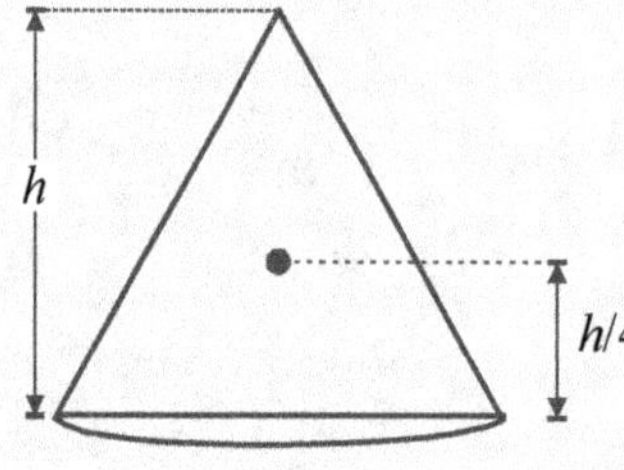

Cone

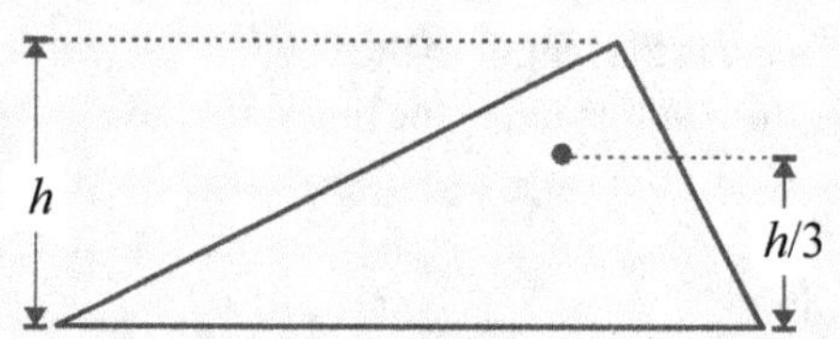

Triangular Plate

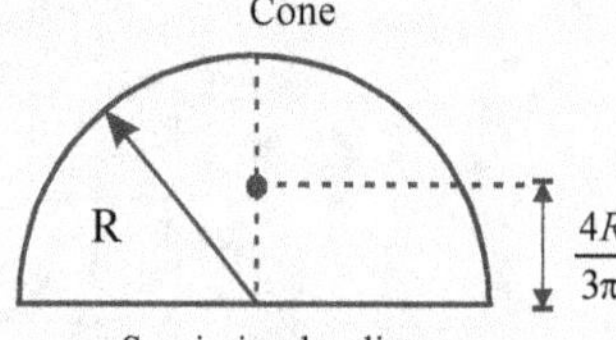

Semi-circular disc

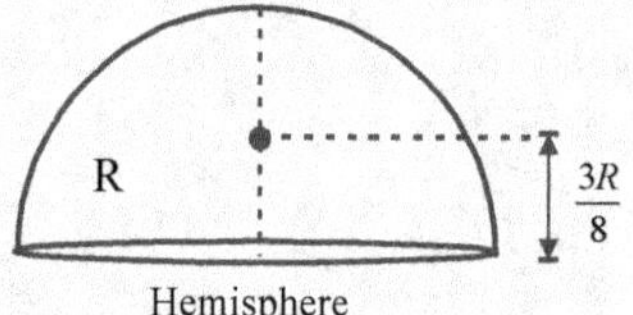

Hemisphere

8.   CM of the remaining body $= \dfrac{M\vec{R} - m\vec{r}}{(M - m)}.$

EXAMPLES BASED ON CENTRE OF MASS

Example 1. Two particles of masses m_1 and m_2 are placed at a separation r. Find centre of mass of the system of two particles.

Sol. Let c.m. is at a distance x_{cm} from m_1, we have

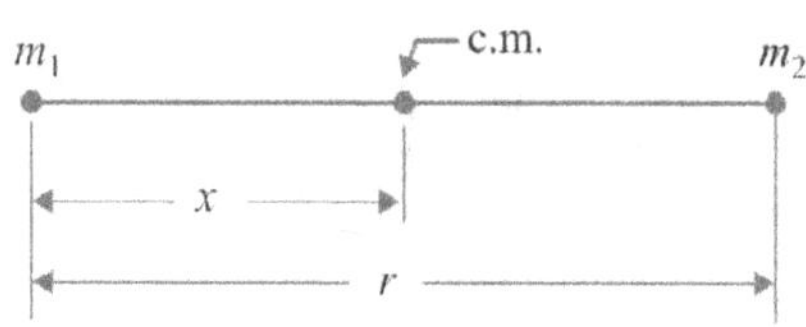

Figure. 8.46

$$x_{cm} = \frac{m_1 x_1 + m_2 x_2}{m_1 + m_2}.$$

Let $x_1 = 0$, then $x_2 = r$

$$\therefore \qquad x_{cm} = \frac{m_1 0 + m_2 r}{m_1 + m_2} = \left[\frac{m_2 r}{m_1 + m_2}\right].$$

Thus the c.m. of the system is at a distance $\left[\dfrac{m_2 r}{m_1 + m_2}\right]$ from m_1 and

$r - x_{cm} = \left[\dfrac{m_1 r}{m_1 + m_2}\right]$ from m_2.   **Ans.**

Example 2. The mass per unit length of a rod varies as

$m = \left(\dfrac{M_0}{L}\right) x$, where M_0 is a constant and x is the distance of any

point on rod measured from one end. If L is the length of rod, then find its centre of mass.

Sol.

Choose an element of rod of length dx at a distance x from one of its ends. The mass of the element

$$dm = \left[\frac{M_0}{L} x\right] dx$$

Centre of mass of the rod can be defined as;   **Figure. 8.47**

$$x_{cm} = \frac{m_1 x_1 + m_2 x_2}{m_1 + m_2}.$$

$$x_{cm} = \frac{\displaystyle\int_0^L dm\,x}{\displaystyle\int_0^L dm} = \frac{\displaystyle\int_0^L \left[\frac{M_0}{L} x\,dx\right] x}{\displaystyle\int_0^L \left[\frac{M_0}{L} x\,dx\right]}$$

$$= \frac{\displaystyle\int_0^L x^2 dx}{\displaystyle\int_0^L x\,dx} = \frac{\left. x^3/3 \right|_0^L}{\left. x^2/2 \right|_0^L} = \frac{2L}{3} \quad \textit{Ans.}$$

Example 3. Find the centre of mass of a uniform *L*-shaped lamina (a thin flat plate) with dimensions as shown in *figure* 8.48.

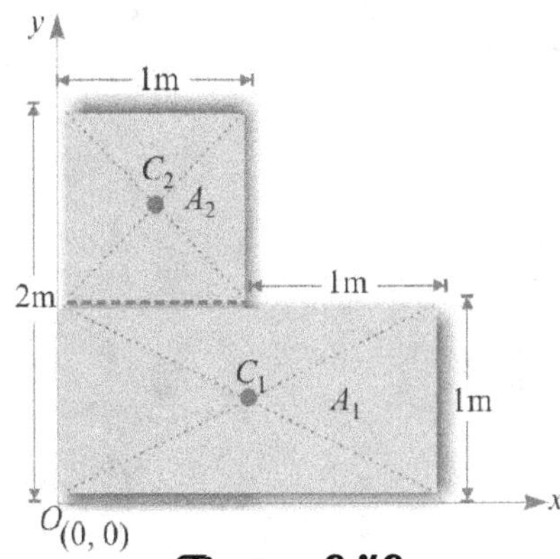

Figure. 8.48

Sol. The plate is of uniform density and same thickness everywhere. So its C.M. will coincide with the centroid.

Divide the given plate into two parts of area A_1 and A_2 as shown in figure. We have

$A_1 = 2 \times 1 = 2\text{m}^2$ with its centroid C_1 (1, 1/2) and

$A_2 = 1 \times 1 = 1\text{m}^2$ with its centroid C_2 (1/2, 3/2)

The centroid of whole plate can be defined as;

$$\bar{x} = \frac{A_1 x_1 + A_2 x_2}{A_1 + A_2} = \frac{2 \times 1 + 1 \times \frac{1}{2}}{2 + 1} = \frac{5}{6}\text{m}$$

and

$$\bar{y} = \frac{A_1 y_1 + A_2 y_2}{A_1 + A_2} = \frac{2 \times \frac{1}{2} + 1 \times \frac{3}{2}}{2 + 1} = \frac{5}{6}\text{m} \; \textit{Ans.}$$

Example 4. From a uniform disc of radius *R*, a circular hole of radius *R/2* is cut. The centre of the hole is at *R/2* from the centre of the original disc. Locate the centre of gravity of the resulting flat body.

Sol.

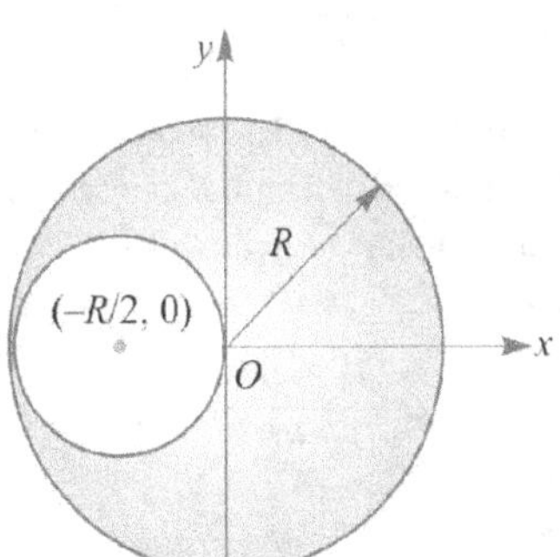

Figure. 8.49

The mass of the cut out hole

$$m = \frac{M}{\pi R^2} \times \pi \left(\frac{R}{2}\right)^2 = \frac{M}{4}.$$

Let the centre of disc be at the origin of coordinates. Then C.M. coordinates of cutout hole are (–R/2, 0). Thus by the definition of C.M, we have

$$x_{\text{cm}} = \frac{M\vec{R} - m\vec{r}}{M - m}$$

$$= \frac{M \times 0 - \frac{M}{4} \times \left(\frac{-R}{2}\right)}{M - \frac{M}{4}} = \frac{R}{6} \text{ and } y_{\text{cm}} = 0.$$

The centre of mass of remaining disc is at a distance of $\dfrac{R}{6}$ from the origin.

Example 5. *Figure* 8.50 shows a uniform disc of radius *R*, from which a hole of radius *R/2* has been cut out from left of the centre and is placed on right of the centre of disc. Find the C.M. of the resulting disc.

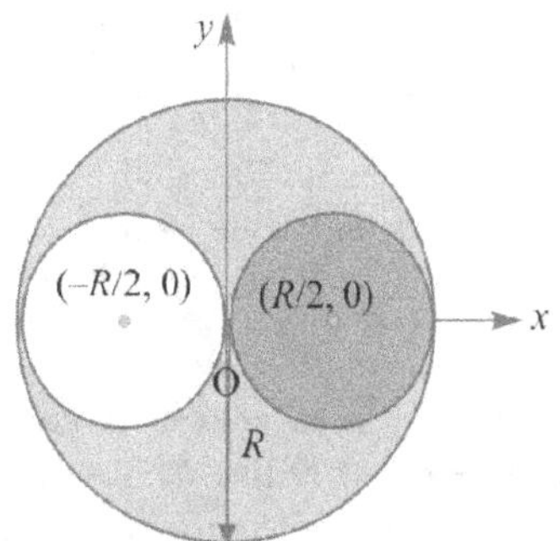

Figure. 8.50

Sol.

Mass of the cut out disc

$$m = \frac{M}{\pi R^2} \times \pi \left(\frac{R}{2}\right)^2 = \frac{M}{4}.$$

Let centre of the disc is at the origin of coordinates, then we can write the C.M. of the system as ;

$$\vec{x}_{\text{cm}} = \frac{M\vec{R} - m\vec{r} + m\vec{r}'}{M - m + m}$$

$$= \frac{M \times 0 - \frac{M}{4}\left(\frac{-R}{2}\right) + \frac{M}{4}\left(\frac{R}{2}\right)}{M - \frac{M}{4} + \frac{M}{4}} = \frac{R}{4}$$

and $\quad y_{\text{cm}} = 0.$ *Ans.*

Example 6. Two small identical bodies are at a separation equal to radius of the earth (*R*), are situated in such a way, that one of them is at the earth surface. Find :

(i)   CM of the system of bodies   (ii) CG of the system of bodies.

Sol.

(i)   If *m* is the mass of each body, then CM

$$y_{\text{cm}}$$

$$= \frac{m \times 0 + mR}{m + m} = \frac{R}{2} \textit{Ans.}$$

(ii)   If g the value of gravity at earth surface, then its value at a

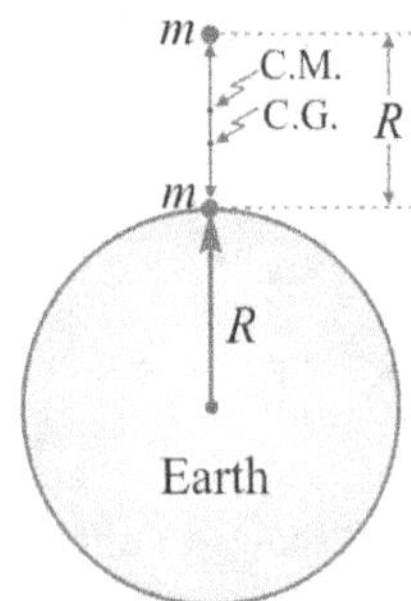

Figure. 8.51

height R,

$$g' = \frac{g}{\left(1+\dfrac{h}{R}\right)^2} = \frac{g}{\left(1+\dfrac{R}{R}\right)^2} = \frac{g}{4}.$$

The centre of gravity

$$y_{cg} = \frac{mg \times 0 + \dfrac{mg}{4} \times R}{mg + \dfrac{mg}{4}} = \frac{R}{5}. \qquad Ans.$$

Example 7. A solid circular cone of radius R is joined to a uniform solid hemisphere of radius R. Both are made of same material. The centre of mass of the composite solid lies at the common base. Find the height of cone.

Sol.

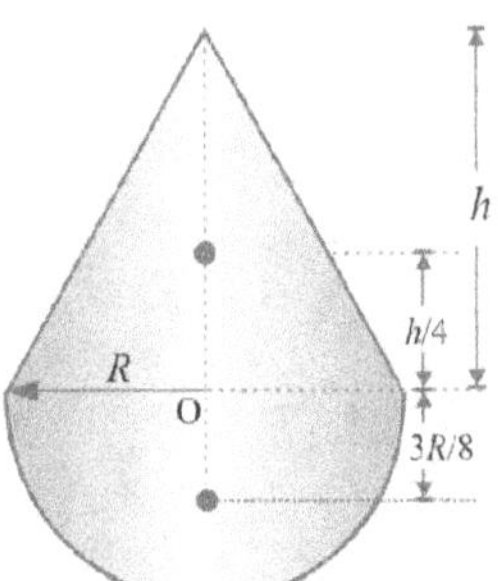

Figure. 8.52

Let the height of the cone be h. Then with respect to its base, the C.M. is at a height of $h/4$. The C.M. of the hemisphere is at $3R/8$ below the base.

If ρ be the density of material, then mass of the cone,

$$m_1 = \rho \times \frac{\pi R^2 h}{3} = \frac{\pi \rho R^2 h}{3}$$

and mass of hemisphere

$$m_2 = \rho \times \frac{2\pi R^3}{3} = \frac{2\pi \rho R^3}{3}.$$

As the C.M. of the whole system lies at the base, thus we have

$$y_{cm} = 0 = \frac{m_1 y_1 + m_2 y_2}{m_1 + m_2}$$

$$0 = \frac{\left(\dfrac{\pi \rho R^2 h}{3}\right) \times \left(\dfrac{h}{4}\right) + \left(\dfrac{2\pi \rho R^3}{3}\right)\left(\dfrac{-3R}{8}\right)}{m_1 + m_2}$$

or $h = \sqrt{3}R. \qquad Ans.$

Example 8. The balloon, the light rope and the monkey shown in *figure* 8.53 are at rest in air. If the monkey reaches the top, by what distance does the balloon descend? Mass of balloon is M, mass of the monkey is m and length of the rope ascended by the monkey is L.

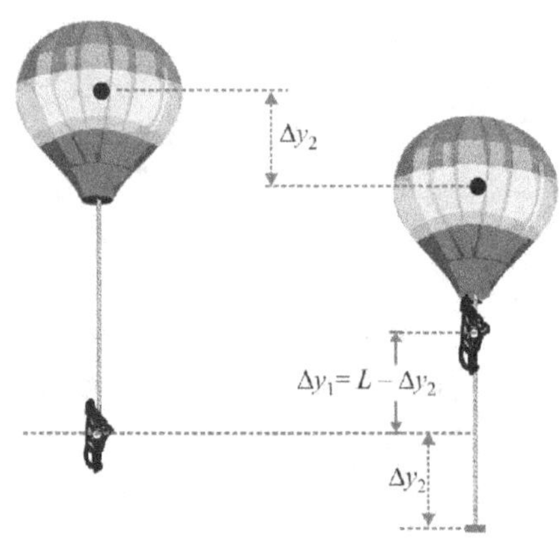

Figure. 8.53

Sol.

Let the C.M. of monkey ascends by Δy_1 while C.M. of balloon descends by Δy_2, where $\Delta y_1 = L - \Delta y_2$.

As the whole system (balloon + monkey) is at rest, so $\vec{F}_{net} = 0$. Therefore the position of C.M. will not change, i.e. $\Delta y_{cm} = 0$. Thus we have

$$\Delta y_{cm} = \frac{m_1 \Delta y_1 + m_2 \Delta y_2}{m_1 + m_2}$$

$$= \frac{m(L - \Delta y_2) + M(-\Delta y_2)}{m + M}$$

After solving, $\Delta y_2 = \left(\dfrac{mL}{m+M}\right). \qquad Ans.$

Example 9. If two like parallel forces of magnitudes P and Q $(P > Q)$, acting on a rigid rod of length L at its ends, are interchanged in position, show that the line of action of the resultant is displaced through a distance,

$$\Delta x = \frac{L(P-Q)}{(P+Q)}.$$

Sol.

Suppose, initially the resultant force $(P + Q)$ passes through A; a distance x from line of action of P, then

$$Px = Q(L - x)$$

$\therefore \qquad x = \dfrac{QL}{P+Q}. \qquad \qquad ...... \text{(i)}$

Now when forces are interchanged, the line of action of resultant force $(P + Q)$, let passes through B, at a distance x' from line of action of Q, then

$$Qx' = P(L - x')$$

Figure. 8.55

$\therefore \qquad x' = \dfrac{LP}{P+Q}.$ ...... (ii)

Now from (i) and (ii), we have

$$\Delta x = x' - x$$

or $\qquad \Delta x = \dfrac{L(P-Q)}{(P+Q)}.$

Example 10. A pulley fixed to the ceiling carries a thread with bodies of masses m_1 and m_2 attached to its ends. The masses of the pulley and the thread are negligible, friction is absent. Find the acceleration of the centre of inertia of this system.

Sol.

The magnitude of acceleration of masses is

$$= \frac{(m_1 - m_2)g}{m_1 + m_2}.$$

Let acceleration of mass m_1 is, a_1

$$= -\left(\frac{m_1 - m_2}{m_1 + m_2}\right) g$$

Then acceleration of mass

$$m_2, a_2 = +\left(\frac{m_1 - m_2}{m_1 + m_2}\right) g.$$

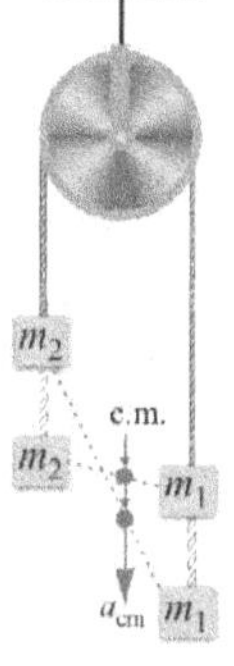

Figure. 8.56

The acceleration of centre of inertia (centre of mass) can be defined as;

$$\vec{a}_{cm} = \frac{m_1 \vec{a}_1 + m_2 \vec{a}_2}{m_1 + m_2}$$

$$= \frac{m_1 \left[-\dfrac{m_1 - m_2}{m_1 + m_2}\right] g + m_2 \left[\dfrac{m_1 - m_2}{m_1 + m_2}\right] g}{m_1 + m_2} = -\left(\frac{m_1 - m_2}{m_1 + m_2}\right)^2 g.$$

That is, the acceleration of C.M. is $\left(\dfrac{m_1 - m_2}{m_1 + m_2}\right)^2 g$ downward.

In Chapter Exercise 8.4

1. Two skaters, one with mass 60 kg and the other with mass 40 kg, stand on an ice holding a pole of length 6 m and negligible mass. Starting from the ends of the pole the skaters pull themselves along the pole until they meet. The 40 kg skater moves a distance $1.8x$. Find the value of x.
   [Integer] *Ans.. $x = 2$*

2. A 10 kg boy stands on a 20 kg boat and is 5 m from the shore. He walks 3m along the boat towards the shore and then stops. The distance of the boy now from the shore is $3x$ m. Find the value of x. Assaming there is no friction between the boat and the water. **[Integer]** *Ans.. $x = 1$*

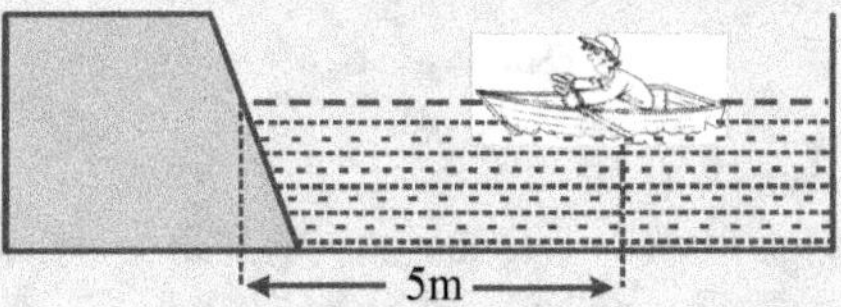

3. A boy of mass 40 kg clings to a rope ladder suspended below a balloon of mass 80 kg (see figure). The balloon is stationary w.r.t. ground. If the boy begins to climb the ladder at speed 1 m/s with respect to ladder, the balloon moves down at a speed of $\dfrac{1}{x}$ m/s. Find the value of x. **[Integer]**

Ans. $x = 3$

4. A cart of mass M is rest on a frictionless horizontal surface and a pendulum bob of mass m hangs from the roof of the cart (see figure). The string breaks, the bob falls on the floor, makes several collisions on the floor and finally lands up i a small slot made in the floor. The horizontal distance between the string and the slot is L. Find the displacement of the cart during this process.

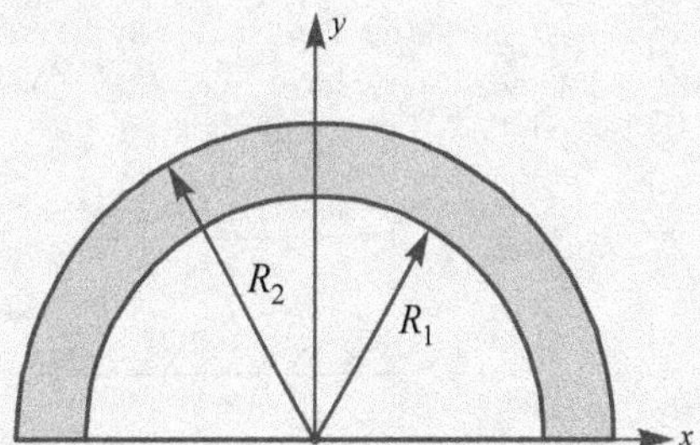

$Ans. \left[\dfrac{mL}{m+M}\right].$

5. Find the centre of mass of a uniform plate having semicircular inner and outer boundaries of radii R_1 and R_2 (see figure).

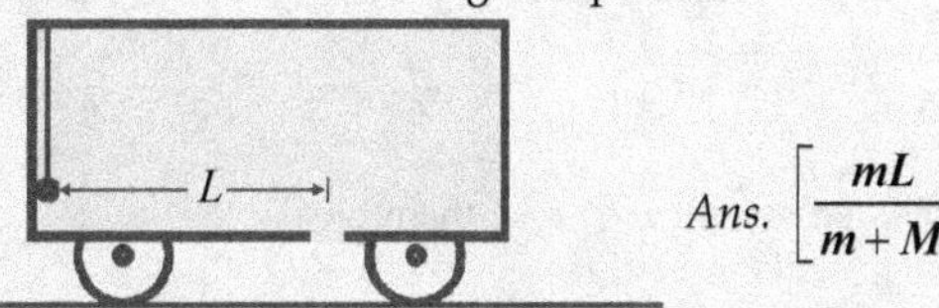

$Ans. x = 0$ and $y = \dfrac{4(R_1^2 + R_1 R_2 + R_2^2)}{3\pi(R_1 + R_2)}$

6. A 20 g bullet pierces through a plate of mass $M_1 = 1$ kg and then comes to rest a second plate of mass $M_2 = 2.98$ kg as shown in the figure. It is found that the two plates, initially at rest, now move with equal velocities.

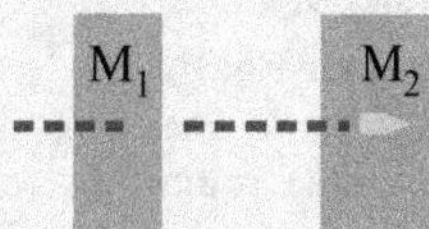

Find the percentage loss in the initial velocity of the bullet when it is between M_1 and M_2. Neglect any loss of material of the plates, due to action of bullet. *Ans. 25%*

EXAMPLES FOR JEE-MAIN AND ADVANCED

Example 1. A man of mass m moves on a plank of mass M with a constant velocity u with respect to the plank, as shown in *figure* 8.57.

(i)   If the plank rests on a smooth horizontal surface, then determine the velocity of the plank.

(ii)   If the man travels a distance L with respect to the plank, then find the distance travelled by the plank with respect to ground.

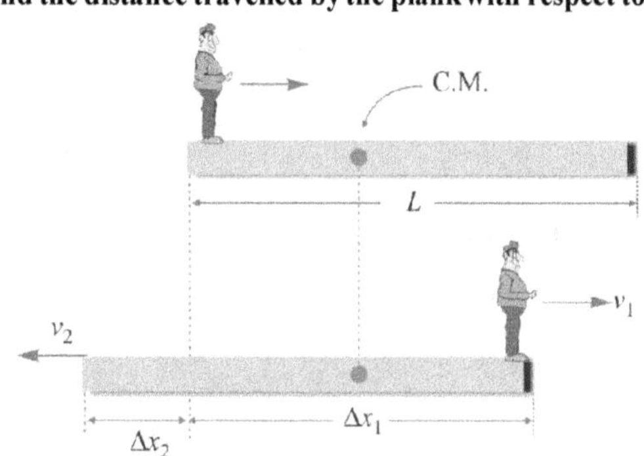

Figure. 8.57

Sol. As no external force is acting on the system in horizontal direction, so its linear momentum remains constant in that direction. Also there will be no shift in position of centre of mass. i.e., $\Delta x_{cm} = 0$.

(i)   Let v_1 and v_2 are the velocities of the man and the plank w.r.t. ground. Then we have

$$[\vec{v}_{man}]_{plank} = [\vec{v}_{man}]_{ground} - [\vec{v}_{plank}]_{ground}$$

then, $[\vec{v}_{man}]_{ground} = [\vec{v}_{man}]_{plank} + [\vec{v}_{plank}]_{ground}$

or $v_1 = u - v_2$

Initially the system is at rest, therefore

$$0 = mv_1 - mv_2$$

or $0 = m(u - v_2) - Mv_2$

or $v_2 = \left[\dfrac{mu}{m+M}\right].$ **Ans.**

(ii)   Let Δx_1 and Δx_2 are the distances moved by the man and the plank relative to ground, then we have $\Delta x_1 = (L - \Delta x_2)$
and shift in position of centre of mass

$$\Delta \vec{x}_{cm} = 0 = \frac{m\Delta \vec{x_1} + M\Delta \vec{x_2}}{m+M}$$

or $0 = \dfrac{m(L - \Delta x_2) + M(-\Delta x_2)}{m+M}$

$\Rightarrow$ $\Delta x_2 = \left(\dfrac{mL}{m+M}\right).$ **Ans.**

Example 2. A ball of mass M and radius R is placed inside a spherical shell of same mass M and the inner radius $2R$. The combination is at rest on a table top in the position shown in figure. The ball is released, rolls back and fourth inside, and finally comes at rest at the bottom of the shell. Find the maximum displacement of the shell during the process.

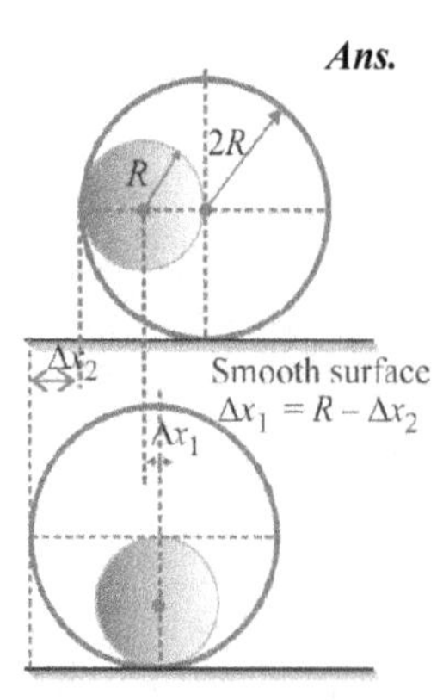

Figure. 8.58

Sol.
Let Δx_1 be the shift in position of C.M. of ball and Δx_2 be the shift in position of C.M. of shell. As there is no external force acting on the system in horizontal direction, so there is no shift in position of C.M. of the system (ball + shell). Thus we have,

$$\Delta x_{cm} = 0 = \frac{m_1 \Delta x_1 + m_2 \Delta x_2}{m_1 + m_2}.$$

From the figure $\Delta x_1 = R - \Delta x_2$

$\therefore$ $0 = \dfrac{M(R - \Delta x_2) + M(-\Delta x_2)}{M + m}$

or $\Delta x_2 = \dfrac{R}{2}.$

This is the displacement of the shell when ball moves down to its lowest position. When ball moves to the right of the centre of the shell, the shell further displaces by $R/2$.

Therefore the total displacement of the shell

$$= \frac{R}{2} + \frac{R}{2} = R. \qquad \textbf{Ans.}$$

Example 3. A square hole is punched out from a circular lamina, the diagonal of the square being a radius of the circle. Show that the centre of mass of the remaining is at a distance $R/(4\pi - 2)$ from the centre of the circle, where R is the radius of the circular lamina.

Sol. Let the mass of the circular lamina having area πR^2 is m.
The side of the square hole can be obtained as
$$a^2 + a^2 = R^2$$
$\Rightarrow$ $a = R/\sqrt{2}$

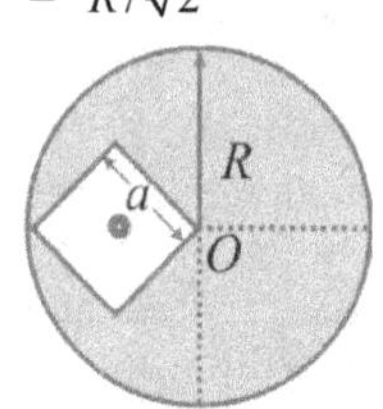

Figure. 8.59

$\therefore$ Area of the hole $= a^2 = R^2/2$
       Mass of the hole $(m') = m/2\pi$

Let O is the origin, then the co-ordinates of the c.m. of the circular lamina is $(0, 0)$ and that of square hole will be $= (- R/2, 0)$.

Centre of mass of the remaining portion

$$\bar{x} = \frac{mx - m'x'}{m - m'}$$

or $x = \dfrac{m.0 - (m/2\pi).(-R/2)}{m - m/2\pi}$

which after solving gives

$$x = R/(4\pi - 2), \qquad \textbf{Ans.}$$

and $y = \dfrac{m.0 - (m/2\pi).0}{m - m/2\pi} = 0.$

As the removed portion is symmetrical about x-axis, the y co-ordinate of the c.m. of the remaining portion remains at $y = 0$.

Example 4. Find the centre of mass of letter E, relative to origin O, whose dimensions are given in *figure* 8.60 Take width of the letter 2 cm everywhere.

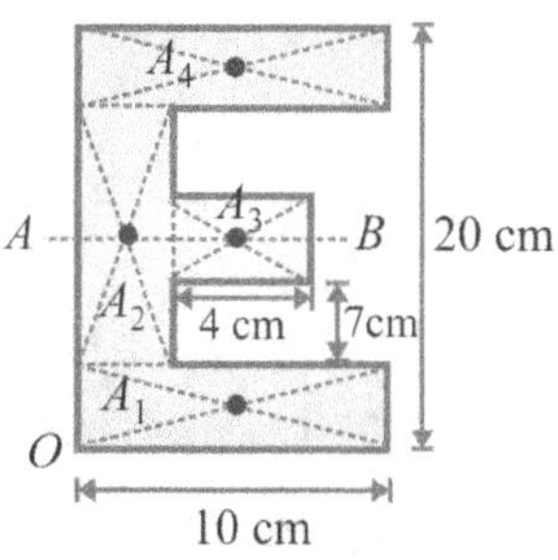

Figure. 8.60

Sol.   Centre of mass of the given letter E can be obtained by area of the different part of the geometry because thickness is same everywhere and density is uniform throughout.

Let the given geometry is divided into 4 segments, having
$$A_1 = 10 \times 2 = 20 \text{ cm}^2, \text{ and c.m.} = (5, 1)$$
$$A_2 = (20 - 4) \times 2 = 32 \text{ cm}^2, \ [1, (2 + 8)] = (1, 10)$$
$$A_3 = 4 \times 2 = 8 \text{cm}^2, \ (2 + 2, 10) = (4, 10)$$
$$A_4 = 10 \times 2 = 20 \text{ cm}^2, \ (5, 20 - 1) = (5, 19)$$

Position of c.m. can be obtained as:
$$\bar{x} = \frac{A_1 x_1 + A_2 x_2 + A_3 x_3 + A_4 x_4}{A_1 + A_2 + A_3 + A_4}$$
$$= \frac{20 \times 5 + 32 \times 1 + 8 \times 4 + 20 \times 5}{20 + 32 + 8 + 20} = 3.3 \text{ cm}$$

and
$$\bar{y} = \frac{A_1 y_1 + A_2 y_2 + A_3 y_3 + A_4 y_4}{A_1 + A_2 + A_3 + A_4}$$
$$= \frac{20 \times 1 + 32 \times 10 + 8 \times 10 + 20 \times 19}{20 + 32 + 8 + 20}$$
$$= 10 \text{ cm} \hspace{2cm} \textbf{Ans.}$$

There is no need of calculation of $\bar{y}$, because the geometry is symmetrical about the dotted line AB which is at a height of 10 cm.

Example 5. A block of mass M with a semicircular track of radius R, rests on a horizontal frictionless surface. A uniform cylinder of radius r and mass m is released from rest at the top point A as shown in *figure* 8.61 The cylinder slips on a semicircular frictionless track. How far has the block moved when the cylinder reaches the bottom (point B) of the track ? How fast is the block moving when the cylinder reaches the bottom of the track?

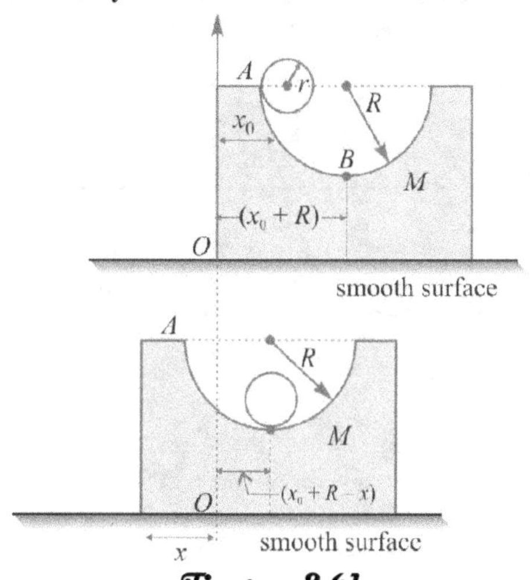

Figure. 8.61

Sol.

Since there is no force acting in the horizontal direction, the centre of mass of the whole system remain fixed throughout.

Let x be the displacement of larger block towards left when the mass m reaches at B.

Taking O as the origin, the initial position of the c.m.
$$x_{cm} = \frac{M(x_0 + R) + m(x_0 + r)}{M + m}. \hspace{1cm} \dots \text{(i)}$$

Final position of the c.m.
$$x_{cm} = \frac{(M + m).(x_0 + R - x)}{M + m} \hspace{1cm} \dots \text{(ii)}$$

Since there should be no change in the position of c.m. Therefore
$$\frac{M(x_0 + R) + m(x_0 + r)}{M + m} = \frac{(M + m).(x_0 + R - x)}{M + m}$$

After solving, we get,
$$x = \frac{m(R - r)}{M + m}.$$

Now according to the principle of conservation of momentum, we have
$$0 = MV + mv \hspace{2cm} \dots \text{(iii)}$$
where V and v are velocities of M and m w.r.t. ground.

Also by conservation of mechanical energy, we have
$$mg(R - r) = \frac{1}{2}MV^2 + \frac{1}{2}mv^2 \hspace{1cm} \dots \text{(iv)}$$

After solving (iii) and (iv), we get
$$V = m\sqrt{\frac{2g(R - r)}{M(M + m)}}. \hspace{1cm} \textbf{Ans.}$$

Example 6. A solid cone of height h and base radius R is placed with its base on a rough inclined plane whose coefficient of friction is μ. The inclination of the plane is increased gradually. Show that the cone slips if $\mu < \dfrac{4R}{h}$ and topple if $\mu > \dfrac{4R}{h}$.

Sol.

The free body is shown in *fig.* 8.62.

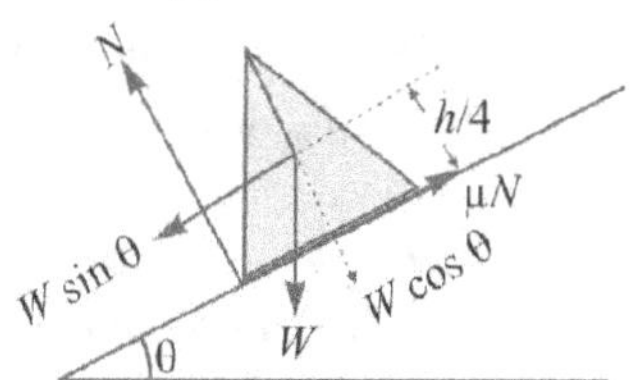

Figure. 8.62

For translational equilibrium along the inclined plane, we have $F = 0$,
or $W \sin\theta = \mu N$, where $N = W \cos\theta$
$$\therefore \hspace{2cm} \mu = \tan\theta \hspace{1.5cm} \dots \text{(i)}$$

For rotational equilibrium,
$$\Sigma\tau = 0.$$
Taking moment of the forces acting on the cone about P, we have
$$W \sin\theta \times \frac{h}{4} - W \cos\theta \times R = 0$$

or
$$\tan\theta = \frac{4R}{h} \hspace{1.5cm} \dots \text{(ii)}$$

From equations (i) and (ii), we have

$$\mu = \frac{4R}{h}.$$

Thus, if $\mu < \frac{4R}{h}$, the cone will slip and if $\mu > \frac{4R}{h}$, the cone will topple.

Example 7. **A pack of cards is laid on a table, and each card is project in the direction of the length of the pack, beyond the one below it, if each project as far as possible, show that the distances between the extremities of successive cards will form a harmonical progression.**

Sol.

Let A, B, C, D, so on are the maximum projecting end of the cards, and let m be the mass and ℓ be the length of each card. The top card can project at most a distance $\ell/2$ beyond the one below it and hence its centre of gravity will be just above B. Again, the centre of gravity of the top two cards is similarly just above C.

Consider the equilibrium of cards 1 and 2 over 3 *fig.* (b) . Let c.g. of combined weight of 1 and 2 is at a distance x_1 from B, then

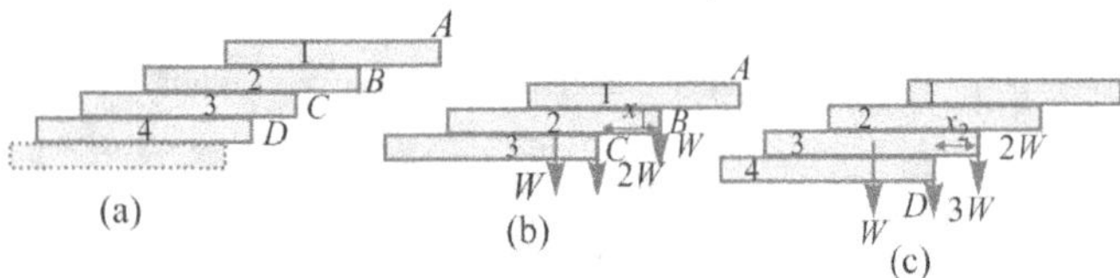

Figure. **8.63**

taking moment of weight about C, we get

$$W.x_1 = W(\ell/2 - x_1)$$

or

$$x_1 = \ell/4.$$

Now consider the equilibrium of card 1,2 and 3 over 4 *fig.* (c). Let c.g. of combined weight of 1, 2 and 3 is at a distance x_2 from C, then taking moment of weights about D, we get

$$W(\ell/2 - x_2) = 2W.x_2$$

or

$$x_2 = 1/6.$$

In general for n cards, we have

$$W(\ell/2 - x) = (n-1)Wx$$

or

$$x = \ell/2n.$$

Hence the distance between the ends of the successive cards are;

$$\ell/2, \ell/4, \ell/6, \ell/8, \dots \qquad \textit{Ans.}$$

If maximum overhang is asked, then

$$x = \ell/2 + \ell/4 + \ell/6 + \ell/8 + \dots \qquad .$$

Example 8. **Two blocks of masses m_1 and m_2 are connected by a spring of force constant k. Block of mass m_1 is pulled by a constant force F_1 and other block is pulled by a constant force F_2. Find the maximum elongation that the spring will suffer.**

Sol.

Let us take the two blocks plus spring as the system. The centre of mass of system moves with an acceleration,

$$a_c = \frac{(F_1 - F_2)}{m_1 + m_2}.$$

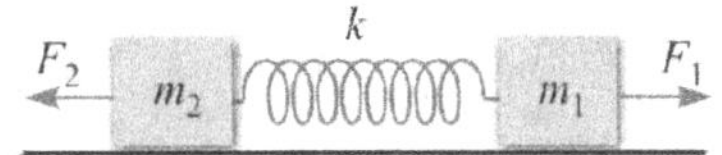

Figure. **8.64**

Supposing $F_1 > F_2$. As this frame is accelerated with respect to ground, we have to apply pseudo force on the blocks.

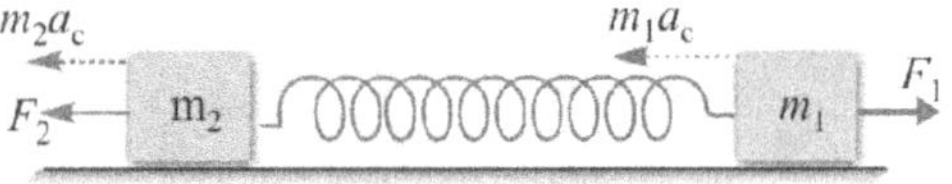

Figure. **8.65**

Therefore net external force on m_1

$$F'_1 = F_1 - m_1 a_c = F_1 - m_1\left(\frac{F_1 - F_2}{m_1 + m_2}\right)$$

$$= \left(\frac{F_1 m_2 + F_2 m_1}{m_1 + m_2}\right) \text{ towards right.}$$

and on m_2,

$$F'_2 = F_2 + m_2 a_c = F_2 + m_2\left(\frac{F_1 - F_2}{m_1 + m_2}\right)$$

$$= \left(\frac{F_1 m_2 + F_2 m_1}{m_1 + m_2}\right) \text{ towards left.}$$

As the centre mass is at rest in this frame, the blocks move in opposite directions and come to instantaneous rest at some instant. The spring will have maximum extension at this instant. Suppose the right block displaces distance x_1 and left displaces a distance x_2 from their initial positions.

Therefore work done by external force = Increase in P.E. of the spring

i.e. $$F_1'x_1 + F_2'x_2 = \frac{1}{2}k(x_1 + x_2)^2$$

or $$F_1'(x_1 + x_2) = \frac{1}{2}k(x_1 + x_2)^2$$

$$\Rightarrow \qquad (x_1 + x_2) = \frac{2F_1'}{k}$$

or $$x_{\max} = \frac{2}{k}\left(\frac{F_1 m_2 + F_2 m_1}{m_1 + m_2}\right). \qquad \textit{Ans.}$$

Example 9. **Two masses m_1 and m_2 are connected by a spring of force constant k and are placed on a frictionless horizontal surface. Initially the spring is stretched through a distance x_0, when the system is released from rest. Find the distance moved by two masses before they again comes to rest.**

Sol.

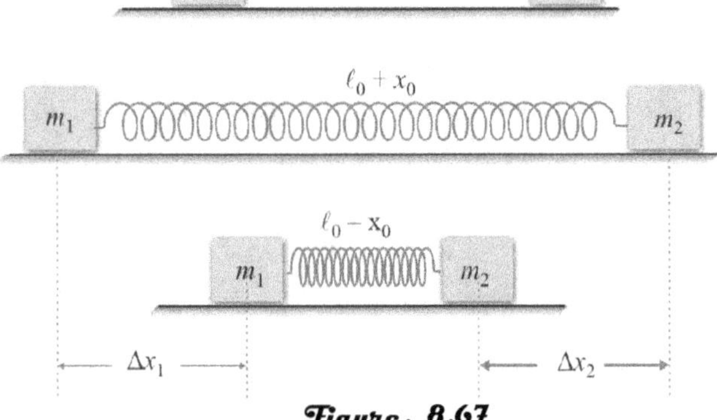

Figure. **8.67**

Blocks again come to rest when spring is compressed by x_0. Since no external force is acting on the system, so there is no change in the position of c.m. of the system. i.e. $\Delta x_{cm} = 0$

Let mass m_1 displaces by Δx_1 and m_2 displaces by Δx_2, then
$$\Delta x_1 + \Delta x_2 = 2x_0 \qquad \text{... (i)}$$

and
$$\Delta x_{cm} = \frac{m_1\Delta x_1 + m_2\Delta x_2}{m_1 + m_2}.$$

As
$$\Delta x_{cm} = 0$$

$\therefore$
$$\frac{m_1\Delta x_1 + m_2\Delta x_2}{m_1 + m_2} = 0 \qquad \text{... (ii)}$$

After solving equations (i) & (ii), we get
$$\Delta x_1 = \frac{2m_2 x_0}{m_1 + m_2}, \ \Delta x_2 = \frac{2m_1 x_0}{m_1 + m_2}. \qquad \textit{Ans.}$$

Example 10. **Two blocks of equal mass m are connected by an unstretched spring and the system is kept at rest on a frictionless horizontal surface. A constant force F is applied on one of the blocks pulling it away from the other as shown in _figure_ 8.68.**

(a) **Find the position of c.m. at time t.**

(b) **If the extension of the spring is x_0 at time t, find the displacement of the blocks at that instant.**

Sol

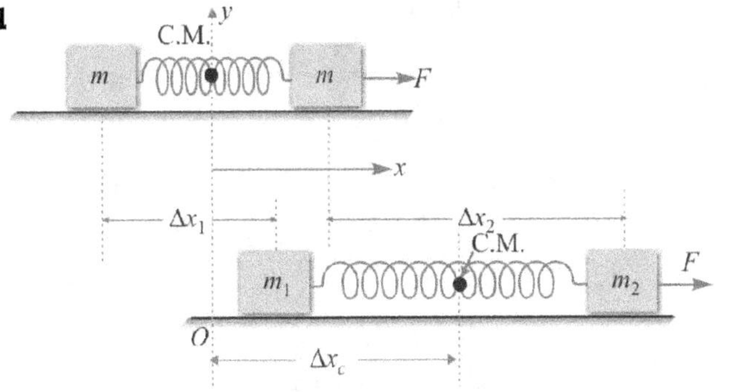

Figure. 8.68

(a) The acceleration of centre of mass
$$\vec{a}_c = \frac{\vec{F}}{M} = \frac{F}{m+m} = \frac{F}{2m}.$$

The position of c.m. at time t
$$\Delta x_c = \frac{1}{2}a_c t^2 = \frac{1}{2}\frac{F}{2m}t^2 = \frac{Ft^2}{4m}. \qquad \textit{Ans.}$$

(b) We have,
$$\Delta x_c = \frac{m_1\Delta x_1 + m_2\Delta x_2}{m_1 + m_2}$$

or
$$\frac{Ft^2}{4m} = \frac{m\Delta x_1 + m\Delta x_2}{m+m}$$

or
$$\Delta x_1 + \Delta x_2 = \frac{Ft^2}{2m}. \qquad \text{... (i)}$$

The extension of spring is,

$\therefore \quad \Delta x_2 - \Delta x_1 = x_0 \qquad \text{... (ii)}$

After solving equations (i) and (ii), we get
$$\Delta x_1 = \frac{1}{2}\left[\frac{Ft^2}{2m} - x_0\right]$$

and
$$\Delta x_2 = \frac{1}{2}\left[\frac{Ft^2}{2m} + x_0\right]. \qquad \textit{Ans.}$$

Example 11. **A particle of mass m is released from the top of a smooth wedge of mass M which rests on a smooth horizontal floor.**

(a) **Calculate the velocity of the wedge.**

(b) **And the distance moved by wedge when the mass m just touches the floor.**

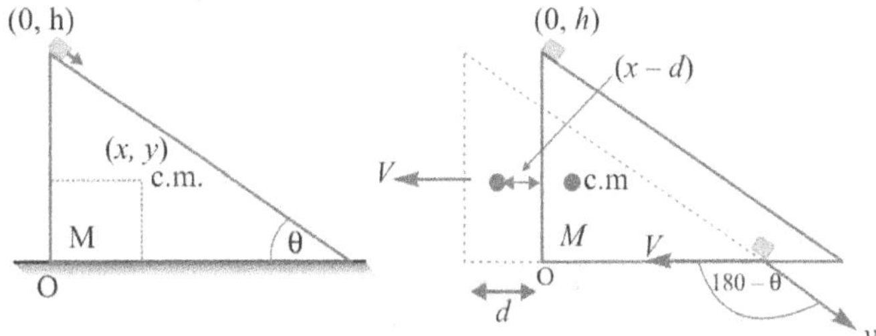

Figure. 8.69

Sol.

(a) Let the velocity of the block be v w.r.t. the wedge at the instant it touches the floor and let the wedge acquires a velocity V in the horizontal direction.

The velocity of the particle w.r.t. ground will be
$$= \sqrt{V^2 + v^2 + 2Vv\cos(180° - \theta)}$$
$$= \sqrt{(V^2 + v^2 - 2Vv\cos\theta)}.$$

Since there is no force acting on the system in horizontal direction, its momentum remains constant in this direction.

$\therefore \quad mv\cos\theta = (M+m)V. \qquad \text{..... (i)}$

Conservation of mechanical energy gives
$$\frac{1}{2}MV^2 + \frac{1}{2}m(\sqrt{V^2 + v^2 - 2Vv\cos\theta})^2 = mgh. \qquad \text{..... (ii)}$$

Solving above equations, we get
$$V = \sqrt{\frac{2ghm^2\cos^2\theta}{(M+m)^2 - m(M+m)\cos^2\theta}}. \qquad \textit{Ans.}$$

(b) Since there is no external force in the x-direction, the centre of mass of the system does not move in this direction. Let the centre of mass of M be located at the point (x, y) before m is released. When m moves down the floor, the centre of mass of M moves to left by an amount d. The centre of mass of m has travelled a distance $(h\cot\theta - d)$ to the right. Thus we have

Initial state of the $c.m.$ of the system = final state of the $c.m.$ of the system
$$\frac{Mx + m.0}{(M+m)} = \frac{M(x-d) + m(h\cot\theta - d)}{(M+m)}$$

After solving above equation, we get
$$d = \frac{mh\cot\theta}{(M+m)}. \qquad \textit{Ans.}$$

Example 12. A body of mass M as shown in *figure* 8.70 with a small disc of mass m place on it rests on a smooth horizontal plane. The disc is set in motion in the horizontal direction with velocity v. To what height (relative to the initial level) will the disc rise after breaking off the body M? The friction is assumed to be absent.

Sol.

Applying the law of conservation of momentum

$$mv = (m + M)v_1$$

$$\therefore \qquad v_1 = \frac{mv}{m+M},$$

where v_1 is the velocity of the combined system

Let disc rises to a height h, then

$$\frac{1}{2}mv^2 = mgh + \frac{1}{2}(m+M)v_1^2$$

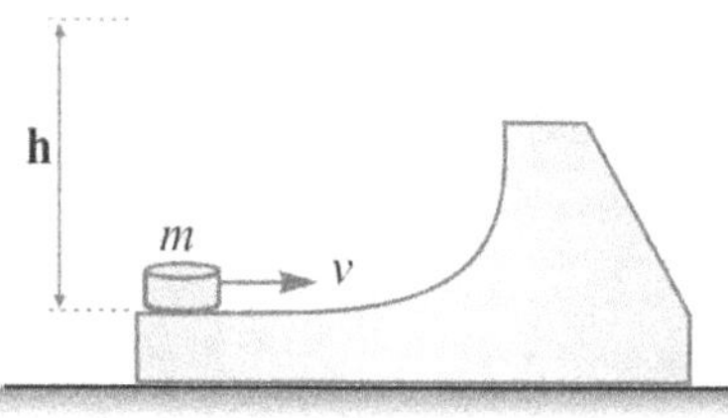

Figure. 8.70

Substituting the value of v_1, we get

$$\Rightarrow \qquad h = \frac{mv^2}{2(m+M)g} \qquad \text{Ans.}$$

Example 13. A small disc of mass m slides down a smooth hill of height h without initial velocity and gets onto a plank of mass M lying on the horizontal plane at the base of the hill shown in the *figure* 8.71. Due to friction between the disc and the plank, the disc slows down and, beginning with a certain moment, moves in one piece with the plank. Find the total work performed by the friction forces in this process.

Sol.

Velocity of the disc just before comes in contact with the plank can be obtained as

$$mgh = \frac{1}{2}mv^2 \Rightarrow v = \sqrt{(2gh)}.$$

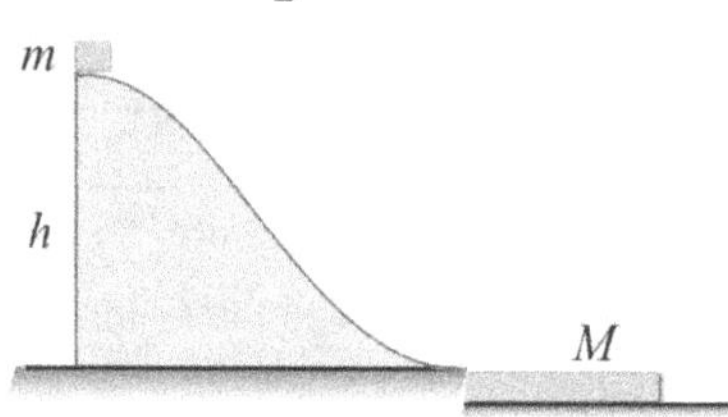

Figure. 8.71

Let v_1 be the combined velocity of both the disc and the plank when they move together. In this process momentum of the system remain constant, therefore

$$mv + 0 = (M + m)v_1$$

or $\qquad v_1 = mv/(M + m).$

Initial K.E. of the system $= \dfrac{1}{2}mv^2$

Final K.E. of the system $= \dfrac{1}{2}(M+m)v_1^2$.

Work performed by the friction in this process

$$W = \text{change in K.E. of the system}$$

or $\qquad = \dfrac{1}{2}(M+m)v_1^2 - \dfrac{1}{2}mv^2$

Substituting the value of v and v_1 in the above expression, we get

$$W = -\left[\frac{ghmM}{m+M}\right]. \qquad \text{Ans.}$$

Example 14. Two bars of masses m_1 and m_2 connected by a weightless spring of stiffness k as shown in *figure* 8.72 rest on a smooth horizontal plane. Bar 2 is shifted a small distance x to the left and then released. Find the velocity of the centre of inertia of the system after bar 1 breaks off the wall.

Sol.

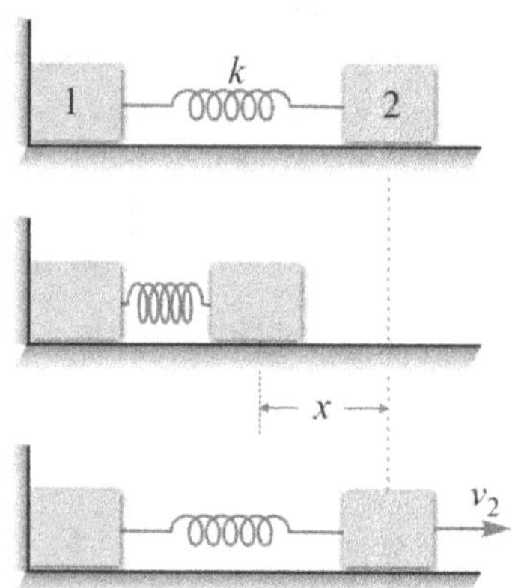

Figure. 8.72

Velocity of the bar 2 at the instant of break off will be obtained as

$$\frac{1}{2}m_2v_2^2 = \frac{1}{2}kx^2$$

$$v_2 = x\sqrt{\frac{k}{m_2}}$$

The velocity of the bar 1 at the instant is zero ($v_1 = 0$).

The velocity of the centre of inertia is given by

$$v_c = \frac{(m_1v_1 + m_2v_2)}{(m_1 + m_2)}.$$

After substituting the value of v_1 and v_2, we get

$$v_c = x\sqrt{\frac{km_2}{(m_1 + m_2)}} \quad \text{Ans.}$$

Mechanics   **MCQ Type 1**   Exercise 8.1

Collision

1. Choose the correct statement (s) from the following ;
  (i)   In an elastic collision of two bodies, the momentum and energy of each body is conserved.
  (ii) The work done by a force on a body in nature, over a closed loop is always zero.
  (iii) In an inelastic collision of two bodies, the final kinetic energy is less than the initial kinetic energy of the system.
  (a) (i)   (b) (ii)
  (c) (iii)   (d) all

2. Consider the following statements (i) and (ii) and identify the correct answer :
  (i)   Coefficient of restitution varies between 0 and 1
  (ii) In inelastic collision, the law of conservation of energy is satisfied.
  (a) (i) and (ii) are true
  (b) (i) and (ii) are false
  (c) (i) is true but (ii) is false
  (d) (i) is false but (ii) is true

3. Consider the following two statements :
  (A) Linear momentum of a system of particles is zero
  (B) Kinetic energy of a system of particles is zero then :
  (a) A implies B and B implies A
  (b) A does not imply B and B does not imply A
  (c) A implies B but B does not imply A
  (d) A does not imply B but B implies A

4. Two bodies A and B have masses M and m respectively, where $M > m$ and they are at a distance d apart. Equal force is applied to them so that they approach each other. The position where they hit each other is
  (a) nearer to B
  (b) nearer to A
  (c) at equal distance from A and B
  (d) cannot be decided

5. Four identical balls are in contact and at rest on a horizontal smooth surface are hit by another identical ball moving initially as shown in the figure. The ball 1 comes to rest after collision. Which of the following can possible represent the motion of balls after collision;

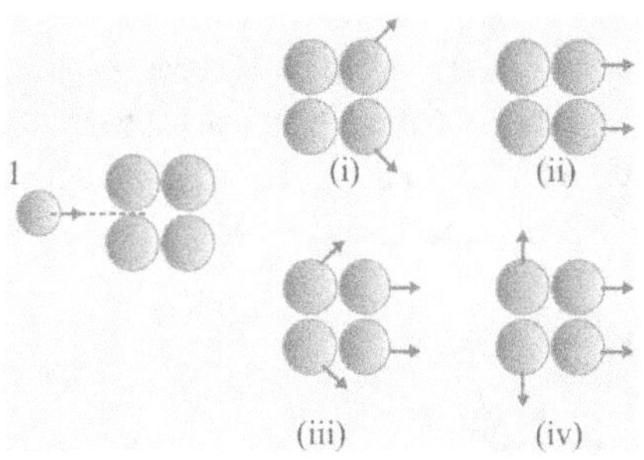

  (a) (i)   (b) (ii)
  (c) (iii)   (d) all

6. A massive ball moving with speed v collides head on with a tiny ball having mass very much smaller than the mass of the first ball. If the collision is completely elastic, then the speed of the second ball after the collision approximately equal to ;
  (a) v (b) $2v$
  (c) $\dfrac{v}{2}$ (d) ∞

7. An object of mass 3m splits into three equal fragments. Two fragments have velocities $v\,\hat{j}$ and $v\,\hat{i}$. The velocity of the third fragment is:
  (a) $v(\hat{j} - \hat{i})$ (b) $v(\hat{i} - \hat{j})$
  (c) $-v(\hat{i} + \hat{j})$ (d) $\dfrac{v(\hat{i} + \hat{j})}{\sqrt{2}}$

8. Two particles having position vectors $\vec{r}_1 = (3\,\vec{i} + 5\,\vec{j})$ meter and $\vec{r}_2 = (-5\,\vec{i} - 3\,\vec{j})$ meter are moving with velocities $\vec{v}_1 = (4\,\vec{i} + 3\,\vec{j})$ m/s and $\vec{v}_2 = (a\,\vec{i} + 7\,\vec{j})$ m/s. If they collide after 2 second, the value of a ;
  (a) 2   (b) 4
  (c) 6   (d) 8

9. A bomb of mass 12 kg explodes into two pieces of masses 4 kg and 8 kg. The velocity of 8 kg mass is 6 m/s. The kinetic energy of the other mass is ;
  (a) 48 J   (b) 32 J
  (c) 24 J   (d) 288 J

10. A ball 'A' of mass 1 kg, moving with speed of 12 m/s, collides obliquely and elastically with another ball B which was initially at rest. Ball A then moves off at right angles to its direction with a speed of 5 m/s. The momentum of ball B after collision is ;
  (a) 5 kg m/s   (b) 11 kg m/s
  (c) 13 kg m/s   (d) 17 kg m/s

Answer	1	(c)	2	(a)	3	(d)	4	(b)	5	(c)
Key	6	(b)	7	(c)	8	(d)	9	(d)	10	(c)

11. A player caught a cricket ball of mass 150 g moving at a rate of 20 m/s. If the catching process is completed in 0.1 s, the force of the blow exerted by the ball on the hand of the player is equal to :
(a) 300 N
(b) 150 N
(c) 3 N
(d) 30 N

12. A particle of mass $4\,m$ which is at rest explodes into three fragments. Two of fragments, each of mass m are found to move with a speed v each in mutually perpendicular directions. The total energy released in the process is ;
(a) $\dfrac{1}{2}\,mv^2$
(b) mv^2
(c) $\dfrac{3}{2}\,mv^2$
(d) $\dfrac{5}{2}\,mv^2$

13. A shell of mass 200 g is ejected from a gun of mass 4 kg by an explosion that generates 1.05 kJ of energy. The initial velocity of the shell is :
(a) 40 m/s
(b) 80 m/s
(c) 100 m/s
(d) 120 m/s

14. A neutron of mass m collides elastically with a nucleus of mass M, which is initially at rest. If the neutron's initial kinetic energy is k_0, the maximum kinetic energy that it can lose during the collision is ;
(a) k_0
(b) $\dfrac{k_0}{2}$
(c) $\dfrac{m\,M\,k_0}{(M+m)^2}$
(d) $\dfrac{4m\,M\,k_0}{(M+m)^2}$

15. A ball A, moving with kinetic energy K, makes a head on elastic collision with a stationary ball with mass n times that of A. The maximum potential energy stored in the system during the collision is
(a) K/n
(b) $\dfrac{(n-1)K}{n}$
(c) $\dfrac{(n+1)K}{n}$
(d) $\dfrac{nK}{(n+1)}$

16. A body A is released from a condition of rest on a frictionless circular surface. It then moves on a horizontal surface BD whose coefficient of friction with the body is 0.1. A spring having a spring constant $k = 2 \times 10^4$ N/ m is positioned at D as shown in the diagram. The mass of the body is 10 kg. The comparison of the spring approximately is (Take $g = 10$ m/s^2) ;

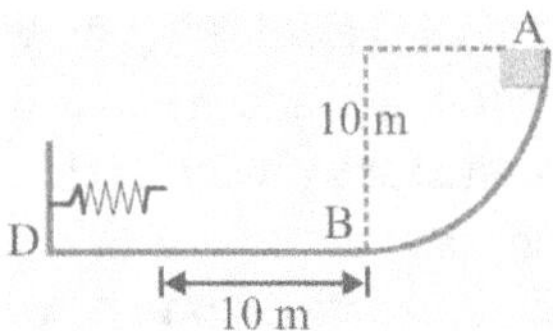

(a) 0.1 m
(b) 0.2 m
(c) 0.3 m
(d) 1 m

17. A ^{238}U nucleus decays by emitting an alpha particle of speed $v\,ms^{-1}$. The recoil speed of the residual nucleus is (in ms^{-1})
(a) $-4v/234$
(b) $v/4$
(c) $-4v/238$
(d) $4v/238$

18. A ball is dropped from a height h. It the coefficient of restitution be e, then to what height will it rise after jumping twice from the ground
(a) $eh/2$
(b) $3eh$
(c) eh
(d) e^4h

19. A particle of mass m moving with horizontal speed 6 m/sec as shown in figure. If $m \ll M$ then for one dimensional elastic collision, the speed of lighter particle after collision will be

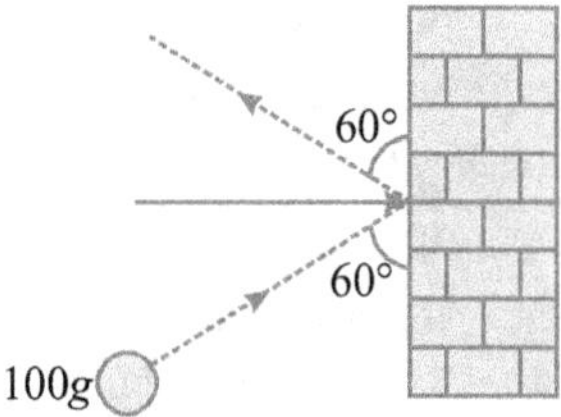

(a) 2m/s in original direction
(b) 2 m/s opposite to the original direction
(c) 2 m/s opposite to the original direction
(d) 4 m/s in original direction

20. A body falling from a height of 10m rebounds from hard floor. If it loses 20% energy in the impact, then coefficient restitution is
(a) 0.89
(b) 0.56
(c) 0.23
(d) 0.18

21. A mass of 100g strikes the wall with speed 5m/s at an angle as shown in figure and it rebounds with the same speed. If the contact time is 2×10^{-3} sec, what is the force applied on the mass by the wall

(a) $250\sqrt{3}N$ to right
(b) $250\,N$ to right
(c) $250\sqrt{3}N$ to left
(d) $250\,N$ to left

22. A particle of mass m moving eastward with a speed v collides with another particle of the same mass moving northward with the same speed v. The two particles coalesce on collision. The new particle of mass $2m$ will move in the north-easterly direction with a velocity
(a) $v/2$
(b) $2v$
(c) $v/\sqrt{2}$
(d) v

Answer	11	(d)	12	(c)	13	(c)	14	(d)	15	(d)	16	(c)
Key	17	(a)	18	(d)	19	(a)	20	(a)	21	(c)	22	(c)

23. Two identical mass M moving with velocity u_1 and u_2 collide perfectly inelastically. The loss in energy is

(a) $\dfrac{M}{2}(u_2 - u_1)^2$ 　　(b) $\dfrac{M}{2}(u_1 - u_2)^2$

(c) $\dfrac{M}{4}(u_1 - u_2)^2$ 　　(d) $\dfrac{M}{8}(u_2 - u_1)^2$

24. If the masses of two balls be as $3 : 2$ and their respective velocities before impact be as $2 : 3$ and in opposite directions, and the coefficient of restitution is $2/3$, find with what velocity will each ball move back with respect to the original velocity.

(a) 1/3 times the original velocity

(b) 2/3 times the original velocity

(c) 3/1 times the original velocity

(d) 3/2 times the original velocity

Centre of Mass

25. Two bodies of mass 1 kg and 3 kg have position vectors $\hat{i} + 2\hat{j} + \hat{k}$ and $-3\hat{i} - 2\hat{j} + \hat{k}$, respectively. The centre of mass of this system has a position vector

(a) $-2\hat{i} + 2\hat{k}$ 　　(b) $-2\hat{i} - \hat{j} + \hat{k}$

(c) $2\hat{i} - \hat{j} + \hat{k}$ 　　(d) $-\hat{i} + \hat{j} + \hat{k}$

26. Three identical spheres each of radius R are placed touching each other on a horizontal table as shown in figure. The co-ordinates of centre of mass are ;

(a) (R, R) 　　(b) $(0, 0)$

(c) $\left(\dfrac{R}{2}, \dfrac{R}{2}\right)$

(d) $\left(R, \dfrac{R}{\sqrt{3}}\right)$

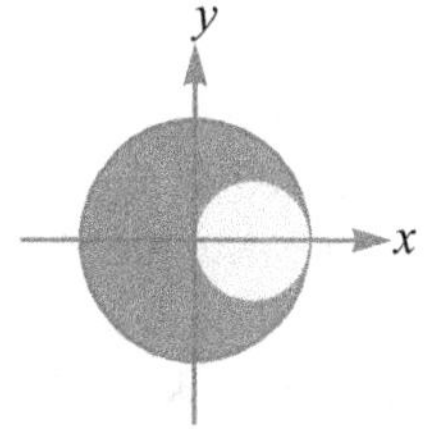

27. The mass per unit length of a non - uniform rod of length L varies as $m = \lambda x$ where λ is constant. The centre of mass of the rod will be at ;

(a) $\dfrac{2}{3}L$ 　　(b) $\dfrac{3}{2}L$

(c) $\dfrac{1}{2}L$ 　　(d) $\dfrac{4}{3}L$

28. Two blocks of masses 10 kg and 4 kg are connected by a spring of negligible mass and are placed on a frictionless horizontal surface. An impulse gives a speed of 14 m/s to the heavier block in the direction of the lighter block. Then, the velocity of the centre of mass is :

(a) $30\ \text{ms}^{-1}$ 　　(b) $20\ \text{ms}^{-1}$

(c) $10\ \text{ms}^{-1}$ 　　(d) $5\ \text{ms}^{-1}$

29. The centre of mass coordinates of a block of shape shown in the figure is

(a) $\left(\dfrac{L}{2}, \dfrac{L}{2}\right)$

(b) $\left(\dfrac{5}{12}L, \dfrac{5}{12}L\right)$

(c) $\left(\dfrac{2}{3}L, \dfrac{2}{3}L\right)$

(d) $\left(\dfrac{L}{4}, \dfrac{L}{4}\right)$

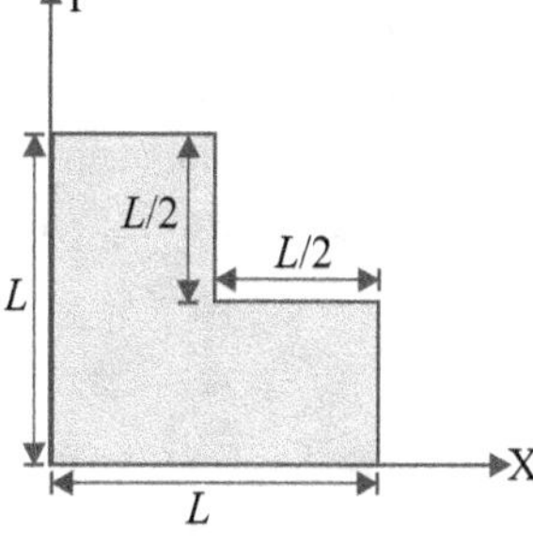

30. One end of a thin rod of length L and mass M_1 is riveted to the centre of a circular uniform disc of radius R and mass M_2, such that they are coplanar. The centre of mass of system relative to centre of the disc is: **[PET–2008]**

(a) $\dfrac{(M_1 + M_2)L}{2M_1}$ 　　(b) $\dfrac{M_1 L}{(M_1 + M_2)}$

(c) $\dfrac{M_1 L}{2(M_1 + M_2)}$ 　　(d) $\dfrac{M_1 L + M_2 R}{M_1 + M_2}$

31. A hole of radius $\dfrac{r}{2}$ is cut in a disc of radius having mass m. The centre of mass system will be: **[PET–2004]**

(a) at the centre

(b) at distance $\dfrac{r}{3}$ from centre away from the hole

(c) at distance $\dfrac{r}{4}$ from centre away from the hole

(d) at distance $\dfrac{r}{6}$ from centre away from the hole along the common diameter.

32. Consider a two particle system with particles having masses m_1 and m_2. If the first particle is pushed towards the centre of mass through a distance d, by what distance should the second particle be moved, so as to keep the centre of mass at the same position :

(a) d 　　(b) $\dfrac{m_2}{m_1}d$

(c) $\dfrac{m_1}{m_1 + m_2}d$ 　　(d) $\dfrac{m_1}{m_2}d$

Answer	23	(c)	24	(b)	25	(b)	26	(d)	27	(a)
Key	28	(c)	29	(b)	30	(c)	31	(d)	32	(d)

33. Three thin rods, each of length L, are arranged in an inverted U, as shown in figure. The two rods on the arms of the U each have mass M; the third rod has mass $3M$. The centre of mass of the system from upper rod is

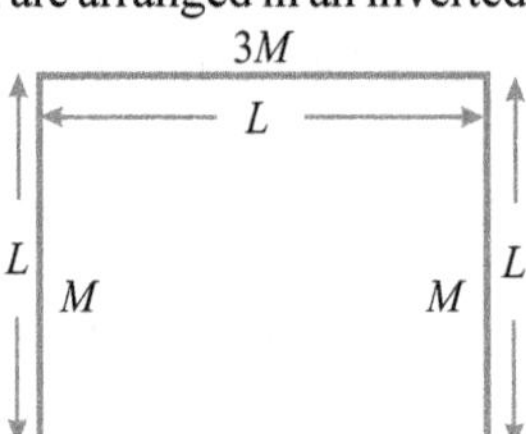

(a) $\dfrac{L}{3}$ (b) $\dfrac{L}{2}$

(c) $\dfrac{L}{5}$ (d) $\dfrac{2L}{3}$

34. A particle of mass m moves on the x-axis under the influence of a force of attraction towards the origin O given by

$$\vec{F} = -k\left(\frac{1}{x^2}\right)\hat{i}.$$

If the particle starts from rest at $x = a$, the speed it will attain to reach at a distance x from the origin will be :

(a) $\sqrt{\dfrac{2k}{m}\left(\dfrac{a-x}{ax}\right)^{1/2}}$ (b) $\sqrt{\dfrac{2k}{m}\left(\dfrac{a+x}{ax}\right)^{1/2}}$

(c) $\sqrt{\dfrac{k}{m}\left(\dfrac{ax}{a-x}\right)}$ (d) $\sqrt{\dfrac{m}{2k}\left(\dfrac{a-x}{ax}\right)^{1/2}}$

35. Two astronauts each of mass 150 kg are travelling in a closed skylab moving at a speed of 5 km/s in the outer space far removed from all other material objects. The total mass of the skylabe is 800 kg. If the astronauts do slimming exercise and thereby reduce their masses to 100 kg each, the velocity now with which the skylab is moving:

(a) 5.5 km/s   (b) 11 km/s

(c) 5 km/s   (d) 3 km/s

36. A child is sitting at one end of a long trolley moving with a uniform speed v on a smooth horizontal track. If the child starts running towards the other end of the trolley with a speed u, the speed of the centre of mass of the system will;

(a) $u + v$ (b) $v - u$

(c) v (d) none

37. Two particle A and B initially at rest. Move towards each other under a mutual force of attraction. At the instant, when the speed of A is v and the speed of B is $2\,v$, the velocity of centre of the system is ;

(a) 0   (b) v

(c) $1.5\,v$ (d) $3\,v$

38. Two bodies of masses 1 kg and 2 kg are moving in two perpendicular direction with velocities 1 m/s and 2 m/s as shown in figure. The velocity of the centre of mass (in magnitude) of the system will be ;

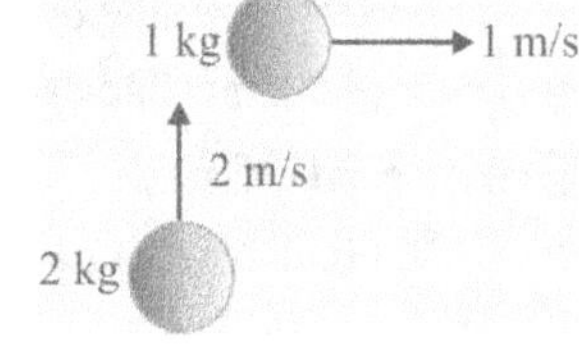

(a) 3 m/s   (b) 1.67 m/s

(c) 1.5 m/s   (d) 1.37 m/s

39. Two masses $3\,m$ and m are suspended from a light frictionless pulley with the help of a massless string. If system is set free the acceleration of centre of mass will be:

(a) g   (b) $\dfrac{g}{2}$

(c) $\dfrac{g}{4}$ (d) none of these

Answer	33	(c)	34	(a)	35	(c)	36	(c)	37	(a)
Key	38	(d)	39	(c)						

Collision

1. A particle of mass m moving with a velocity u makes an elastic one dimensional collision with a stationary particle of mass m establishing a contact with if for extremely small time T. Their force of contact increases form zero to F_0 linearly in time $T/4$, remains constant for a further time $T/2$ and decreases linearly from F_0 to zero in further time $T/4$ as shown. The magnitude possessed by F_0 is

(a) $\dfrac{mu}{T}$ (b) $\dfrac{2mu}{T}$

(c) $\dfrac{4mu}{3T}$ (d) $\dfrac{3mu}{4T}$

2. In a gamma decay process, the internal energy of a nucleus of mass M decreases, a gamma photon of energy E and linear momentum E/c is emitted and the nucleus recoils. The decrease in internal energy ;

(a) E (b) $E + \dfrac{E^2}{2Mc^2}$

(c) $\dfrac{E^2}{2Mc^2}$ (d) zero

3. A trolley of mass 200 kg moves with a uniform speed of 10 m/s on a frictionless track. A child of mass 20 kg runs on the trolley from one end to the other with a speed of 4 m/s relative to the trolley in a direction opposite to its motion, and jumps out of the trolley. The final speed of the trolley is

(a) 10.4 m/s
(b) 12.4 m/s
(c) 16 m/s
(d) none of these

4. A car having a mass of 200 kg is rolling at a speed of 1 m/s towards a spring - stop system. If the spring is non - linear such that it develops $300\, x^2$ N force for a deflection of x m. The maximum deceleration that the car A undergoes ;

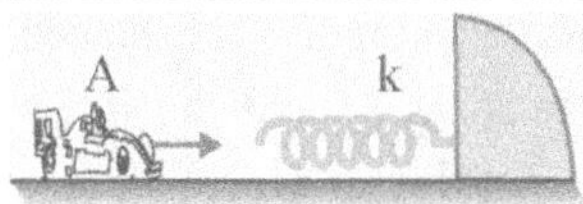

(a) 1 m/s^2
(b) 1.5 m/s^2
(c) 2 m/s^2
(d) 2.5 m/s^2

5. A ball of mass 1 kg bounces against the ground as shown in the figure. The approaching velocity is 25 m/s and the velocity after hitting the ground is 20 m/s. The impulse exerted on the ball is :

(a) 7.8 N - s
(b) 27.68 N - s
(c) 31 N - s
(d) 62 N - s

6. Two equal balls are in contact on a table are in equilibrium. A third ball collides them simultaneously symmetrically and remains at rest after impact. The coefficient of restitution is ;

(a) $\dfrac{2}{3}$
(b) $\dfrac{1}{3}$
(c) $\dfrac{1}{4}$
(d) $\dfrac{3}{5}$

7. An intense stream of water of cross–sectional area A strikes a wall at an angle θ with the normal to the wall and returns back elastically. If the density of water is ρ and its velocity is v, then the force exerted in the wall will be

(a) $2Av^2\rho \cos\theta$
(b) $2Av^2\rho \cos\theta$
(c) $2Av^2\rho$
(d) $2Av\rho$

8. A ball of mass 1 kg is attached to an inextensible string. The ball x released from the position shown in figure. The impulse imparted by the string to the ball just after string becomes taut is $(g = 10 m/s^2)$

(a) $\sqrt{20}\ N\text{-}s$
(b) $\sqrt{40}\ N\text{-}s$
(c) $\sqrt{10}\ N\text{-}s$
(d) none of these

9. Block A of mass m is hanging from a vertical spring of force constant k. Another identical block B strikes the block A with velocity v and sticks to it. The value of v for which the spring just attains natural length is

(a) $\sqrt{\dfrac{6m}{k}g}$
(b) $\sqrt{\dfrac{8m}{k}g}$
(c) $\sqrt{\dfrac{24m}{k}g}$
(d) $\sqrt{\dfrac{12m}{k}g}$

10. A body of mass $m_1 + m_2$ is split into two parts of masses m_1 and m_2 by an internal explosion which generates a kinetic energy E. If after explosion the parts move in the same line as before, then their relative speed is

(a) $\sqrt{\dfrac{E(m_1+m_2)}{m_1+m_2}}$
(b) $\sqrt{\dfrac{2E(m_1+m_2)}{m_1 m_2}}$
(c) $\sqrt{\dfrac{E(m_1+m_2)}{m_1+m_2}}$
(d) $\sqrt{\dfrac{E(m_1+m_2)}{2m_1\times m_2}}$

11. A particle of mass $2m$ is projected at an angle of 45° with horizontal with a velocity of $20\sqrt{2}$ m/s. After 1 second explosion takes place and the particle is broken into two equal pieces. As a result of explosion one part comes to rest. The maximum height from the ground attained by the other part is $(g = 10 m/s^2)$

(a) 50 m
(b) 25 m
(c) 40 m
(d) 35 m

12. Two balls having masses m and $2m$ are fastened to two light strings of same length l as shown in figure. The other ends of the strings are fixed at O. The strings are kept in the same horizontal line and the system is released from rest. The collision between the balls is elastic. Point A is the lowest point at which either ball can reach. The speed of ball of $2\,m$ just after collision is:

(a) $2\dfrac{\sqrt{2gl}}{3}$
(b) $2\dfrac{\sqrt{50gl}}{3}$
(c) $\dfrac{\sqrt{2gl}}{3}$
(d) $\dfrac{\sqrt{50gl}}{3}$

13. In figure, if the coefficient of restitution is 0.8, what is the maximum angle from the vertical that body B will reach after the first impact :

(a) 30°
(b) $\cos^{-1}(0.45)$
(c) $\cos^{-1}(0.9995)$
(d) none

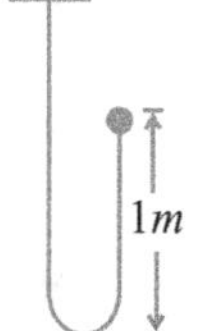

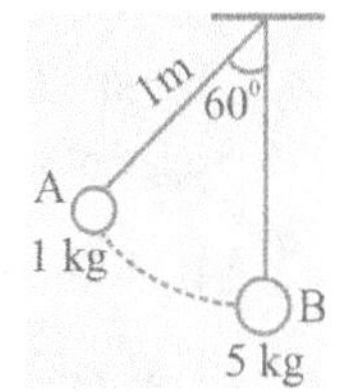

Answer	1	(c)	2	(b)	3	(a)	4	(b)	5	(b)	6	(a)	7	(a)
Key	8	(b)	9	(b)	10	(b)	11	(b)	12	(c)	13	(c)		

14. A ball is projected from a point on a smooth horizontal plane with a velocity u at an angle θ with the horizontal and continuous to rebound. If the coefficient of restitution is e, then range after first rebound is

(a) $\dfrac{u^2 \sin 2\theta}{g}$

(b) $\dfrac{e u^2 \sin 2\theta}{g}$

(c) $\dfrac{e u^2 \sin 2\theta}{2g}$

(d) none of these

15. Figure shows a smooth spherical ball of mass m striking two identical equilateral triangular wedges, each of mass m. The velocity of ball at the instant of impact is v_0. If e is the coefficient of restitution, then velocity of either wedge after impact is

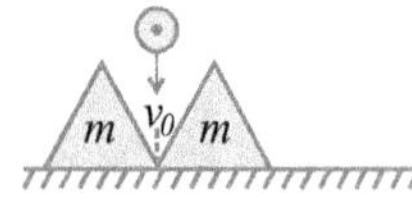

(a) $\dfrac{\sqrt{3}}{5}(1+e)v_0$

(b) $\dfrac{5}{\sqrt{3}}(1+e)v_0$

(c) $\sqrt{3}(1+e)v_0$

(d) $\dfrac{e v_0}{3}$

Centre of Mass

16. Centre of mass of 3 particles 10 kg , 20 kg and 30 kg is at $(0, 0, 0)$. Where should a particle of mass 40 kg be placed so that the combination centre of mass will be at $(3, 3, 3)$

(a) $(0, 0, 0)$

(b) $(7.5, 7.5, 7.5)$

(c) $(1, 2, 3)$

(d) $(4, 4, 4)$

17. Consider a particle of two particles having masses m_1 and m_2. It the particle of mass m_1 is pushed towards the centre of mass of particles through a distance d, by what distance would be particle of mass m_2 move so as to keep the centre of mass of particles at the original position

(a) $\dfrac{m_1}{m_1 + m_2} d$

(b) $\dfrac{m_1}{m_2} d$

(c) d

(d) $\dfrac{m_2}{m_1} d$

18. Two identical uniform rectangular blocks (with longest side ℓ) and a solid sphere of radius R are to be balanced at the edge of a heavy table such that the centre of the sphere remains at the maximum possible horizontal distance from the vertical edge of the table without toppling as indicated in the figure. If the mass of each block is M and of the sphere is $\dfrac{M}{2}$, the maximum distance x that can be achieved is: **[KVPY -2013]**

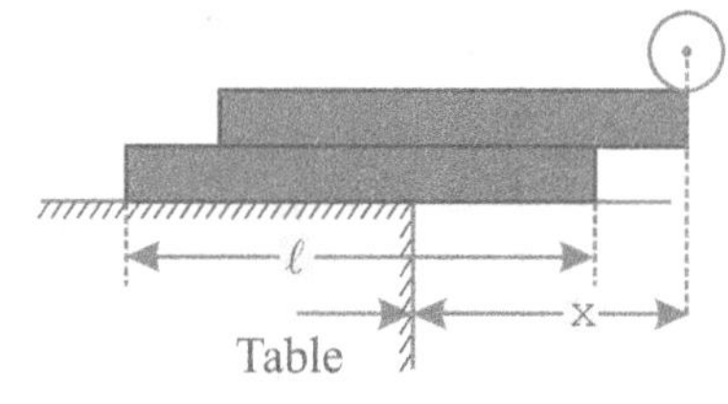

(a) $\dfrac{8\ell}{15}$

(b) $\dfrac{5\ell}{6}$

(c) $\dfrac{3\ell}{4} + R$

(d) $\dfrac{7\ell}{15} + R$

19. A ball of mass M and radius R is placed inside a spherical shell of same mass M and the inner radius $2R$. The combination is at rest on a table top in the position shown in figure. The ball is released, rolls back and fourth inside and finally comes to at rest of the bottom of the shell. The maximum displacement of the shell during this process is

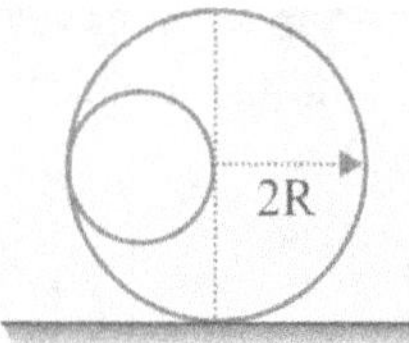

(a) $\dfrac{R}{2}$

(b) R

(c) $\dfrac{3}{2}R$

(d) $2R$

20. Two spherical bodies of mass M and $5M$ and radius R and $2R$ respectively are released in free space with initial separation between their centres equal to $12R$. If they attract each other due to gravitational force only, then the distance covered by the smaller body just before collision is

(a) $1.5 R$

(b) $2.5 R$

(c) $4.5 R$

(d) $7.5 R$

21. Particles of masses $m, 2m, 3m, \ldots\ldots\ldots\ldots nm$ grams are placed on the same line at distances $l, 2l, 3l, \ldots\ldots nl$ cm from a fixed point. The distance of centre of mass of the particles from the fixed point in centimetres is

(a) $\dfrac{(2n+1)l}{3}$

(b) $\dfrac{1}{n+1}$

(c) $\dfrac{n(n^2+1)l}{2}$

(d) $\dfrac{2l}{n(n^2+1)}$

22. A strip of wood of length l is placed on a smooth horizontal surface. An insect starts from one end of the strip, walks with constant velocity and reaches the other end in time t_1. It then flies off vertically. The strip moves a further distance

Answer	14	(b)	15	(a)	16	(b)	17	(b)	18	(a)	19	(b)
Key	20	(d)	21	(a)								

l in time t_2.

(a)　$t_1 = t_2$　　　　　(b)　$t_1 > t_2$

(c)　$t_1 < t_2$　　　　　(d)　none of these

23. A block of mass M is tied to one end on a massless rope. The other end of the rope is in the hands of a man of mass $2M$ as shown in figure. The block and the man are resting on a rough wedge of mass M as shown in figure. The whole system is resting of a smooth horizontal surface. The man pulls the rope. Pulley is massless and frictionless. What is the displacement of the wedge. When the block meets the pulley. (Man does not leave his position during the pull).

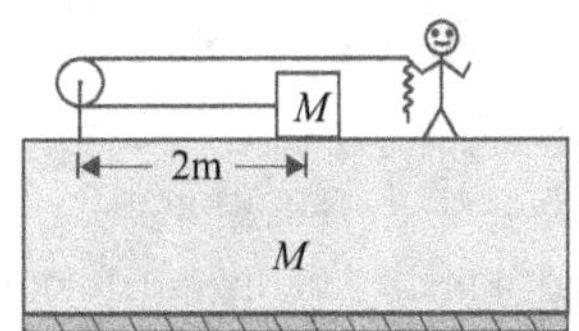

(a)　0.5 m　　　　　(b)　1 m

(c)　$\dfrac{2}{3}m$　　　　　(d)　zero

24. Two blocks A and B of masses m and $2m$ respectively, attached at opposite ends of a spring of force constant k, placed on smooth horizontal surface. Spring is initially at its natural length ℓ. A is given a velocity $2v_0$ and B given velocity v_0 as shown. The maximum separation between $2m$ and centre of mass of the system will be:

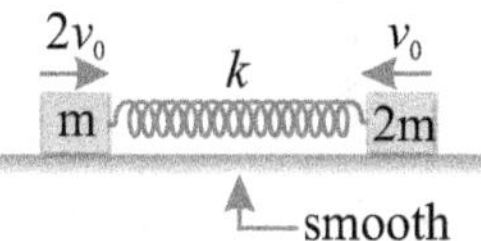

(a)　$\dfrac{\ell}{3} + \sqrt{\dfrac{8mv_0^2}{k}}$　　　　　(b)　$\dfrac{2\ell}{3} + \sqrt{\dfrac{2mv_0^2}{3k}}$

(c)　$\dfrac{\ell}{3} + \sqrt{\dfrac{2mv_0^2}{3k}}$　　　　　(d)　none of these

Answer Key	22	(c)	23	(a)	24	(c)

Mechanics　　　　　**MCQ Type 2**　　　　　Exercise 8.2

MULTIPLE OPTIONS CORRECT

1. A ball hits the floor and rebounds after an inelastic collision. In this case, choose the correct alternative ;

(a)　the momentum of the ball just after the collision is the same as that just before the collision

(b)　the total energy of the ball and the earth is conserved

(c)　the mechanical energy of the ball remains the same in the collision

(d)　the total momentum of the ball and the earth is conserved

2. A bomb at rest explodes into large number of tiny fragments. Then:

(a)　the momentum of all the fragments is zero

(b)　the momentum of all the fragments increases

(c)　the K. E. of all the fragment remain zero

(d)　the K. E. of all the fragment is more than zero

3. A body moves towards another stationary body and collides. Then

(a)　both the bodies move after collision

(b)　the moving body may come to rest and other starts moving

(c)　both comes to rest

(d)　stationary body may move with a velocity help the velocity of rolling body

4. In head on collision of two identical bodies

(a)　the momenta are interchanged

(b)　the velocities are interchanged

(c)　the kinetic energies are interchanged

(d)　none of the above

5. A sphere A moving with a speed u and rotating with an angular velocity ω, makes a head-on elastic collision with an identical stationary sphere B. There is no friction between the surfaces of A and B. Disregard gravity.

(a)　A will stop moving but continue to rotate with an angular velocity ω.

(b)　A will come to rest and stop rotating

(c)　B will move with a speed u without rotating

(d)　B will move with a speed u and rotate with an angular velocity ω.

6. A man of mass m is stationary on a stationary flat car. The car can move without friction along horizontal rails. The man starts walking with velocity v relative to the car. Work done by him:

(a)　is less than $\dfrac{1}{2}mv^2$, if he walks along the rails

(b)　is equal $\dfrac{1}{2}mv^2$, if he walks normal to rails

(c)　can never be less than $\dfrac{1}{2}mv^2$

(d)　is greater than $\dfrac{1}{2}mv^2$, if he walks along the rails

7. In each of three figure shown, two blocks are connected by a light spring and the system is placed on smooth horizontal surface. A constant horizontal force of magnitude F is applied to left block as shown. Assuming force constant in all three cases to be same and if x_1, x_2 and x_3 are their maximum compression, then

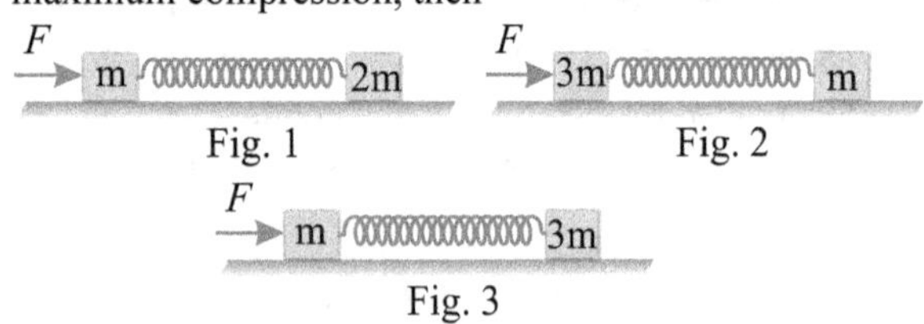

Fig. 1   Fig. 2

Fig. 3

(a) $x_1 = x_2 = x_3$ (b) $x_1 > x_2$
(c) $x_1 < x_3$ (d) $x_2 < x_3$

8. A set of n identical cubical blocks lies at rest parallel to each other along a line on a smooth horizontal surface. The separation between the near surfaces of any two adjacent blocks is L. The block of one end is given a speed v towards the next one at time $t = 0$. All collisions are completely inelastic, then ;

(a) the last block starts moving at $t = \dfrac{(n-1)L}{v}$

(b) the last block starts moving at $t = \dfrac{n(n-1)L}{2v}$

(c) the centre of mass of the system will have a final speed v

(d) the centre of mass of the system will have a final speed $\dfrac{v}{n}$

9. In a one - dimensional collision between two identical particles A and B, B is stationary and A has momentum P before impact. During impact, B gives impulse J to A ;

(a) the total momentum of the 'A plus B' system is P before and after the impact, and $(P - J)$ during the impact.

(b) during the impact, A gives impulse J to B.

(c) the coefficient of restitution is $\dfrac{2J}{P} - 1$.

(d) the coefficient of restitution is $\dfrac{J}{P} + 1$.

10. A ball strikes a wall at an angle α with the normal of the wall. It rebounds at an angle θ :

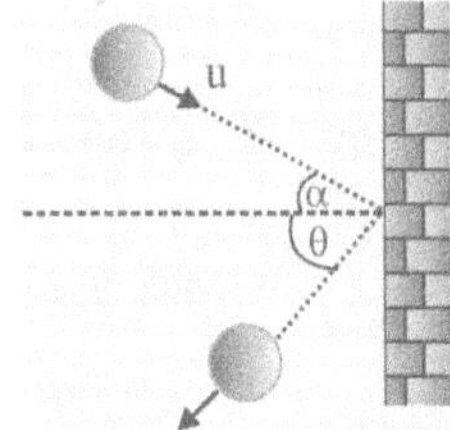

(a) the speed of the ball after collision will be less than u

(b) the angle θ will be greater than angle α

(c) the coefficient of restitution between ball and wall is 1

(d) the coefficient of restitution between ball and wall is $e = \dfrac{\tan \alpha}{\tan \theta}$

11. Two balls A and B having masses m kg and $2m$ kg, moving with speeds 21 m/s and 4 m/s respectively in opposite directions, collide head-on. After collision, A moves with a speed of 1 m/s in the same direction. Then :

(a) the velocity of B after collision is 6 m/s opposite to the direction before collision

(b) the coefficient of restitution is 0.2

(c) the loss of kinetic energy due to collision is 200 m J.

(d) the impulse of the force between the two balls is 20 m Ns.

12. A body of mass 3 kg, moving with a speed of 4 m/s, collides head-on with a stationary body of mass 2 kg. Their velocity of separation after the collision is 2 m/s. Then:

(a) the coefficient of restitution is 0.5

(b) the impulse of collision is 7.2 Ns

(c) the loss of kinetic energy due to collision is 3.6 J.

(d) the loss of kinetic energy due to collision is 7.2 J

13. A horizontal block A is at rest on a smooth horizontal surface. A small block B, whose mass is half of A, is placed on A at one end and project along other end with some velocity u. The coefficient of friction between blocks is μ. Then:

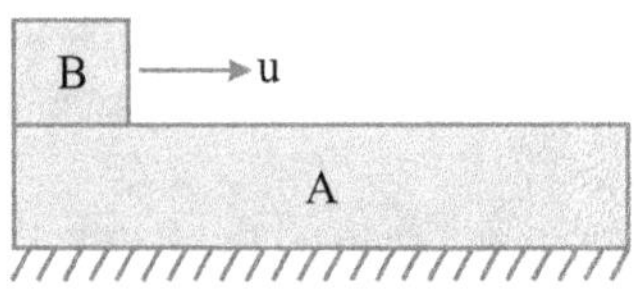

(a) the blocks will reach a final common velocity $u/3$

(b) the work done against friction is two-third of the initial kinetic energy of B

(c) before the blocks reach a common velocity, the acceleration of A relative to B is $(2/3)\,\mu g$

(d) before the block reach a common velocity, the acceleration of A relative to B is $(3/2)\,\mu g$

14. A ball of mass 1 kg strikes a wedge of mass 4 kg horizontally with a velocity of 10 m/s. Just after collision velocity of wedge becomes 4 m/s. Friction is absent every where and collision is elastic. Select the correct alternative (s):

Answer	1	(b, d)	2	(a, d)	3	(a, b, d)	4	(a, b, c)	5	(a, c)	6	(a, b)	7	(c)
Key	8	(b, d)	9	(a, b, c)	10	(a, b, d)	11	(a, b, d)	12	(a, b, d)	13	(a, b, d)		

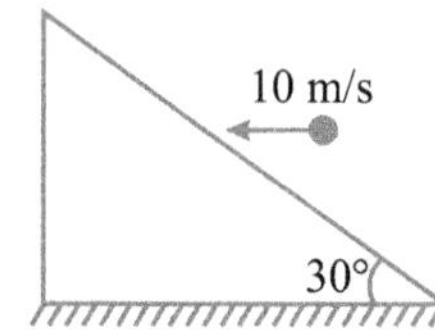

(a) Speed of ball after collision is 6 m/s
(b) Speed of ball after collision is 8 m/s
(c) Impulse between ball and wedge during collision is 16 N-s
(d) Impulse between ball and wedge during collision is 32 N-s

15. A block of mass m moving with a velocity v_0 collides with a stationary block of mass M at the back of which a spring of spring constant k is attached, as shown in the figure. Select the correct alternatives(s)

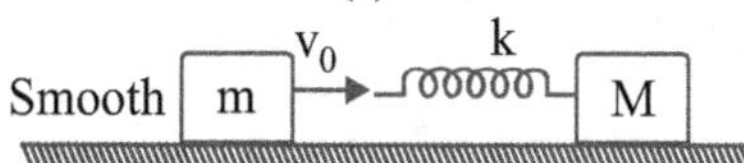

(a) The velocity of centre of mass is $\left(\dfrac{m}{m+M}\right)v_0$

(b) The initial kinetic energy of the system in the centre of mass frame is $\dfrac{1}{4}\left(\dfrac{mM}{M+m}\right)v_0^2$

(c) The maximum compression in the spring is $v_0\sqrt{\dfrac{mM}{(M+m)}\dfrac{1}{k}}$

(d) When the spring is in the state of maximum compression the kinetic energy in the centre of mass frame is zero.

16. A block of mass 1 kg is pushed towards another block of mass 2 kg from 6 m distance as shown in figure. Just after collision velocity of 2 kg block becomes 4 m/s.

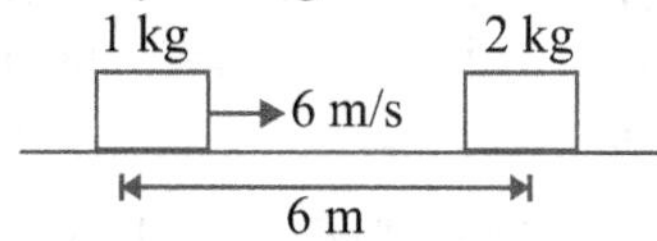

(a) coefficient of restitution between two blocks is 1
(b) coefficient of restitution between two blocks is 1/2
(c) velocity of centre of mass after 2 s is 2 m/s
(d) velocity of centre of mass after 2 s is 1 m/s

17. A block of mass m slides down an inclined wedge of same mass m shown in figure. Friction is absent everywhere.

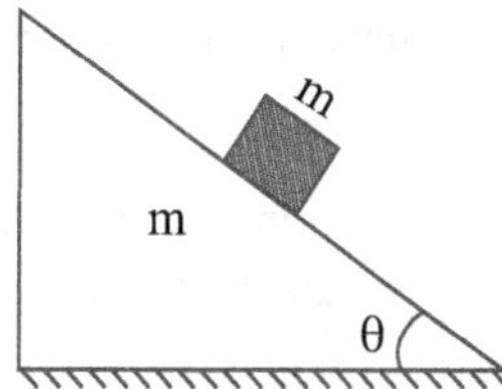

(a) The acceleration of block vertically downwards is $\dfrac{g\cos^2\theta}{(1+\sin^2\theta)}$

(b) The acceleration of centre of mass is $\dfrac{g\sin^2\theta}{(1+\sin^2\theta)}$

(c) The acceleration of centre of mass is $\dfrac{g\cos\theta}{1+\sin^2\theta}$

(d) The acceleration of block vertically downwards is $\dfrac{2g\sin^2\theta}{(1+\sin^2\theta)}$

18. A smooth sphere of mass m is moving on a horizontal plane with a velocity $(3\hat{i}+\hat{j})$, when it collides with a vertical wall which is parallel to the vector $\hat{j}$. If the coefficient of restitution between the sphere and the wall is $\dfrac{1}{2}$, then

(a) velocity of the sphere after impact $\dfrac{-3}{2}\hat{i}+\hat{j}$

(b) the loss in kinetic energy caused by the impact $\dfrac{27m}{8}\hat{j}$

(c) the impulse $\vec{j}$ that acts on the sphere $= -m\hat{i}$

(d) none of these.

Answer Key	14	(a, d)	15	(a, c, d)	16	(a, c)	17	(b, d)	18	(a, b, c)

Mechanics **Reasoning Type Questions** Exercise 8.3

Read the two statements carefully to mark the correct option out of the options given below:

(a) **Statement - 1** is true, **Statement - 2** is true; **Statement - 2** is correct explanation for **Statement - 1**.

(b) **Statement -1** is true, **Statement - 2** is true; **Statement - 2** is not correct explanation for **Statement - 1**.

(c) **Statement - 1** is true, **Statement - 2** is false.

(d) **Statement - 1** is false, **Statement - 2** is true

1. **Statement - 1**

In an elastic collision between two bodies, the relative speed of the bodies after collision is equal to the relative speed before the collision. **because**

Statement - 2

In an elastic collision the linear momentum of the system is conserved.

2. Statement - 1

If there is no external torque on a body about its centre of mass, then the velocity of the centre of mass remains constant. **because**

Statement - 2

The linear momentum of isolated system remains constant.

3. Statement - 1

In case of bullet fired from gun, the ratio of kinetic energy of gun and bullet is equal to ratio of mass of bullet and gun

Statement - 2

In firing total momentum of system remain conserved.

4. A particle of mass m strikes a wedge of mass M horizontally as shown in the figure.

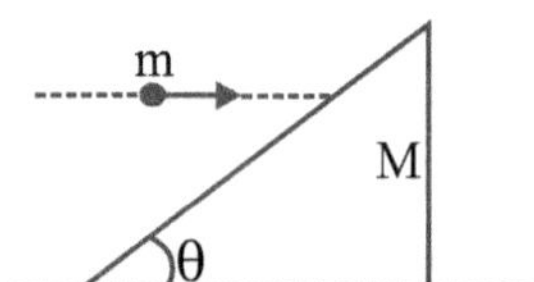

Statement - 1 : If collision is perfectly inelastic then, it can be concluded that the particle sticks to the wedge.

Statement - 2: In perfectly inelastic collision velocity of both bodies is same along common normal just after collision.

5. Statement - 1 : In an elastic collision of two billiard balls, the total kinetic energy is conserved during the short time of collision of the balls (i.e., when they are in contact).

Statement - 2 : Energy spent against friction follows the law of conservation of energy.

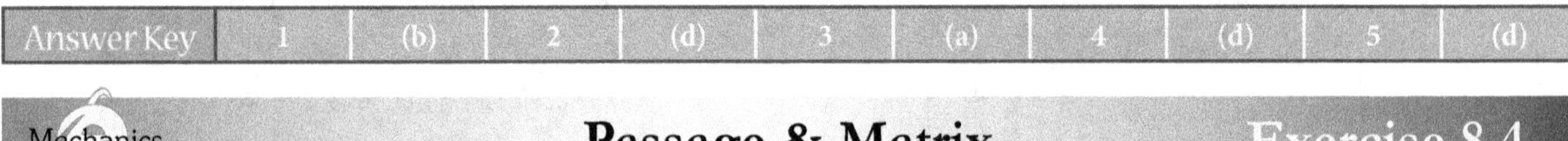

Answer Key	1	(b)	2	(d)	3	(a)	4	(d)	5	(d)

Mechanics   **Passage & Matrix**   **Exercise 8.4**

PASSAGES

Passage for (Questions 1 & 2) :
A jet of liquid of cross - sectional area A and density ρ moves with speed v in the positive x-direction and impinges against a perfectly smooth blade B, which deflects the stream at right angle but does not slow it down, as shown in figure. The blade moves to the right with a speed v_B.

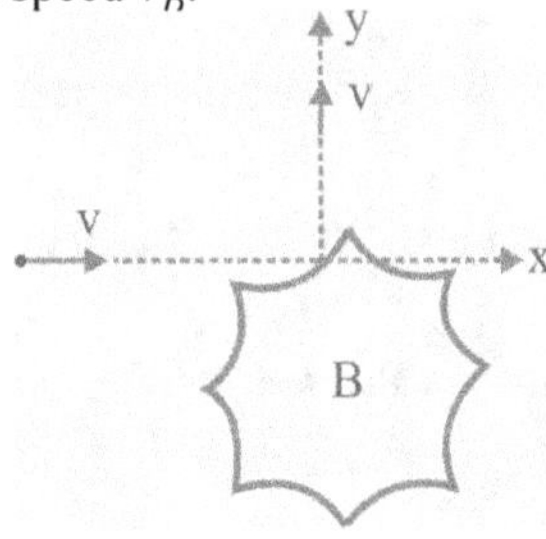

1. The force exerted by the jet, F_x on the blade is :

(a) $\rho A (v - v_B)$ (b) $\rho A (v - v_B)^2$

(c) $\rho A v_B (v - v_B)$ (d) $\rho A v^2$

2. The power delivered on the blade :

(a) $\rho A (v - v_B)^2$ (b) $\rho A v_B^2 (v - v_B)$

(c) $\rho A v_B (v - v_B)^2$ (d) $\rho A v^2 v_B$

Passage for (Questions 3 & 4) :
Block A in figure has a mass of 1 kg, and block B has a mass of 2 kg. The blocks are forced together, compressing a spring S between them, and the system is released from rest on a level frictionless surface. The spring is not fastened to either block and drops to the surface after it has expended. Block B acquires a speed of 0.5 m/s.

3. The kinetic energy of the block A is :

(a) 0.5 J   (b) 1 J

(c) 2.0 J   (d) 2.5 J

4. The potential energy stored in the spring was :

(a) 0.5 J   (b) 0.75 J

(c) 1.0 J   (d) 2.5 J

Passage for (Question 5 to 7) :
A small block of mass M moves on a frictionless surface of an inclined plane as shown in figure. The angle of the incline suddenly changes from $60°$ to $30°$ at point B. The block is initially at rest at A. Assume that collision between the block and the incline are totally inelastic ($g = 10$ m/s^2).   **[IIT-JEE 2008]**

5. The speed of the block at B immediately after it strikes the second incline is

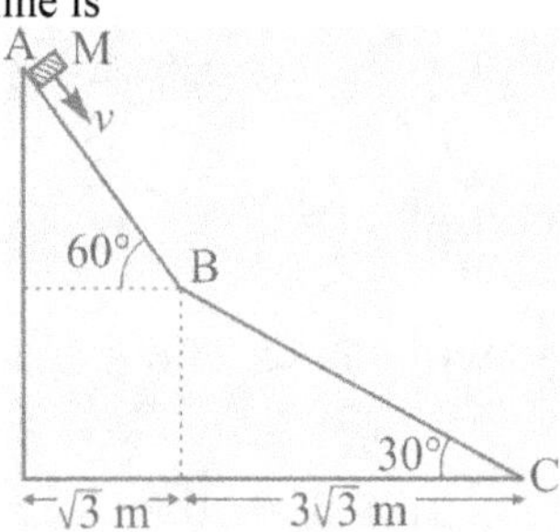

(a) $\sqrt{60}$ m/s   (b) $\sqrt{45}$ m/s

(c) $\sqrt{30}$ m/s   (d) $\sqrt{15}$ m/s

6. The speed of the block at point C immediately before it leaves the second incline is

(a) $\sqrt{120}$ m/s   (b) $\sqrt{105}$ m/s

(c) $\sqrt{90}$ m/s   (d) $\sqrt{75}$ m/s

7. If collision between the block and the incline is completely elastic then the vertical (upward) component of the velocity of the block at point B, immediately after it strikes the second incline is
   (a) $\sqrt{30}$ m/s
   (b) $\sqrt{15}$ m/s
   (c) 0
   (d) $-\sqrt{15}$ m/s

Passage for (Questions 8 & 9) :
A ball is dropped on an inclined plane and is observed to move horizontally after the impact. The coefficient of restitution between plane and ball is e.

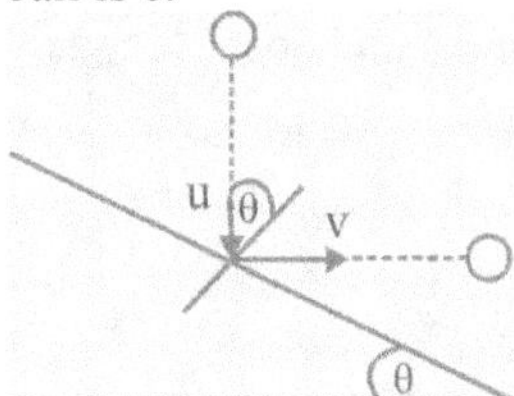

8. The inclination θ is :
   (a) 45^0
   (b) $\tan^{-1} e$
   (c) $\tan^{-1} \sqrt{e}$
   (d) $\tan^{-1} \dfrac{e}{2}$

9. The velocity of ball after impact is :
   (a) $v = u/2$
   (b) $v = e\,u$
   (c) $v = u\sqrt{e}$
   (d) $v = e^2 u$

Passage for (Questions 13 - 15) :
A sphere projected from a given point 0 with given velocity u at an inclination α to horizontal. After hitting a smooth vertical wall at a distance d form 0, returns to 0. The coefficient of restitution between sphere and wall is e.

10. The time of journey of sphere is

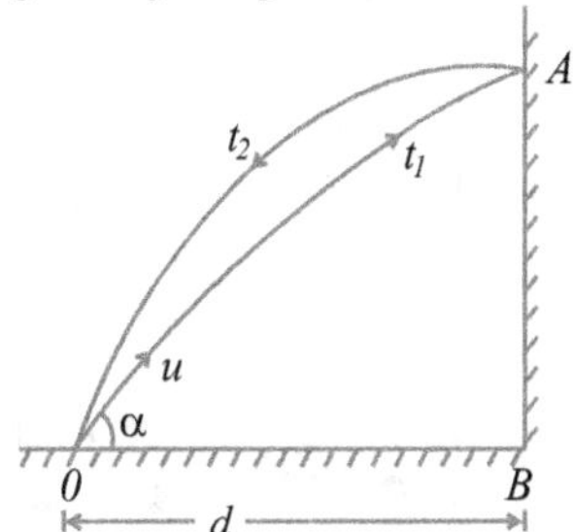

   (a) $u \sin \alpha /g$
   (b) $2u \cos \alpha/g$
   (c) $2u \cos \alpha/g$
   (d) $\dfrac{u \tan \alpha}{2g}$

11. The horizontal distance d from the wall is
   (a) $\dfrac{u^2 \sin 2\alpha}{g}$
   (b) $\dfrac{u^2 \cos 2d}{g} = \dfrac{(1+e)}{e}$
   (c) $\dfrac{u^2 \sin 2\alpha}{g} = \dfrac{(1+e)}{e}$
   (d) none of these

12. If the line joining the point of projection and the point of impact makes an angle θ with the horizontal, then tan θ is
   (a) $e \tan \alpha$
   (b) $\dfrac{\tan \alpha}{(1+e)}$
   (c) $(1 + e) \cot \alpha$
   (d) $\dfrac{\tan \alpha}{(1+e)}$

Passage for (Questions 13 to 15) :
Block A(1 kg) is placed on smooth horizontal surface and connected with a block B (2 kg), as shown in the figure, by an inextensible string. A bullet of mass 250 gm, strikes the block A horizontally with speed 200 m/s. The bullet penetrates through the block A and comes out with velocity 100 m/s.

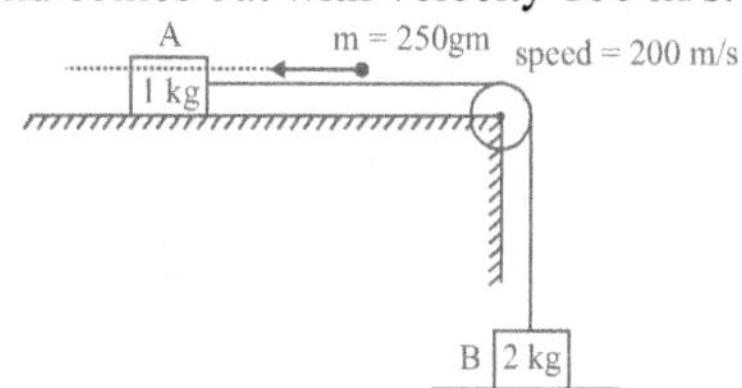

13. Velocity of 2 kg block just after bullet comes out of block A
   (a) 8 m/s
   (b) $\dfrac{15}{3} m/s$
   (c) $\dfrac{25}{3} m/s$
   (d) $\dfrac{25}{7} m/s$

14. Impulse produced by string on block B
   (a) 50 N-s
   (b) 25 N-s
   (c) $\dfrac{50}{3} N-s$
   (d) $\dfrac{50}{4} N-s$

15. Maximum displacement of block A in left direction is approximately $(g = 10m/s^2)$
   (a) 2.2 m
   (b) 3.2 m
   (c) 4.2 m
   (d) 5.2 m

16.

Column I	Column II
A. Collision of two light nuclei to form a heavier nucleus	(p) Elastic collision
B. Speeding bullet getting embedded in a wooden plank	(q) Perfectly inelastic collision
C. Collision of neutron with heavy unstable nucleus	(r) Nuclear fission
D. Collision in which there is no loss of external kinetic	(s) Nuclear fusion.

Answer Key	1	(b)	2	(c)	3	(a)	4	(b)	5	(b)	6	(b)	7	(c)
	8	(c)	9	(c)	10	(b)	11	(c)	12	(d)	13	(c)	14	(c)
	15	(d)	16	A→q, s; B→q; C→r; D→p, r, s									

17. A particle of mass m, kinetic energy K and momentum p collides head on elastically with another particle of mass 2 m at rest. Match the following (after collision):

Column I		Column II
A.	Momentum of first particle	(p) $\dfrac{4}{3}p$
B.	Momentum of second particle	(q) K/9
C.	Kinetic energy of first particle	(r) $-p/3$
D.	Kinetic energy of second particle	(s) 8K/9

18. A body initially moving towards the right explodes into two pieces 1 and 2. The magnitudes of v_1 and v_2 (the final velocities) are completely arbitrary. Directions of motion of the pieces are shown in Column I and possible mass ratios are shown in Column II.

Column I	Column II

A. 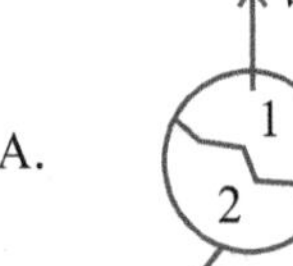

(p) $m_1 > m_2$

B.

(q) $m_1 = m_2$

C. 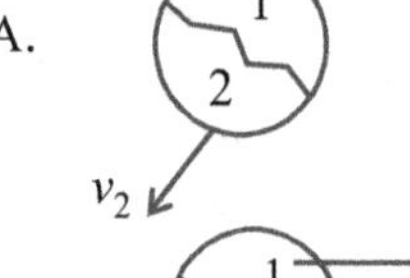

(r) $m_1 < m_2$

D.

(s) impossible for any masses

JEE- (Main)

1. A mass m moves with a velocity v and collides inelastically with another identical mass. After collision the Ist mass moves with velocity $\dfrac{v}{\sqrt{3}}$ in a direction perpendicular to the initial direction of motion. Find the speed of the 2nd mass after collision: **[AIEEE 2005]**

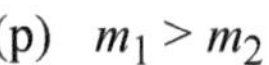

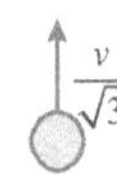

(a) $\dfrac{2}{\sqrt{3}}v$ (b) $\dfrac{v}{\sqrt{3}}$

(c) v (d) $\sqrt{3}v$

2. A thin rod of length 'L' is lying along the x-axis with its ends at $x = 0$ and $x = L$. Its linear density (mass/length) varies with x as $k\left(\dfrac{x}{L}\right)^n$; where n can be zero or any positive number. If the position x_{cm} of the centre of mass of the rod is plotted against 'n', which of the following graphs best approximates the dependence of x_{cm} on n   **[AIEEE 2008]**

(a) 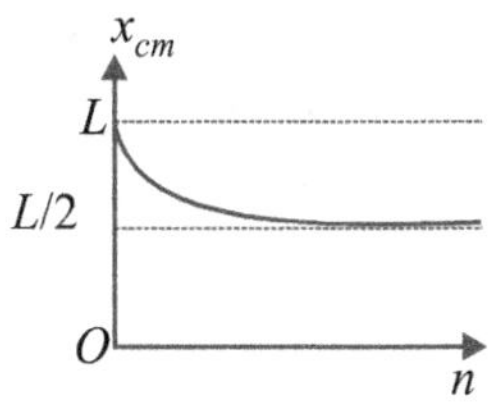

(b) 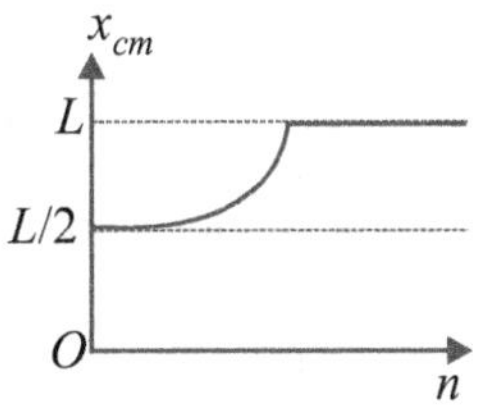

(c) 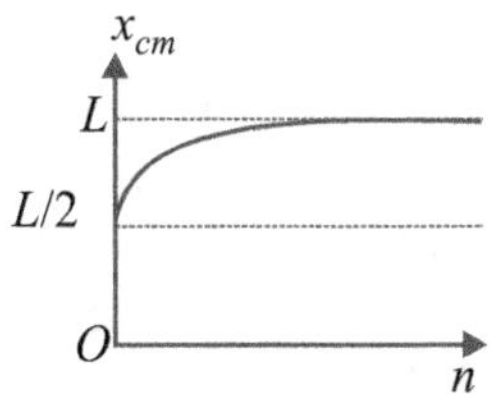

(d) 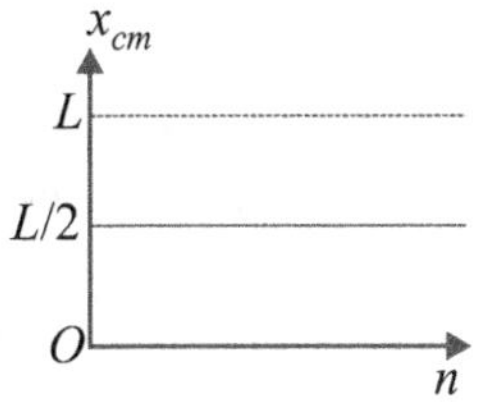

3. **Statement 1 :** Two particles moving in the same direction do not lose all their energy in a completely inelastic collision.
Statement 2 : Principle of conservation of momentum holds true for all kinds of collisions. **[AIEEE 2010]**

(a) Statement -1 is true, Statement -2 is true ; Statement -2 is the correct explanation of Statement -1.

(b) Statement -1 is true, Statement -2 is true; Statement -2 is not the correct explanation of Statement -1

(c) Statement -1 is false, Statement -2 is true.

(d) Statement -1 is true, Statement -2 is false.

JEE- (Advanced)

4. Two balls, having linear momenta $\vec{\mathbf{P}}_1 = P\hat{\mathbf{i}}$ and $\vec{\mathbf{P}}_2 = -P\hat{\mathbf{i}}$, undergo a collision in free space. There is no external force acting on the balls. Let $\vec{\mathbf{P}}_1{}'$ and $\vec{\mathbf{P}}_2{}'$ be their final momenta. The following option (s) is (are) not allowed for any non-zero value of P, a_1, a_2, b_1, b_2, c_1 and c_2. **[IIT-JEE 2008]**

(a) $\vec{\mathbf{P}}_1{}' = a_1\hat{\mathbf{i}} + b_1\hat{\mathbf{j}} + c_1\hat{\mathbf{k}};\ \vec{\mathbf{P}}_2{}' = a_2\hat{\mathbf{i}} + b_2\hat{\mathbf{j}}$

(b) $\vec{\mathbf{P}}_1{}' = c_1\hat{\mathbf{k}};\ \vec{\mathbf{P}}_2{}' = c_2\hat{\mathbf{k}}$

(c) $\vec{\mathbf{P}}_1{}' = a_1\hat{\mathbf{i}} + b_1\hat{\mathbf{j}} + c_1\hat{\mathbf{k}};\ P_2{}' = a_2\hat{\mathbf{i}} + b_2\hat{\mathbf{j}} - c_1\hat{\mathbf{k}}$

(d) $\vec{\mathbf{P}}_1{}' = a_1\hat{\mathbf{i}} + b_1\hat{\mathbf{j}};\ \vec{\mathbf{P}}_2{}' = a_2\hat{\mathbf{i}} + b_1\hat{\mathbf{j}}.$

5. Two small particles of equal masses start moving in opposite directions from a point A in a horizontal circular orbit. Their tangential velocities are v and $2v$, respectively, as shown in the figure. Between collisions, the particles move with constant speeds. After making how many elastic collisions, other than that at A, these two particles will again reach the point A. **[IIT-JEE 2009]**

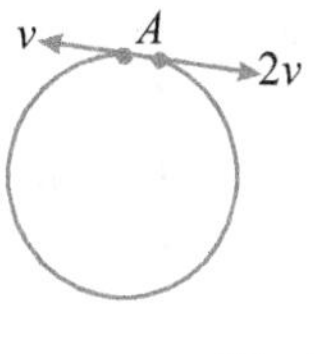

(a) 4 (b) 3
(c) 2 (d) 1

6. Look at the drawing given in the figure which has been drawn with ink of uniform line-thickness. The mass of ink used to draw each of the two inner circles, and each of the two line segments is m. The mass of the ink used to draw the outer circle is 6 m. The coordinates of the centres of the different parts are: outer circle (0, 0), left inner circle (–a, a), right inner circle (a, a) vertical line (0, 0) and horizontal line (0, –a). The y-coordinate of the centre of mass of the ink in this drawing is **[IIT-JEE 2009]**

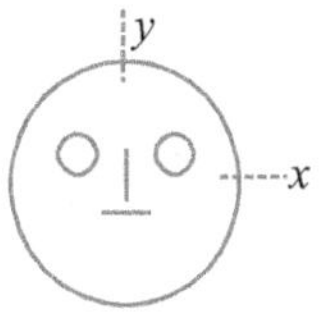

(a) $\frac{a}{10}$ (b) $\frac{a}{8}$
(c) $\frac{a}{12}$ (d) $\frac{a}{3}$

7. A ball of mass 0.2 kg rests on a vertical post of height 5 m. A bullet of mass 0.01 kg, traveling with a velocity V m/s in a horizontal direction, hits the centre of the ball. After the collision, the ball and bullet travel independently. The ball hits the ground at a distance of 20 m and the bullet at a distance of 100 m from the foot of the post. The velocity V of the bullet is **(IIT-JEE 2011)**

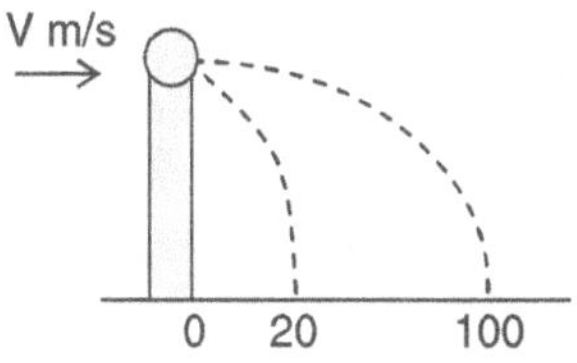

(a) 250 m/s (b) $250\sqrt{2}$ m/s
(c) 400 m/s (d) 500 m/s

8. A particle of mass m is projected from the ground with an initial speed u_0 at an angle α with the horizontal. At the highest point of its trajectory, it makes a completely inelastic

Answer Key	1	(a)	2	(c)	3	(a)	4.	(a, d)	5	(c)
	6	(a)	7	(d)						

collision with another identical particle, which was thrown vertically upward from the ground with the same initial speed u_0. The angle that the composite system makes with the horizontal immediately after the collision is

(JEE Adv. 2013)

(a) $\dfrac{\pi}{4}$　　　　(b) $\dfrac{\pi}{4}+\alpha$

(c) $\dfrac{\pi}{2}-\alpha$　　　(d) $\dfrac{\pi}{2}$

9. This question has statement I and statement II. of the four choices given after the statements, choose the one that best describes the two statements. **[JEE-Adv 2013]**

Statement I : A point particle of mass m moving with speed v collides with stationary point particle of mass M. If the maximum energy loss possible is given as $f\left(\dfrac{1}{2}mv^2\right)$ then

$$f=\left(\dfrac{m}{M+m}\right).$$

Statement II : Maximum energy loss occurs when the particles get stuck together as a result of the collision.

(a) Statement I is true, Statment II is true, Statement - II is the correct explanation of Statement - I.

(b) Statement I is true, Statment II is true, Statement - II is not the correct explanation of Statement - II.

(c) Statement I is true, Statment II is false.

(d) Statement I is false, Statment II is true.

Hints & Solutions

In Chapter Exercise -8.1

1. See examples

2. The average force exerted, $F = mg = 1 \times 10 = 10$ N

   Given $\qquad 10 = 5x$

   $\therefore \qquad x = 2.$

3. $1 \times 200 + 0 = 1 \times 100 + 5v_2$

   $\therefore \quad v_2 = 20$ m/s

   If h is the height attained, then

   $$h = \frac{v_2^2}{2g} = \frac{20^2}{1 \times 10} = 20\,\text{m}$$

   so $\qquad 10x = 20, \therefore x = 2$

4. The velocity of the sphere just before impact with the block

   $$u = \sqrt{2g \times 1.2} = 4.85 \text{ m/s}$$

   If v_1 and v_2 are the velocities of ball and the block after impact, then

   $$1 \times u = 1 \times v_1 + 5v_2$$

   or $\qquad u = v_1 + 5v_2 \qquad \text{...(i)}$

   and $\qquad e = -\left[\dfrac{v_1 - v_2}{u_1 - u_2}\right]$

   or $\qquad 0.70 = -\left[\dfrac{v_1 - v_2}{u - 0}\right]$

   or $\qquad 0.7\,u = -v_1 + v_2 \qquad \text{...(ii)}$

   From equations (i) and (ii), we get

   $$v_2 = \frac{1.7u}{6} = \frac{1.7 \times 4.85}{6} = 1.37 \text{ m/s}$$

   The retardation of the block,

   $$a = \mu g = 0.3 \times 9.8$$
   $$= 2.94 \text{ m/s}^2$$

   If x is the distance travelled by the block, then

   $$0 = v_2^2 - 2ax$$

   $\therefore \qquad x = \dfrac{1.37^2}{2 \times 2.94} = 0.32$ m   **Ans.**

5. By conservation of momentum, we have

   $$m_1\vec{v}_1 + m_2\vec{v}_2 = (m_1 + m_2)\vec{v}$$

   $\therefore \qquad \vec{v} = \left[\dfrac{m_1\vec{v}_1 + m_1\vec{v}_2}{m_1 + m_2}\right]$

   $$= \frac{1 \times (3.0\hat{i} - 2.0\hat{j}) + 2(4.0\hat{j} - 6.0\hat{k})}{1 + 2}$$

   $$= (\hat{i} + 2.0\hat{j} - 4.0\hat{k}) \text{ m/s.} \quad \textbf{\textit{Ans.}}$$

6. (a) The situation is shown in figure.

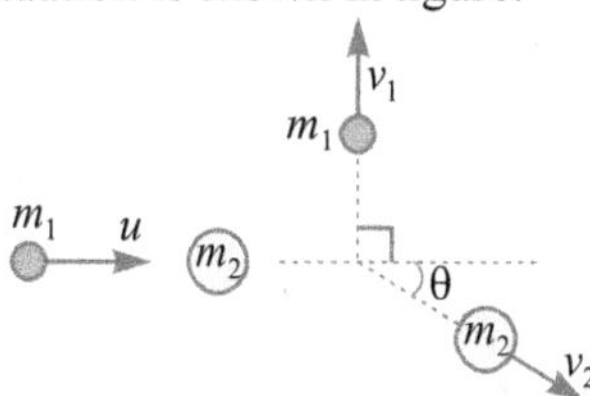

   By conservation of momentum, we have

   $$m_1 u = m_2 v_2 \cos\theta \qquad \text{...(i)}$$

   and $\qquad m_1 v_1 = m_2 v_2 \sin\theta \qquad \text{...(ii)}$

   Fractional loss in $K.E.$ of the striking particle

   $$\eta = \frac{K_i - K_f}{K_i} = \frac{\frac{1}{2}m_1 u^2 - \frac{1}{2}m_1 v_1^2}{\frac{1}{2}m_1 u^2}$$

   $$= \frac{u^2 - v_1^2}{u^2} \qquad \text{...(iii)}$$

   After solving above equations, we get

   $$\eta = \left[\frac{2m_1}{m_1 + m_2}\right] \qquad \textbf{\textit{Ans.}}$$

   (b) $\qquad m_1 u = m_1 v_1 + m_2 v_2$

   and $\qquad \dfrac{1}{2}m_1 u^2 = \dfrac{1}{2}m_1 v_1^2 + \dfrac{1}{2}m_2 v_2^2$

   $$\eta = \frac{K_i - K_f}{K_i} = \frac{u^2 - v_1^2}{u^2}$$

   After solving, we get $\eta = \dfrac{4m_1 m_2}{(m_1 + m_2)^2} \qquad \textbf{\textit{Ans.}}$

7. If u and v are the velocities of ball before and after collision, then

   $$mu = (m + M)v$$

   $\therefore \qquad v = \left[\dfrac{mu}{m + M}\right]$

   The energy stored in the spring

   $$\Delta K = \frac{1}{2}mu^2 - \frac{1}{2}(M + m)v^2$$

   $$= \frac{1}{2}mu^2 - \frac{1}{2}(M + m)\left[\frac{mu}{m + M}\right]^2$$

   $$= \frac{M\left(\frac{1}{2}mu^2\right)}{(m + M)}$$

The fraction $f = \dfrac{\Delta K}{K} = \dfrac{M\left(\frac{1}{2}mu^2\right)}{(m+M)\left(\frac{1}{2}mu^2\right)} = \left[\dfrac{M}{m+M}\right]$ ***Ans.***

8.   If v is the speeds of the blocks at the instant of maximum compression, then

$$m_1u_1 + m_2u_2 = (m_1 + m_2)v$$

and $\dfrac{1}{2}m_1u_1^2 + \dfrac{1}{2}m_2u_2^2 = \dfrac{1}{2}(m_1 + m_2)v^2 + \dfrac{1}{2}kx_{max}^2$

After substituting the given values and simplifying, we get

$$x_{max} = 0.25 \text{ m} \qquad \textbf{\textit{Ans.}}$$

In Chapter Exercise -8.2

1.   The velocity of the body after slide from height h, $v_0 = \sqrt{2gh}$. Its component along horizontal direction will be $v_0 \cos\alpha$.

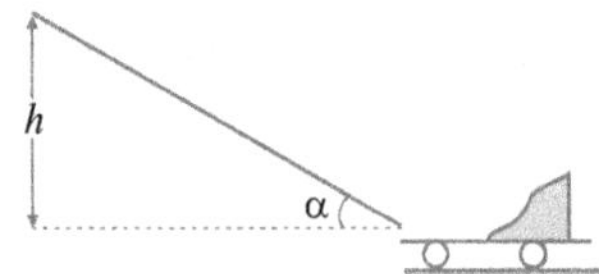

By conservation of momentum, we can write

$$P \times v_0 \cos\alpha = (P+Q)v$$

$$\therefore \qquad v = \dfrac{Pv_0 \cos\alpha}{(P+Q)} = \dfrac{P\sqrt{2gh}\,\cos\alpha}{(P+Q)} \qquad \textbf{\textit{Ans.}}$$

2.   (a) After falling from height h, the velocity of the ball will be

$$u = \sqrt{2gh}$$

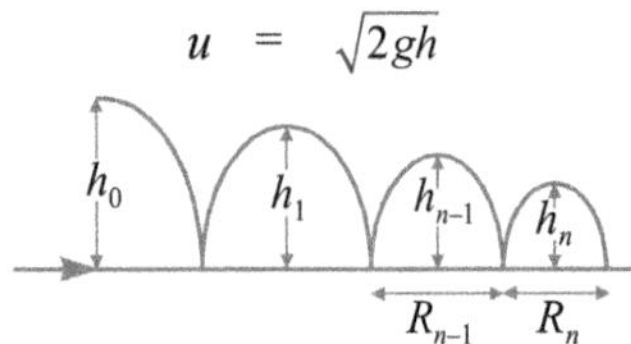

Before collision, $h = h_{n-1}, u_1 = \sqrt{2gh_{n-1}}$

After collision, $h = h_n, v_1 = -\sqrt{2gh_n}$

Thus $e = -\left[\dfrac{v_1 - v_2}{u_1 - u_2}\right]$

$$= -\left[\dfrac{-\sqrt{2gh_n} - 0}{\sqrt{2gh_{n-1}} - 0}\right] = \sqrt{\dfrac{h_n}{h_{n-1}}} \quad \textbf{\textit{Ans.}}$$

(b) We have $R = \dfrac{2u_x u_y}{g}$

$$\therefore \qquad u_y = \dfrac{Rg}{2u_x} \qquad [\,u_x \text{ constant}]$$

Before collision, $u_1 = \dfrac{R_{n-1}g}{2u_x}$

After collision, $v_1 = \dfrac{-R_n g}{2u_x}$

$$e = -\left[\dfrac{v_1 - v_2}{(u_1 - u_2)}\right]$$

$$= -\left[\dfrac{-R_n g/2u_x - 0}{-R_{n-1}g/2u_x - 0}\right]$$

$$= \dfrac{R_n}{R_{n-1}} \qquad \textbf{\textit{Ans.}}$$

For n^{th} bounce, the time of flight

$$T_n = 2t_n = 2\sqrt{\dfrac{2h_n}{g}}$$

3.   The situation is shown in figure.

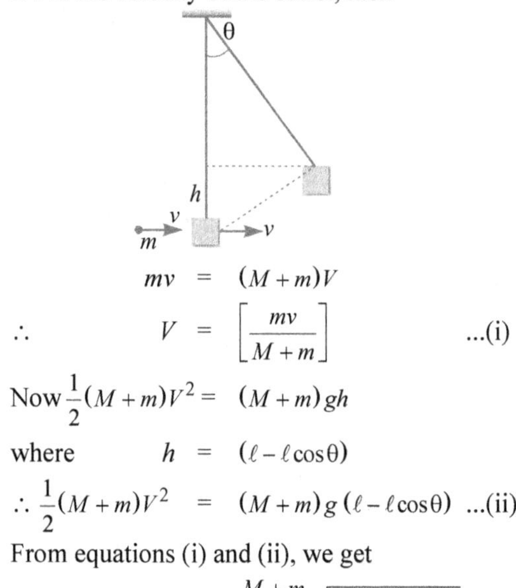

By conservation of momentum, we have

$$mv = Mv_2 \cos\theta \qquad \text{...(i)}$$

$$mv_1 = Mv_2 \sin\theta \qquad \text{...(ii)}$$

Percentage change in *K.E.*

$$\dfrac{\Delta K}{K} \times 100 = \dfrac{\left(\frac{1}{2}mv_1^2 + \frac{1}{2}Mv_2^2\right) - \frac{1}{2}mv^2}{\frac{1}{2}mv^2} \times 100$$

After solving above equations, we get

$$\dfrac{\Delta K}{K} \times 100 = -40\,\% \qquad \textbf{\textit{Ans.}}$$

4.   (a) If v is the velocity of the bullet, then

$$mv = (M+m)V$$

$$\therefore \qquad V = \left[\dfrac{mv}{M+m}\right] \qquad \text{...(i)}$$

Now $\dfrac{1}{2}(M+m)V^2 = (M+m)gh$

where $h = (\ell - \ell\cos\theta)$

$$\therefore \dfrac{1}{2}(M+m)V^2 = (M+m)g\,(\ell - \ell\cos\theta) \;\text{...(ii)}$$

From equations (i) and (ii), we get

$$V = \dfrac{M+m}{m}\sqrt{2g\ell(1-\cos\theta)}$$

$$= \dfrac{M+m}{m} \times \sqrt{2g\ell \times 2\sin^2\dfrac{\theta}{2}}$$

As $m << M$, $\therefore$ $M + m \simeq M$

and $v \simeq \dfrac{2M}{m}\sqrt{g\ell}\,\sin\dfrac{\theta}{2} \qquad \textbf{\textit{Ans.}}$

(b) $\dfrac{\Delta K}{K} = \left(\dfrac{\frac{1}{2}(M+m)V^2 - \frac{1}{2}mv^2}{\frac{1}{2}mv^2}\right)$

$$\simeq 1 - \dfrac{m}{M}$$

In Chapter Exercise -8.3

1. The velocity of B just after collision with A is

$$v_B = \frac{(m_B - m_A)u_B}{m_B + m_A} + \frac{2m_A u_A}{m_A + m_B}$$

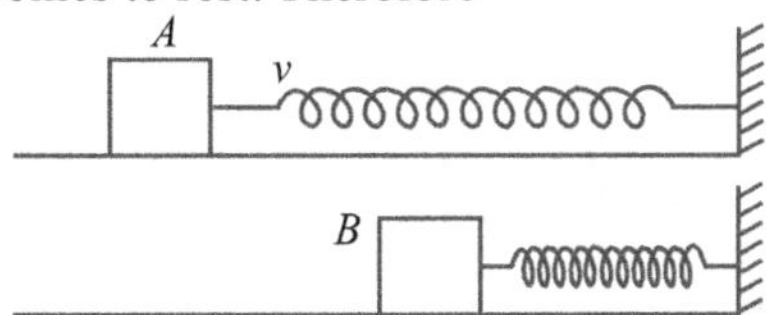

$$= \frac{0 + 2m \times 9}{m + 2m} = 6\,\text{m/s}$$

The collision between B and C is completely inelastic.

$\therefore \quad m_B v_B = (m_B + m_c) v$

$\therefore \quad v = \frac{6 \times 2m}{2m + m} = 4\,\text{m/s}.$

2. Let v be the speed of the block just after impulse. At B, the block comes to rest. Therefore

Loss in K.E. of the block = Gain in P.E. of the spring
$\qquad\qquad\qquad\qquad\qquad$ + Work done against friction

$$\frac{1}{2}mv^2 = \frac{1}{2}kx^2 + \mu mg.x$$

$$\therefore\ v = \sqrt{\frac{k}{m}x^2 + \mu gx}\ .$$

$$\therefore\ v = \sqrt{\frac{2}{0.18} \times 0.06 \times 0.06 + 0.1 \times 10 \times 0.06}$$

$$\therefore\ v = \frac{4}{10}$$

$$\therefore\ \text{N} = 4$$

3. Here Δ K.E. = W = P $\times$ t

$$\therefore \frac{1}{2}mv^2 = P \times t$$

$$\therefore v = \sqrt{\frac{2Pt}{m}} = \sqrt{\frac{2 \times 0.5 \times 5}{0.2}} = 5\,ms^{-1}$$

4. Velocity at the highest point of bob tied to string ℓ_1 is acquired by the bob tied to string ℓ_2 due to elastic head-on collision of equal masses

$$\text{Therefore}\ \sqrt{g\ell_1} = \sqrt{5g\ell_2}$$

$$\therefore \frac{\ell_1}{\ell_2} = 5$$

In Chapter Exercise -8.4

1. $60(\Delta x_1) - 40(6 - \Delta x_1) = 0$

$$\therefore \qquad\qquad \Delta x_1 = 2.4\ \text{m}$$

The distance moved by 40 kg skater = 6 – 2.4 = 3.6 m
Given $\quad 3.6 = 4.8\ x,\ \therefore x = 2$

2. $10 \times (3 - \Delta x) + 20(-\Delta x) = 0$

$$\therefore \qquad\qquad \Delta x = 1\ \text{m}$$

The distance moved by him towards, shore is 3– 1 = 2 m.
So his distance from shore = 5 – 2 = 3 m. Given 3 = 3x,
$\therefore x = 1.$

3. $40(1 + v) + 80 \times v = 0$

$$\therefore \qquad\qquad v = -\frac{1}{3}$$

$$\therefore \qquad\qquad x = 3$$

4. As there is no external force is acting in horizontal direction, so there is no shift in position of CM in this direction. If Δx_1 and Δx_2 are the displacements of bob and cart respectively, then

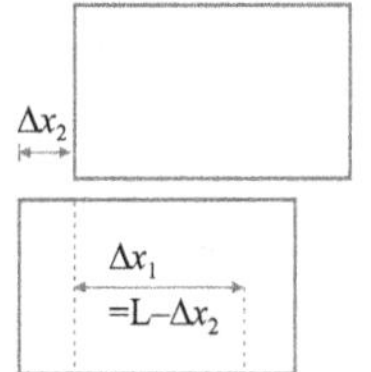

$$m\Delta \vec{x}_1 + M\Delta \vec{x}_2 = 0$$

$\text{Here} \qquad \Delta x_1 = (L - \Delta x_2)$

$\therefore\quad m(L - \Delta x_2) + M(-\Delta x_2) = 0$

$\text{or} \qquad\qquad \Delta x_2 = \frac{mL}{m + M}.$ $\qquad$ ***Ans.***

5. The area of the element, $dA = (2\pi r dr)$

This behaves like a wire of radius r, whose centre of mass is at a height of $\frac{2r}{\pi}$ from base.

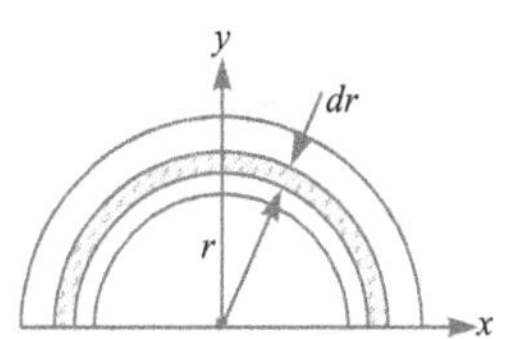

Mass of the element, $\quad dm = \dfrac{m}{\pi(R_2{}^2 - R_1{}^2)} \times (2\pi r dr)$

Now $\qquad\qquad y_{cm} = \dfrac{1}{m}\int\limits_{R_1}^{R_2} dmy = \dfrac{1}{m}\int\limits_{R_1}^{R_2}(dm)\left(\dfrac{2r}{\pi}\right)$

After substituting the values and simplifying, we get

$$y_{cm} = \frac{4\left(R_1{}^2 + R_1 R_2 + R_2{}^2\right)}{3\pi(R_1 + R_2)}.$$

6. The velocities of bullet and plates are shown in figure. If u is the initial velocity of the bullet, then

$$mu + 0 = M_1 v_1 + mv \qquad \text{...(i)}$$

$$\text{and} \qquad mv = (m + M_2)v_1 \qquad \text{...(ii)}$$

After solving, above equations, we get

$$v = \frac{u(m + M_2)}{(m + M_1 + M_2)}$$

$$= \frac{u(0.02 + 2.98)}{(0.02 + 1 + 2.98)} = \frac{3u}{4}$$

$$\text{Percentage loss in velocity} = \left[\frac{u - v}{u}\right] \times 100$$

$$= \left[\frac{u - \dfrac{3u}{4}}{u}\right] \times 100 = 25\%\ \textit{Ans.}$$

1. (c) In an inelastic collision, some part of KE will convert into heat energy.

2. (a) $0 \le e \le 1$ and total energy of the system remains constant.

3. (d) If linear momentum of the system is zero, then KE of the system need not be zero. But if KE of the system is zero, then momentum of the system must be zero.

4. (b)

5. (c) Collision between ball 1 and first two balls is oblique collision, while between these and next two is head on collision, so option (iii) is the right.

6. (b) $$Mv + 0 = Mv_1 + mv_2$$

$$\frac{1}{2}Mv^2 + 0 = \frac{1}{2}Mv_1^2 + \frac{1}{2}mv_2^2$$

Simplifying for $m \ll M$, we get $v_z \simeq 2v$.

7. (c) $$0 = m\vec{v}_1 + m\vec{v}_2 + m\vec{v}_3$$

or $$0 = m(v\hat{i} + v\hat{j}) + m\vec{v}_3$$

$\therefore$ $$\vec{v}_3 = -v(\hat{i} + \hat{j}).$$

8. (d) For collision,

$$\vec{r}_1 + \vec{v}_1 t = \vec{r}_2 + \vec{v}_2 t$$

or $(3\hat{i} + 5\hat{j}) + (4\hat{i} + 3\hat{j}) \times 2 = (-5\hat{i} - 3\hat{j}) + (a\hat{i} + 7\hat{j}) \times 2$

$\therefore$ $a = 8$

9. (d) $4v_1 + 8 \times 6 = 0$

$\therefore$ $v_1 = -12 \ m/s.$

Now $K_1 = \frac{1}{2} \times 4 \times (12)^2 = 288$ J.

10. (c) $$\vec{P} = \vec{P}_1 + \vec{P}_2$$

$\therefore$ $$\vec{P}_2 = \vec{P} - \vec{P}_1$$

or $$P_2 = \sqrt{P^2 + P_1^2} = \sqrt{12^2 + 5^2}$$

$$= 13 \text{ kgm/s}.$$

11. (d) $$F = \frac{\Delta P}{\Delta t} = \frac{0.15 \times 20}{0.1} = 30 \ N.$$

12. (c) $\vec{P}_1 + \vec{P}_2 + \vec{P}_3 = 0,$

and so $\vec{P}_3 = -(\vec{P}_1 + \vec{P}_2)$

or $(2m) v_3 = \sqrt{(mv)^2 + (mv)^2}$

$\therefore$ $v_3 = \dfrac{v}{\sqrt{2}}.$

Total energy released in the process

$$= \frac{1}{2}mv^2 + \frac{1}{2}mv^2 + \frac{1}{2}(2m)\left(\frac{v}{\sqrt{2}}\right)^2$$

$$= \frac{3}{2}mv^2.$$

13. (c) $0.2 \, v_1 + 4v_2 \ ...(i)$

$$\frac{1}{2} \times 0.2 \times v_1^2 + \frac{1}{2} \times 4 \times v_2^2 = 1050 \ ...(ii)$$

After simplifying, we get
$v_1 = 100$ m/s.

14. (d) $$K_0 = \frac{1}{2}mu^2$$

$$mu + 0 = mv_1 + mv_2$$

and $$k_0 + 0 = \frac{1}{2}mv_1^2 + \frac{1}{2}Mv_2^2$$

After simplifying above equations, we get

$$\frac{1}{2}Mv_2^2 = \frac{4mMk_0}{(M+m)^2}$$

15. (d) Given, $K = \frac{1}{2}mv^2$

If v' is the velocity of the balls during collision, then

$$mv + 0 = (m + nm)v'$$

$$v' = \left(\frac{v}{n+1}\right)$$

The maximum potential energy stored during collision

$$= \frac{1}{2}mv^2 - \frac{1}{2}(m + nm)v'^2$$

$$= \frac{1}{2}mv^2 - \frac{1}{2}(n+1)\frac{mv^2}{(n+1)^2}$$

$$= K - \frac{K}{n+1}$$

$$= \frac{nK}{n+1}$$

16. (c) The kinetic energy of the body at B

$$K = mgh = 10 \times 10 \times 10 = 1000 \text{ J}$$

Work done by friction on the body in moving from

$$B \text{ to } C = -f_r \times s$$

$$= -\mu \, mg \times s = -0.1 \times 10 \times 10 \times 10$$

$$= -100 \text{ J}$$

Thus the kinetic energy of the body at C

$$= 1000 - 100 = 900 \text{ J}$$

Let spring get compressed by x, then we have

$$\frac{1}{2}kx^2 = 900$$

or $\frac{1}{2}(2 \times 10^4) x^2 = 900$

or $x = 0.3$ m

17. (a) $$0 = 4v + (234) v_2$$

$\therefore$ $$v_2 = \frac{-4v}{234}.$$

18. (d) $\quad h^n = e^4 h.$

19. (a) $\quad m \times 6 + M \times 4 = mv_1 + Mv_2$

and $\dfrac{1}{2} m \times 6^2 + \dfrac{1}{2} M \times 4^2 = \dfrac{1}{2} mv_1^2 + \dfrac{1}{2} Mv_2^2$

After simplifying for, $m << M$, we get
$$v_1 = 2 \ m/s.$$

20. (a) $\quad h = 10 \ m,$

$\therefore \quad u_1 = \sqrt{2g \times 10}$

$h_1 = 0.8 \ h = 8 \ m,$

$\therefore \quad v_1 = \sqrt{2g \times 8}$

Now, $\quad e = -\left[\dfrac{v_2 - v_1}{u_2 - u_1}\right]$

$$= -\left[\dfrac{0 - (-\sqrt{2g \times 8})}{0 - \sqrt{2g \times 10}}\right] = 0.89$$

21. (c) $\quad \Delta P = 2mv \sin 60°$

$$F = \dfrac{\Delta P}{\Delta t} = \dfrac{2mv \times \sqrt{3}/2}{2 \times 10^{-3}}$$

$$= \dfrac{2 \times 0.1 \times 5 \times \sqrt{3}/2}{2 \times 10^{-3}}$$

$$= 250 \ \sqrt{3} \ N.$$

22. (c) $\quad 2m(v') = \sqrt{(mv)^2 + (mv)^2}$

$\therefore \quad v' = \dfrac{v}{\sqrt{2}}.$

23. (c) Loss in KE in inelastic collision is given by

$$\Delta K = \dfrac{1}{2}\left(\dfrac{m_1 m_2}{m_1 + m_2}\right)(u_1 - u_2)^2$$

$$= \dfrac{1}{2}\left(\dfrac{MM}{M + M}\right)(u_2 - u_1)^2$$

$$= \dfrac{M}{4}(u_2 - u_1)^2$$

24. (b) $\quad 3 \times 2 - 2 \times 3 = 3v_1 + 2v_2$

and $\quad \dfrac{2}{3} = -\dfrac{[v_2 - v_1]}{[3 - (-2)]}$

After simplifying, we get

$$v_1 = -4/3, \ v_2 = 2$$

25. (b) $\quad \vec{r}_{cm} = \dfrac{m_1 \vec{r_1} + m_2 \vec{r_2}}{m_1 + m_2}$

$$= \dfrac{1 \times (\hat{i} + 2\hat{j} + \hat{k}) + 3(-3\hat{i} - 2\hat{j} + \hat{k})}{1 + 3}$$

$$= -2\hat{i} - \hat{j} + \hat{k}.$$

26. (d) Coordinates of spheres are : $(0, 0)$, $(2R, 0)$ and $(R, \sqrt{3}R)$

$$X_{cm} = \dfrac{m \times 0 + m \times 2R + m \times R}{m + m + m} = R$$

and $\quad Y_{cm} = \dfrac{m \times 0 + m \times 0 + m\sqrt{3}R}{m + m + m} = \dfrac{R}{\sqrt{3}}.$

27. (a) $\quad X_{cm} = \dfrac{\displaystyle\int_0^L (dm)x}{\displaystyle\int_0^L (dm)} = \dfrac{\displaystyle\int_0^L (\lambda x dx)x}{\displaystyle\int_0^L (\lambda x dx)} = \dfrac{2L}{3}$

28. (c) $\quad v_{cm} = \dfrac{10 \times 14 + 4 \times 0}{10 + 4} = 10 \ m/s.$

29. (b)

$A_1 = L \times \dfrac{L}{2} = \dfrac{L^2}{2}$ and its centroid $\left(\dfrac{L}{2}, \dfrac{L}{4}\right)$

$A_2 = \dfrac{L}{2} \times \dfrac{L}{2} = \dfrac{L^2}{4}$, its centroid $\left(\dfrac{L}{4}, \dfrac{3L}{4}\right)$

$\therefore \quad \bar{x} = \dfrac{A_1 x_1 + A_2 x_2}{A_1 + A_2}$

$$= \dfrac{\dfrac{L^2}{2} \times \dfrac{L}{2} + \dfrac{L^2}{4} \times \dfrac{L}{4}}{\left(\dfrac{L^2}{2} + \dfrac{L^2}{4}\right)} = \dfrac{5L}{12}$$

Similarly $\bar{y} = \dfrac{5L}{12}$

30. (c) $\quad x_{cm} = \dfrac{M_2 \times 0 + M_1 L/2}{M_1 + M_2} = \dfrac{M_1 L}{2(M_1 + M_2)}$

31. (d) Mass of removed disc, $m' = \dfrac{m}{\pi r^2} \times \pi \left(\dfrac{r}{2}\right)^2 = \dfrac{m}{4}$

Thus, $x_{cm} = \dfrac{m \times 0 - \dfrac{m}{4}\left(\dfrac{r}{2}\right)}{\left(m - \dfrac{m}{4}\right)} = \dfrac{r}{6}$

32. (d) $\quad m_1 \Delta x_1 + m_2 \Delta x_2 = 0$

$\therefore \quad \Delta x_2 = -\dfrac{m_1 \Delta x_1}{m_2}$

$$= -\dfrac{m_1 d}{m_2}$$

33. (c)
$$y_{cm} = \frac{M \times \dfrac{L}{2} + 3M \times 0 + M \times \dfrac{L}{2}}{M + 3M + M} = \frac{L}{5}.$$

34. (a)
$$W = \Delta K$$

or
$$\int_a^0 F\,dx = \frac{1}{2} m(v_f^2 - 0)$$

$$\int_a^0 \frac{-k}{x^2}\,dx = \frac{1}{2} m v_f^2$$

$$\left| \frac{k}{x} \right|_a^0 = \frac{1}{2} m v_f^2$$

$$\therefore \qquad v_f = \sqrt{\frac{2k}{m}\left(\frac{a-x}{ax}\right)}.$$

35. (c) In isolated system, its total mass remains constant and so its velocity remains constant ($\vec{P}$ = const).

36. (c) Child is the internal part of the system, so velocity of centre of mass will not change due to his movement.

37. (a) Initially, $\quad v_{cm} = \dfrac{m_1 \times 0 + m_2 \times 0}{m_1 + m_2} = 0$

As no external force acts on the system, and so v_{cm} remains constant.

38. (d) $v = \dfrac{\sqrt{P_1^2 + P_2^2}}{m_1 + m_2} = \dfrac{\sqrt{(1 \times 1)^2 + (2 \times 2)^2}}{1 + 2} = 1.37\ m/s.$

39. (c)
$$a = \frac{(3m - m)g}{3m + m} = \frac{g}{2}$$

$$a_{cm} = \frac{3m \times g/2 + m(-g/2)}{3m + m} = \frac{g}{4}\ m/s^2$$

1. (c)
$$\frac{F_0\left(T + \dfrac{T}{2}\right)}{2} = m\,(0 - u)$$

$$\therefore \qquad F_0 = \frac{4mu}{3T}.$$

2. (b)
$$0 = \vec{P}_{gamma} + \vec{P}_{nucleus}$$

$$\therefore \quad \vec{P}_{nucleus} = \vec{P}_{gamma}$$

or $\quad P_{nucleus} = E/c$

$$\therefore \text{Energy released} = \frac{P_{nucleus}^2}{2M} + E$$

$$= \frac{E^2}{2Mc^2} + E$$

3. (a) The speed of the child $= -4 + v = 6$ m/s.
Now $220 \times 10 = 20 \times (-4 + v) + 200\,v$
$\therefore \qquad v = 10.4$ m/s.

4. (b) For the deflection of spring by x, the energy stored in the spring,

$$U = \int_0^x F\,dx$$

$$= \int_0^x 300 x^2\,dx = 300\,\frac{x^3}{3} = 100\,x^3$$

Thus by conservation of mechanical energy, we have

$$100\,x^3 = \frac{1}{2}\,mv^2$$

or $\quad 100\,x^3 = \dfrac{1}{2} \times 200 \times (1.0)^2$

or $\qquad x = 1$ m

The maximum restoring force acts on the car
$$F = 300\,x^2 = 300\,(1)^2 = 300\ N$$

$\therefore$ Deceleration of the car $= \dfrac{F}{m} = \dfrac{300}{200} = 1.5\ m/s^2$

5. (b) $J = m(v_f - v_i)_y = 1\,(25 \sin 45° + 20 \sin 30°)$
$$= 27.67\ \text{N-s}$$

6. (a) $\quad mu = mv \cos 30° + mv \cos 30°$

and $\quad e = -\left(\dfrac{0 - v}{u \cos 30° - 0}\right)$

After solving, we get $e = 2/3$.

7. (a) $\quad F = \rho AQ = \rho AV^2$
$\therefore \quad F_{wall} = 2F \cos\theta = 2\rho Av^2 \cos\theta.$

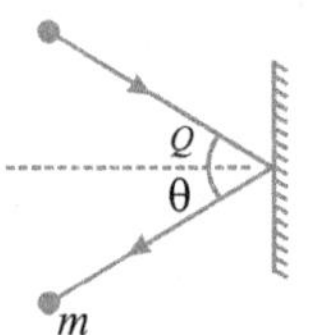

8. (b)
$$J = (mv - 0)$$
$$= 1 \times \sqrt{2gh} = 1 \times \sqrt{2 \times 10 \times 2} = \sqrt{40}\ N\text{-}s$$

9. (a) The initial extension of the spring

$$y_0 = \frac{mg}{k} \qquad \qquad \text{... (i)}$$

The velocity of combined block after collision
$$mv = (m + m)\,v$$

$$\therefore \qquad v' = \frac{v}{2}$$

Now from conservation of mechanical energy, we have

$$\frac{1}{2}(2m)\left(\frac{v}{2}\right)^2 + \frac{1}{2} k y_0^2 = 2m\,g y_0 \qquad \text{...(ii)}$$

After solving above equations, we get

$$v = \sqrt{\frac{6m}{k}}\,g$$

10. **(b)**
$$0 = m_1 v_1 - m_2 v_2$$

and $\dfrac{1}{2} m_1 v_1^2 + \dfrac{1}{2} m_2 v_2^2 = E$

After simplifying above equations, we get

$$v_1 + v_2 = \sqrt{\dfrac{2E(m_1 + m_2)}{m_1 m_2}}$$

11. **(b)** After 1 second,

$v_y = u_y - gt = 20\sqrt{2}\,\sin 45° - 10 \times 1 = 10$ m/s.

Now $2m \times 10 = m \times 0 + mv$

$\therefore \qquad v = 20$ m/s.

Height attained in addition to previous height

$$h = \dfrac{10^2}{2g} = 5 \text{ m.}$$

Previous height,

$$h_0 = \dfrac{U_y^2}{2g} = \dfrac{(20\sqrt{2}\,\sin 45°)^2}{2g} = 20 \; m.$$

Thus, $\; h_0 + h = 20 + 5 = 25$ m.

12. **(c)** Speed of each ball just before collision, $v = \sqrt{2gl}$

Now, $mv - 2mv = mv_1 + 2mv_2$

and $1 = \dfrac{-(v_1 - v_2)}{v - (-v)}$

After solving, we get $v_2 = \dfrac{v}{3} = \dfrac{\sqrt{2gl}}{3}$.

13. **(c)** The velocity of body A, before collision

$$u = \sqrt{2g\,y} = \sqrt{2g(1 - 1\cos 60°)} = 3.13 \; m/s.$$

Now $1 \times 3.13 + 5 \times 0 = v_1 + 5v_2$ ...(i)

and $\qquad 0.8 = -\left[\dfrac{v_2 - v_1}{0 - 3.13}\right]$ ...(ii)

After solving, we get $h = 0.0005 \, m$

Now $\quad \cos\theta = \dfrac{h}{L} = \left(\dfrac{1 - 0.0005}{1}\right)$

$= 0.995 \, m.$

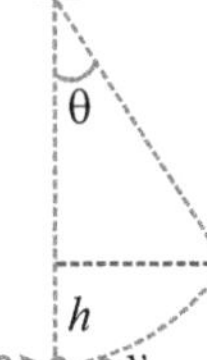

14. **(b)** Range, $\quad R = \dfrac{2 u_x u_y}{g} = \dfrac{2(u\cos\theta)\,(e\,u\sin\theta)}{2}$

$$= \dfrac{e\,u^2\,\sin 2\theta}{g}$$

15. **(a)** If v_1 and v_2 are the velocity of ball and the wedge after collision, then

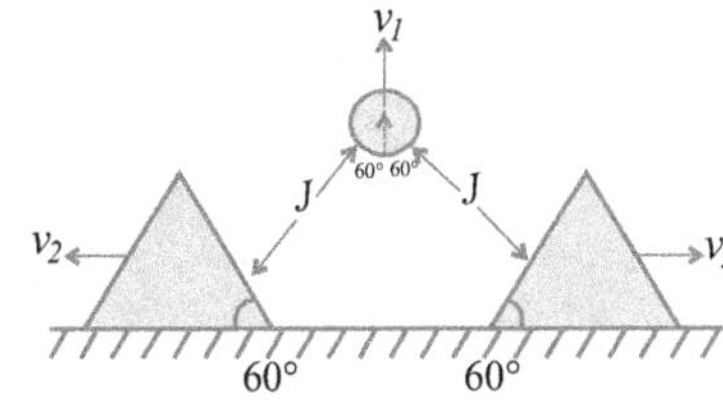

For ball:

$2J\cos 60° = mv_1 - (-mv_0)$

or $\qquad J = mv_1 + mv_0$

And $J\sin 60° = mv_2 - 0$

From above equations, we get

$$\dfrac{2v_2}{\sqrt{3}} = v_1 + v_0 \qquad \text{...(i)}$$

Also $\qquad e = \dfrac{[v_1\cos 60° - (-v_2\cos 30°)]}{(v_0\cos 60° - 0)}$

$$= \dfrac{v_1 + \sqrt{3}v_2}{v_0} \qquad \text{...(ii)}$$

After simplifying above equations, we get

$$v_2 = \dfrac{\sqrt{3}}{5}(1 + e)v_0 .$$

16. **(b)** $\quad 3\hat{i} + 3\hat{j} + 3\hat{k} = \dfrac{(10 + 20 + 30) \times 0 + 40 \times \vec{r}_2}{(10 + 20 + 30 + 40)}$

$\therefore \qquad \vec{r}_2 = 7.5\hat{i} + 7.5\hat{j} + 7.5\hat{k}.$

17. **(b)** $\quad m_1 d - m_2 x_2 = 0$

$\therefore \qquad x_2 = \dfrac{m_1 d}{m_2}$

18. **(a)** If x_1 is the overhang length on second blocks, then,

$$M\left(\dfrac{\ell}{2} - x_1\right) = \dfrac{M}{2}(x_1)$$

$\therefore \qquad x_1 = \dfrac{\ell}{3}$

Now if x_2 is the overhang from table, then

$$M\left(\dfrac{\ell}{2} - x_2\right) = \dfrac{3M}{2}x_2$$

$\therefore \qquad x_2 = \dfrac{\ell}{5}$

Now $\quad x = x_1 + x_2 = \dfrac{\ell}{3} + \dfrac{\ell}{5} = \dfrac{8\ell}{15}.$

19. **(b)** Solution is given in the example.

20. **(d)** Total distance moved by the bodies,

$x_1 + x_2 = 12R - 3R = 9R$ ...(i)

Also $\qquad Mx_1 = 5Mx_2$ ...(ii)

After solving above equations, we get

$x_1 = 7.5R$

$x_2 = 1.5\,R.$

21. **(a)** $\quad x_{cm} = \dfrac{m \times \ell + 2m \times 2\ell + 3m \times 3\ell + ... + nm \times n\ell}{m + 2m + 3m + .. + nm}$

$$= \dfrac{(1 + 4 + 9 + .. + n^2)\ell}{1 + 2 + .. + n}$$

$$= \dfrac{\ell\,n(n+1)(2n+1)/6}{n(n+1)/2}$$

$$= \dfrac{(2n+1)\ell}{3}$$

22. **(c)** If v is the velocity of insect and u is the velocity of strip (opposite direction), then

$$l = (v+u)t_1$$

$$\therefore \quad t_1 = \frac{\ell}{(v+u)}$$

When insect fly off, $t_2 = \dfrac{\ell}{u}$

Clearly, $t_2 > t_1$

23. **(a)** Man and wedge will displace as one unit of mass $3M$. If its displacement is Δx_1, towards left, then

$$0 = M\left(2 - \Delta x_1\right) + 3M\left(-\Delta x_1\right)$$

$$\therefore \quad \Delta x_1 = \frac{2}{4} = 0.5 \text{ m}$$

24. **(c)** Initial position of centre of mass from $2m$

$$x_0 = \frac{\times \ell}{m \quad 2m} \quad \frac{\ell}{3}.$$

Now $\dfrac{1}{2}k(x_1 + x_2)^2 = \dfrac{1}{2}m(2v_0)^2 + \dfrac{1}{2}(2m)v_0^2$

and $mx_1 = (2m)x_2$

After solving above equations, we get

$$x_2 = \sqrt{\frac{2mv_0^2}{3k}}.$$

Thus maximum separation between centre of mass and $2m$ (it happens when m moves away from centre of mass) $= x_0 + x_2$.

---

1. **(b,d)**

The total momentum and total energy of (earth + ball) system remain conserved.

2. **(a, d)**

The initial momentum of the bomb is zero, and so after explosion, it must be zero. Some internal energy will convert into external K.E.

3. **(a,b,d)**

System has non-zero initial momentum, so it must be after collision. Therefore both the bodies can not be at rest after collision.

4. **(a,b,c)**

5. **(a,c)** Linear momentum of A will transfer to B, but not angular momentum.

6. **(a, b)**

If the man walks along the rails, some velocity say V is imparted to car also. Let M be the mass of car. Then from conservation of linear momentum.

$$M.V = m(v - V)$$

$$\therefore \quad V = \frac{mv}{m+M}$$

$\therefore$ Work done by man

$$= \frac{1}{2}m(v-V)^2 + \frac{1}{2}mV^2$$

$$= \frac{1}{2}\left(\frac{mM}{m+M}\right)v^2 < \frac{1}{2}mv^2$$

Hence, option (a) is correct. If the man moves normal to the rails then car will not move. Hence, work done by him in this case will be $\dfrac{1}{2}mv^2$ and option (b) is also correct.

7. **(c)** Spring gets most compressed is case when force is applied from smaller block.

8. **(b,d)**

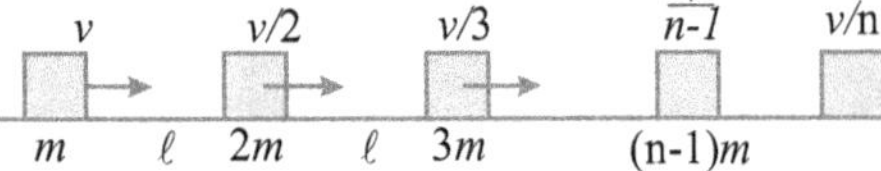

$$t_1 = \frac{\ell}{v}, \; t_2 = \frac{\ell}{v/2} = \frac{2\ell}{v}$$

$$t_3 = \frac{3\ell}{v}, \; ..... , \; t_{n-1} = \frac{(n-1)\ell}{v}$$

So

$$T = \frac{\ell}{v} + \frac{2\ell}{v} + \frac{3\ell}{v} + ... + \frac{(n-1)\ell}{v}$$

$$= \frac{\ell}{v}\left[1 + 2 + 3 + ... + (n-1)\right]$$

$$= \frac{n(n-1)\ell}{2v}$$

$$v_{\text{cm}} = \frac{mv + 0 + 0 + ... + 0}{nm} = \frac{v}{n}.$$

9. **(a,b,c)**

According to conservation of momentum (a,b) are obviously correct.

By the definition

$$e = -\left[\frac{v_2 - v_1}{u_2 - u_1}\right]$$

If v is the velocity during collision, then

$$= -\frac{m}{m}\left[\frac{(v_1 - v) - (v - v_2)}{u_2 - u_1}\right]$$

$$= -\frac{m(v_1 - v) - m(v - v_2)}{m(u_2 - 0)}$$

$$= -\frac{(P - J) - J}{P}$$

$$= \frac{2J - P}{P}.$$

10. **(a,b,d)**

11. **(a, b, d)** $m \times 21 - 2m \times 4 = m \times 1 + 2m \times v_2$

$$\therefore \quad v_2 = 6 \text{ m/s}$$

$$e = -\left[\frac{v_2 - v_1}{u_2 - u_1}\right] = -\left[\frac{6 - 1}{-4 - 21}\right] = 0.2$$

$$J = m(v_1 - u_1) = m\,[21 - 1]$$
$$= 20\ m\ \text{N–s.}$$

12. (a,b,d)

$$e = \frac{\text{velocity of separation}}{\text{velocity of approach}} = \frac{2}{4 - 0}$$

$$= 0.5.$$

Now $3 \times 4 - 2 \times 0 = 3v_1 + 2v_2$

and $\qquad 0.5 = -\left[\dfrac{v_2 - v_1}{0 - 4}\right]$

After simplifying above equations, we get
$$v_1 = 1.5\ \text{m/s.}$$

Thus $\qquad J = m_1(v_1 - u_1) = 3\,(4 - 1.6)$
$$= 7.2\ \text{N-s.}$$

13. (a, b, d)

From conservation of momentum,
$$\left(\frac{m}{2}\right)u = \left(m + \frac{m}{2}\right).v$$
$$\therefore \qquad v = \frac{u}{3}$$

Work done against friction $= E_\text{i} - E_\text{f}$

$$= \frac{1}{2}\left(\frac{m}{2}\right)u^2 - \frac{1}{2}\left(\frac{3m}{2}\right)\left(\frac{u}{3}\right)^2$$

$$= \frac{1}{6}mu^2 = \frac{2}{3}\left(\frac{1}{4}mu^2\right)$$

Force of friction on the two blocks before the blocks reach a common velocity is as shown below,

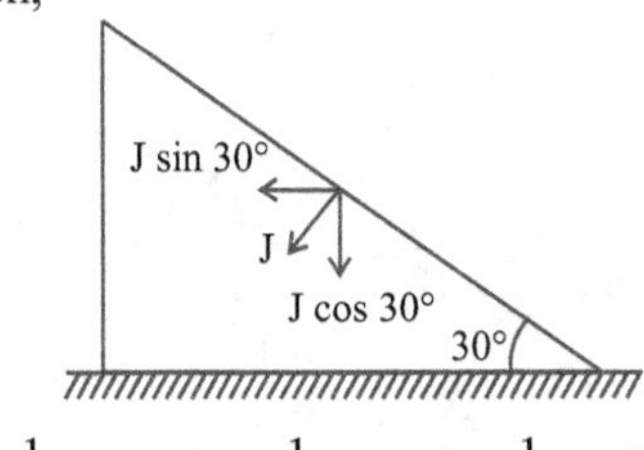

$$f = \frac{\mu}{2}mg$$

$$a_1 = \mu g \text{ and } a_2 = \frac{\mu}{2}g \quad \therefore a_r = \frac{3}{2}\mu g$$

14. (a, d)

Collision is elastic. Therefore, kinetic energy will be conserved. Let v be the speed of ball after collision. Then,

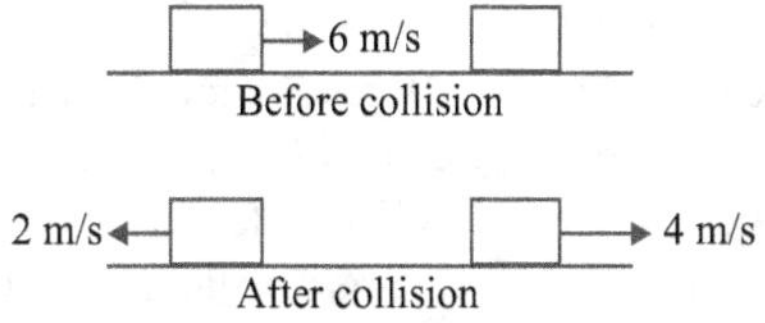

$$\frac{1}{2}(1)(10)^2 = \frac{1}{2}(4)(4)^2 + \frac{1}{2}(1)v^2$$

or $\qquad v = 6$ m/s

Let J be the impulse between the two during collision.

Applying impulse = Change in linear momentum
$$J \sin 30° = (4)\,(4)$$

or $\qquad J = 32\ \text{N - S}$

15. (a,c,d)

Clearly, the velocity of centre of mass $= \left(\dfrac{m}{m + M}\right)v_0$

Initial K.E. in the centre of mass frame (K_cm)

$$= \frac{1}{2}(m + M)v_\text{cm}^2$$

$$= \frac{1}{2}(m + M)\left[\left(\frac{m}{m + M}\right)v_0\right]^2$$

$$= \frac{1}{2}\frac{m^2 v_0^2}{m + M}$$

The maximum compression (x_m) in spring is given by

$$\frac{1}{2}kx_\text{m}^2 = E - K_{cm}$$

or $\qquad \dfrac{1}{2}kx_\text{m}^2 = \dfrac{1}{2}mv_0^2 - \dfrac{1}{2}\dfrac{m^2 v_0^2}{m + M}$

or $\qquad kx = mv_0^2\left(1 - \dfrac{m}{m + M}\right)$

$$= mv_0^2\left(\frac{M}{m + M}\right)$$

$$= \left(\frac{mM}{m + M}\right)v_0^2$$

$\Rightarrow \qquad x_\text{m} = v_0\sqrt{\left(\dfrac{mM}{m + M}\right)\dfrac{1}{k}}$

16. (a,c) From conservation of linear momentum we can see that velocity of 1 kg block just after collision is 2 m/s leftwards.

Now relative velocity of approach = 6 m/s
and relative velocity of separation = 6 m/s

$$e = \frac{\text{relative velocity of separation}}{\text{relative velocity of approach}} = 1$$

Initially $v_\text{cm} = \dfrac{m_1v_1 + m_2v_2}{m_1 + m_2} = \dfrac{1 \times 6 + 2 \times 0}{1 + 2} = 2\,m/s$

During collision v_cm will not change.

17. (b,d) Let a be the acceleration of wedge leftwards and a_r the relative acceleration of block down the plane. Then absolute acceleration of block in horizontal direction will be $(a_r \cos\theta - a)$ towards right. Net force on the system in horizontal direction is zero. Therefore, acceleration of COM in horizontal direction will be zero or acceleration of wedge towards left is equal to the acceleration of block towards right.

$\therefore\ a_r \cos\theta - a = a$

or $\qquad 2a = a_r \cos\theta \qquad\qquad ....(1)$

Now let N be the normal reaction between the block and the wedge. Then free body diagram of wedge gives

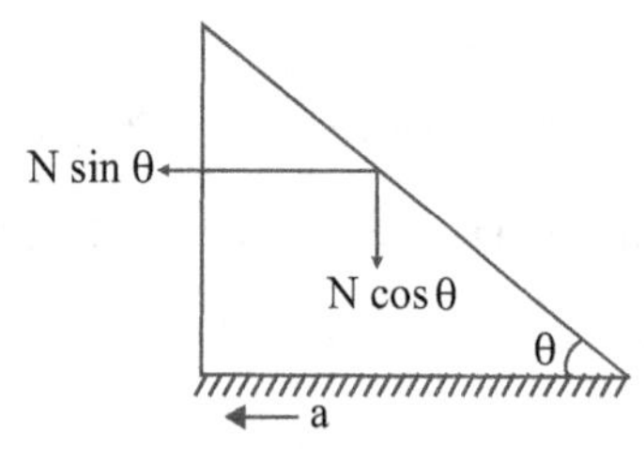

$$N \sin \theta = ma \qquad \text{....(2)}$$

Free body diagram of block with respect to wedge is:

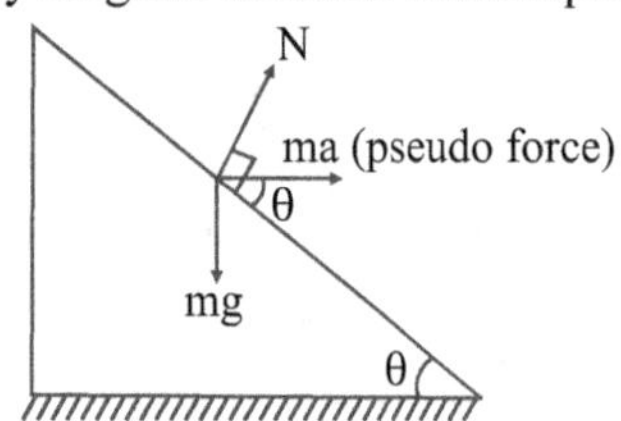

Net force on block perpendicular to plane is zero .
Hence, $N + ma \sin \theta = mg \cos \theta$ .... (3)
Solving eqs. (1), (2) and (3), we get,

$$a_r = \frac{2g \sin \theta}{1 + \sin^2 \theta}$$

acceleration of block vertically downwards

$$a_y = a_r \sin \theta$$

$$a_y = \frac{2g \sin^2 \theta}{1 + \sin^2 \theta}$$

$\therefore$ acceleration of COM is

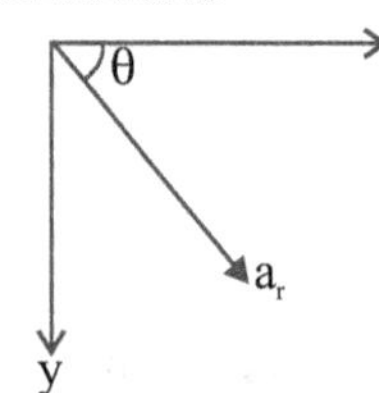

$$a_{com} = \frac{a_y}{2} = \frac{g \sin^2 \theta}{(1 + \sin^2 \theta)}$$

18. **(a,b,c)**

If we resolve the initial velocity along x-and y-axis, then it is clear that u_y will remain constant after collision but u_x will change. Also, $m_2 \gg m_1$, therefore m_1 can be neglected. Hence,

$$(v_x)_1 = \left(\frac{-em_2}{m_2} \right)(u_x)_1 = -e(u_x)_1 = -\frac{1}{2} \times 3 = -\frac{3}{2}$$

$\therefore$ Velocity after collision is

$$\vec{v} = -\frac{3}{2}\hat{i} + \hat{j}.$$

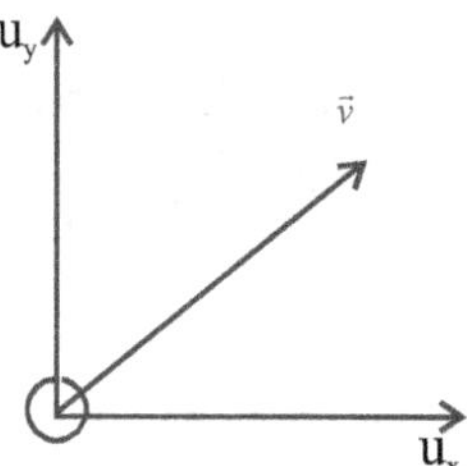

Similarly we can find that

$$\text{loss in K.E.} = \frac{27}{8m}\hat{j}$$

and impulse $= -\dfrac{9m}{2}\hat{i}$

---

1. (b) Both the statements are separately correct. Relative speed of bodies after collision comes out equal to relative speed after collision, when we K.E. before collision is equal to K.E. after collision.

2. (d) Velocity of c.m. remains constant, when external force on the system is zero.

3. (a)
$$0 = \vec{P}_{gun} + \vec{P}_{bullet}$$

or
$$P_{gun} = P_{bullet}$$

$$\frac{K_{gun}}{K_{bullet}} = \frac{P_{gun}^2 / 2m_{gun}}{P_{bullet}^2 / 2m_{bullet}} = \frac{m_{bullet}}{m_{gun}}.$$

4. (d) When e = 0 velocity of separation along common normal zero, but there may be relative velocity along common tangent.

5. (d) In an elastic collision, no conversion of energy, so K.E. remains constant during the time of collision. There is no friction acting in this case. In case of friction too conservation of energy is followed provided we take into account all the transformations there.

Passage for (Questions 1 & 2)

1. (b), 2. (c)

Let v_{jb} is the velocity of jet w.r.t. moving blade, then,

$$v_{jb} = v - v_B.$$

The force exerted by jet on the blade,

$$F_x = \rho A v_{jb}^2 = \rho A (v - v_B)^2$$

The power delivered to the blade

$$P = F_x v_B$$
$$= \rho A v_B (v - v_B)^2$$

Passage for (Questions 3 & 4)

3. (a)
$$0 = u_1 + 2 \times 0.5$$
$$\therefore \quad u, = -1 \ m/s.$$
$$K = \frac{1}{2}m_1 u_1^2 = \frac{1}{2} \times 1 \times (-1)^2 = 0.5 \text{ J.}$$

4. (b)
$$U = \frac{1}{2}m_1 u_1^2 + \frac{1}{2}m_2 u_2^2$$
$$= \frac{1}{2} \times 1 \times (-1)^2 + \frac{1}{2} \times 2 \times (0.5)^2$$
$$= 0.75 \text{ J.}$$

Passage for (Questions 5 to 7)

5. (b) The vertical height of AB is $\sqrt{3}\tan 60° = 3$m. The velocity of block before collision $v_0 = \sqrt{2g \times 3} = \sqrt{60}$ m/s. Its perpendicular component get absorbed by the plane while component along the plane

$$v_x = v_0 \cos 30°$$
$$= \sqrt{60} \times \frac{\sqrt{3}}{2} = \sqrt{45} \text{ m/s.}$$

6. (b) $\dfrac{1}{2}\, m \left(\sqrt{45}\right)^2 + mg \times 3 = \dfrac{1}{2}\, m\, v_c^2$

$$\therefore \qquad v_c = \sqrt{105} \text{ m/s}$$

7. (c) The vertical component after collision with second incline

$$v = \sqrt{15}\cos 30° - \sqrt{45}\cos 60°$$
$$= \frac{\sqrt{45}}{2} - \frac{\sqrt{45}}{2} = 0$$

Passage for (Questions 8 & 9)

8. (c) Along the inclined plane

$$mu\sin\theta = mv\cos\theta$$
$$\therefore \qquad u\sin\theta = v\cos\theta$$
$$\Rightarrow \qquad \frac{v}{u} = \tan\theta$$

Now $\qquad e = -\left[\dfrac{v_2 - v_1}{u_2 - u_1}\right]$

$$= -\left[\frac{0 - (-v\sin\theta)}{0 - u\cos\theta}\right]$$
$$e = \frac{v}{u}\tan\theta = (\tan\theta)(\tan\theta)$$
$$\therefore \qquad \theta = \tan^{-1}\sqrt{e}\,.$$

9. (c) $v = u\tan\theta$

$$= u\sqrt{e}\,.$$

Passage for (Questions 10 to 12)

10. (b) **11.** (c) **12.** (d)

The horizontal component of velocities before and after impact are: $u\cos\alpha$ and $eu\cos\alpha$ respectively. Thus,

$$d = u\cos\alpha\, t_1 \text{ and } d = eu\cos\alpha\, t_2 \qquad \text{...(i)}$$
$$\text{or} \qquad t_1 + t_2 = \frac{2u\sin\alpha}{g} \qquad \text{...(ii)}$$

The coordinates of points of impact are $(d, d\tan\theta)$ so from,

$$d\tan\theta = \delta\tan\alpha - \frac{gd^2}{2u^2\cos^2\alpha} \qquad \text{...(iii)}$$

From equations (ii) and (iii), we get

$$\tan\theta = \frac{\tan\alpha}{(1+e)}$$

Passage for (Questions 13 to 15)

13. (c) Use impulse momentum equation

$$\vec{p}_2 - \vec{p}_1 = \text{impulse} = F.\Delta T$$
$$-0.25 \times 200 + 0.25 \times 100 = F.\Delta T \qquad \text{... (i)}$$

Block A
$$-1 \times v = T.\Delta t - F.\Delta T \qquad \text{... (ii)}$$

Block B
$$2 \times v = T.\Delta t \qquad \text{... (iii)}$$

Solving we get, $v = \dfrac{25}{3}$ m/s.

14. (c) From equation (iii)

$$T.\Delta t = 2.v = \frac{50}{3} N - s.$$

15. (d) Δ K.E. = W.d. by all forces

$$-\frac{1}{2}(1+2)v^2 = -(2)(10)h$$
$$h = \frac{3}{4 \times 10} \times \frac{25 \times 25}{3 \times 3} = \frac{625}{12 \times 10} = 5.2\,m.$$

16. **A→q, s; B→q; C→r; D→p, r, s**

In perfectly inelastic collision bodies combine together after collision. It is similar to nuclear fusion process.

17. **A → (r); B→ (p); C → (q); D → (s)**

18. **A→s; B→s; C→p, q, r; D→p, q, r**
(A) not possible, P_x cannot be conserved
(B) not possible, P_y cannot be conserved
(C) possible, for any mass ratio – p, q, r
(D) possible for any mass ratio – p, q, r

1. (a) $\vec{P}_1 + \vec{P}_2 = \vec{P}_1{}' + \vec{P}_2{}'$

$$mv\hat{i} + 0 = m\frac{v}{\sqrt{3}}\hat{j} + m\vec{v}_2$$
$$\therefore \qquad v_2 = \sqrt{v^2 + \left(\frac{v}{\sqrt{3}}\right)^2} = \frac{2v}{\sqrt{3}}\,.$$

2. (c) $x_{cm} = \dfrac{\displaystyle\int_0^L x\,dm}{\displaystyle\int_0^L dm} = \dfrac{\displaystyle\int_0^L xK\left(\dfrac{x}{L}\right)^n dx}{\displaystyle\int_0^L K\left(\dfrac{x^n}{L^n}\right)dx}$

$$= \frac{\displaystyle\int_0^L x^{n+1}dx}{\displaystyle\int_0^L x^n dx} = \left.\frac{x^{(n+2)/(n+2)}}{x^{(n+1)/(n+1)}}\right|_0^L$$

$$= \frac{L(1+n)}{(2+n)} = \frac{Ln\left(1+\frac{1}{n}\right)}{n\left(1+\frac{2}{n}\right)} = \frac{L\left(1+\frac{1}{n}\right)}{\left(1+\frac{2}{n}\right)}$$

For n = 0, $x_{cm} = \dfrac{L}{2}$

and $n = \infty$, $x_{cm} = L$

Clearly option (c) is correct.

3. (a) In completely inelastic collision, all energy is not lost (so, statement -1 is true) and the principle of conservation of momentum holds good for all kinds of collisions (so, statement -2 is true) . Statement -2 explains statement -1 correctly because applying the principle of conservation of momentum, we can get the common velocity and hence the kinetic energy of the combined body.

4. (a,d) Momentum before collision,

$$\vec{P} = \vec{P_1} + \vec{P_2} = P\hat{i} - P\hat{i} = 0$$

Option (a) and (d), add together can not give zero momentum.

5. (c) The time taken in first collision

$$= \frac{2\pi r}{3v} = \frac{120°}{\omega}$$

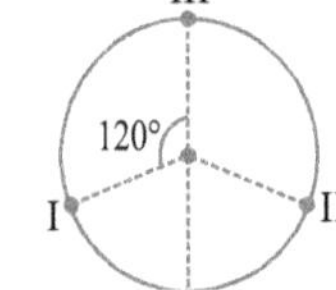

The second collision will be at $\dfrac{240°}{\omega}$ and third $\dfrac{360°}{\omega}$.

So there are two collision, excluding at A.

6. (a) $y_{cm} = \dfrac{6m \times 0 + m \times a + m \times a + m \times 0 + m(-a)}{6m + m + m + m + m} = \dfrac{a}{10}$

7. (d) For vertical motion of bullet or ball

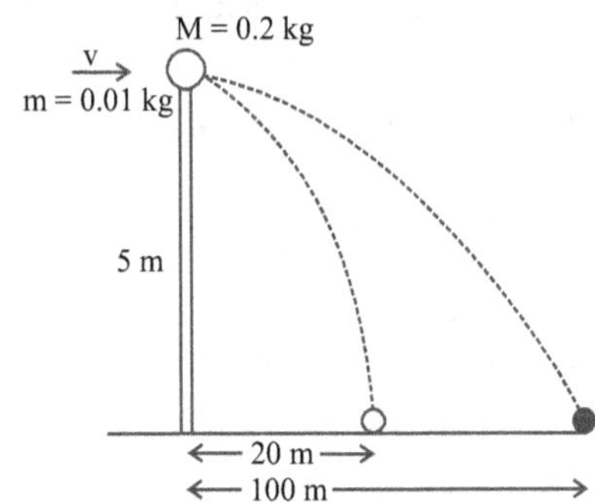

$$S = ut + \frac{1}{2}at^2 \Rightarrow 5 = \frac{1}{2} \times 10 \times t^2$$

$$\Rightarrow \quad t = 1 \text{ sec}$$

For horizontal motion of ball

$x_{ball} = v_{ball}\, t \Rightarrow 20 = v_{ball} \times 1 = v_{ball}$

For horizontal motion of bullet

$x_{bullet} = v_{bullet} \times t \Rightarrow 100 = v_{bullet} \times 1 = v_{bullet}$

Applying conservation of linear momentum during collision, we get

$$mv = mv_{bullet} + Mv_{ball}$$

$$0.01\, v = 0.01 \times 100 + 0.2 \times 20$$

$$\therefore \qquad v = \frac{5}{0.01} = 500 \text{ m/s}$$

8. (a) $v_1^2 - u_0^2 = 2(-g)\left[\dfrac{u_0^2 \sin^2 \alpha}{2g}\right]$

$\therefore v_1^2 = u_0^2(1 - \sin^2 \alpha) = u_0^2 \cos^2 \alpha$

$\therefore v_1 = u_0 \cos \alpha$ ...(i)

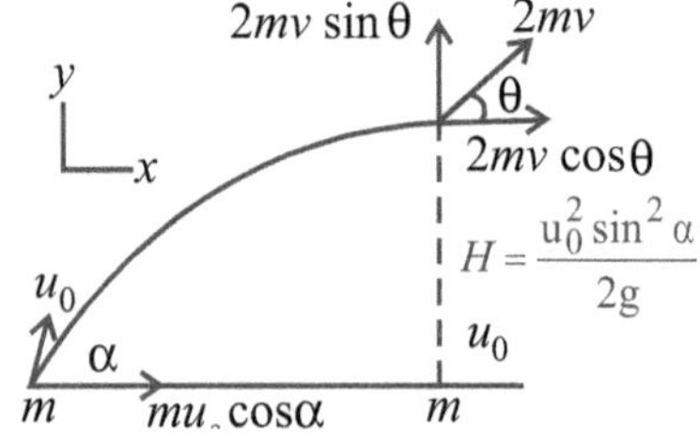

Applying conservation of linear momentum in Y-direction

$2mv \sin \theta = mv_1 = mu_0 \cos \alpha$ (ii) [from (i)]

Applying conservation of linear momentum in X-direction

$2mv \cos \theta = mu_0 \cos \alpha$ ...(iii)

on dividing (ii) and (iii) we get

$\tan \theta = 1 \qquad \therefore \theta = \dfrac{\pi}{4}$

option (a) is correct

9. (d) Maximum energy loss $= \dfrac{P^2}{2m} - \dfrac{P^2}{2(m+M)}$

$$\left[\because K.E. = \frac{P^2}{2m} = \frac{1}{2}mv^2\right]$$

$$= \frac{P^2}{2m}\left[\frac{M}{(m+M)}\right] = \frac{1}{2}mv^2\left\{\frac{M}{m+M}\right\}$$

Statement II is a case of perfectly inelastic collision. By comparing the equation given in statement I with above equation, we get

$$f = \left(\frac{M}{m+M}\right) \text{ instead of } \left(\frac{m}{M+m}\right)$$

Hence statement I is wrong and statement II is correct.

Chapter

9

Gravitation

(423 - 480)

Chapter contents

Johonnes Keper

Mathematician and astronomer Johonnes Keper (1571-1630) supported the ideas of Copernicus. The Earth was not the centre of the Universe, with everything going around it. Earth and the other planets went around the Sun. Kepler worked out the orbits of Earth and other planets known at the time, in mathematical detail – Kepler's three laws of planetary motion. ....

Definitions, Explanations and Derivations

9.1 HELIOCENTRIC MODEL

Around 100 A.D. Ptolemy wrote in his book that stars including Sun revolved around earth. The similar geo-centric theory was proposed by Indian astronomers in nearly about 5th century A.D. Aryabhata in his Aryabhatia described a heliocentric theory. According to this theory Earth revolves in circular orbit around the sun in a year's time. In 1543 Nicolaus Copernicus stated that all the planets moved in circular path around sun, which was considered to be fixed.

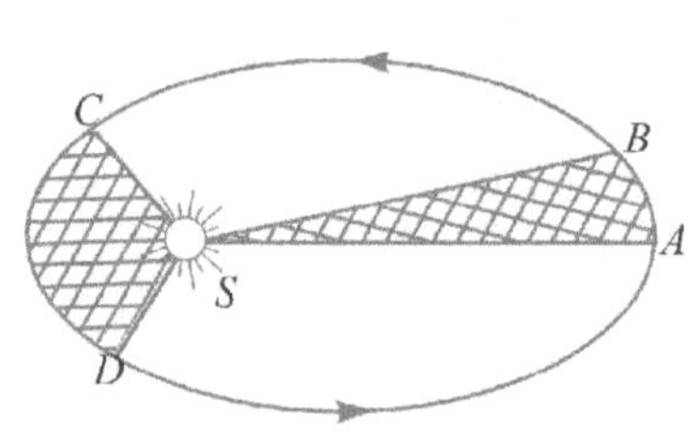

Figure. 9.1

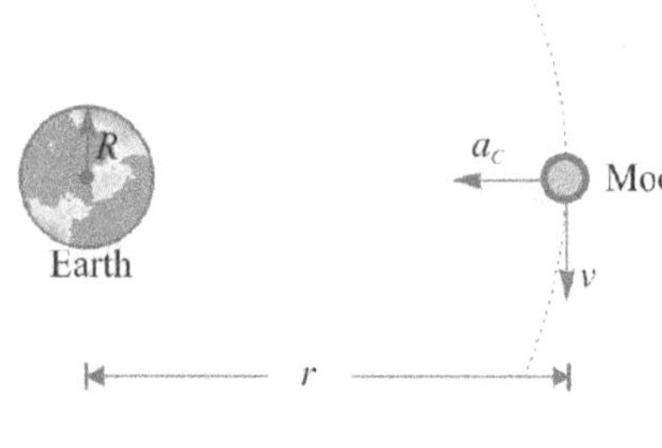

Figure. 9.2

9.2 KEPLER'S LAWS

On the basis of observations Johannes Kepler (1571–1630) presented three famous laws about planetary motion. These are :

1. **Law of orbits (Kepler's first law)**
    Each planet revolves around sun in an elliptical orbit with the sun at one of the foci.
    Elliptical orbit of a planet: $PA = 2a =$ major axis
    $$BC = 2b = \text{minor axis}.$$
    The distance of planet closest to sun is called **perihelion** and farthest to sun is called **aphelion**.

2. **Law of areas (Kepler's second law)**
    The radius vector drawn from the sun to planet sweeps out equal areas in equal intervals of time i.e., the areal velocity of a planet around the sun is constant. The linear speed of a planet is greater when it is closer to the sun than its linear speed when away from the sun.

3. **Law of periods (Kepler's third law)**
    The square of the time period of revolution of a planet around the sun is proportional to the cube of the semi major axis of its elliptical orbit.
    If T is the time period of revolution of a planet and a is the length of the semi major axis of it, then

$$T^2 \propto a^3.$$

Steps towards law of gravitation

On seeing a falling apple, Newton was inspired to think about the law of gravitation. He realised that for the falling apple on his head and the overhead moon, the same gravitational force was responsible for both phenomenon. Newton assumed that the moon revolved around the earth in a circular orbit of radius r ($= 3.84 \times 10^8$ m). Moon completes a revolution around earth in 27.3 days, so

$$T = 27.3 \times 24 \times 60 \times 60 = 27.3 \times 86400 \text{ s}.$$

Figure. 9.3

Speed of moon around earth
$$v = \frac{2\pi r}{T} = \frac{2\pi \times (3.84 \times 10^8)}{27.3 \times 86400}$$
$$= 1.02 \times 10^3 \text{ m/s}.$$

Centripetal acceleration of the moon towards the centre of orbit

$$a_c = \frac{v^2}{r} = \frac{(1.02 \times 10^3)^2}{3.84 \times 10^8}$$
$$= 2.72 \times 10^{-3} \text{ m/s}^2.$$

Acceleration due to gravity at the surface of earth is $g = 9.8$ m/s^2.

Newton proposed that the gravitational force should be inversely proportional to the square of the distance. If R is the radius of earth, then

$$\frac{\text{acceleration of moon}}{\text{acceleration of body near earth}} = \frac{a_c}{g} = \frac{1/r^2}{1/R^2} = \frac{R^2}{r^2}$$

Newton knew that

$$\frac{R}{r} = \frac{1}{60}$$

$\therefore$

$$a_c = \frac{R^2}{r^2}g = \left(\frac{1}{60}\right)^2 \times 9.8$$

$$= 2.72 \times 10^{-3} \text{ m/s}^2.$$

This value is in close agreement with the value obtained otherwise.

9.3 NEWTON'S LAW OF GRAVITATION

"Every particle in the universe attracts every other particle with a force which is directly proportional to the product of their masses and inversely proportional to the square of the distance between them".

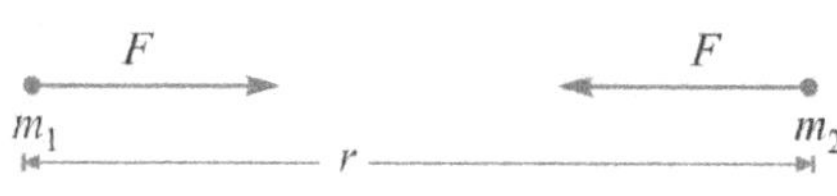

Figure. 9.4

Consider two particles of masses m_1 and m_2 placed at a separation r, the force between them is given by;

$$F = \frac{Gm_1m_2}{r^2},$$

where **G is called universal gravitational constant.** In SI system, its value is $G = 6.67 \times 10^{-11}$ N-m²/kg². The value of G does not depend on the nature and size of the bodies. It also does not depend on the nature of the medium between the bodies. That is why G is called universal gravitational constant.

Vector form of law of gravitation

Consider two particles of masses m_1 and m_2 placed at a separation r.

Let $\hat{r}_{12}$ is the unit vector from particle 1 to particle 2,

$\hat{r}_{21}$ is the unit vector from particle 2 to particle 1, then

Figure. 9.5

$$\vec{F}_{21} = -G\frac{m_1m_2}{r^2}\hat{r}_{12}.$$

The negative sign indicates that the direction of $\vec{F}_{21}$ is opposite to the vector $\hat{r}_{12}$.

Similarly,

$$\vec{F}_{12} = -\frac{Gm_1m_2}{r^2}\hat{r}_{21}.$$

As $\hat{r}_{21} = -\hat{r}_{12}$, so $\vec{F}_{21} = -\vec{F}_{12}$

Clearly, the universal law of gravitation is consistent with Newton's third law of motion.

As $\vec{F}_{12}$ and $\vec{F}_{21}$ are directed towards the centres of the particles so gravitational force is **central force.**

The following points about the gravitational force are to be noted

(i) The gravitational force is a conservative force.

(ii) The law of gravitation holds for point masses.

(iii) For bodies of finite sizes if the distance between them is much greater than their sizes, one may take r to be the distance between their centres of mass.

(iv) For a spherically symmetric body the force on an object outside the body acts as if the entire mass of the body is concentrated at the centre. Newton proved this important assertion, called shell theorem in his book principia.

(v) The gravitational force between two point masses is the central force. This force has no angular dependence. Its magnitude depends on r. We can say that gravitational force possesses spherical symmetry.

(vi) The gravitational force does not depend on the medium between the bodies. In other words the forces between the bodies remain the same whether, they are in air or in water, other things remain the same.

(vii) The resultant force acting on a particle m due to a number of masses $M_1, M_2, \ldots\ldots M_n$; we can use the principle of superposition. Let $\vec{F_1}, \vec{F_2}, \ldots\ldots, \vec{F_n}$ be the individual forces due to M_1,

$M_2, ..., M_n$, each given by the law of gravitation. The resultant force on the particle m is given by ;

$$\vec{F} = \vec{F}_1 + \vec{F}_2 + ... + \vec{F}_n = \sum_{i=1}^{n} \vec{F}_i.$$

This shows that each force acts independently and uninfluenced by the other bodies. This is called the **principle of superposition**.

9.4 SHELL THEOREM

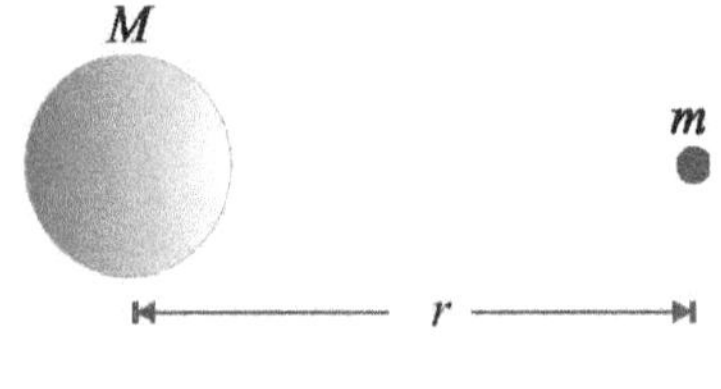

According to this theorem :

(i)   If a point mass lies outside the spherical shell/sphere with a spherically symmetric mass distribution, the shell/sphere attracts the point mass as if the whole mass of the shell/sphere were concentrated at its centre.

(ii)   If the point mass lies inside the uniform spherical shell, the gravitational force on the point mass is zero.

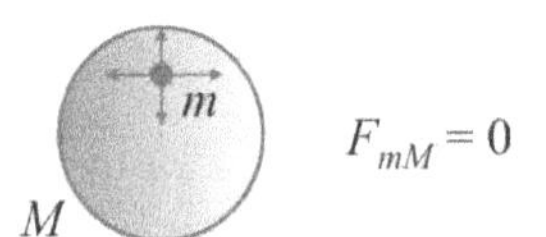

$F_{mM} = 0$

Figure. 9.6

Is gravitational shielding possible ?
Gravitational shielding is not possible. If we place a particle inside a shell, the gravitational force on the particle due to shell is zero, yet the shell does not shield the other bodies outside it which exert gravitational force on the particle lying inside it.

9.5 DERIVATION OF KEPLER'S LAWS

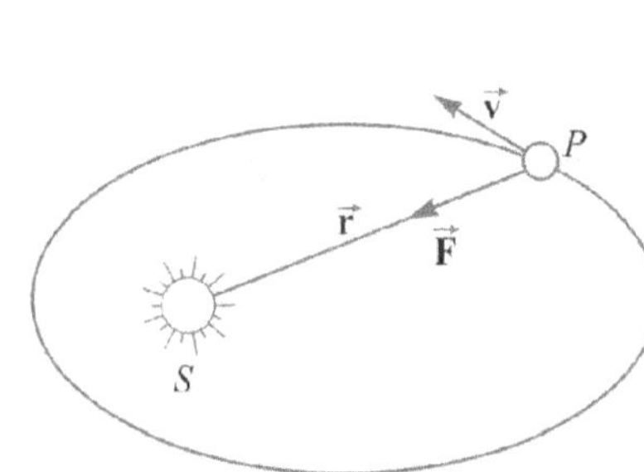

Figure. 9.7

Kepler's first law : The orbit of a body under the gravitational force of a massive body is a circle, ellipse, parabola or a hyperbola depends on the initial condition. The proof of the first law at this level is not possible.

Kepler's second law : Let a planet P revolves round sun. It experiences a force

$$\vec{F} = -\frac{GM_s m_p}{r^2}\hat{r}$$

$$= -\frac{GM_s m_p \vec{r}}{r^3} \qquad \left(\hat{r} = \frac{\vec{r}}{r}\right)$$

The torque exerted on the planet P about the sun S

$$\vec{\tau} = \vec{r} \times \vec{F} = \vec{r} \times \left[\frac{-GM_s m_p \vec{r}}{r^3}\right]$$

$$= \left[\frac{-GM_s m_p}{r^3}\right](\vec{r} \times \vec{r}) = 0 \qquad (\text{As } \vec{r} \times \vec{r} = 0)$$

Here M_S and m_p are the masses of sun and the planet respectively.

The angular momentum $\vec{L}$ of planet about sun is given by

$$\vec{L} = \vec{r} \times \vec{P}$$

$$= \vec{r} \times m_p \vec{v}$$

Since $\vec{\tau} = \dfrac{d\vec{L}}{dt}$ is zero , so momentum $\vec{L}$ is constant.

Kepler's second law of the constancy of areal velocity is a consequence of angular momentum conservation

Consider a planet whose radius vector $\vec{r}$ sweeps out an area ΔA in time Δt. We know that

$$\Delta \vec{A} = \frac{1}{2}(\vec{r} \times \overrightarrow{\Delta r})$$

Since
$$\Delta\vec{r} \;=\; \vec{v}\,\Delta t$$

$\therefore$
$$\Delta\vec{A} \;=\; \frac{1}{2}(\vec{r}\times\vec{v}\Delta t)$$

or
$$\frac{\Delta\vec{A}}{\Delta t} \;=\; \frac{1}{2}(\vec{r}\times\vec{v})$$

or
$$\frac{\Delta\vec{A}}{\Delta t} \;=\; \frac{1}{2m}(\vec{r}\times m\vec{v})$$

or
$$\frac{\Delta\vec{A}}{\Delta t} \;=\; \frac{\vec{L}}{2m}.$$

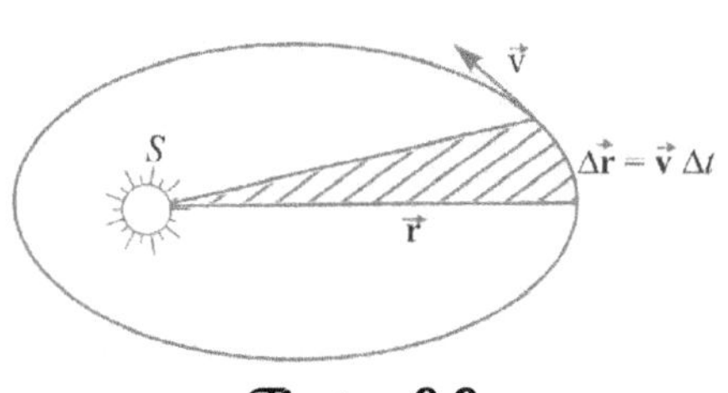

Figure. 9.8

Since $\vec{L}$ is constant, so that areal velocity $\left(\dfrac{d\vec{A}}{dt}\right)$ is constant.

Kepler's third law : Assuming that the orbit of planet is a circle of radius r with the sun at the centre. The sun's gravitational attraction is responsible for the planet's centripetal acceleration i.e.,

$$\frac{GM_s m_p}{r^2} \;=\; \frac{m_p v^2}{r}$$

which gives
$$v \;=\; \sqrt{\frac{GM_s}{r}}.$$

The time period of revolution

$$T \;=\; \frac{2\pi r}{v} = \frac{2\pi r}{\sqrt{\dfrac{GM_s}{r}}} = 2\pi\sqrt{\frac{r^3}{GM_s}}$$

or
$$T^2 \;=\; 4\pi^2\,\frac{r^3}{GM_s}$$

Here $[4\pi^2/GM_s]$ is constant.

$\therefore$
$$T^2 \;\propto\; r^3.$$

9.6 Intensity of Gravitational Field

A body attracts the other by the gravitational force even if they are not in direct contact. It can be explained by the concept of field.

The space surrounding a body in which other body experiences gravitational force is called **gravitational field**. The intensity of gravitational field at any point is the force experienced by a unit mass placed at that point provided the presence of unit mass does not affect the original gravitational field. The gravitational field intensity is a vector quantity, it can be denoted by $\vec{E}$. Its direction is towards the mass producing field.

Consider a body of mass M. The intensity of gravitational field due to this body at a distance r is given by

$$\vec{E} \;=\; \frac{\vec{F}}{m},$$

where m is the test mass , $m \ll M$.

According to Newton's law of gravitation,

$$F \;=\; \frac{GMm}{r^2}$$

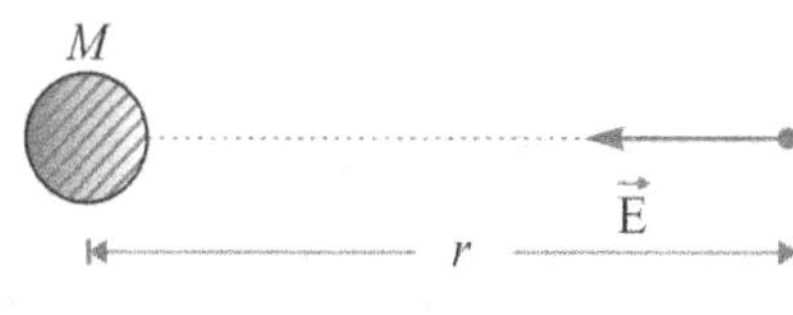

Figure. 9.9

$$\therefore \qquad E = \frac{F}{m} = \frac{\left(\dfrac{GMm}{r^2}\right)}{m}$$

or

$$E = \frac{GM}{r^2}.$$

Intensity of gravitational field due to earth

Let us assume, earth as a uniform sphere and non-rotating. The gravitational force acting on a particle of mass m located outside the earth at a distance r from the centre of earth, is given by

$$F = \frac{GMm}{r^2}$$

In which M is the mass of the earth.

Intensity of gravitational field is given by

$$E_g = \frac{F}{m} = \frac{GM}{r^2}. \qquad \ldots(i)$$

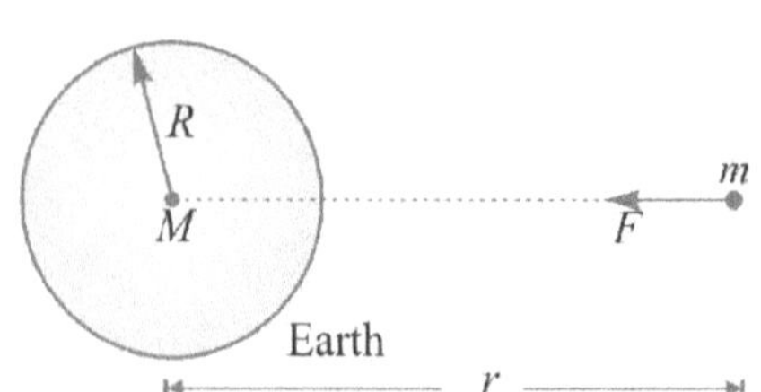

Figure. 9.10

The gravitational force produces an acceleration to each particle towards the centre of earth. We shall call this as gravitational acceleration, and it is equal to

$$a_g = \frac{F}{m} = \frac{GM}{r^2}. \qquad \ldots(ii)$$

Thus for the assumed model of earth, intensity of gravitational field and gravitational acceleration are equal.

At the surface of the earth the gravitational acceleration

$$g = \frac{GM}{R^2}, \qquad (r = R).$$

Note: The gravitational acceleration a_g is due to the gravitational force exerted on the particle by the earth. It differs from free fall acceleration that would measure for a falling particle, because earth is not spherical and also rotating.

The effect on value of *g*

1. **The earth is not uniform**

   The density of the earth varies radially. The density is nearly 13.6×10^3 kg/m^3 at the inner core of earth and 2.3×10^3 kg/m^3 at the outer crust. This variation in density affects the value of g when we go inside earth.

2. **Effect of shape of earth**

   The earth is not spherical . It is approximately an ellipsoid flattened at the poles and bulging at the equator. Its equatorial radius is nearly 21 km greater than its polar radius. If R_e and R_p be the radius at equator and poles, then we have

$$R_e = (R_p + 21)km .$$

The acceleration due to gravity,

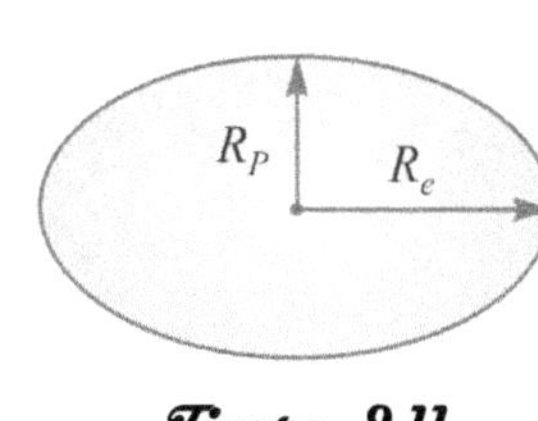

Figure. 9.11

$$g_e = \frac{GM}{R_e^{\,2}} \quad \text{(Assuming earth is not rotating)}$$

and

$$g_p = \frac{GM}{R_p^{\,2}}$$

Since $\qquad R_e > R_p, \ \therefore g_e < g_p.$

3. **Effect of rotation of earth**

Now suppose the earth to be a perfect sphere of radius R and mass M. It rotates with angular velocity ω about polar axis. As the earth rotates, every particle lying on its surface revolves in a horizontal circle with the same angular velocity ω.

Consider a particle of mass m lying at a point whose latitude is λ. The particle revolves in a circle of radius $r = R\cos\lambda$. The particle has centrifugal force $F_c = m\omega^2 r$ in addition to gravitational force mg.

Let g' be the acceleration due to gravity in the presence of rotation of the earth, then we have

$$g' = \frac{F_{net}}{m}$$

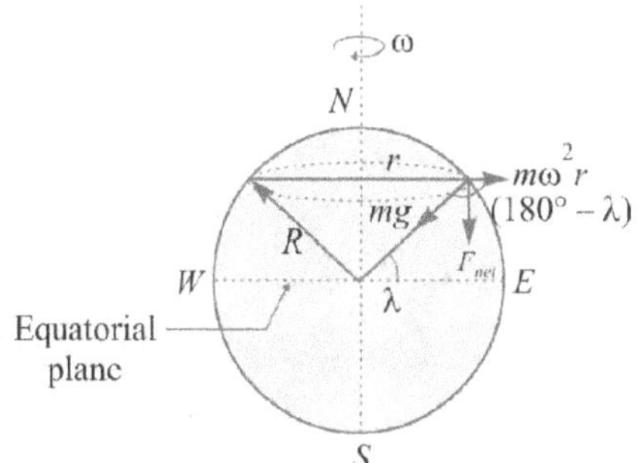

Figure. **9.12**

$$= \sqrt{\frac{(mg)^2 + (m\omega^2 R\cos\lambda)^2 + 2(mg)(m\omega^2 R\cos\lambda)\cos(180° - \lambda)}{m}}$$

$$= \left[g^2 + R^2\omega^4\cos^2\lambda - 2gR\omega^2\cos^2\lambda\right]^{1/2}$$

$$= g\left[1 + \left(\frac{R\omega^2}{g}\right)^2\cos^2\lambda - \frac{2R\omega^2}{g}\cos^2\lambda\right]^{1/2}.$$

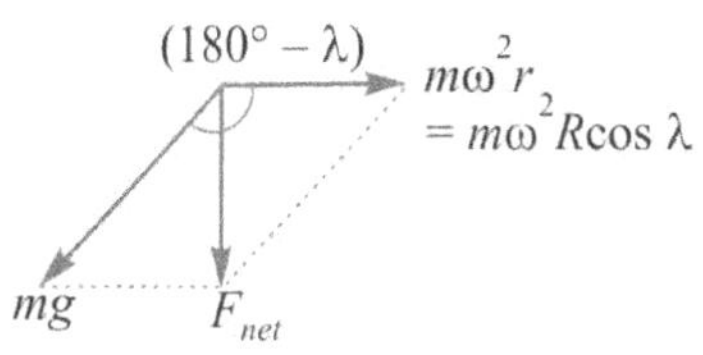

Figure. **9.13**

As $R = 6.38 \times 10^6$ m and $g = 9.8$ m/s^2

$$\therefore \quad \frac{R\omega^2}{g} = \frac{6.38 \times 10^6}{9.8} \times \left(\frac{2\pi}{24 \times 60 \times 60}\right)^2 = \frac{1}{291}$$

Since $\dfrac{R\omega^2}{g}$ is small, so its square is very small. Thus we can write

$$g' \simeq g\left[1 - 2\frac{R\omega^2}{g}\cos^2\lambda\right]^{1/2}$$

Expanding by binomial theorem, we get

$$g' = g\left[1 - \frac{R\omega^2}{g}\cos^2\lambda\right]$$

or $$g' = g - \omega^2 R\cos^2\lambda.$$

Special cases :

1. At poles $\lambda = 90°$; $g' = g$.

The highest value of g will occur at poles. It is nearly 9.83 m/s^2.

2. At equator $\lambda = 0°$; $\qquad g' = g - \omega^2 R$

or $$g - g' = \omega^2 R$$

$$= \left(\frac{2\pi}{T}\right)^2 R$$

$$\simeq 0.034 \, \text{m/s}^2.$$

Thus the free-fall acceleration $g'(9.78 \, \text{m/s}^2 \simeq 9.8 \, \text{m/s}^2)$ measured on the equator of the rotatory earth is slightly less than the gravitation acceleration g.

3. The effective value of g at equator to be zero : Let ω' be the angular velocity of rotation of earth, then

$$g - \omega'^2 R = 0$$

or $$\omega' = \sqrt{\frac{g}{R}}.$$

This value is nearly 17 times the present value of rotation.

As $\omega' = 17\omega$, $\therefore$ $T' = \dfrac{T}{17} = \dfrac{24}{17} \simeq 1.41$ h . Thus, if time period of rotation of earth becomes 1.41 h, the body of equator will fly off.

Variation of *g* with height

Consider a point at a height h from the earth's surface, then distance from earth's centre $r = R + h$. The value of g at height h is given by ;

$$g_h = \frac{GM}{r^2} = \frac{GM}{(R+h)^2}$$

$$= \frac{GM}{R^2\left(1+\dfrac{h}{R}\right)^2}$$

Since $$g = GM / R^2$$

$$\therefore \qquad g_h = \frac{g}{\left(1+\dfrac{h}{R}\right)^2}.$$

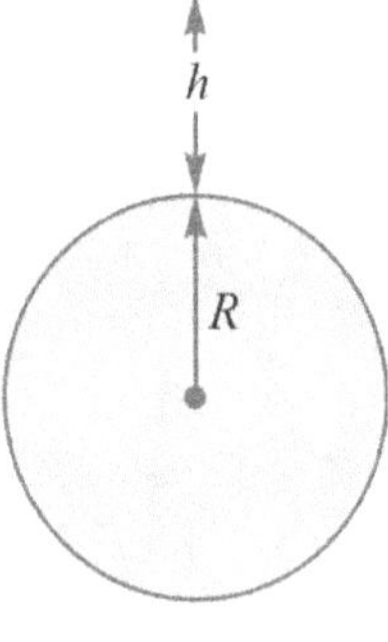

Figure. 9.14

The value of *g*
(i) At a height of geostationary satellite $g_h = 0.225$ m/s^2.
(ii) At a distance as moon from earth's centre $g_h = 0.0027$ m/s^2.

Variation of *g* with depth

Consider a point, at a depth d from earth's surface. We assume that the earth is a homogeneous sphere. It can be shown that the gravitational force on the mass m is only due to the inner solid sphere of radius $(R - d)$. The outer shell of thickness d exterior to the mass exerts no force on it. Thus the mass of the earth included in a sphere of radius $r = (R - d)$

$$M' = \left[\frac{M}{\dfrac{4}{3}\pi R^3}\right]\frac{4}{3}\pi(R-d)^3$$

$$= \frac{M}{R^3}(R-d)^3.$$

This mass can be assumed at the centre of the earth, then

$$g_d = \frac{F'}{m} = \frac{GM'm}{(R-d)^2}\bigg/ m$$

$$= \frac{GM'}{(R-d)^2}$$

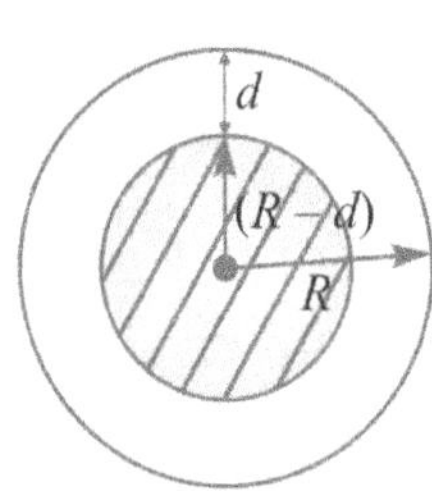

Figure. 9.15

$$= \frac{G\left[\dfrac{M(R-d)^3}{R^3}\right]}{(R-d)^2}$$

$$= \frac{GM}{R^2}\frac{(R-d)}{R}$$

or $$g_d = g\left(1-\frac{d}{R}\right) = \frac{g(R-d)}{R} = \frac{gr}{R}.$$

Special cases :

1. At the centre of earth, $d = R$; $\therefore g_d = 0$
2. At the surface of earth, $d = 0$; $g_d = g$.

Variation in value of g :

$$g_h = \frac{GM}{r^2}, \; r > R$$

$$g = \frac{GM}{R^2}, \; r = R$$

$$g_d = \frac{GM}{R^3}r, \; r < R.$$

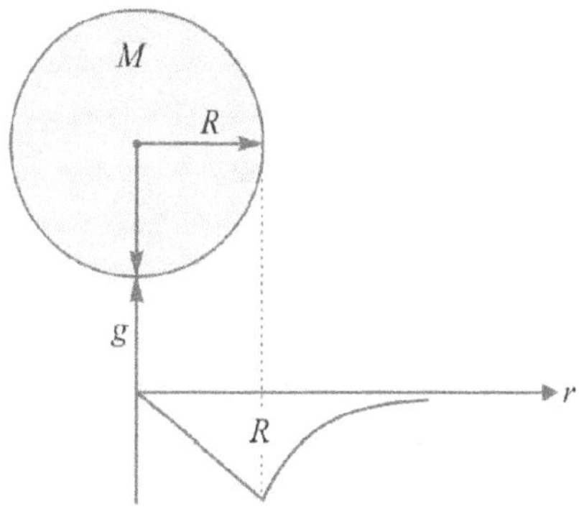

Figure. 9.16

Note: Intensity of gravitational field is towards the centre of earth, i.e. $\vec{g} \propto (-\vec{r})$. Therefore it is plotted on negative side.

Change in value of 'g' due to change in radius of earth, keeping mass of earth constant

g at the surface of the earth

$$g = \frac{GM}{R^2}$$

$$= (GM)R^{-2}$$

For small change in radius (ΔR), the change in value of g,

$$\therefore \quad \frac{\Delta g}{g} = -2\frac{\Delta R}{R}$$

or $$\frac{\Delta g}{g} \times 100 = -2\left(\frac{\Delta R}{R} \times 100\right)$$

Thus 1% decrease in radius of earth will increase the value of g by 2%.

9.7 GRAVITATIONAL POTENTIAL ENERGY

We have discussed gravitational potential energy of a particle due to the earth in chapter (Work, Energy and Power). We had kept the particle very close to earth's surface. So that we could regard the gravitational force as constant. We arbitrarily defined the potential energy of the particle-earth system to be zero when the particle was on the earth surface.

Now we take our zero potential energy reference to one in which the particles are separated at infinite distance. The potential energy of the particle-earth system is the negative of the work done W by the gravitational force as the particle moves from infinite to the some finite distance.

We have $$\Delta U = W_{\text{agent}} = -W_{\text{gravitational force}}$$

or $$U_f - U_i = -W_{\text{gravitational force}}$$

For $r = \infty$, $$U_i = 0$$

and $r = r$, $$U_f = U$$

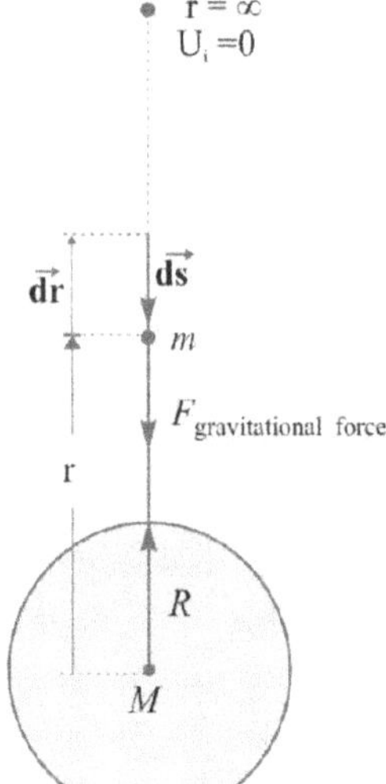

Figure. 9.17

$$\therefore \quad U = -W_{\text{gravitational force}}$$

$$= -\int \vec{F}.d\vec{s}$$

$$= -\int F ds \cos 0°$$

As displacement vector and position vector are opposite, so $d\vec{s} = -d\vec{r}$

$$\therefore \quad U = -\int_{\infty}^{r} F(-dr)$$

$$= \int_{\infty}^{r} \frac{GMm}{r^2} dr$$

$$= GMm \int_{\infty}^{r} r^{-2} dr$$

$$= GMm \left[\frac{r^{-1}}{-1}\right]_{\infty}^{r}$$

$$= -GMm \left[\frac{1}{r}\right]_{\infty}^{r}$$

$$= -GMm \left[\frac{1}{r} - \frac{1}{\infty}\right]$$

or

$$U = -\frac{GMm}{r}.$$

Other Definition of Potential Energy

The potential energy can also be defined as; The work done in bringing the particle from infinite distance to a finite distance. So we can write,

$$U = \left[W_{\text{agent}}\right]_{\infty}^{q} \qquad ...(i) \qquad [U_{\infty} = 0, \text{ at } r = \infty]$$

The gravitational force on the body at a distance x from its centre, $F = \dfrac{GMm}{x^2}$.

Now work done by agent,

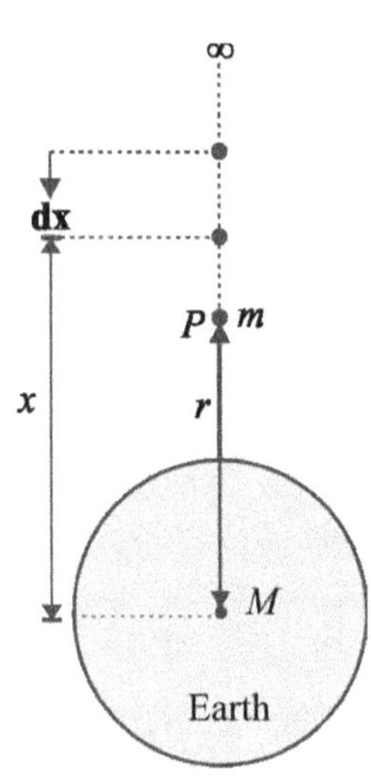

Figure. 9.18

$$W_{\text{agent}} = \int_{\infty}^{r} F dx$$

$$= \int_{\infty}^{r} \frac{GMm}{x^2} dx$$

$$= GMm \int_{\infty}^{r} x^{-2} dx$$

$$= -\frac{GMm}{r}.$$

On substituting this value in equation (i), we get

$$U = -\frac{GMm}{r}.$$

Change in potential energy

With respect to infinity as reference level, the potential energy of particle at earth surface, $r = R$

$$U = \frac{-GMm}{R}.$$

The potential energy of particle at height h

$$U_h = \frac{-GMm}{R+h}.$$

The change in potential energy

$$\Delta U = U_h - U$$

$$= -\frac{GMm}{R+h} - \left[\frac{-GMm}{R}\right]$$

$$= GMm\left[\frac{1}{R} - \frac{1}{R+h}\right]$$

or

$$\Delta U = GMm\left[\frac{R+h-R}{R(R+h)}\right]$$

$$= \frac{GMmh}{R^2\left(1+\dfrac{h}{R}\right)}$$

$$\Delta U = \frac{mgh}{1+\dfrac{h}{R}} \qquad \left(g = \frac{GM}{r^2}\right)$$

For $h << R,\ \dfrac{h}{R} \rightarrow 0$

$$\therefore \qquad \Delta U \simeq mgh.$$

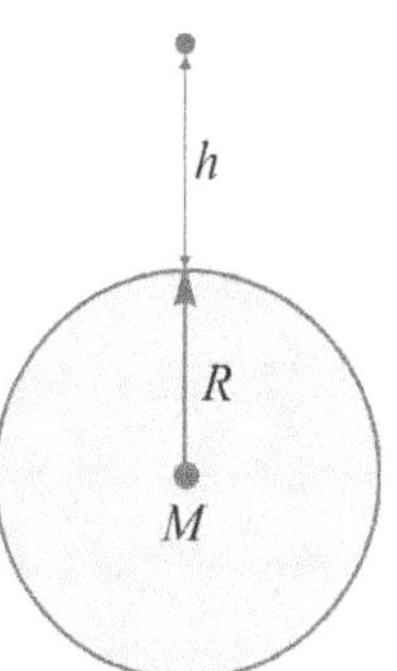

Figure. **9.19**

> **Note :** The potential energy given by equation $U = -\dfrac{GMm}{r}$ is a property of the system of two particles rather than of either particle alone. For particle-earth system , $M >> m$, so we often speak of "the potential energy of the particle."

Height attained by a particle

Suppose a particle is projected with a speed v. We wish to find maximum height attained by the particle. Neglecting air resistance etc., its mechanical energy remains constant, so we have
decrease in kinetic energy = increase in potential energy

i.e.,

$$-\Delta K = \Delta U$$

or

$$-\left(0 - \frac{1}{2}mv^2\right) = \frac{mgh}{1+\dfrac{h}{R}}.$$

After solving, we get

$$h = \frac{v^2}{2g - \dfrac{v^2}{R}}$$

Special case : If v is small, then $\dfrac{v^2}{R} \rightarrow 0$

$$\therefore \qquad h = \frac{v^2}{2g}.$$

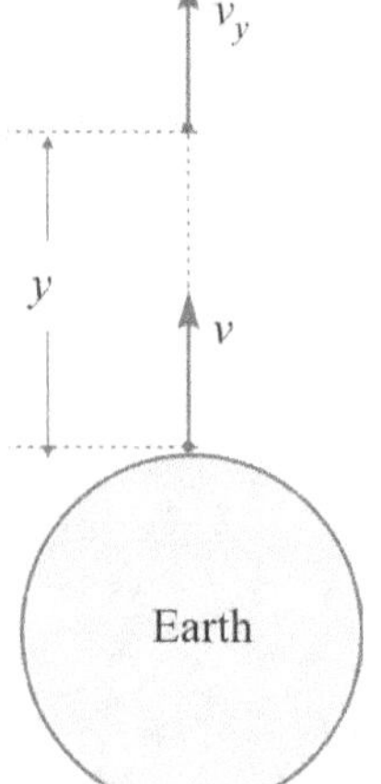

Figure. **9.20**

Time to get the maximum height

Suppose at any height y, the speed of the particle is v_y, so by conservation of mechanical energy, we have

$$-\left(\frac{1}{2}mv_y^2 - \frac{1}{2}mv^2\right) = \frac{mgy}{1+\dfrac{y}{R}}$$

or

$$\frac{1}{2}mv^2 - \frac{1}{2}mv_y^2 = \frac{mgy}{1+\dfrac{y}{R}}$$

or

$$v_y = \left[v^2 - \frac{2gy}{1+\dfrac{y}{R}}\right]^{1/2}$$

or

$$\frac{dy}{dt} = \left[v^2 - \frac{2gy}{1+\dfrac{y}{R}}\right]^{1/2}$$

or

$$\int_0^h \frac{dy}{\left[v^2 - \dfrac{2gy}{1+y/R}\right]^{1/2}} = \int_0^t dt$$

After solving above equation, we can get t.

Self energy of earth

The energy possesse due to interactions between particles of the body itself is called self energy. Consider an element of thickness dr at a radial distance r.

Let m_1 and m_2 be the masses of sphere of radius r and element respectively. If M and R are the mass and radius of earth, then

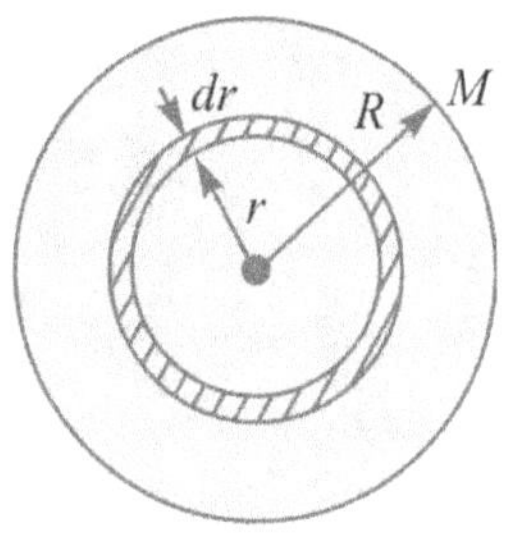

Figure. **9.21**

$$m_1 = \left(\frac{M}{\dfrac{4}{3}\pi R^3}\right) \times \frac{4}{3}\pi r^3 = \frac{Mr^3}{R^3}$$

$$m_2 = \left(\frac{M}{\dfrac{4}{3}\pi R^3}\right) \times 4\pi r^2 dr = \frac{3Mr^2 dr}{R^3}.$$

The potential energy of system of masses m_1 and m_2 is given by

$$dU = \frac{-Gm_1 m_2}{r}$$

The total potential energy (self energy) of the earth

$$U = -\int_0^R \frac{Gm_1 m_2}{r}$$

$$= -G\int_0^R \frac{\left(\dfrac{Mr^3}{R^3}\right)\left(\dfrac{3Mr^2}{R^3}dr\right)}{r}$$

$$= -\frac{3GM^2}{R^6}\int_0^R r^4 dr$$

$$= -\frac{3GM^2}{R^6}\left.\frac{r^5}{5}\right|_0^R$$

or
$$U_{\text{self}} = -\frac{3}{5}\frac{GM^2}{R}.$$

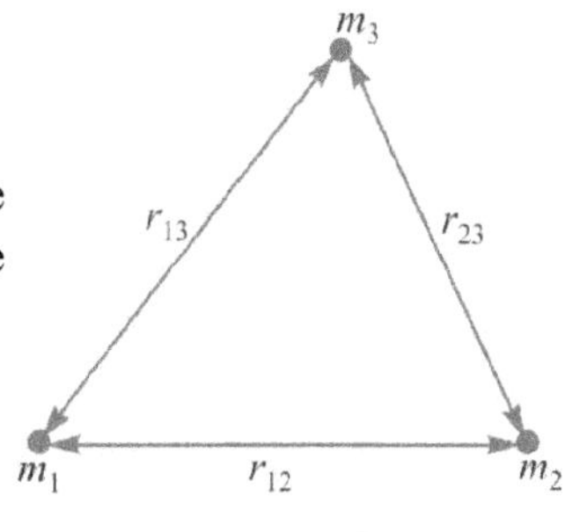

Figure. **9.22**

Potential energy of system of particles

If our system contains more than two particles , we consider each pair of particles in turn, calculate the gravitational potential energy of that pair as if the other particles were not there and then sum the result. The potential energy of the system of three particles shown in *figure 9.22*.

$$U = -\left(\frac{Gm_1m_2}{r_{12}} + \frac{Gm_1m_3}{r_{13}} + \frac{Gm_2m_3}{r_{23}}\right).$$

Note: If there are n particles in the system, then number of pairs formed are $\dfrac{n(n-1)}{2}$. For

three- particle system, it is $\dfrac{3\times 2}{2} = 3$. For n $= 4$, total pairs will be $\dfrac{4\times(4-1)}{2} = 6$.

Potential energy of multi-particles system

In case the system has *n*-particles, the total gravitational potential energy of the system is given by

$$U = \sum\left\{-G\frac{m_im_j}{r_{ij}}\right\} = -G\left\{\sum\frac{m_im_j}{r_{ij}}\right\}$$
$$\text{all pairs, } i \neq j$$

where the summation extends to all pairs of *i* and *j* excluding the case $i = j$, which contributes nothing to the potential energy of the system. We have to count all possible pairs, which obviously means counting each pair twice, first as *i*, *j* and then *j*, *i* (i.e. 1, 2 and 2, 1) excluding the case $i = j$, thus the total number counted is twice the actual number of pairs. Therefore to get correct pairs, we divide the expression of *U* by 2. Thus we have

$$U = -\frac{1}{2}G\sum_{i=1}^{n}\sum_{\substack{j=1\\j\neq i}}^{n}\frac{m_im_j}{r_{ij}}.$$

9.8 Gravitational potential

The gravitational potential at a point in the gravitational field of a body is defined as the amount of work done in bringing a body of unit mass from infinity to that point. Thus gravitational potential,

$$V_p = \frac{[W_\infty^P]_{\text{agent}}}{m}.$$

The gravitational potential is a scalar quantity. Its SI unit is J/kg.

Gravitational potential at a point due to earth

The work done in bringing a body of mass *m* from infinity to a point at a distance *r* from the

centre of the earth is $W = \dfrac{-GMm}{r}$ for $r > R.$

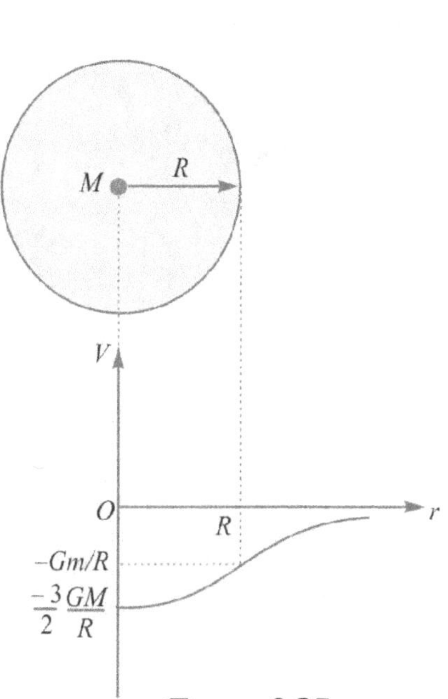

Figure. **9.23**

Hence gravitational potential, $\quad V \;=\; \dfrac{W}{m}$

$$= \dfrac{-GMm/r}{m}$$

or $\qquad V \;=\; \dfrac{-GM}{r}.$

Other cases :

(i) $\quad V = \dfrac{-GM}{r}, \;\; r > R$

(ii) $\quad V = \dfrac{-GM}{R}, \;\; r = R$

(iii) $\quad V = -GM\left[\dfrac{3R^2 - r^2}{2R^3}\right], \;\; r < R$

(iv) $\quad V = \dfrac{3}{2}\left(\dfrac{-GM}{R}\right), \;\; r = 0$

or $\quad V_{\text{centre}} = \dfrac{3}{2} V_{\text{surface}}.$

Potential at, $r < R$

Potential at point P

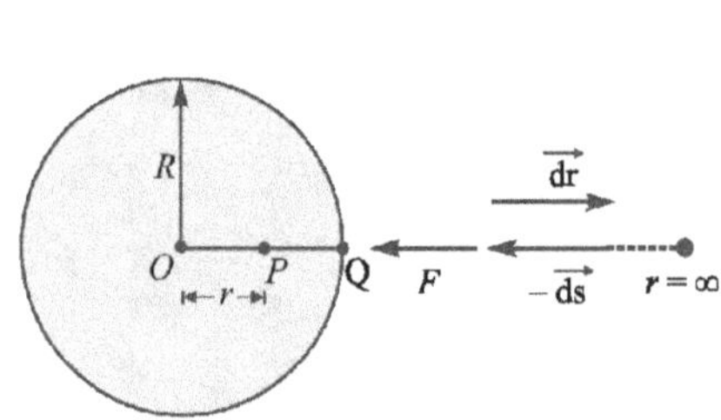

Figure. 9.24

$$V_P \;=\; \dfrac{\left[W_\infty^P\right]_{\text{agent}}}{m} = -\left[W_\infty^P\right]_{\text{gravitational force}}$$

$$= \; -\left[\dfrac{W_\infty^Q + W_Q^P}{m}\right]$$

$$= \; -\dfrac{1}{m}\left[\int_\infty^R \vec{\mathbf{F}}\cdot d\vec{\mathbf{s}} + \int_R^r \vec{\mathbf{F}}\cdot d\vec{\mathbf{s}}\right]$$

$$= \; -\dfrac{1}{m}\left[\int_\infty^R F\,ds + \int_R^r F'\,ds\right]\left[\vec{\mathbf{F}}.d\vec{\mathbf{s}} = \mathrm{F}\,ds\cos 0^\circ = \mathrm{F}\,ds\right]$$

$$= \; -\dfrac{1}{m}\left[\int_\infty^R \dfrac{GMm}{r^2}(-dr) + \int_R^r \dfrac{GMmr}{R^3}(-dr)\right]$$

After solving, we get

$$V_P \;=\; -GM\left[\dfrac{3R^2 - r^2}{2R^3}\right].$$

Spherical shell of mass M and radius R

1. Intensity of gravitational field

   (i) $E = -\dfrac{GM}{r^2},\ r > R$ (ii) $E = -\dfrac{GM}{R^2},\ r = R$

   (iii) $E = 0,\ r < R$.

2. Gravitational potential

   (i) $V = -\dfrac{GM}{r},\ r > R$ (ii) $V = -\dfrac{GM}{R},\ r = R$

   (iii) $V = -\dfrac{GM}{R},\ r < R$.

Relation between gravitational field and potential

Gravitational potential at any point is defined as ;

$$V = \frac{W_{\text{agent}}}{m} = \frac{-W_{\text{gravitational force}}}{m}$$

$$= -\frac{\int \vec{F}.d\vec{r}}{m}$$

$$= -\int \left(\frac{\vec{F}}{m}\right).d\vec{r}$$

As $\quad \dfrac{\vec{F}}{m} = \vec{E},$

$$\therefore \quad V = -\int \vec{E}.d\vec{r}.$$

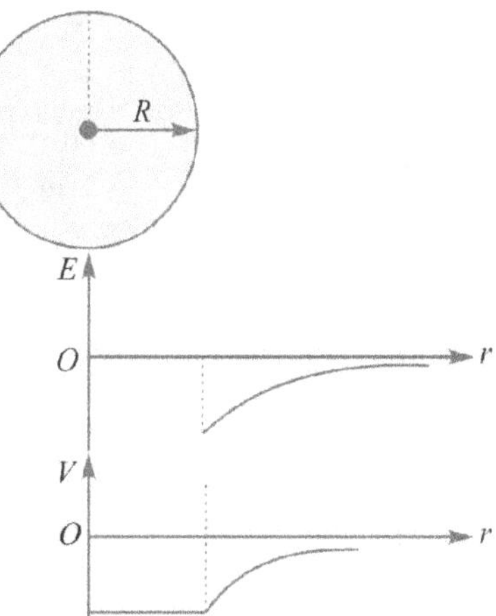

Figure. 9.25

Differentiating both sides of above expression, we get

$$E = \frac{-dV}{dr}.$$

For three dimensional field, we can write

$$E_x = \frac{-\partial V}{\partial x},\ E_y = -\frac{\partial V}{\partial y}\ \text{and}\ E_z = -\frac{\partial V}{\partial z}.$$

Thus resultant field can be written as;

$$\vec{E} = -\left(\frac{\partial V}{\partial x}\hat{\mathbf{i}} + \frac{\partial V}{\partial y}\hat{\mathbf{j}} + \frac{\partial V}{\partial z}\hat{\mathbf{k}}\right).$$

FORMULAE USED

1. Kepler's law of areas : $\dfrac{\Delta \vec{A}}{\Delta t} = \dfrac{\vec{L}}{2m}.$

2. Kepler's law of periods : $T^2 \propto r^3.$

3. Newton's law of gravitation, $F = \dfrac{Gm_1 m_2}{r^2}.$

4. Intensity of gravitation field on the earth's surface $E_g = g = \dfrac{GM}{R^2}.$

5. Mass of the earth, $M = \dfrac{gR^2}{G}.$

6. The value of g at some height, $g' = \dfrac{g}{\left(1+\dfrac{h}{R}\right)^2} \simeq g(1-\dfrac{2h}{R})$ for $h << R$

7. The value of g at some depth, $g' = g\left(1-\dfrac{h}{R}\right)$.

8. Effect of rotation, at an latitude λ
$$g' = g - \omega^2 R \cos^2\lambda$$

9. At equator, $\lambda = 0$, $g' = g - \omega^2 R$.

10. At equator $g' \to 0$, $\omega = \sqrt{\dfrac{g}{R}} = 17$ times present value of rotation

11. Gravitation potential, outside the body $V_g = -\dfrac{GM}{r}$. Also $E_g = -\dfrac{dV}{dr}$

12. Gravitational Potential energy (earth-body system) $U_g = -\dfrac{GMm}{r}$.

13. Self energy of earth, $U = -\dfrac{3}{5}\dfrac{GM^2}{R}$.

14. Change in potential energy, $\Delta U = \left(\dfrac{mgh}{1+\dfrac{h}{R}}\right) \simeq mgh, \quad h << R.$

EXAMPLES BASED ON NEWTONS LAW OF GRAVITATION, INTENSITY OF FIELD AND POTENTIAL

Example 1. **Answer the following:**

(a) **You can shield a charge from electrical forces by putting it inside a hollow conductor. Can you shield a body from the gravitational influence of nearby matter by putting it inside a hollow sphere or by some other means?**

(b) **An astronaut inside a small spaceship orbiting around the Earth cannot detect gravity. If the space station orbiting around the Earth has a large size, can he hope to detect gravity?**

(c) **If you compare the gravitational force on the Earth due to the Sun to that due to the Moon you would find that the Sun's pull is greater than the Moon's pull. (You can check this yourself using the data available in the succeeding exercises). However, the tidal effect of the Moon's pull is greater than the tidal effect of Sun. Why?** **[NCERT]**

Sol. (a) No. Gravitational forces are independent of medium. A body cannot be shielded from the gravitational influence of nearby matter.

(b) Yes. If the size of the spaceship is extremely large, then the gravitational effect of spaceship may become measurable. The variation in g can also be detected.

(c) Tidal effect depends inversely on the cube of the distance, unlike force which depends inversely on the square of the distance. Since the distance of moon from the earth is very small as compared to the distance of sun from the earth. Therefore, the tidal effect of Moon's pull is greater than the tidal effect of sun.

Example 2. **A rocket is fired from the earth towards the sun. At what point on its path is the gravitational force on the rocket zero? Mass of sun = 2×10^{30} kg, Mass of earth = 6×10^{24} kg. Neglect the effect of the other planets. Orbital radius of the earth = 1.5×10^{11} m** **[NCERT]**

Sol. $M_s = 2 \times 10^{30}$ kg. $M_e = 6 \times 10^{24}$ kg $r = 1.5 \times 10^{11}$ m

Let at a distance x from the earth the gravitational force on the rocket due to sun and the earth are equal and opposite.

$\therefore$ Distance of the rocket from the sun $= r - x$

If m is the mass of the rocket then

$$\frac{GM_s m}{(r-x)^2} = \frac{GM_e m}{x^2} \Rightarrow \frac{(r-x)^2}{x^2} = \frac{M_s}{M_e}$$

$$\Rightarrow \frac{r-x}{x} = \sqrt{\frac{M_s}{M_e}} \Rightarrow \sqrt{\frac{2 \times 10^{30}}{6 \times 10^{24}}} = \frac{10^3}{\sqrt{3}}$$

$\therefore x = 2.59 \times 10^8$ m *Ans.*

Example 3. How will you 'weigh the sun', that is estimate its mass? The mean orbital radius of the earth around the sun is 1.5×10^8 km. [NCERT]

Sol. The mean orbital radius of the Earth around the Sun

$R = 1.5 \times 10^8$ km $= 1.5 \times 10^{11}$ m

Time period, $T = 365.25 \times 24 \times 60 \times 60$ s

Let the mass of the Sun be M and that of Earth be m.

According to law of gravitation

$$F = G \frac{Mm}{R^2} \qquad ...(i)$$

Centripetal force,

$$F = \frac{mv^2}{R} = m\omega^2 R \qquad ...(ii)$$

From eqn. (i) and (ii), we have

$$\frac{GMm}{R^2} = mR\omega^2$$

$$= \frac{mR4\pi^2}{T^2} \qquad \left[\because \omega = \frac{2\pi}{T} \right]$$

$$\therefore \quad M = \frac{4\pi^2 R^3}{GT^2}$$

$$= \frac{4 \times (3.14)^2 \times (1.5 \times 10^{11})^3}{6.67 \times 10^{-11} \times (365.25 \times 24 \times 60 \times 60)^2}$$

$$= 2.009 \times 10^{30} \text{ kg} = 2.0 \times 10^{30} \text{ kg.} \qquad \textbf{Ans.}$$

Example 4. Assuming the earth to be a sphere of a uniform mass density, how much would a body weigh half way down to the centre of earth if it weighed 250 N on the surface? [g on the surface of the earth = 9.8 m/s^2] [NCERT]

Sol. Acceleration due to gravity at a depth 'd' is $g' = g\left(1 - \dfrac{d}{R}\right)$

$$\therefore \quad \text{Weight} = mg' = mg\left(1 - \frac{d}{R}\right)$$

$$= 250\left(1 - \frac{R/2}{R}\right) = 125 \text{ N} \qquad \textbf{Ans.}$$

Example 5. A geostationary satellite orbits the earth at a height of nearly 36,000 km from the surface of the earth. What is the potential due to earth's gravity at the site of this satellite? (Consider the P.E. at infinity to be zero.) Mass of the earth = 6×10^{24} kg, Radius = 6400 km . [NCERT]

Sol. Gravitational potential at a height h above the surface of the

earth, $V = \dfrac{-GM}{R+h}$

$$= \frac{-6.67 \times 10^{-11} \times 6 \times 10^{24}}{(6.4 \times 10^6 + 36 \times 10^6)} = -9.4 \times 10^6 \text{ J/kg.}$$

Example 6. A spherical hollow is made in a lead sphere of radius R. Such that its surface touches the outside surface of the lead sphere and passes through its centre. The mass of the sphere before hollowing was M. With what gravitational force will the hollowed-out lead sphere attract a small sphere of mass m, which lies at a distance d from the centre of the lead sphere on the straight line connecting the centres of the sphere and of the hollow?

Sol.

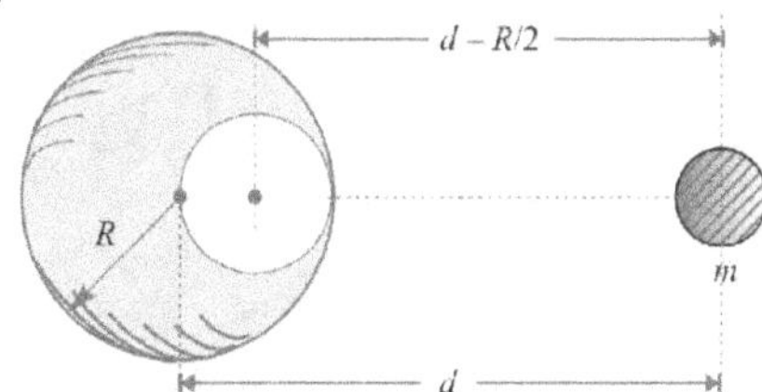

Figure. 9.26

Volume of the sphere removed

$$V = \frac{4}{3}\pi\left(\frac{R}{2}\right)^3$$

Mass of the sphere removed

$$M' = \frac{M}{\frac{4}{3}\pi R^3} \times \frac{4}{3}\pi\left(\frac{R}{2}\right)^3 = \frac{M}{8}.$$

The force on the small sphere of mass m

= Force due to sphere of radius R with the distance d

    – force due to sphere of radius $R/2$ with the distance $(d - R/2)$

i.e.,
$$F = \frac{GMm}{d^2} - \frac{GM'm}{(d - R/2)^2}$$

$$= \frac{GMm}{d^2} - \frac{G\left(\dfrac{M}{8}\right)m}{(d - R/2)^2}$$

$$= GMm\left[\frac{1}{d^2} - \frac{1}{8(d - R/2)^2}\right]$$

$$= \frac{GMm}{d^2}\left[1 - \frac{1}{8(1 - R/2d)^2}\right]. \qquad \textbf{Ans.}$$

Example 7. Two bodies of masses m_1 and m_2 are placed at a distance r apart. Show that the position where the gravitational field due to them is zero, the potential is given by

$$V = -\frac{G}{r}\left[m_1 + m_2 + 2\sqrt{m_1 m_2}\right].$$

Sol. Let the gravitational field be zero at a distance x from m_1. Then we have

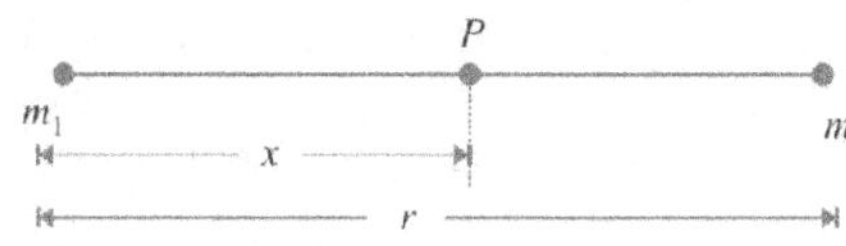

Figure. 9.27

$$\frac{Gm_1}{x^2} = \frac{Gm_2}{(r-x)^2}$$

or $\qquad \dfrac{\sqrt{m_1}}{x} = \dfrac{\sqrt{m_2}}{r-x}$

or $\quad \sqrt{m_1}(r-x) = \sqrt{m_2}\,x$

$\therefore \qquad x = \dfrac{r\sqrt{m_1}}{\sqrt{m_1}+\sqrt{m_2}}$

or $\qquad \dfrac{1}{x} = \dfrac{\sqrt{m_1}+\sqrt{m_2}}{r\sqrt{m_1}}$

and $\quad (r-x) = r - \dfrac{r\sqrt{m_1}}{\sqrt{m_1}+\sqrt{m_2}} = \dfrac{r\sqrt{m_2}}{\sqrt{m_1}+\sqrt{m_2}}$

or $\qquad \dfrac{1}{r-x} = \dfrac{\sqrt{m_1}+\sqrt{m_2}}{r\sqrt{m_2}}$

Gravitational potential at the point P due to both masses

$$V = V_1 + V_2 = -\frac{Gm_1}{x} - \frac{Gm_2}{r-x}$$

$$= -G\left[\frac{m_1(\sqrt{m_1}+\sqrt{m_2})}{r\sqrt{m_1}} + \frac{m_2(\sqrt{m_1}+\sqrt{m_2})}{r\sqrt{m_2}}\right]$$

$$= -\frac{G}{r}\left[m_1 + m_2 + 2\sqrt{m_1 m_2}\right]. \qquad \textbf{Proved}$$

Example 8. **A non-homogeneous sphere of radius R has the following density variation :**

$$\rho = \rho_0 \quad \text{for} \quad r \le R/3$$

$$\rho = \frac{\rho_0}{2} \quad \text{for} \quad \frac{R}{3} < r \le \frac{3R}{4}$$

$$\rho = \frac{\rho_0}{8} \quad \text{for} \quad \frac{3R}{4} < r \le R.$$

What is the gravitational field due to the sphere at $r = \dfrac{R}{4}, \dfrac{R}{2}, \dfrac{5R}{6}$ **and** $2R$ **?**

Sol. The gravitational field at a distance r due to a spherical body of mass M is given by

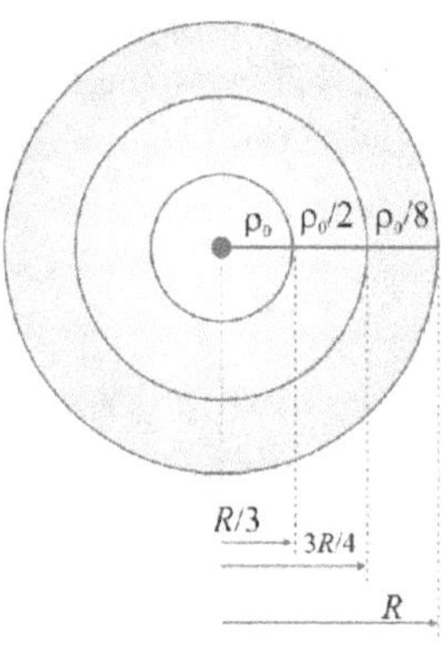

Figure. **9.28**

$$E = \frac{GM}{r^2}$$

(i) For $\quad r = \dfrac{R}{4}$, density $\rho = \rho_0$

The mass of the sphere of radius $R/4$

$$M = \frac{4}{3}\pi\left(\frac{R}{4}\right)^3 \rho_0$$

$$= \pi R^3 \rho_0 / 48.$$

Gravitational field at a distance $R/4$ from the centre of sphere

$\therefore \qquad E_1 = \dfrac{GM}{r^2}$

$$= \frac{G \times \left[\pi R^3 \rho_0 / 48\right]}{(R/4)^2}$$

$$= 0.33\pi GR\rho_0. \qquad \textit{Ans.}$$

In Chapter Exercise 9.1

1. How is gravitational force between two point masses affected when they are dipped in water keeping the separation between them the same? [NCERT Exemplar]
   Ans: gravitational force is independent of medium

2. Is it possible for a body to have inertia but no weight?
   Ans: Yes [NCERT Exemplar]

3. Out of aphelion and perihelion, where is the speed of the earth more and why? **Ans :** $v \propto \dfrac{1}{r}$ [NCERT Exemplar]

4. An object of mass m is raised from the surface of the earth to the height equal to the radius of the earth, that is, taken from a distance R to 2R from the centre of the earth. What is the gain in its potential energy?

   Ans: $\Delta U = \dfrac{mgR}{2}$. [NCERT Exemplar]

5. A mass m is placed at point P at a distance h along the normal through the centre O of a thin circular ring of mass M and radius r as shown in figure.
   If the mass is removed further away such that OP becomes 2h, by what factor, the force of gravitation will decrease, if $h = r$?

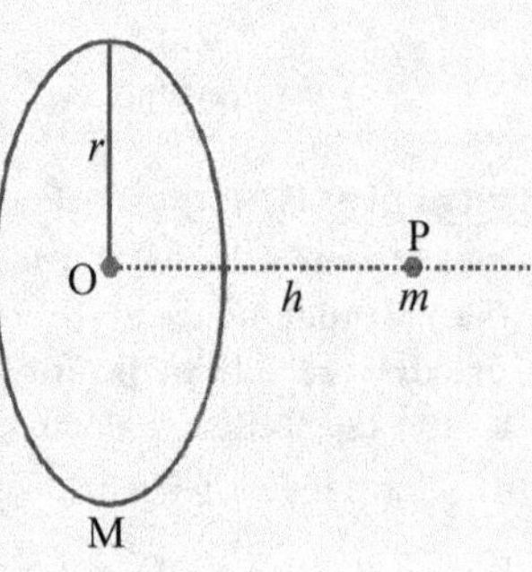

[NCERT Exemplar]

Ans : $\dfrac{F'}{F} = \dfrac{4\sqrt{2}}{5\sqrt{5}}$

9.9 SATELLITE

A satellite is a body which continuously revolves around a much heavier body in a stable orbit. Moon is the natural satellite of the earth, which in turn, is a satellite of sun. A man made satellite is called artificial satellite. Aryabhata, INSAT etc. are the India's artificial satellites.

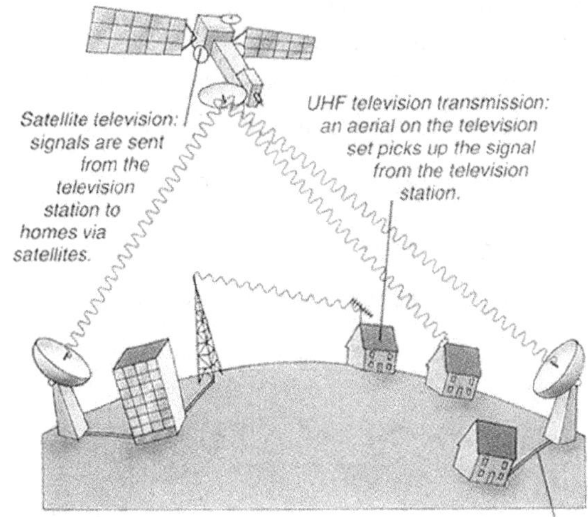

Figure. 9.29

Principle of launching a satellite

Let us throw a body horizontally from the top of the tower. The body describes a parabolic path under the influence of gravity and hits the earth's surface. At a certain horizontal velocity, the body will not hit the earth, but it will always be in state of free fall under gravity. The body will follow a circular path around the earth and will become a satellite of the earth. This horizontal velocity is called orbital velocity. Hence to establish a satellite into an orbit around the earth, it requires;

1. A minimum vertical velocity to take the satellite to its orbit.
2. Orbital velocity to make it move in a circular orbit around the earth.

9.10 ORBITAL VELOCITY

Let a satellite is to revolve in a circular orbit at a height h from earth surface. The orbital radius of

satellite, $r = R + h$. The centripetal force required to keep the satellite in orbit is $\dfrac{mv_0^2}{r}$, which is

provided by the gravitational pull of the earth. Therefore

$$\frac{mv_0^2}{r} = \frac{GMm}{r^2}$$

or
$$v_0 = \sqrt{\frac{GM}{r}}.$$

If g is the acceleration due to gravity on the surface of the earth, then $GM = gR^2$.

$$\therefore \quad v_0 = \sqrt{\frac{gR^2}{r}} = \sqrt{\frac{gR^2}{(R+h)}}.$$

When satellite revolves close to earth surface, then $h \ll R$ and $R + h \simeq R$.

$$\therefore \quad v_0 \simeq \sqrt{gR}.$$

As $g = 9.8 \text{ m/s}^2$ and $R = 6.4 \times 10^6$ m.

So
$$v_0 \simeq \sqrt{9.8 \times 6.4 \times 10^6}$$
$$= 7.92 \text{ km/s}$$
$$= 8 \text{ km/s} \quad (\text{say}).$$

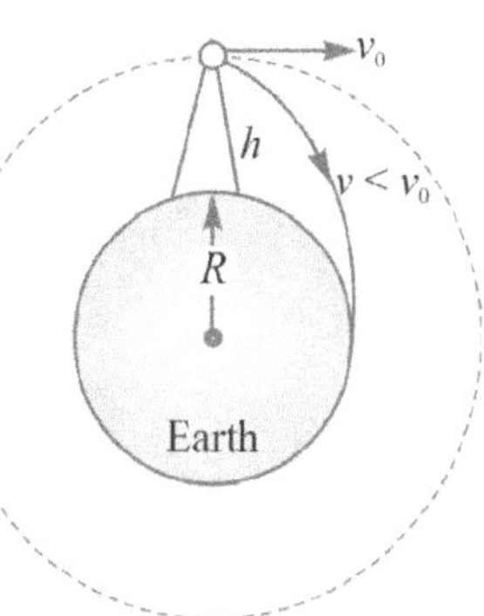

Launching a satellite
Figure. 9.30

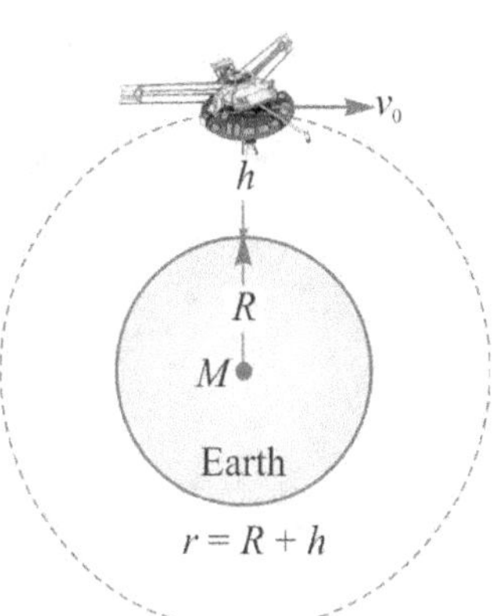

Figure. 9.31

Important points

It is clear from the formula $\quad v_0 = \sqrt{\dfrac{GM}{r}}\quad$ that

(i)   orbital velocity is independent of the mass of the satellite,

(ii)   it decreases with the increase in radius of the orbit,

(iii)   it depends on the mass and radius of the planet about which the satellite revolves,

(iv)   the escape velocity of a body from the earth's surface is $v_e = \sqrt{2gR}$. The orbital velocity of a satellite revolving close to the earth's surface is $v_0 = \sqrt{gR}$. Therefore, $v_e = \sqrt{2}\,v_0$.

9.11 TIME PERIOD OF REVOLUTION

It is the time taken by a satellite to complete one revolution around the earth. It is given by

$$T = \frac{\text{circumference of the orbit}}{\text{orbital velocity}}$$

or

$$T = \frac{2\pi r}{v_0} = \frac{2\pi r}{\sqrt{\dfrac{GM}{r}}}.$$

or

$$T = 2\pi\sqrt{\frac{r^3}{GM}}.$$

We have, $GM = gR^2$ and $r = R + h$

$$\therefore \qquad T = 2\pi\sqrt{\frac{(R+h)^3}{gR^2}}$$

When satellite revolves close to the earth surface, then $h \ll R$ and $R + h \simeq R$

$$\therefore \qquad T \simeq 2\pi\sqrt{\frac{R}{g}}.$$

Putting $g = 9.8 \text{ m/s}^2$ and $R = 6.4 \times 10^6$ m, we get

$$T = 2\pi\sqrt{\frac{6.4 \times 10^6}{9.8}}$$
$$= 5078 \text{ s}$$
$$= 84.6 \text{ min.}$$

9.12 ENERGY OF A SATELLITE

(i)   **Kinetic energy :** The kinetic energy of a satellite due to its orbital motion is

$$\text{K.E.} = \frac{1}{2}mv^2$$
$$= \frac{1}{2}m\left[\sqrt{\frac{GM}{r}}\right]^2$$
$$= \frac{GMm}{2r}.$$

(ii)   **Potential energy :** Because of gravitational pull of the earth, the potential energy of the satellite is given by

$$U = -\frac{GMm}{r}.$$

Total mechanical energy of the satellite

$$E = K + U$$

$$= \frac{GMm}{2r} + \left[-\frac{GMm}{r}\right]$$

or
$$E = -\frac{GMm}{2r}.$$

The total energy of the satellite is negative. It indicates that the satellite is bound to the earth. It can be concluded that

$$K = -\frac{U}{2} = -E.$$

9.13 BINDING ENERGY

The energy required by a satellite to free it from the bondage of earth and escape it to infinity is called binding energy. The total energy of a satellite is $-\dfrac{GMm}{2r}$. In order to escape to infinity, it must be supplied an extra energy equal to $+\dfrac{GMm}{2r}$ so that its total energy becomes equal to zero. Hence binding energy of a satellite

$$\text{B.E.} = \frac{GMm}{2r}.$$

Energy required to establish a satellite into its orbit

The energy of the satellite at the earth's surface
$$E_i = -\frac{GMm}{R}.$$

The energy of the satellite into its orbit
$$E_f = -\frac{GMm}{2r}.$$

The energy needed to establish the satellite into its orbit
$$\Delta E = E_f - E_i$$
$$= -\frac{GMm}{2r} - \left[-\frac{GMm}{R}\right]$$
$$= -\frac{GMm}{2(R+h)} + \frac{GMm}{R}$$
$$= \frac{GMm(R+2h)}{2R(R+h)}.$$

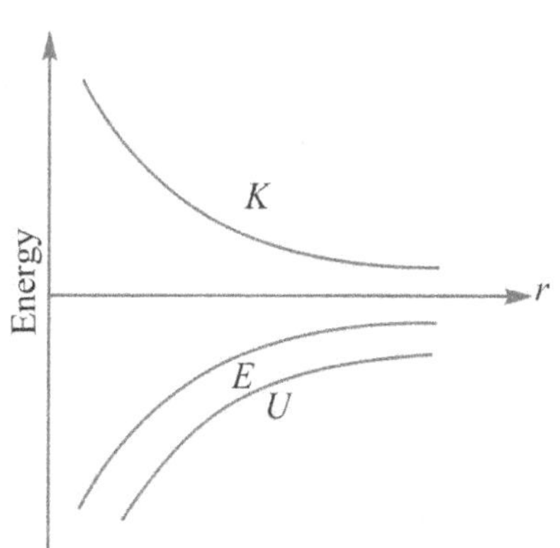

Figure. **9.32**

9.14 GEOSTATIONARY SATELLITE (GSS)

A satellite which appears stationary to an observer on earth's surface is called **geostationary satellite**. When such a satellite is used for communication purposes, it is called **communication satellite**. The first communication satellite was sent by USA in space in 1962 named telstar.

Necessary conditions for a geostationary satellite

1. The orbital plane of the geostationary satellite must lie in the equatorial plane of the earth.
2. Its sense of rotation should be same as that of the earth i.e., from west to east.
3. Its period of revolution around earth will equal to that of the period of rotation of the earth about its axis i.e., 24 hours.

Note: For the stability of satellite into circular orbit, there should not be any torque produced by the force acting on it about the centre of the orbit, when the centre of orbit of satellite does not passes through the centre of the planet, the gravitational pull will cause a torque about the centre and satellite falls on the planet.

Height of geostationary satellite

The time period of revolution of the satellite is given by

$$T = 2\pi \sqrt{\frac{(R+h)^3}{gR^2}}$$

or

$$h = \left[\frac{T^2 gR^2}{4\pi^2}\right]^{1/3} - R.$$

Here $T = 24\,h = 86400$ s, $R = 6.4 \times 10^6$ m, $g = 9.8$ m/s^2

$\therefore$ $h = 35920 \times 10^3$ m

$= 36000$ km (say)

Orbital radius $r = R + h = 6400 + 35923 \simeq 42000$ km.

Orbital velocity of geostationary satellite

Orbital velocity, $\quad v_0 = \omega r$

$$= \frac{2\pi}{T} r$$

$$= \frac{2\pi \times 42000 \times 10^3}{86400} \,\text{m/s}$$

$$\simeq 3 \text{ km/s}.$$

Use of geostationary satellite in global transmission

A satellite cannot make link over the entire earth. This is because of the curvature of the earth keeps a large part of the earth out of sight. However three equally spaced satellites placed in a geostationary orbit can be used to establish link over the entire earth. It can easily be understood by the *figure* 9.33. Such satellites are called synchronous communication satellites (SYNCOMS).

Three equally spaced satellites used for global communication.

Polar satellite

A satellite whose orbital plane is perpendicular to equatorial plane is called polar satellite. IERS is the India's polar satellite. A polar orbit passes over north and south poles of the earth and has a height of 500– 800 km. The polar satellite successively passes across the different parts of earth's surface as the earth rotates about its axis. Thus the polar satellite can photograph entire surface of the earth. They are used in *spying* work for military purposes.

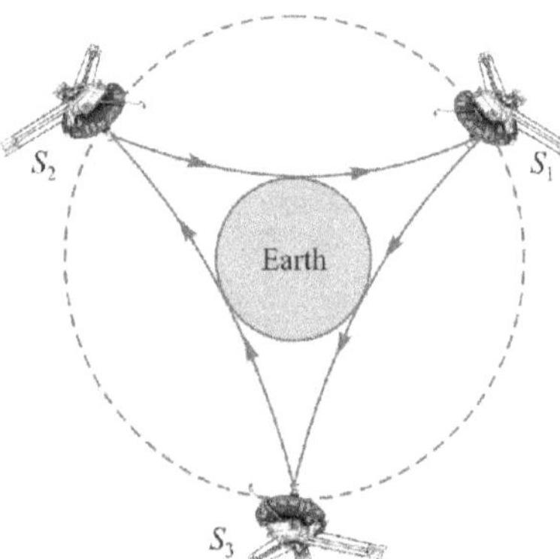

Figure. **9.33**

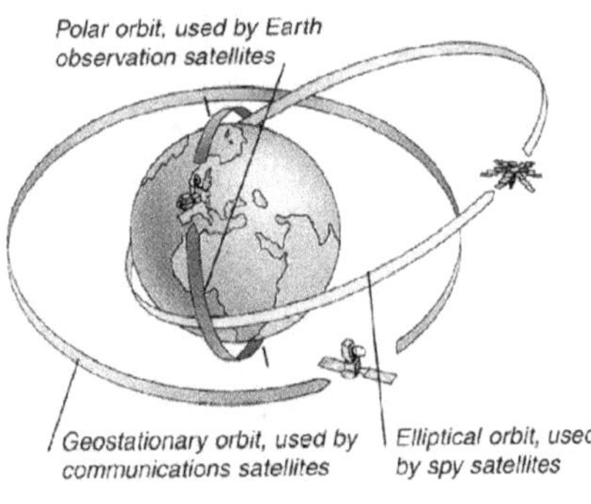

Figure. **9.34**

Table showing path of body at different speeds

Velocity of projection v	Nature of path
$v = v_0$	Circular path around the earth
$v > v_0$ $< v_e$	Elliptical path around the earth
$v = v_e$	Parabolic path, body escapes from earth
$v > v_e$	Hyperbolic path, body escapes from earth

Satellite in elliptical orbit

Eccentricity of the elliptical path $\qquad e \;=\; \dfrac{c}{a}$

$\Rightarrow \qquad\qquad c \;=\; ea$

$\qquad\qquad\qquad r_p \;=\; a - c = a - ea = a(1-e).$

Using conservation of angular momentum at perigee and apogee, we have

$$mv_p r_p \;=\; mv_a r_a \qquad\qquad \ldots(i)$$

$\Rightarrow \qquad\qquad \dfrac{v_p}{v_a} \;=\; \dfrac{r_a}{r_p} = \dfrac{1+e}{1-e}. \qquad\qquad \ldots(ii)$

Mechanical energy of revolving satellite remains constant

$$\therefore \qquad -\dfrac{GMm}{r_p} + \dfrac{1}{2}mv_p{}^2 \;=\; \dfrac{-GMm}{r_a} + \dfrac{1}{2}mv_a{}^2$$

or $$v_p{}^2 - v_a{}^2 \;=\; 2GM\left[\dfrac{1}{r_p} - \dfrac{1}{r_a}\right]$$

We have from equation (i), $\qquad v_p \;=\; \dfrac{v_a r_a}{r_p}$

$$\therefore \qquad \left(\dfrac{v_a r_a}{r_p}\right)^2 - v_a{}^2 \;=\; 2GM\left[\dfrac{1}{r_p} - \dfrac{1}{r_a}\right]$$

or $$v_a{}^2\left(\dfrac{r_a{}^2 - r_p{}^2}{r_p{}^2}\right) \;=\; 2GM\left[\dfrac{r_a - r_p}{r_p r_a}\right]$$

or $$v_a{}^2 \;=\; \dfrac{2GM r_p}{r_a(r_a + r_p)}$$

We have $r_a = a + c$ and $r_p = a - c$, therefore

$$v_a{}^2 \;=\; \dfrac{2GM}{(a+c)+(a-c)}\left[\dfrac{a-c}{a+c}\right]$$

$$=\; \dfrac{GM}{a}\left[\dfrac{a-c}{a+c}\right]$$

$$=\; \dfrac{GM}{a}\left[\dfrac{1-e}{1+e}\right]$$

or $$v_a \;=\; \sqrt{\dfrac{GM}{a}\left[\dfrac{1-e}{1+e}\right]}$$

and $$v_p \;=\; \sqrt{\dfrac{GM}{a}\left[\dfrac{1+e}{1-e}\right]}$$

$$\therefore \qquad \dfrac{v_a}{v_p} \;=\; \left[\dfrac{1-e}{1+e}\right].$$

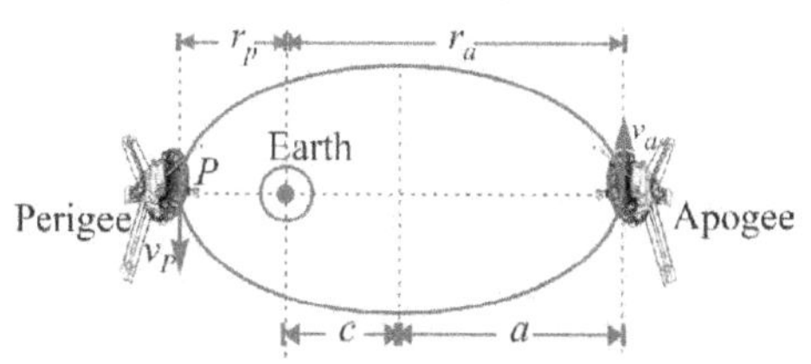

Figure. **9.35**

MISCELLANEOUS TOPICS

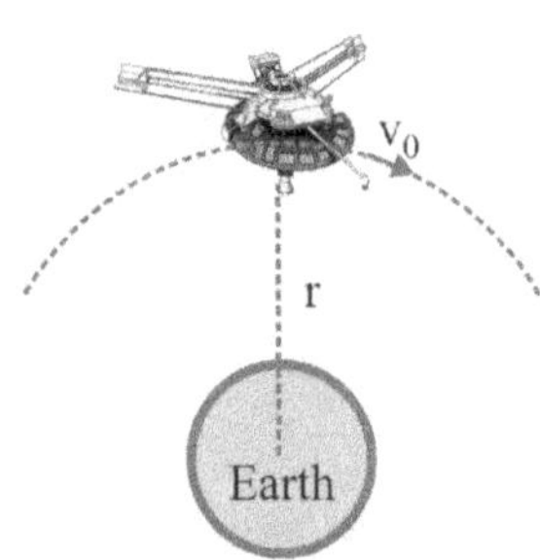

Figure. 9.36

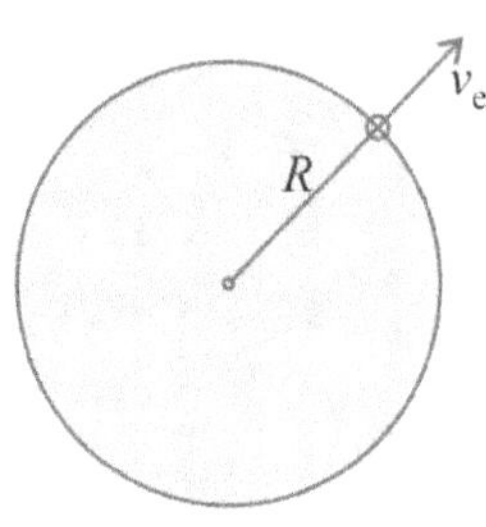

Figure. 9.37

Weightlessness : A body is said to be in a state of weightlessness when the reaction of the supporting surface is zero. For a body in a satellite, by Newton's second law

$$\frac{GMm}{r^2} - N = ma$$

$$= \frac{mv_0^2}{r} = \frac{m}{r}\left(\sqrt{\frac{GM}{r}}\right)^2$$

$$\Rightarrow \qquad N = 0.$$

Thus the surface of satellite exerts no force on the body and hence it experiences weightlessness.

9.15 ESCAPE VELOCITY (ESCAPE SPEED)

When a body is thrown upward, it rises to a certain height and comes back on earth surface. If we throw it with a sufficient velocity, it will never come back. It will escape from the gravitational pull of the earth.

Thus escape velocity is the minimum velocity with which a body be projected in order that it may just escape from the gravitational field of the earth.

Suppose a body is projected from the surface of the earth with a velocity v_e. The total mechanical energy of the body at the surface of earth

$$E = \left[\frac{-GMm}{R} + \frac{1}{2}mv_e^2\right]$$

The body to escape, it will reach at infinity. Therefore by conservation of mechanical energy, we have M.E. of the body at earth surface = M.E. of the body at infinity

or $\qquad -\dfrac{GMm}{R} + \dfrac{1}{2}mv_e^2 = 0 + 0 \qquad$ (As P.E. at infinity is zero, K.E. also becomes zero)

or $\qquad v_e = \sqrt{\dfrac{2GM}{R}}.$

Since $GM = gR^2$, $\quad \therefore v_e = \sqrt{\dfrac{2gR^2}{R}} = \sqrt{2gR}.$

More about escape velocity

1. It is clear from the expression that, escape velocity does not depend on the mass of the projected body. It depends on the mass and radius of the planet from which the body is projected. Some escape velocities:

Heavenly body	Escape velocity
Earth	11.2 Km/s
Moon	2.3 km/s
Jupiter	60 km/s
Sun	618 km/s
Neutron star	2×10^5 km/s

2. In deriving the escape velocity, from earth we have ignored the air resistance on the body. So in actual practice, the value of escape velocity will be greater than 11.2 km/s.

3. The escape velocity does not depend on the angle of projection from the surface of the earth. But it depends on the rotation of the earth about its axis. It becomes easier to attain escape velocity if the body is projected in the direction in which the launch site is moving.

4. If body is projected at a place, h above the earth surface, then

$$\frac{-GMm}{(R+h)} + \frac{1}{2}mv_e'^2 = 0 + 0$$

or $\qquad v_e' = \sqrt{\dfrac{2GM}{(R+h)}} < v_e.$

5. When body is projected from between the planets :
   By conservation of mechanical energy, we have

   $$-\left[\frac{GM_1m}{d_1}+\frac{GM_2m}{d_2}\right]+\frac{1}{2}mv_e^2 = 0+0$$

   or
   $$v_e = \sqrt{2\left[\frac{GM_1}{d_1}+\frac{GM_2}{d_2}\right]}.$$

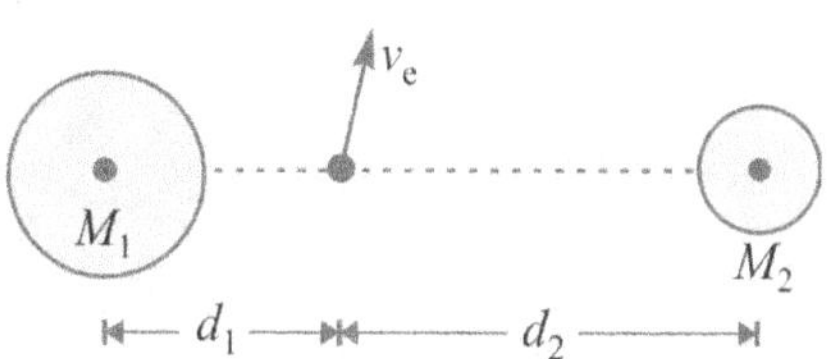

Figure. **9.38**

6. A planet will have atmosphere if the root mean square velocity, $v_{rms} < v_e$.
7. When body is projected with a velocity greater than escape velocity kv_e, $(k > 1)$, then its velocity at infinity will not be zero. It can very easily be calculated by using conservation of mechanical energy. Let v be the velocity at infinity, then

   Mechanical energy at earth's surface = Mechanical energy at infinity

   $$\frac{1}{2}m(kv_e)^2 - \frac{GMm}{R} = \frac{1}{2}mv^2 + 0$$

   or
   $$v = \sqrt{k^2v_e^2 - \frac{2GM}{R}}$$

   As
   $$\sqrt{\frac{2GM}{R}} = v_e$$

   $\therefore$
   $$v = \sqrt{k^2v_e^2 - v_e^2} = v_e\sqrt{k^2-1}.$$

Special cases :

   (i) For $k = 1$, $v = 0$

   (ii) For $k = 2$, $v = \sqrt{3}v_e$.

9.16 BLACK HOLE

A black hole is a body from the surface of which nothing can be escaped, even light. From Einstein's theory of relativity, speed of any object cannot exceed the speed of light , $c = 3 \times 10^8$ m/s. Thus c is the upper limit to the projectile's escape velocity. Hence for a body to be a black hole,

$$v_e \geq c$$

or
$$\sqrt{\frac{2GM}{R}} \geq c$$

or
$$R \leq \frac{2GM}{c^2}.$$

FORMULAE USED

1. Orbital velocity of satellite $(r = R + h)$;

   $$v_0 = \sqrt{\frac{GM}{r}} = \sqrt{\frac{gR^2}{r}} \text{ and time period, } T = 2\pi\sqrt{\frac{r^3}{GM}}$$

2. For a satellite close to earth, $h << R$, $r \simeq R$

   $$v_0 = \sqrt{gR} \simeq 8 \text{ km/s}$$

   and $T = 2\pi\sqrt{\dfrac{R}{g}} \simeq 84.6$ min.

Mechanics

PROBLEM SOLVING STRATEGY

3.   Satellite in elliptical orbit : (a semi-major axis)

$$v_{max} = \sqrt{\left(\frac{1+e}{1-e}\right)\frac{GM}{a}}, \quad v_{min} = \sqrt{\left(\frac{1-e}{1+e}\right)\frac{GM}{a}}.$$

4.   Kinetic energy of a satellite, $K = \dfrac{GMm}{2r}$.

5.   Potential energy, $U = -\dfrac{GMm}{r}$.

6.   Total mechanical energy of satellite $E = K + U = -\dfrac{GMm}{2r}$.

7.   Also $K = -E = -\dfrac{U}{2}$.

8.   Geostationary satellite : $T = 24$ hour, $v_0 \approx 3$ km/s, $h = 36000$ km from earth surface

9.   Escape velocity, $v_e = \sqrt{\dfrac{2GM}{R}} = \sqrt{2gR} = 11.2$ km/s.

10.   For block hole, $v_e \geq c,$

     or $\sqrt{\dfrac{2GM}{R}} \geq c \Rightarrow R \leq \dfrac{2GM}{c^2}.$

PROBLEM SOLVING STRATEGY

1.   **Orbital velocity of Satellite :** To get the orbital velocity of satellite or planet at any point of orbit we can write;

$$\text{Centripetal force} = \frac{mv_0^2}{r}$$

2.   **Escape velocity :** Assuming no air resistance, we can use conservation of mechanical energy;

$$[K + U]_{earth} = [K + U]_{infinity}$$

3.   **For motion of satellite** around earth or motion of planet around sun, we can use;

$$[K + U] = \text{constant},$$

and $\quad m(\vec{r} \times \vec{v}) = \text{constant}.$

4   **At perigee and apogee,** we can have

$$v_2 r_1 = v_2 r_2$$

EXAMPLES BASED ON SATELLITE, ORBITAL SPEED AND EXCAPE VELOCITY

Example 9. Two heavy spheres each of mass 100 kg and radius 0.1m are placed 1 m apart on a horizontal table. What is the gravitational field and potential at the mid point of the line joining the centres of the spheres? Is an object placed at that point in equilibrium? If so, is the equilibrium stable or unstable.

         [NCERT]

Sol.

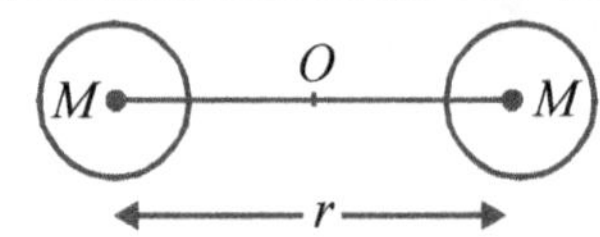

***Figure.* 9.39**

Gravitational field at the mid point O of the line joining the two spheres is equal and opposite

Net field $= -\dfrac{GM}{(r/2)^2} + \dfrac{GM}{(r/2)^2} = 0$

$\therefore$ Net field zero.

Potential at O $V = -\dfrac{GM}{r/2} - \dfrac{GM}{r/2} = \dfrac{-4GM}{r}$

$= \dfrac{-4 \times 6.67 \times 10^{-11} \times 100}{1} = -2.7 \times 10^{-8}$ J/kg $\qquad$ *Ans.*

Example 10. Two stars each of 1 solar mass (= 2×10^{30}kg) are approaching each other for a head on collision. When they are at a distance10^9 km, their speeds are negligible. What is the speed with which they collide? The radius of each star is 10^4 km. Assume the stars to remain undistorbed until they collide. Use the known value of *G*. **[NCERT]**

Sol. Mass of each star, $M = 2 \times 10^{30}$kg.

Radius, $R = 10^4$ km $= 10^7$ m

Initial distance between 2 stars, $r = 10^9$km $= 10^{12}$m

Initial P.E. of the system $= \dfrac{-GM^2}{r}$;

Total K.E. of the system $= \dfrac{1}{2}Mv^2 + \dfrac{1}{2}Mv^2 = Mv^2$

v = speed of collision of each star.

Distance between the centres of the stars when they are about to collide $= r' = R + R = 2R$

$\therefore$ $\quad$ Final P.E. of the system $= \dfrac{-GM^2}{2R}$

$\because$ $\quad$ Gain in K.E. = Loss in P.E.

$\therefore$ $\quad$ $Mv^2 = -\dfrac{GM^2}{r} - \left(-\dfrac{GM^2}{2R}\right)$

$2 \times 10^{30} \times v^2 = -GM^2 \left[\dfrac{1}{10^{12}} - \dfrac{1}{2 \times 10^7}\right]$

$\Rightarrow$ $\quad$ $2 \times 10^3 \times v^2$

$= -6.67 \times 10^{-11} \times (2 \times 10^{30})^2 \left[\dfrac{2 - 10^5}{2 \times 10^{12}}\right]$

$v^2 = \dfrac{1.334 \times 10^{43}}{2 \times 10^{30}}$

$\Rightarrow v = 2.583 \times 10^6$ m/s.

Example 11. A satellite orbits the earth at a height of 400 km above the surface. How much energy must be expended to rocket the satellite out of the gravitational influence of the earth? Mass of the satellite is 200 kg, mass of the earth = 6×10^{24} kg, radius of the earth = 6.4×10^6 m, G = 6.67×10^{-11} Nm²/kg² . **[NCERT]**

Sol. Total energy of the satellite at a height

$h = -\dfrac{GMm}{(R+h)} + \dfrac{1}{2}mv^2$

$= -\dfrac{GMm}{R+h} + \dfrac{1}{2}m\dfrac{GM}{R+h} = -\dfrac{GMm}{2(R+h)}$

Energy expended to rocket the satellite out of the earth's gravitational field = – (T.E. of the satellite) = $\dfrac{GMm}{2(R+h)}$

$= \dfrac{6.67 \times 10^{-11} \times 6 \times 10^{24} \times 200}{2(6.4 \times 10^6 + 4 \times 10^5)} = 5.9 \times 10^9$ J.

Example 12. Two uniform solid spheres of equal radii *R*, but masses *M* and *4 M* have a centre to centre separation *6 R*, as shown in *fig.* 9.40. The two spheres are held fixed. A projectile of mass *m* is projected from the surface of the sphere of mass *M* directly towards the centre of the second sphere. Obtain an expression for the minimum speed *v* of the projectile so that it reaches the surface of the second sphere.

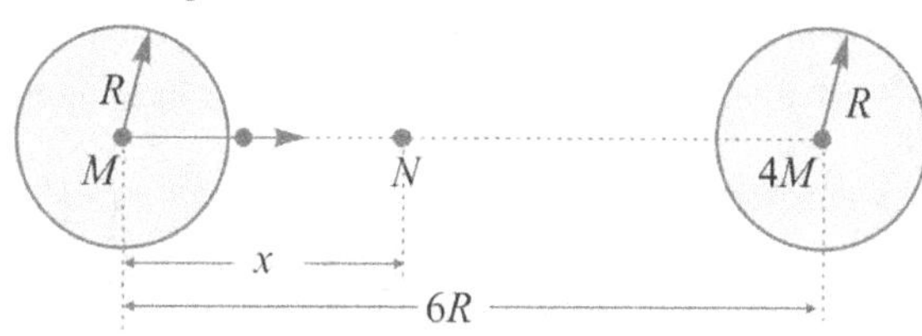

Figure. 9.40

Sol. Let *N* be the position at a distance *x* from the centre of sphere of mass *M* at which two spheres exert equal amount of forces in opposite directions. So we have

$\dfrac{GMm}{x^2} = \dfrac{G(4M)m}{(6R-x)^2}$

or $\qquad\qquad x = 2R.$

For the minimum speed it is sufficient to project the particle on to the point *N*. Thereafter, the particle *m* gets attracted by the gravitational pull of 4 *M*.

Now by conservation of mechanical energy, we have

Mechanical energy of *m* at the surface of *M* = Mechanical energy of *m* at *N*

$\therefore$ $\quad$ $-\left[\dfrac{GMm}{R} + \dfrac{G(4M)m}{5R}\right] + \dfrac{1}{2}mv^2$

$= -\left[\dfrac{GMm}{x} + \dfrac{G(4M)m}{(6R-x)}\right]$

Here $x = 2 R$. After solving, we get

$v = \sqrt{\dfrac{3GM}{5R}}.$ $\qquad$ *Ans.*

Example 13. To what latitude does the syncoms coverage extend?

Sol. The latitude of the coverage extends upto the tangent *SP*.

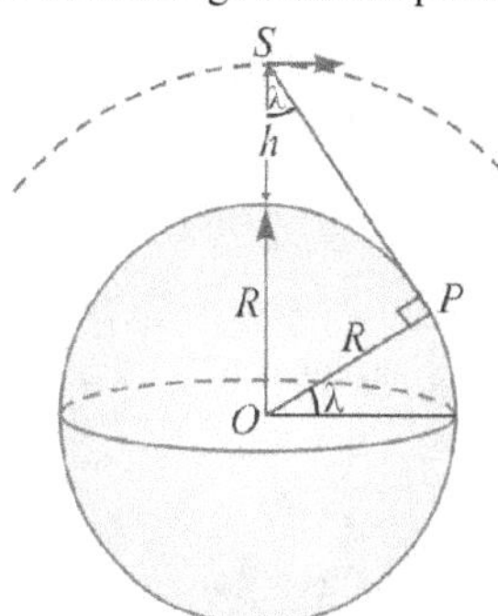

Figure. 9.41

From right $\Delta\ OPS$,

$$\sin\lambda = \frac{OP}{OS} = \frac{R}{R+h} = \frac{6.4\times10^6}{4.2\times10^7}$$

or $\qquad \lambda = \sin^{-1}(0.15)$ **Ans.**

Example 14. A spaceship is stationed on Mars. How much energy must be expended on the spaceship to rocket it out of the solar system? Mass of the space ship = 1000 kg, Mass of the sun $= 2\times10^{30}$ kg, Mass of the Mars = 6.4×10^{23} kg, Radius of Mars = 3395 km, Radius of the orbit of Mars = 2.28×10^{11} m G $= 6.67\times10^{-11}$ Nm²/kg².

Sol. Let R' = radius of the Mars, R = radius of the orbit of Mars, M = mass of the sun M' = mass of the Mars, m = mass of the space-ship.

$\therefore$ P.E. of space-ship due to gravitational attraction of the Sun

$$= \frac{-GMm}{R}$$

P.E. of space-ship due to gravitational attraction of $Mars$

$$= \frac{-GM'm}{R'}$$

$\because$ The K.E. of space-ship is zero.
$\therefore$ Total energy of the ship

$$= \frac{-GMm}{R} - \frac{GM'm}{R'} = -Gm\left(\frac{M}{R} + \frac{M'}{R'}\right)$$

Energy required to rocket out the space ship from the solar system = – (total energy)

$$= -\left[-Gm\left(\frac{M}{R} + \frac{M'}{R'}\right)\right] = Gm\left(\frac{M}{R} + \frac{M'}{R'}\right)$$

$$= 6.67\times10^{-11}\times1000\left[\frac{2\times10^{30}}{2.28\times10^{11}} + \frac{6.4\times10^{23}}{3395\times10^3}\right]$$

$$= 6.67\times10^{-8}\left[\frac{20}{2.28} + \frac{6.4}{33.95}\right]\times10^{18} = 5.98\times10^{11}\text{J. } \textit{Ans.}$$

Example 15. Two masses m_1 and m_2 at an infinite distance from each other are initially at rest, start interacting gravitationally. Find their velocity of approach when they are at a distance r apart.

Sol. Let v_r is the velocity of approach at the required separation. Then by conservation of mechanical energy. Here by using the concept of reduce mass, we have

$$0+0 = \frac{1}{2}\mu v_r^2 - \frac{Gm_1m_2}{r} \qquad \ldots\text{(i)}$$

where $\qquad \mu = \frac{m_1m_2}{m_1+m_2}$

Substituting the value of μ in equation (i) we get

$$v_r = \sqrt{\frac{2G(m_1+m_2)}{r}}. \qquad \textit{Ans.}$$

Example 16. Three particles each of mass m, are situated at the vertices of an equilateral triangle of side length a. The only forces acting on the particles are their mutual gravitational forces.

It is desired that each particle moves in a circle while maintaining the original separation a. Find the initial velocity that should be given to each particle and also the time period of the circular motion.

Sol. Let the particles are located at vertices A, B and C of equilateral triangle. The centre of their circular path is O. The radius of circular path

$$r = OA = OB = OC = \frac{a/2}{\cos30°} = \frac{a}{\sqrt{3}}.$$

The force exerted by any particle on the other particle $F = \dfrac{Gmm}{a^2}$.

Each particle experiences the force due to other two particles. The resultent force on any of the particles

$$F' = \sqrt{F^2 + F^2 + 2FF\cos60°}$$

$$= \sqrt{3}F = \frac{Gmm}{a^2}\sqrt{3}.$$

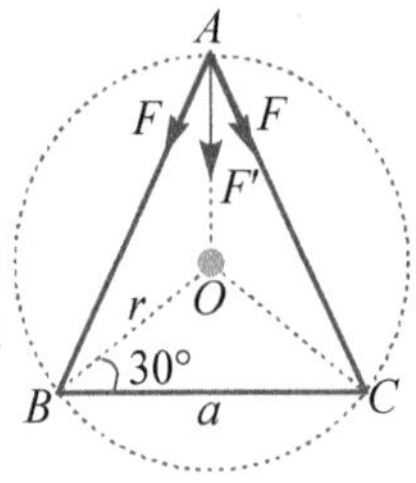

This force provides the necessary centripetal force.i.e.,

$$\frac{mv^2}{r} = \frac{Gmm}{a^2}\sqrt{3}.$$

Substituting the value of r and after solving, we get

$$v = \sqrt{\frac{Gm}{a}}$$

$$\text{Time period} = \frac{2\pi r}{v} = \frac{2\pi(a/\sqrt{3})}{\sqrt{\dfrac{Gm}{a}}} = \frac{2\pi a^{3/2}}{(3Gm)^{1/2}}. \qquad \textit{Ans.}$$

Figure. 9.42

Example 17. The mass of railway train is 100 metric tons. What will be its weight when it is (i) moving due east (ii) moving due west along the equator at 72 km/h ? Radius of earth is 6400 km.

Sol. Suppose W_0 is the weight of the train when it is not moving; earth is also not rotating. Let W is the weight of the train when earth is rotating with angular velocity ω_e; train is at rest with respect to earth, we have

$$W = W_0 - \frac{mv_e^2}{R}$$

or $\qquad W_0 = W + \dfrac{mv_e^2}{R} \qquad \ldots\text{(i)}$

where $v_e = \omega_e R$ and $\omega_e = \dfrac{2\pi}{T} = \dfrac{2\pi}{24\times60\times60} = 7.27\times10^{-5}$ s

(i) Apprent weight of the train when it is moving along east, with velocity v w.r.t. earth

$$W' = W_0 - \frac{m(v_e+v)^2}{R}$$

$$= \left(W + \frac{mv_e^2}{R}\right) - \frac{m(v_e+v)^2}{R} \qquad \ldots\text{(ii)}$$

Simplifying equation (ii) and noting that $v << v_e$ and $W = mg$, we get

$$W' = W\left(1 - \frac{2\omega_e v}{g}\right)$$

Here $v = 72$ km/h $= 20$ m/s and $\omega_e = 7.27\times10^{-5}$ s

$$\therefore W' = 100\times1000g\left(1 - \frac{2\times7.27\times10^{-5}\times20}{9.8}\right)$$

$$= 99.63 \text{ metric ton weight.} \qquad \textit{Ans.}$$

In Chapter Exercise 9.2

1. A Saturn year is 29.5 times the earth year. How far is the Saturn from the Sun if the Earth is 1.5×10^8 km away from the sun? **Ans. 1.43×10^9 km**

2. A body weighs 63N on the surface of the earth. What is the gravitational force on it due to the earth at a height equal to half the radius of the earth? **Ans. 28 N**

3. A rocket is fired vertically with a speed of 5 km/s from the earths surface. How far from the earth does the rocket go before returning to the earth? Mass of the earth = 6×10^{24} kg,
Mean radius of the earth = 6.4×10^6 m
$G = 6.67 \times 10^{-11}$ Nm^2/kg^2 **Ans. 1.6×10^6 km**

4 The escape velocity of a projectile on the surface of earth is 11.2 km/s. If a body is projected out with thrice of this speed, find the speed of the body far away from the earth. Ignore the presence of other planets and sun.
Ans. 31.68 km/s

5. The largest and the shortest distance of the earth from the sun are r_1 and r_2 respectively. Calculate the distance from the sun when it is at perpendicular distance to the major axis of the orbit drawn from sun. **Ans. $\left(\dfrac{2r_1 r_2}{r_1 + r_2}\right)$**

6. A planet moves around the sun along an ellipse so that its minimum distance from the sun is equal to r and the maximum distance to R. Making use of Kepler's laws, find its period of revolution around the sun.
Ans. $\pi \sqrt{\dfrac{(R+r)^3}{2GM}}$

7. An artificial satellite of the moon revolves in a circular orbit whose radius exceeds the radius of the moon η times. The process of motion the satellite experiences a slight resistance due to cosmic dust. Assuming the resistance force to depend on the velocity of the satellite as $F = \alpha v^2$, where α is a constant, find how long the satellite will stay in orbit until it falls onto the moon's surface.
Ans. $t = \dfrac{m}{\alpha} \dfrac{[\sqrt{\eta R} - \sqrt{R}]}{\sqrt{GM}}$

8. Gravitational acceleration on the surface of a planet is $\dfrac{\sqrt{6}}{11} g$, where g is the gravitational acceleration on the surface of the earth. The average mass density of the planet is $\dfrac{2}{3}$ times that of the earth. If the escape speed on the surface of the earth is taken to be 11 kms^{-1}, the escape speed on the surface of the planet in kms^{-1} will be
[Integer] **[IIT-JEE 2010]**
Ans. 3

9.17 REDUCTION OF TWO-BODY PROBLEM TO ONE-BODY PROBLEM:

A two-body problem, involving central forces, can be reduced to a one-body problem and thereby simplifying calculations.

Suppose we have two particles of masses m_1 and m_2 whose positions at any time are $\vec{r}_1$ and $\vec{r}_2$ with respect to origin O.

The vector distance of particle m_1 from m_2 is $\vec{r} = \vec{r}_1 - \vec{r}_2$.
The force exerted by the second particle on the first,

$$\vec{F}_{12} = m_1\left(\frac{d^2\vec{r}_1}{dt^2}\right), \qquad \text{...(i)}$$

and the force exerted by the first particle on the second, $\vec{F}_{21}$ is given by

$$\vec{F}_{21} = m_2\left(\frac{d^2\vec{r}_2}{dt^2}\right) \qquad \text{...(ii)}$$

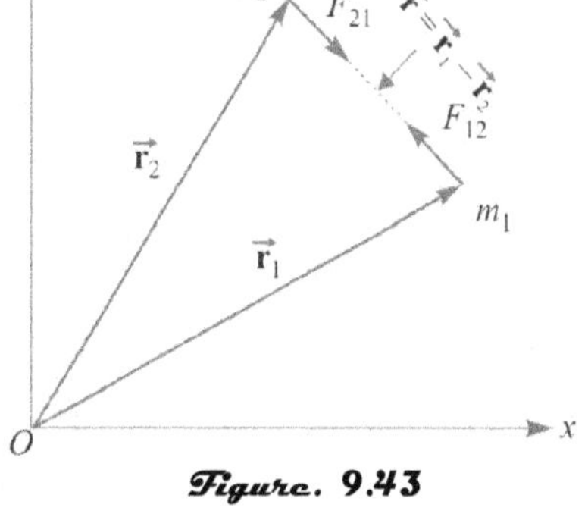

Figure. 9.43

Both the forces act along the line joining m_1 and m_2. Since no external forces are acting on the system,

and in according with Newton's third law of motion, we have $\vec{F}_{12} = -\vec{F}_{21} = \vec{F}$.
The above equations now can be written as

$$m_1\left(\frac{d^2\vec{r}_1}{dt^2}\right) = \vec{F} \qquad \text{...(iii)}$$

and

$$m_2\left(\frac{d^2\vec{r}_2}{dt^2}\right) = -\vec{F} \qquad \text{...(iv)}$$

Multiplying equation (iii) by m_2 and (iv) by m_1 and subtracting equation (iv) from (iii), we get

$$m_1 m_2 \left(\frac{d^2 \vec{r}_1}{dt^2} - \frac{d^2 \vec{r}_2}{dt^2} \right) = (m_1 + m_2)\vec{F}$$

or

$$\frac{d^2}{dt^2}(\vec{r}_1 - \vec{r}_2) = \left(\frac{m_1 + m_2}{m_1 m_2} \right) \vec{F}$$

Substituting $\vec{r}_1 - \vec{r}_2 = \vec{r}$ and $\dfrac{m_1 m_2}{m_1 + m_2} = \mu$, is called reduced mass, we have

$$\frac{d^2 \vec{r}}{dt^2} = \frac{\vec{F}}{\mu} \quad or \quad \mu \frac{d^2 \vec{r}}{dr^2} = \vec{F} .$$

This equation will be seen as the equation of motion of a particle of mass μ at a vector distance $\vec{r}$ from one of the particles relative to other. In other words, take m_2 as a fixed particle which exerts a force $\vec{F}$ on m_1 at vector distance $\vec{r}$ from it, we can get the relative motion of m_1 by using μ in place of m_1.

Gravitational force

The gravitational force between two particles of masses m_1 and m_2 is given by

$$\vec{F} = -G \frac{m_1 m_2}{r^2} \hat{r}$$

where $\hat{r}$ is the unit vector along r, the distance of particle m_1 from m_2. Thus we have

$$\mu \left(\frac{d^2 \vec{r}}{dt^2} \right) = -G \frac{m_1 m_2}{r^2} \hat{r}$$

or

$$\frac{d^2 \vec{r}}{dt^2} = -\frac{G m_1 m_2}{\mu r^2} \hat{r}$$

as

$$\mu = \frac{m_1 m_2}{m_1 + m_2}$$

$\therefore$

$$\frac{d^2 \vec{r}}{dt^2} = -\left(\frac{m_1 + m_2}{m_1 m_2} \right) \frac{G m_1 m_2}{r^2} \hat{r}$$

or

$$\frac{d^2 \vec{r}}{dt^2} = -G \frac{m_1 + m_2}{r^2} \hat{r} .$$

Here the motion of particle m_1 with respect to particle m_2 would be the same as that of the particle of mass μ under the force of a fixed mass m_2 at a vector distance $\vec{r}$ from it.

Motion of a body of mass m around a body of mass M

In the absence of any external force acting on the system, the total linear momentum and hence the velocity of centre of mass remains constant in the inertial frame and zero in centre of mass frame. The two particles rotate about the centre of mass with same angular velocity.

Let r_1 and r_2 be the distances of m and M from the centre of mass and r be the distance between them, then we have

$$r_1 + r_2 = r \qquad \text{...(i)}$$

and

$$mr_1 = Mr_2 \qquad \text{...(ii)}$$

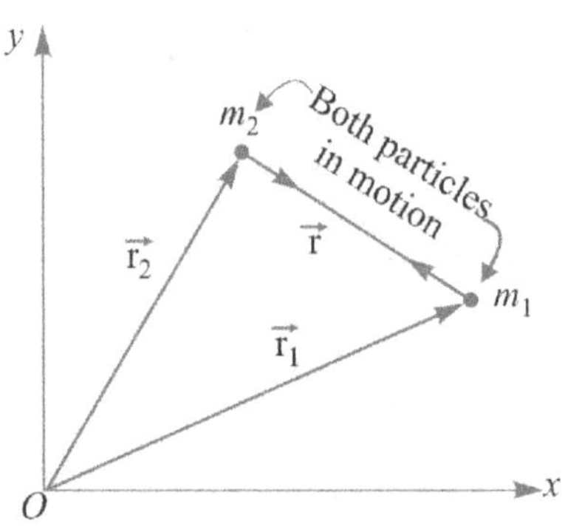

(a)   Two - body problem

(b)   One-body problem

Figure. 9.44

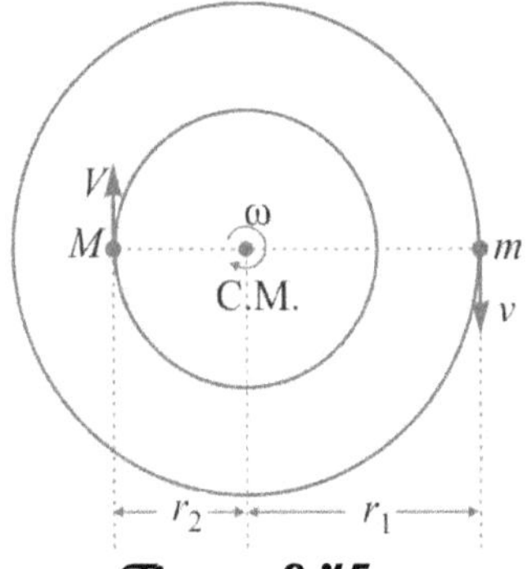

Figure. 9.45

Solving (i) and (ii), we get

$$r_1 = \frac{Mr}{M+m}$$

$$= \left(\frac{mM}{M+m}\right)\frac{r}{m} = \frac{\mu r}{m}$$

and

$$r_2 = \frac{mr}{M+m} = \frac{\mu r}{M}$$

Orbital velocity

Let v be the orbital velocity of m, then

$$\frac{GMm}{r^2} = \frac{mv^2}{r_1}$$

or

$$\frac{GMm}{r^2} = \frac{mv^2}{\left(\dfrac{Mr}{M+m}\right)}$$

$$\therefore \quad v = \sqrt{\frac{GM^2}{(M+m)r}}.$$

Similarly orbital velocity of M will be

$$V = \sqrt{\frac{Gm^2}{(M+m)r}}.$$

Time period

Method I :

Let T be the time-period of revolution of m, then

$$T = \frac{2\pi r_1}{v} = \frac{2\pi\left(\dfrac{Mr}{M+m}\right)}{\sqrt{\dfrac{GM^2}{(M+m)r}}}$$

or

$$T = 2\pi\sqrt{\frac{r^3}{G(M+m)}}$$

For $m << M$, $V = 0$ and $v \simeq \sqrt{\dfrac{GM}{r}}$ and $T \simeq 2\pi\sqrt{\dfrac{r^3}{GM}}$.

These are the results which we have obtained earlier.

Method II :

We can assume the body of mass μ orbiting in a circle of radius r about a fixed mass M.

For the motion of μ, we have

$$\frac{GMm}{r^2} = \mu\omega^2 r$$

$$= \left(\frac{mM}{M+m}\right)\omega^2 r$$

$$\therefore \quad \omega = \sqrt{\frac{G(M+m)}{r^3}}$$

and

$$T = \frac{2\pi}{\omega} = 2\pi\sqrt{\frac{r^3}{G(M+m)}}.$$

EXAMPLES FOR JEE (MAIN AND ADVANCED)

Example 1. In *figure* 9.46 a spherical body of mass M is a distance 'a' from one end of a uniform rod of length L and mass m. What is the force between them.

Sol.

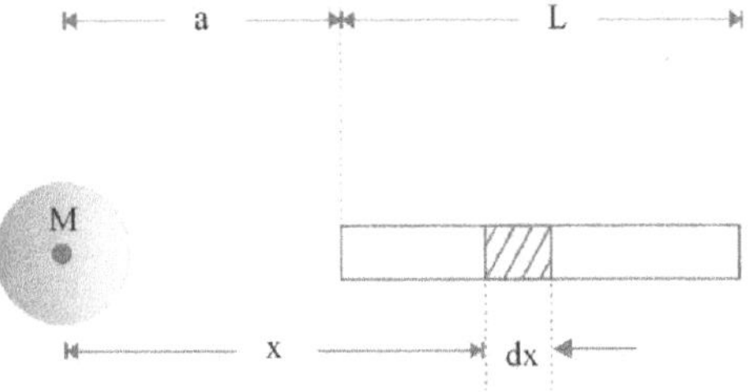

Figure. 9.46

Take an element of width dx of the rod at a distance x from the centre of the spherical body. The mass of the element,

$$dm = \left(\frac{m}{L}dx\right).$$

The force between the spherical body and the element of mass dm

$$dF = \frac{GM(dm)}{x^2}$$

$$= \frac{GM\left(\frac{m}{L}dx\right)}{x^2}$$

The force between body and whole rod

$$F = \int_a^{(a+L)} \frac{GM\left(\frac{m}{L}dx\right)}{x^2} = \frac{GMm}{L}\left|\frac{x^{-1}}{(-1)}\right|_a^{(a+L)}$$

$$= \frac{GMm}{a(a+L)} \qquad \textit{Ans.}$$

If $L \ll a$, $\qquad F \simeq \dfrac{GMm}{a^2}$

Example 2. Consider a homogeneous ring of mass M and radius R. What gravitational attraction does it exert on a particle of mass m located a distance x from the centre of the ring along its axis?

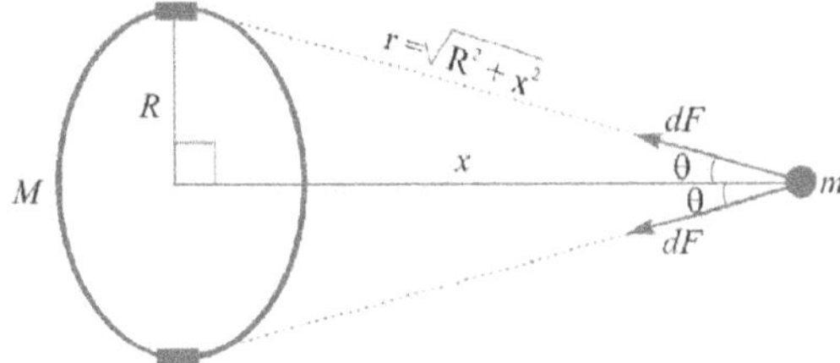

Figure. 9.47

Sol. Take an element of ring of length $d\ell$, its mass

$$dm = \left(\frac{M}{2\pi R}\right)d\ell$$

The force between the element of mass (dm) and particle of mass m is

$$dF = \frac{G(dm)m}{r^2}$$

$$= \frac{G\left(\frac{M}{2\pi R}d\ell\right)m}{r^2}$$

Take another element of length $d\ell$, diametrically opposite to first element. The resultant force due to these two elements on the particle will be
$$= 2dF\cos\theta$$
The effective force on the particle due to one element
$$= dF\cos\theta.$$
The force on the particle due to whole ring

$$F = \int_0^{2\pi R} dF\cos\theta$$

$$= \int_0^{2\pi R} \frac{G\left(\frac{M}{2\pi R}d\ell\right)m}{r^2}\cos\theta$$

$$= \frac{GMm}{r^2}\frac{\cos\theta}{(2\pi R)}\int_0^{2\pi R} d\ell$$

$$= \frac{GMm}{r^2}\times\left(\frac{x}{r}\right)\times\frac{[\ell]_0^{2\pi R}}{2\pi R}$$

$$= \frac{GMm}{r^2}\left(\frac{x}{r}\right)\frac{(2\pi R-0)}{2\pi R}$$

$$= \frac{GMmx}{r^3}$$

$$= \frac{GMmx}{\left[R^2+x^2\right]^{3/2}} \qquad \textit{Ans.}$$

If $x = 0$, $F = 0$, i.e., when particle is placed at the centre of a ring, it experiences zero force.

Example 3. A thin rod of mass M is bent in a arc of circle of radius R, which sustained an angle 2θ at the centre. What is its gravitational force on a particle of mass m at the centre of curvature.

Sol. Take two identical elements as shown in *figure* 9.48.

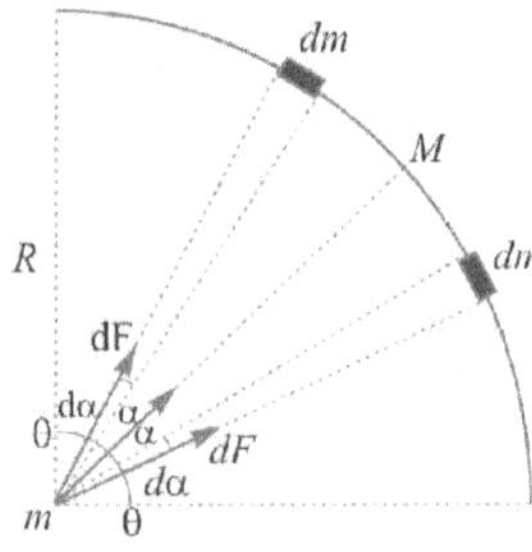

Figure. 9.48

Mass of each element, $dm = \left(\dfrac{M}{2\theta}d\alpha\right).$

The resultant force on the particle m due to the elements
$$= 2dF\cos\alpha$$

where $\qquad dF = \dfrac{G(dM)m}{R^2}$

The resultant force on the particle due to whole arc,

$$F = \int_0^\theta (2dF\cos\alpha)$$

$$= \int_0^\theta 2\frac{G(dM)m}{R^2}\cos\alpha$$

$$= \frac{2Gm}{R^2}\int_0^\theta \left(\frac{M}{2\theta}.d\alpha\right)\cos\alpha$$

$$= \frac{GMm}{R^2}\left|\frac{\sin\alpha}{\theta}\right|_0^\theta$$

$$= \frac{GMm}{R^2}\left(\frac{\sin\theta}{\theta}\right) \qquad Ans.$$

For $,\ \theta \to 0°,\quad \dfrac{\sin\theta}{\theta} = 1$

$$\therefore \qquad F = \frac{GMm}{R^2}.$$

Example 4. A planet moves around the sun along an ellipse so that its minimum distance from the sun is equal to r and the maximum distance to R. Making use of Kepler's laws, find its period of revolution around the sun.

Sol. The motion of the planet can be approximated to be along a circle of radius $\left(\dfrac{R+r}{2}\right)$.

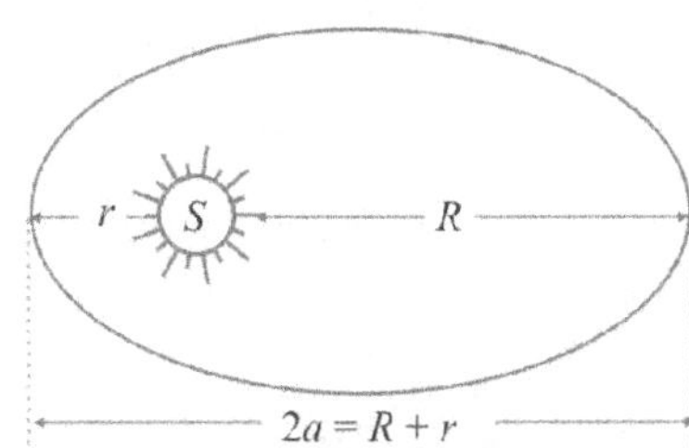

Figure. 9.49

The time period will be given by

$$T = 2\pi\sqrt{\frac{\left[\dfrac{R+r}{2}\right]^3}{G(M+m)}}$$

Here m is the mass of the planet and M is the mass of sun. As $m << M$

$$\therefore \qquad T = \pi\sqrt{\frac{(R+r)^3}{2GM}} \qquad Ans.$$

Example 5. An artificial satellite of the moon revolves in a circular orbit whose radius exceeds the radius of the moon η times. The process of motion the satellite experiences a slight resistance due to cosmic dust. Assuming the resistance force to depend on the velocity of the satellite as $F = \alpha v^2$, where α is a constant, find how long the satellite will stay in orbit until it falls onto the moon's surface.

Sol. The energy of the satellite in a orbit of radius r,

$$E = \frac{-GMm}{2r}.$$

Here m is the mass of satellite and M is the mass of the moon. If dE/dt is the instantaneous rate of decrease of energy of the satellite, then we have

$$\left(\frac{dE}{dt}\right) = Fv$$

Given $\qquad F = \alpha v^2$

$$\therefore \qquad \frac{d\left[\dfrac{-GMm}{2r}\right]}{dt} = (\alpha v^2)v$$

or $\qquad \dfrac{GMm}{2r^2}dr = -\alpha v^3 dt$

Orbital velocity of satellite,

$$v = \sqrt{\frac{GM}{r}} .$$

$$\therefore \qquad \frac{GMm}{2r^2}dr = -\alpha\left[\frac{GM}{r}\right]^{3/2}dt$$

or $\qquad \dfrac{mr^{-1/2}}{2}dr = -\alpha(GM)^{1/2}dt$

Integrating above expression, we get

$$\frac{m}{2}\int_{\eta R}^R r^{-1/2}dr = -\alpha(GM)^{1/2}\int_0^t dt$$

$$m\left|\sqrt{r}\right|_{\eta R}^R = -\alpha\sqrt{GM}\,t$$

or $\quad m[\sqrt{\eta R}-\sqrt{R}] = \alpha\sqrt{GM}\,t$

$$\therefore \qquad t = \frac{m}{\alpha}\frac{[\sqrt{\eta R}-\sqrt{R}]}{\sqrt{GM}} \qquad Ans.$$

Example 6. The largest and the shortest distance of the earth from the sun are r_1 and r_2 respectively. Calculate the distance from the sun when it is at perpendicular distance to the major axis of the orbit drawn from sun.

Sol. Since $e = \dfrac{c}{a} \Rightarrow c = ea$

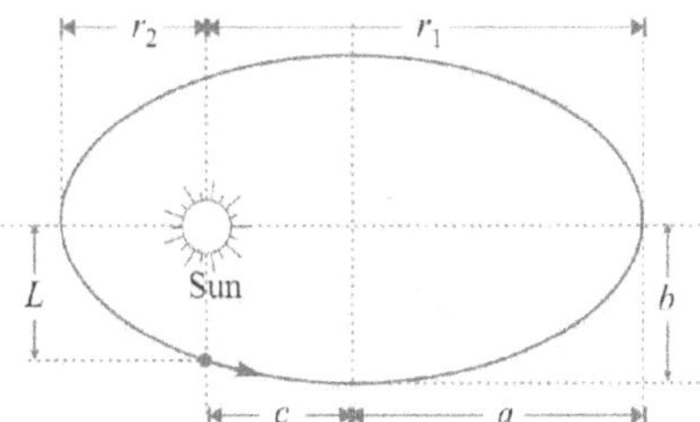

Figure. 9.50

$$\therefore \qquad r_1 = a + c = a + ea = a(1+e)$$
$$r_2 = a - c = a - ea = a(1-e)$$

Required distance $= \dfrac{1}{2}$ of latus rectum $= \dfrac{b^2}{a}$

$$\therefore \qquad L = \frac{b^2}{a}$$

We have $\quad r_1 + r_2 = 2a$

and $\qquad r_1 - r_2 = a(1+e) - a(1-e) = 2ae$

$$\Rightarrow \qquad e = \left(\frac{r_1 - r_2}{r_1 + r_2}\right).$$

Also $\qquad e = \sqrt{1 - b^2/a^2} \Rightarrow b^2 = a^2(1 - e^2)$

$$\therefore \qquad L = \frac{b^2}{a} = \frac{a^2}{a}(1 - e^2)$$

$$= a(1 - e^2)$$

$$= \left(\frac{r_1 + r_2}{2}\right)\left[1 - \left(\frac{r_1 - r_2}{r_1 + r_2}\right)^2\right]$$

$$= \left(\frac{2r_1 r_2}{r_1 + r_2}\right). \qquad\qquad \textit{Ans.}$$

Example 7. *A planet of mass m moves along an ellipse around the sun of mass M_s, so that its maximum and minimum distances from sun are r_1 and r_2 respectively. Find the angular momentum L of this planet relative to the center of sun.*

Sol. By conservation of angular momentum at given two positions, we have

$$m\,v_1 r_1 = m\,v_2 r_2$$

or $\qquad v_2 = \dfrac{v_1 r_1}{r_2}.$ $\qquad\qquad$ ....(i)

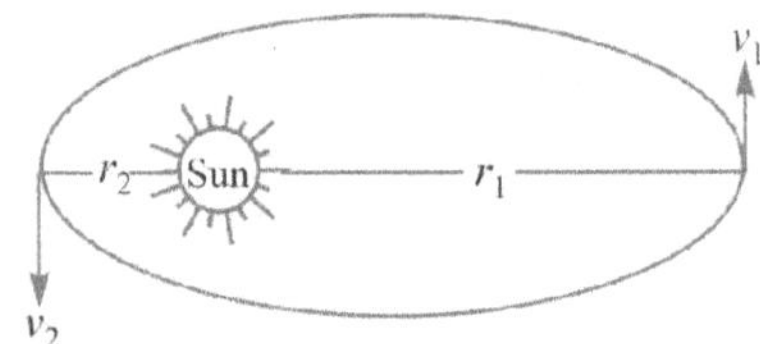

Figure. 9.51

Applying principle of conservation of mechanical energy at the given positions, we have

$$\frac{1}{2}mv_1^2 - \frac{GM_s m}{r_1} = \frac{1}{2}mv_2^2 - \frac{GM_s m}{r_2} \qquad ....(ii)$$

Solving equations (i) and (ii), we get

$$v_1 = \sqrt{\frac{2Gm_s r_2}{r_1(r_1 + r_2)}}$$

Angular momentum $\quad L = mv_1 r_1$

$$= m\sqrt{\frac{2Gm_s r_1 r_2}{(r_1 + r_2)}}. \qquad \textit{Ans.}$$

Example 8. *A chord of length 64 m is used to connect a 100 kg astronaut spaceship whose mass is much larger than that of the astronaut. Estimate the value of tension in the chord assuming that the spaceship is orbiting near earth's surface. Also assume that the spaceship and the astronaut fall in a straight line from the earth centre. The radius of earth $R = 6400$ km.*

Sol. If h is the length of the chord, then radius of path of astronaut (neglecting height of spaceship) is $(R + h)$. The gravitational force on the astronaut due to earth

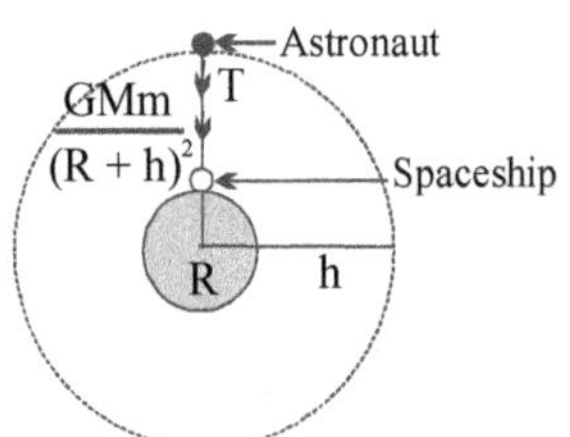

Figure. 9.52

$$F = \frac{GMm}{(R + h)^2}$$

If T is the tension in the chord then by Newton's second law

$$\frac{GMm}{(R + h)^2} + T = m\omega^2 (R + h)$$

or $\qquad T = m\omega^2(R + h) - \dfrac{GMm}{(R + h)^2} \qquad$ ....(i)

For the astronaut,

$$\frac{GMm}{(R + h)^2} = m\omega^2(R + h)$$

or $\qquad \omega^2 = \dfrac{GM}{(R + h)^3} = \dfrac{gR^2}{(R + h)^3} = \dfrac{g}{R} \quad$ (As $h \ll R$).

Substituting value of ω^2 and $GM = gR^2$ in equation (i), we have

$$T = \frac{mg(R + h)}{R} - \frac{mgR^2}{(R + h)^2}$$

$$= mg + \frac{mgh}{R} - mg\left(\frac{1}{\left(1 + \dfrac{h}{R}\right)^2}\right)$$

$$= mg + \frac{mgh}{R} - mg\left[\left(1 + \frac{h}{R}\right)^{-2}\right]$$

$$= mg + \frac{mgh}{R} - mg\left[\left(1 - \frac{2h}{R}\right)\right]$$

$$= \frac{mgh}{R} + \frac{2mgh}{R}$$

$$= \frac{3mgh}{R}$$

$$= \frac{3 \times 100 \times 10 \times 64}{6400 \times 10^3} = 3 \times 10^{-2} \ N. \ \textit{Ans.}$$

Example 9. *There is a crater of depth $\dfrac{R}{100}$ on the surface of moon of $R =$ radius of moon. A projectile is fired vertically upward from the crater, with a velocity, which is equal to excape velocity on the moon. Find the maximum height obtained by the projectile*

Sol. If M is the mass of the moon, then escape velocity from the moon surface

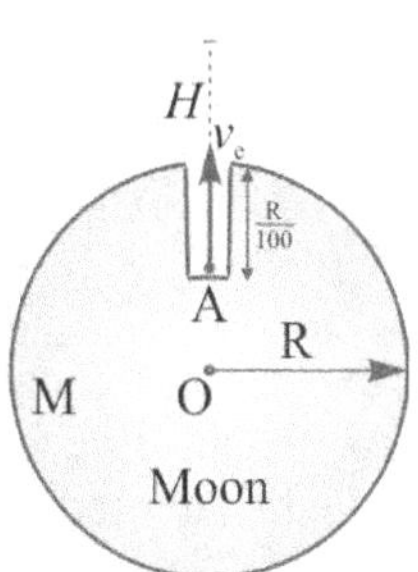

Figure. 9.53

$$v = \sqrt{\frac{2GM}{R}}.$$

By conservation of mechanical energy, we can write

$$K_i + U_i = K_f + U_f \qquad \qquad ...(i)$$

where $$K_i = \frac{1}{2}mv^2 = \frac{1}{2}m\left(\frac{2GM}{R}\right) = \frac{GMm}{R}.$$

$$K_f = 0.$$

$$U_i = m \times \text{potential of point } A$$

$$= m\left[\frac{-GM}{2R^3}\left(3R^2 - r\right)\right]$$

$$= m\left[\frac{-GM}{2R^3}\left\{3R^2 - \left(R - \frac{R}{100}\right)^2\right\}\right]$$

$$= \frac{-1.01\,GM}{R}$$

If H is the height attained, then

$$U_f = \frac{-GMm}{R + H}.$$

On substituting these values in equation (i) and simplifying, we get

$$H = 99.5\,R. \qquad \qquad \textbf{\textit{Ans.}}$$

Example 10. **An artificial satellite is moving in a circular orbit around the earth with a speed equal to half the magnitude of escape velocity from the earth :**

(i)   **Determine the height of the satellite above the earth's surface.**

(ii) **If the satellite is stopped suddenly in its orbit and allowed to fall freely into the earth, find the speed with which it hits the surface of the earth.**

Sol. (i)   If M and R are the mass and radius of the earth, then orbital speed of the satellite

$$v_0 = \frac{1}{2}\sqrt{\frac{2GM}{R}}.$$

If h is the height of satellite, then

$$v_0 = \sqrt{\frac{GM}{R + h}}$$

Thus $$\sqrt{\frac{GM}{R + h}} = \frac{1}{2}\sqrt{\frac{2GM}{R}}$$

$$\therefore \qquad h = R. \qquad \qquad \textbf{\textit{Ans.}}$$

(ii) By conservation of mechanical energy, we have

$$K_i + U_i = K_f + U_f$$

$$O - \frac{GMm}{(R + h)} = -\frac{GMm}{R} + \frac{1}{2}mv^2$$

or $$-\frac{GMm}{(R + R)} = \frac{-GMm}{R} + \frac{1}{2}mv^2$$

After solving, we get

$$v = \sqrt{gR}. \qquad \qquad \textbf{\textit{Ans.}}$$

(In Chapter Exercise 9.3)

1. Three particles of mass m each are placed at the three corners of an equilateral triangle of side a. Find the work which should be done on this system to increase the side of the triangle to $2a$.

    $$\text{Ans. } \frac{3Gm^2}{2a}.$$

2. An earth satellite is revolving in a circular orbit of radius 'a' with velocity v_0. A gun is in the satellite and is aimed directly towards the earth. A bullet is fired from the gun with muzzle velocity $v_0/2$. Neglecting resistance offered by cosmic dust and recoil of gun, calculate the maximum and minimum distance of bullet from the centre of earth during its subsequent motion. *Ans.* **$2a$ and $2a/3$.**

3. A satellite of mass M_s is orbiting the earth in a circular orbit of radius R. It starts losing energy slowly at a constant rate C due to friction. If M_e and R_e denote the mass and radius of the earth respectively, show that the satellite falls on the earth in a time $t = \dfrac{GM_s M_e}{2C}\left(\dfrac{1}{R_e} - \dfrac{1}{R}\right).$

4. Use the conservation of mechanical energy and show that if an object is in an elliptical orbit about a planet, then its distance r from the planet and speed v are related by

    $$v^2 = GM\left(\frac{2}{r} - \frac{1}{a}\right); \text{ where } a \text{ is the semimajor axis.}$$

5. A certain triple-star system consists of two stars, each of mass m, revolving about a central star of mass M in the same circular orbit of radius r. The two stars are always at opposite ends of a diameter of the circular orbit (see figure). Derive an expression for the period of revolution of the stars.

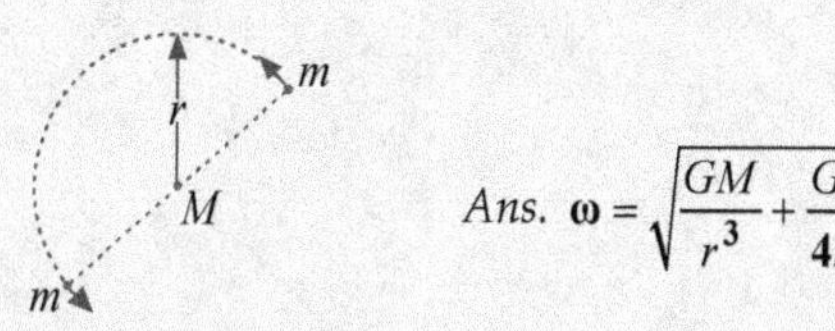

$$\text{Ans. } \omega = \sqrt{\frac{GM}{r^3} + \frac{Gm}{4r^3}}.$$

LEVEL - 1 (ONLY ONE OPTION CORRECT)

Newton's Law of Gravitation, Gravitational Field Intensity and Potential

1. Kepler's second law regarding constancy of aerial velocity of a planet is a consequence of the law of conservation of
   (a) energy   (b) angular momentum
   (c) linear momentum   (d) none of these

2. A planet is revolving around the sun as shown in elliptical path

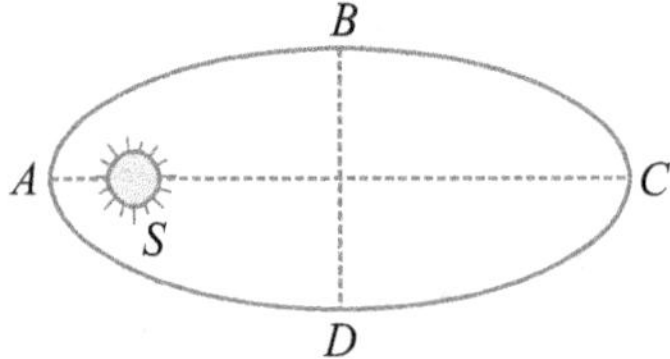

The correct option is
   (a) the time taken in travelling DAB is less than that for BCD
   (b) the time taken in travelling DAB is greater than that for ABC
   (c) the time taken in travelling CDA is less than that for ABC
   (d) the time taken in travelling CDA is greater than that for ABC

3. A satellite S is moving in an elliptical orbit around the earth. The mass of the satellite is very small compared to the mass of earth:
   (a) the acceleration of S is always directed towards the centre of the earth
   (b) the angular momentum of S about the centre of the earth changes in direction but its magnitude remains constant
   (c) the total mechanical energy of S varies periodically with time
   (d) the linear momentum of S remains constant in magnitude

4. Two sphere of mass m and M are situated in air and the gravitational force between them is F. The space around the masses is now filled with a liquid of specific gravity 3. The gravitational force will now be
   (a) F (b) $\dfrac{F}{3}$
   (c) $\dfrac{F}{4}$ (d) $3F$

5. A mass M is split into two parts m and $(M-m)$, which are then separated by a certain distance. What ratio of m/M maximizes the gravitational force between the two parts:
   (a) $\dfrac{1}{3}$ (b) $\dfrac{1}{2}$
   (c) $\dfrac{1}{4}$ (d) $\dfrac{1}{5}$

6. Two metal spheres of equal radius r are touching each other. The force of attraction F between them is :
   (a) $F \propto r^6$ (b) $F \propto r^4$
   (c) $F \propto r^2$ (d) $F \propto \dfrac{1}{r^2}$

7. The figure shows four arrangement of three particles of equal masses. Arrange them according to the magnitude of the net gravitational force on the particle labeled m, in decreasing order: **[AMU B.Tech.-2013]**

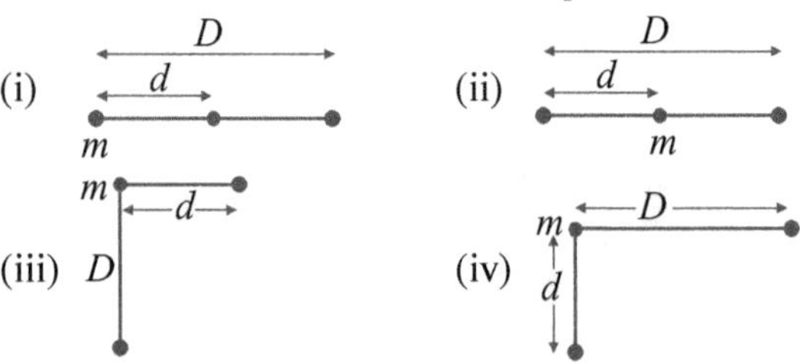

   (a) (i), (iii) = (iv), (ii)   (b) (i) = (iii), (ii), (iv)
   (c) (i), (ii), (iii), (iv)   (d) (iv), (iii), (ii), (i)

8. The gravitational field strength due to a solid sphere (mass M, radius R) varies with distance r from centre as :

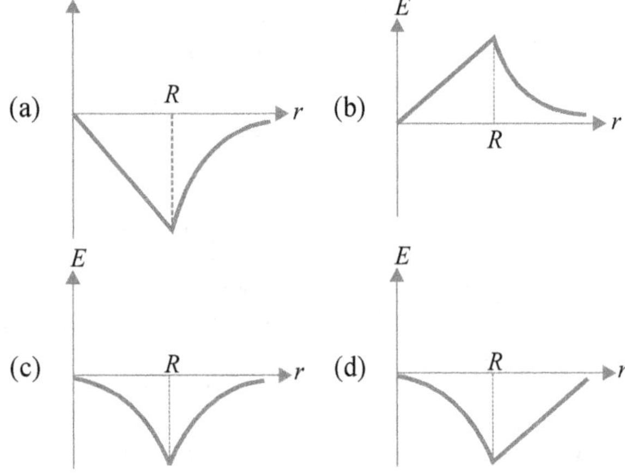

Answer	1	(b)	2	(a)	3	(a)	4	(a)
Key	5	(b)	6	(b)	7	(c)	8	(a)

9. The gravitational potential due to a hollow sphere (mass M, radius R) varies with distance r from centre as :

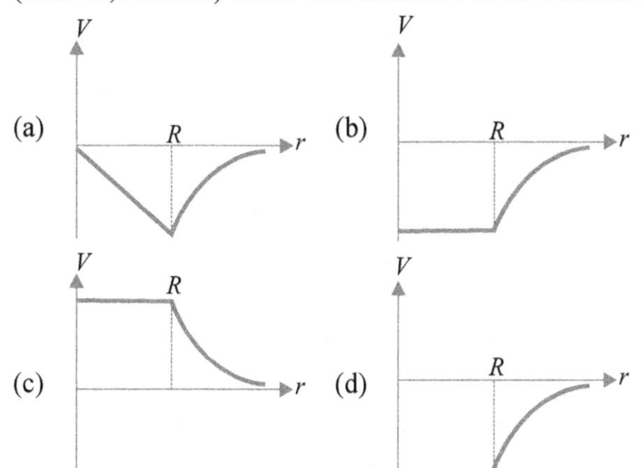

10. The radii of two planets are respectively R_1 and R_2 and their densities are respectively ρ_1 and ρ_2. The ratio of the accelerations due to gravity at their surfaces is

(a) $g_1 : g_2 = \dfrac{\rho_1}{R_1^2} : \dfrac{\rho_2}{R_2^2}$

(b) $g_1 : g_2 = R_1 : R_2 : \rho_1 \rho_2$

(c) $g_1 : g_2 = R_1 \rho_2 : R_2 \rho_1$

(d) $g_1 : g_2 = R_1 \rho_1 : R_2 \rho_2$

11. An object weight $72\,N$ on earth. Its weight at a height of $R/2$ from earth is

(a) $32\,N$ (b) $56\,N$

(c) $72\,N$ (d) zero

12. If radius of earth is R then the height 'h' at which value of 'g' becomes one-fourth is

(a) $\dfrac{R}{4}$ (b) $\dfrac{3R}{4}$

(c) R (d) $\dfrac{R}{8}$

13. Two spheres each of mass M are situated at a distance $2d$ (see figure). A particle of mass m ($m << M$) is taken along the path shown in figure. The work done in the process from A to B is

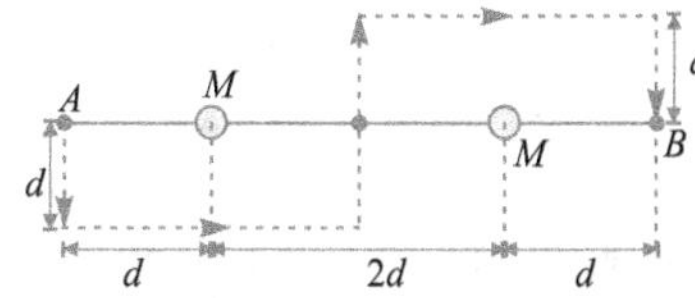

(a) $\dfrac{7\,GMm}{d}$ (b) $\dfrac{8\,GMm}{d}$

(c) $-\dfrac{8\,GMm}{d}$ (d) zero

14. Two satellites of masses m and $2m$ are revolving around a planet of mass M with different speeds in orbits of radii r and $2r$ respectively. The ratio of minimum and maximum forces on the planet due to satellites is

(a) $\dfrac{1}{2}$

(b) $\dfrac{1}{4}$

(c) $\dfrac{1}{3}$

(d) none of these

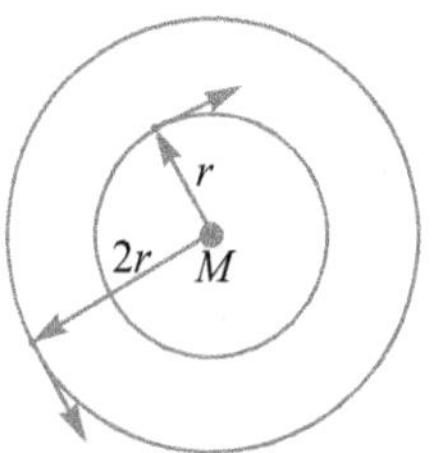

15. The tail of a comet Halley is directed away from the sun due to the fact that :

(a) as the comet rotates around the sun, the lighter mass of comet is pushed away due to centrifugal force only.

(b) as the comet rotates, the lighter mass of comet is attracted by some star situated in the direction of tail.

(c) the radiation emitted by sun exerts a radial pressure on the comet throwing its tail away from the sun

(d) the tail of comet always exists in same orientation.

16. A satellite is in elliptical orbit about the earth (radius = 6400 km). At perigee it has an altitude of 1100 km and at the apogee its altitude is 4100 km. The major axis of the orbit is :

(a) 5200 km   (b) 10400 km

(c) 11600 km   (d) 18000 km

17. A body of mass m is taken from earth surface to the height equal to radius of earth, the change in potential energy will be :

(a) $mg\,R$ (b) $\dfrac{1}{2}\,mg\,R$

(c) $2\,mg\,R$ (d) $\dfrac{1}{4}\,mg\,R$

18. A point mass m is placed inside a spherical shell of radius R and mass M at a distance $R/2$ from the centre of the shell. The gravitational force exerted by the shell on the point mass is

(a) $\dfrac{GMm}{R^2}$ (b) $-\dfrac{GMm}{R^2}$

(c) zero   (d) $4\dfrac{GMm}{R^2}$

19. Two particles of equal mass go round a circle of radius R under the action of their mutual gravitational attraction. The speed of each particle is

(a) $v = \dfrac{1}{2R}\sqrt{\dfrac{1}{Gm}}$ (b) $v = \sqrt{\dfrac{Gm}{2R}}$

(c) $v = \dfrac{1}{2}\sqrt{\dfrac{Gm}{R}}$ (d) $v = \sqrt{\dfrac{4Gm}{R}}$

| Answer | 9 | (b) | 10 | (d) | 11 | (a) | 12 | (c) | 13 | (d) | 14 | (c) |
| Key | 15 | (c) | 16 | (d) | 17 | (b) | 18 | (c) | 19 | (c) | | |

20. The earth (mass $= 6 \times 10^{24}$ kg) revolves round the sun with angular velocity 2×10^{-7} rad/s in a circular orbit of radius 1.5×10^8 km. The force exerted by the sun on the earth in newtons, is

  (a) 18×10^{25} (b) zero

  (c) 27×10^{39} (d) 36×10^{21}

21. The kinetic energy needed to project a body of mass m from the earth surface (radius R) to infinity is

  (a) $mgR/2$ (b) $2mgR$

  (c) mgR (d) $mgR/4$

22. The distance of the centres of moon and earth is D. The mass of earth is 81 times the mass of the moon. At what distance from the centre of the earth, the gravitational force will be zero

  (a) $\dfrac{D}{2}$ (b) $\dfrac{2D}{3}$

  (c) $\dfrac{4D}{3}$ (d) $\dfrac{9D}{10}$

23. The depth d at which the value of acceleration due to gravity becomes $1/n$ times the value at the surface, is [R = radius of the earth]

  (a) $\dfrac{R}{n}$ (b) $R\left(\dfrac{n-1}{n}\right)$

  (c) $\dfrac{R}{n^2}$ (d) $R\left(\dfrac{n}{n+1}\right)$

24. Four particles each of mass M, are located at the vertices of a square with side L. The gravitational potential due to this at the centre of the square is

  (a) $-\sqrt{32}\,\dfrac{GM}{L}$ (b) $-\sqrt{64}\,\dfrac{GM}{L^2}$

  (c) zero   (d) $-\sqrt{32}\,\dfrac{GM}{L}$

25. 3 particles each of mass m are kept at vertices of an equilateral triangel of side L. The gravitational field at centre due to these particles is

  (a) zero   (b) $\dfrac{3GM}{L^2}$

  (c) $\dfrac{9GM}{L^2}$ (d) $\dfrac{12}{\sqrt{3}}\dfrac{GM}{L^2}$

26. The potential energy of 4-particles each of mass 1 kg placed at the four vertices of a square of side 1 m is :

  [AMU B. Tech. -2010]

  (a) $+4.0$ G   (b) -7.5 G

  (c) -5.4 G   (d) $+6.3$ G

Satellites, Orbital Velocity & Escape Velocity

27. A satellite is orbiting a planet at a certain height in a circular orbit. If the mass of planet is suddenly reduced to half, the satellite would :

  (a) continue to revolve around the planet at the same speed

  (b) falls freely on the planet

  (c) orbit the planet at the lesser speed

  (d) escape from the planet

28. An astronaut orbiting the earth in a circular orbit 120 km above the surface of earth, gently drops a spoon out of the spaceship. The spoon will :

  (a) fall vertically down to the earth

  (b) move towards the moon

  (c) will move along with the space ship

  (d) will move in an irregular way and then fall down to earth

29. A missile is launched with a velocity less than the escape velocity. The sum of its kinetic and potential energy is

  (a) positive   (b) negative

  (c) zero

  (d) may be positive or negative depending upon its initial velocity

30. A geostationary satellite is orbiting the earth at a height of $6R$ above the surface of earth, R being radius of earth. The time period of another satellite at a height of $2.5R$ from the surface of earth is :

  (a) $6\sqrt{2}$ h   (b) 6 h

  (c) 6/2 h   (d) 10 h

31. Two satellites A and B go around a planet P in circular orbits having radii $4R$ and R respectively. If the speed of satellite A is $3v$, the speed of satellite B would be :

  (a) $12v$ (b) $6v$

  (c) $\dfrac{4}{3}v$ (d) $\dfrac{3}{2}v$

32. If the gravitational force between two objects were proportional to $1/R$ (instead of $1/R^2$), where R is separation between them ; then a particle in circular orbit under such a force would have its orbital speed v proportional to :

  (a) $\dfrac{1}{R^2}$ (b) R^0

  (c) R (d) $\dfrac{1}{R}$

Answer	20	(d)	21	(c)	22	(d)	23	(b)	24	(a)	25	(a)	26	(c)
Key	27	(c)	28	(c)	29	(b)	30	(a)	31	(b)	32	(b)		

33. An artificial satellite moving in a circular orbit around the earth has a total (kinetic + potential) energy E_0. Its potential energy is :

(a) $-E_0$ (b) $1.5\,E_0$
(c) $2\,E_0$ (d) E_0

34. A satellite is moving in a circular orbit around a planet. If T, the period of revolution and R, the radius of orbit are known, the velocity v is unknown, then which of the following equations would you use to compute its velocity or acceleration :

(a) $v = a\,T,\ a = \dfrac{v^2}{R}$ (b) $v = \dfrac{2\pi R}{T},\ v = a\,T$

(c) $v = \dfrac{2\pi R}{T},\ a = \dfrac{v^2}{R}$ (d) $v = \dfrac{1}{2}\,(aT^2)$ only

35. A satellite is moving round the earth. In order to escape it, its velocity must be increased by :

(a) $20\,\%$ (b) $41.4\,\%$
(c) $1.41\,\%$ (d) not possible

36. In a satellite if the time of revolution is T, then $K.E.$ is proportional to

(a) $\dfrac{1}{T}$ (b) $\dfrac{1}{T^2}$

(c) $\dfrac{1}{T^3}$ (d) $T^{-2/3}$

37. The satellite of mass m revolving in a circular orbit of radius r around the earth has kinetic energy E. Then its angular momentum will be

(a) $\sqrt{\dfrac{E}{mr^2}}$ (b) $\dfrac{E}{2mr^2}$

(c) $\sqrt{2Emr^2}$ (d) $\sqrt{2Emr}$

38. A small asteroid is orbiting around the sun in a circular orbit of radius r_0 with speed v_0. A rocket is lunched from the asteroid with speed $v = \alpha v_0$, where v is the speed relative to the sun. The highest value of α for which the rocket will remain bound to the solar system is : (ignoring gravity due to asteroid and effects of other planets) **[KVPY -2012]**

(a) $\sqrt{2}$ (b) 2
(c) $\sqrt{3}$ (d) 1

39. A planet moving along an elliptical orbit is closest to the sun at a distance r_1 and farthest away at a distance of r_2 . If v_1 and v_2 are the linear velocities at these points respectively, then the ratio $\dfrac{v_1}{v_2}$ is :

(a) $(r_1/r_2)^2$ (b) (r_2/r_1)
(c) $(r_2/r_1)^2$ (d) (r_1/r_2)

40. A satellite moves around the earth in a circular orbit of radius R with speed v. If the mass of the satellite is M, its total energy is

(a) $-\dfrac{1}{2}Mv^2$ (b) $\dfrac{1}{2}Mv^2$

(c) $\dfrac{3}{2}Mv^2$ (d) Mv^2

41. The time period of a satellite of earth is 5 hours. If the separation between the earth and the satellite is increased to four times the previous value, the new time period will become

(a) 20 hours (b) 10 hours
(c) 80 hours (d) 40 hours

42. A satellite of mass m is circulating around the earth with constant angular velocity. If radius of the orbit is R_0 and mass of the earth M, the angular momentum about the centre of the earth is

(a) $m\sqrt{GMR_0}$ (b) $M\sqrt{GmR_0}$

(c) $m\sqrt{\dfrac{GM}{R_0}}$ (d) $M\sqrt{\dfrac{GM}{R_0}}$

43. The escape velocity of a body projected from the surface of the earth vertically upwards is 11.2 km/s. If the body is projected in a direction making an angle 30° with the vertical, then the new escape velocity will be :

(a) $\dfrac{11.2}{2}$ km/s (b) $11.2 \times \dfrac{\sqrt{3}}{2}$ km/s

(c) 22.4 km/s (d) 11.2 km/s

44. The escape velocity from the earth is about 11 km per second. The escape velocity from a planet having twice the radius and the same mean density as the earth is :

(a) 22 km/s (b) 11 km/s
(c) 5.5 km/s (d) 15.5 km/s

45. The acceleration due to gravity on a planet is same as that on earth and its radius is four times that of earth. What will be the value of escape velocity on that planet if it is v_e on earth

(a) v_e (b) $2v_e$

(c) $4v_e$ (d) $\dfrac{v_e}{2}$

46. The condition for a uniform spherical mass m of radius r to be a black hole is [G = gravitational constant and g = acceleration due to gravity]

(a) $(2Gm/r)^{1/2} \le c$ (b) $(2Gm/r)^{1/2}\ \ c$

(c) $(2Gm/r)^{1/2} \ge c$ (d) $(Gm/r)^{1/2} \ge c$

Answer	33	(c)	34	(c)	35	(b)	36	(d)	37	(c)	38	(a)	39	(b)
Key	40	(a)	41	(d)	42	(a)	43	(d)	44	(a)	45	(b)	46	(c)

Newton's Laws of Gravitation, Gravitational Field and Potential:

1. If the radius of the earth were to shrink by 1% its mass remaining the same, the acceleration due to gravity on the earth's surface would

  (a) decrease by 2%   (b) remain unchanged

  (c) increase by 2%   (d) increase by 1%

2. If earth is supposed to be a sphere of radius R, if $g\,g_{30°}$ is value of acceleration due to gravity at latitude of $30°$ and g at the equator, the value of $g - g_{30°}$ is

  (a) $\dfrac{1}{4}\omega^2 R$ (b) $\dfrac{3}{4}\omega^2 R$

  (c) $\omega^2 R$ (d) $\dfrac{1}{2}\omega^2 R$

3. A certain planet completes one rotation about its axis in time T. The weight of an object placed at the equator on the planet's surface is a fraction f (f is close to unity) of tis weight recorded at a latitude of $60°$. The density of the planet (assumed to be uniform) is given by : **[KVPY- 2010]**

  (a) $\left(\dfrac{4-f}{1-f}\right)\dfrac{3\pi}{4GT^2}$ (b) $\left(\dfrac{4-f}{1+f}\right)\dfrac{3\pi}{4GT^2}$

  (c) $\left(\dfrac{4-3f}{1-f}\right)\dfrac{3\pi}{4GT^2}$ (d) $\left(\dfrac{4-2f}{1-f}\right)\dfrac{3\pi}{3GT^2}$

4. The figure shows a spherical hollow inside a lead sphere of radius R, the surface of the hollow passes through the centre of the sphere and "touches" the right side of the sphere. The mass of the sphere before hollowing was M. With what gravitational force does the hollowed out lead sphere attract a small sphere of mass m that lies at a distance 'd' from the centre of the lead sphere, on the straight line connecting the centres of the sphere and of the hollow :

  (a) $\dfrac{GMm}{d^2}\left[1 - \dfrac{1}{8\left(1 - \dfrac{R}{2d}\right)^2}\right]$

  (b) $\dfrac{GMm}{d^2}\left[1 + \dfrac{1}{4\left(1 - \dfrac{R}{2d}\right)^2}\right]$

  (c) $\dfrac{GMm}{d^2}\left[1 - \dfrac{1}{4\left(1 - \dfrac{R}{2d}\right)^2}\right]$

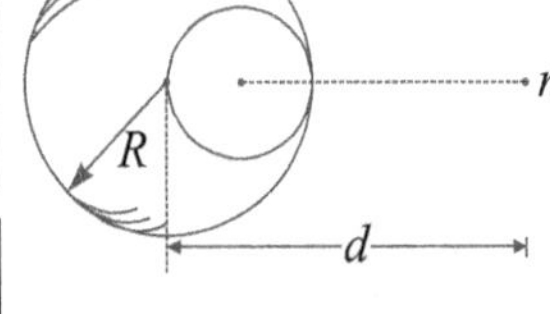

  (d) $\dfrac{GMm}{d^2}\left[1 + \dfrac{1}{8\left(1 - \dfrac{R}{2d}\right)^2}\right]$

5. The gravitational potential difference between the surface of a planet and a point 10 m above is 4.0 J/kg. The gravitational field in this region, assumed uniform is :

  (a) 0.025 N/kg   (b) 0.40 N/kg

  (c) 40 N/kg   (d) 4.0 N/kg

6. Two identical trains are moving on rails along the equator on earth in opposite directions with the same speed. The pressure exerted on rails will be :

  (a) same for both

  (b) zero for both

  (c) more for train moving along the earth's motion

  (d) more for train moving opposite the earth's motion

7. A satellite of mass m is orbiting the earth in a circular path of radius r with velocity v. How much energy is required to take the satellite from an orbit of radius r to one of radius $3\,r$:

  (a) $\dfrac{GMm}{r}$ (b) $\dfrac{GMm}{2r}$

  (c) $\dfrac{GMm}{3r}$ (d) $\dfrac{GMm}{r^2}$

Satellites, Orbital Velocity and Escape Velocity

8. The eccentricity of earth's orbit is e = 0.0167. The ratio of its maximum speed in its orbit to its minimum speed is : **[KVPY 2012]**

  (a) 2.507   (b) 1.033

  (c) 8.324   (d) 1.000

9. A body moves in a circular orbit of radius R under the action of a central force. Potential due to the central force is given by V(r) = kr (k is a positive constant). Period of revolution of the body is proportional to : **[KVPY 2014]**

  (a) $R^{1/2}$ (b) $R^{-1/2}$

  (c) $R^{-3/2}$ (d) $R^{-5/2}$

10. For the earth - moon system, let M and m be the masses of the earth and the moon respectively. Let v be the instantaneous relative velocity. The total kinetic energy of this system in the centre of mass frame will be given by

  (a) $\dfrac{1}{2}\dfrac{mM}{m+M}v^2$ (b) $\dfrac{1}{2}mv^2 + \dfrac{1}{2}Mv^2$

  (c) $\dfrac{1}{2}mv^2$ (d) $\dfrac{1}{2}Mv^2$

Answer	1	(c)	2	(b)	3	(a)	4	(a)	5	(b)
Key	6	(d)	7	(c)	8	(b)	9	(a)	10	(a)

11. A research satellite of mass 200 kg circles the earth in an orbit of average radius $3R/2$ where R is the radius of the earth. Assuming the gravitational pull on a mass of 1 kg on the earth's surface to be 10 N, the pull on the satellite will be

    (a) 880 N   (b) 889 N

    (c) 890 N   (d) 892 N

12. Energy required to move a body of mass m from an orbit of radius $2R$ to $3R$ is

    (a) $GMm/12R^2$ (b) $MGm/3R^2$

    (c) $GMm/8R$ (d) $GMm/6R$

13. A particle of mass 10 g is kept on the surface of a uniform sphere of mass 100 kg and radius 10 cm. Find the work to be done against the gravitational force between them to take the particle far away from the sphere (you may take $G = 6.67 \times 10^{-11} \, Nm^2 / kg^2$)

    (a) $6.67 \times 10^{-9} \, J$ (b) $6.67 \times 10^{-10} \, J$

    (c) $13.34 \times 10^{-10} \, J$ (d) $3.33 \times 10^{-10} \, J$

14. An asteroid of mass m is approaching earth initially at a distance of $10R_e$ with speed v_i. It hits the earth with a speed v_f (R_e and M_e are radius and mass of earth), then

    (a) $v_f^2 = v_i^2 + \dfrac{2Gm}{M_e R}\left(1 - \dfrac{1}{10}\right)$

    (b) $v_f^2 = v_i^2 + \dfrac{2GM_e}{R_e}\left(1 + \dfrac{1}{10}\right)$

    (c) $v_f^2 = v_i^2 + \dfrac{2GM_e}{R_e}\left(1 - \dfrac{1}{10}\right)$

    (d) $v_f^2 = v_i^2 + \dfrac{2Gm}{R_e}\left(1 - \dfrac{1}{10}\right)$

15. A projectile is projected with velocity kv_e in vertically upward direction from the ground into the space. (v_e is escape velocity and $k < 1$). If air resistance is considered to be negligible then the maximum height from the centre of earth to which it can go, will be: (R = radius of earth)

    (a) $\dfrac{R}{k^2 + 1}$ (b) $\dfrac{R}{k^2 - 1}$

    (c) $\dfrac{R}{1 + k^2}$ (d) $\dfrac{R}{k + 1}$

16. A point P lies on the axis of a ring of mass M and radius R at a distance R from its centre C. A small particle starts

from P and reaches at C under gravitational attraction only. Its speed at centre C will be :

(a) $\sqrt{\dfrac{2Gm}{R}}$

(b) $\sqrt{\dfrac{2Gm}{R}\left(1 - \dfrac{1}{\sqrt{2}}\right)}$

(c) $\sqrt{\dfrac{2Gm}{R}\left(\sqrt{2} - 1\right)}$

(d) zero

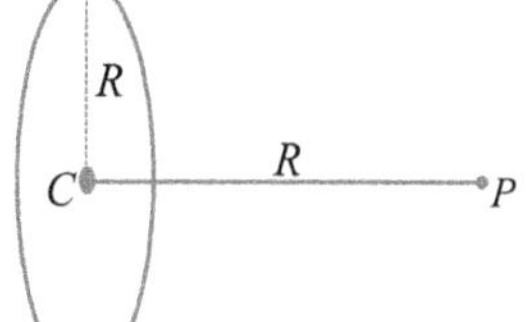

17. A planet was suddenly stopped in its orbit supposed to be circular. The time it takes to fall on to the sun is, if time period of planet's revolution is T

    (a) $\dfrac{T}{2}$ (b) $\dfrac{\sqrt{2}T}{4}$

    (c) $\dfrac{\sqrt{2}T}{8}$ (d) $\sqrt{2}T$

18. The escape velocity from earth is v_e. A body is projected with velocity $2v_e$ with what constant velocity will it move in the inter planetary space

    (a) v_e (b) $3v_e$

    (c) $\sqrt{3}v_e$ (d) $\sqrt{5}v_e$

19. Three equal masses (each m) are placed at the corners of an equilateral triangle of side 'a'. Then the escape velocity of an object from the circumcentre P of triangle is :

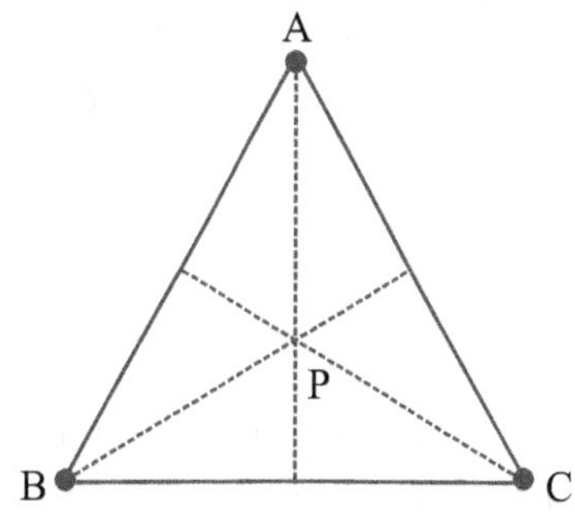

    (a) $\sqrt{\dfrac{2\sqrt{3}\,Gm}{a}}$ (b) $\sqrt{\dfrac{\sqrt{3}\,Gm}{a}}$

    (c) $\sqrt{\dfrac{6\sqrt{3}\,Gm}{a}}$ (d) $\sqrt{\dfrac{3\sqrt{3}\,Gm}{a}}$

| Answer | 11 | (b) | 12 | (d) | 13 | (b) | 14 | (c) | 15 | (c) | 16 | (b) |
| Key | 17 | (c) | 18 | (c) | 19 | (c) | | | | | | |

| Mechanics | **MCQ Type 2** | Exercise 9.2 |

MULTIPLE CORRECT OPTIONS

1. Identical point masses each equal to m are placed at $x = 0$, $x = 1$, $x = 2$, $x = 4$, ... The total gravitational force on mass m at $x = 0$ due to all other masses is :

(a) infinite
(b) $(4/3)\,GM^2$
(c) $(4/3)\,Gm^2$
(d) zero

2. Two masses m_1 and m_2 $(m_1 < m_2)$ are released from rest from a finite distance. They start under their mutual gravitational attraction

(a) acceleration of m_1 is more than that of m_2
(b) acceleration of m_2 is more than that of m_1
(c) centre of mass of system will remain at rest in all the reference frame
(d) total energy of system remains constant

3. The spherical planets have the same mass but densities in the ratio 1 :8. For these planets, the

(a) acceleration due to gravity will be in the ratio 1: 4
(b) acceleration due to gravity will be in the ratio 4 : 1.
(c) escape velocities from their surfaces will be in the ratio $1 : \sqrt{2}$
(d) escape velocities from their surfaces will be in the ratio $\sqrt{2} : 1$.

4. A spherical shell of radius R is cut along a chord AB and slightly displaced as shown in figure. Two points P and Q are such that with P in lower part and Q in upper part of the shell. Then :

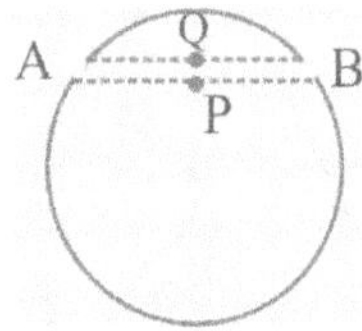

(a) The gravitational field at P and Q are zero.
(b) The sum of gravitational fields at P and Q is zero.
(c) The gravitational potentials at P and Q are equal.
(d) The gravitational potentials at P and Q are unequal.

5. A satellite is revolving in a circular orbit around the earth and an object is placed inside the satellite. Then :

(a) satellite and object both are weightless
(b) satellite has weight while object appears weightless.
(c) object has weight while satellite appears weightless.
(d) satellite behaves as a freely falling body.

6. A satellite is revolving in an elliptical orbit in free space; then which of the following statements are true :

(a) its mechanical energy is constant
(b) its linear momentum is constant
(c) its angular momentum is constant
(d) its areal velocity constant

7. A double star is a system of two stars of masses m and $2m$, rotating about their centre of mass only under their mutual gravitational attraction. If r is the separation between these two stars then their time period of rotation about their centre of mass will be proportional to

(a) $r^{3/2}$
(b) r
(c) $m^{1/2}$
(d) $m^{-1/2}$

8. A tunnel is dug along a chord of the earth at a perpendicular distance $R/2$ from the earth's centre. The wall of the tunnel may be assumed to be frictionless. A particle is released from one end of the tunnel. The pressing force by the particle on the wall and the acceleration of the particle varies with x (distance of the particle from the centre) according to

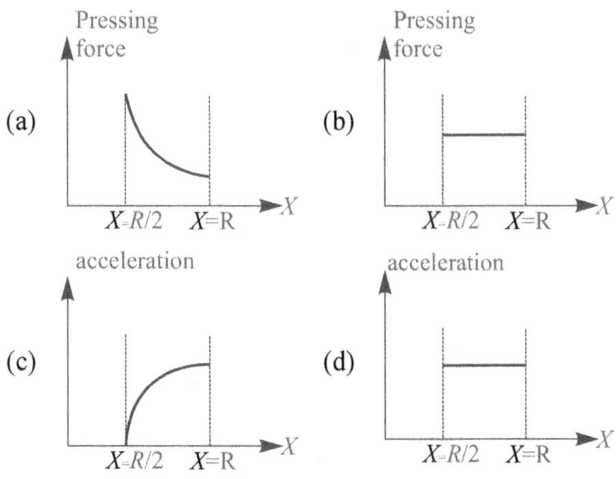

9. Two tunnels are dug from one side of the earth's surface to the other side, one along a diameter and the other along a chord. Now two particles are dropped from one end of each of the tunnels. Both the particles oscillate simple harmonically along the tunnels. Let T_1 and T_2 be the time periods and v_1 and v_2 be the maximum speed of the particles in the two tunnels. Then

(a) $T_1 = T_2$
(b) $T_1 > T_2$
(c) $v_1 = v_2$
(d) $v_1 > v_2$

Answer	1	(b)	2	(a, d)	3	(a, c)	4	(b, d)	5	(b, d)
Key	6	(a, c, d)	7	(a, d)	8	(b, c)	9	(a, d)		

10. Due to a solid sphere magnitude of :

(a) gravitational potential is maximum at centre

(b) gravitational potential is minimum at centre

(c) field strength is maximum at centre

(d) field strength is minimum at centre

11. The magnitude of the gravitational field strengths at distances r_1 and r_2 from the centre of uniform sphere of radius R and mass M are F_1 and F_2 respectively, then :

(a) $\dfrac{F_1}{F_2} = \dfrac{r_1}{r_2}$ if $r_1 < R$ and $r_2 < R$

(b) $\dfrac{F_1}{F_2} = \left(\dfrac{r_2}{r_1}\right)^2$ if $r_1 > R$ and $r_2 > R$

(c) $\dfrac{F_1}{F_2} = \dfrac{r_1}{r_2}$ if $r_1 > R$ and $r_2 > R$

(d) $\dfrac{F_1}{F_2} = \left(\dfrac{r_1}{r_2}\right)^2$ if $r_1 < R$ and $r_2 < R$

12. Two objects of masses m and $4\,m$ are at rest at an infinite separation. They move towards each other under mutual gravitational attraction. G is the universal gravitational constant. Then at separation r:

(a) the total energy of the two objects is zero

(b) their relative velocity of approach is $\left(\dfrac{10\,Gm}{r}\right)^{1/2}$ in magnitude.

(c) the total kinetic energy of the objects is $\dfrac{4\,Gm^2}{r}$

(d) net angular momentum of both the particles is zero about any point

13. A solid sphere of uniform density and radius 4 units is located with its centre at the origin O of coordinates. Two spheres of equal radii 1 unit with their centres at $A\,(-2, 0, 0)$ and $B\,(2, 0, 0)$ respectively are taken

out of the solid leaving behind spherical cavities as shown in figure. Then :

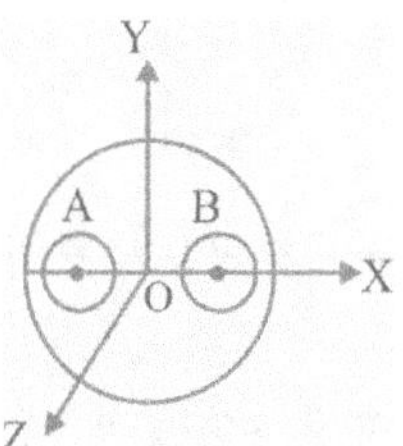

(a) the gravitational force due to this sphere at the origin is zero

(b) the gravitational force at the point B $(2, 0, 0)$ is zero

(c) the gravitational potential is the same at all points of the circle $y^2 + z^2 = 36$

(d) the gravitational potential is the same at all points on the circle $y^2 + z^2 = 4$

14. A geostationary satellite is at a height h above the surface of earth. If earth radius is R

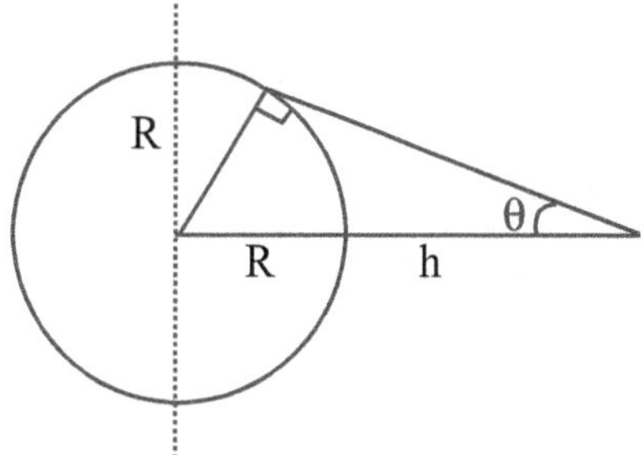

(a) The minimum colatitude on earth upto which the satellite can be used for communicate is $\sin^{-1} R/(R+h)$

(b) The maximum colatitude on earth upto which the satellite can be used for communicate is $\sin^{-1} R/(R+h)$

(c) The area on earth escaped from this satellite is given as $2\pi R^2 (1+\sin\theta)$

(d) The area on earth escaped from this satellite is given as $2\pi R^2 (1+\cos\theta)$

Answer Key	10	(a, d)	11	(a, b)	12	(a, b, c, d)	13	(a, c, d)	14	(a, c)

Mechanics   **Reasoning Type Questions**   Exercise 9.3

Read the two statements carefully to mark the correct option out of the options given below:

(a) **Statement - 1** is true, **Statement - 2** is true; **Statement - 2** is correct explanation for **Statement - 1**.

(b) **Statement -1** is true, **Statement - 2** is true; **Statement - 2** is not correct explanation for **Statement - 1**.

(c) **Statement - 1** is true, **Statement - 2** is false.

(d) **Statement - 1** is false, **Statement - 2** is true

1. **Statement - 1**

Smaller the orbit of the planet around the sun, shorter is the time it takes to complete one revolution.

Statement - 2

According to Kepler's third law of planetary motion, square of time period is proportional to cube of mean distance from sun.

2. **Statement - 1**

Space rocket are usually launched in the equatorial line from west to east

Statement - 2

The acceleration due to gravity is minimum at the equator.

3. **Statement - 1**

A person sitting in an artificial satellite revolving around earth feels weightless.

Statement - 2

There is no gravitational force on the satellite.

4. **Statement - 1**

A body becomes massless at the centre of earth.

Statement - 2

This follows from $g' = g\left(1 - \dfrac{d}{R}\right)$

5. **Statement - 1**

Moon travellers tie heavy weight at their back before landing on the moon.

Statement - 2

The acceleration due to gravity on moon is smaller than that of earth.

6. **Statement - 1**

The tidal waves in sea are primarily due to the gravitational effect of earth.

Statement - 2

The intensity of gravitational field of earth is maximum at the surface of earth.

7. **Statement - 1**

We can not set an artificial satellite into an orbit in such a way that it always remains over New Delhi.

Statement - 2

The orbit of an earth satellite must always lie in a plane contains the centre of earth.

8. **Statement - 1**

If the total energy of a satellite moving around earth is E, its potential energy is $2\,E$.

Statement - 2

Total energy $E = \mathrm{KE} + \mathrm{PE}$.

9. **Statement - 1**

The atmosphere of Jupiter contains light gases, where as earth's atmosphere has little amount of hydrogen gas.

Statement - 2

The escape velocity from the Jupiter is smaller than the escape velocity from the earth.

10. **Statement - 1**

An astronaut in an orbiting space station above the earth experiences weightlessness.

Statement - 2

An object moving around earth under the influence of earth's gravitational force is in a state of free fall.

11. **Statement - 1**

For a mass M kept at the centre of a cube of side $'a'$, the flux of gravitational field passing through its sides is $4\pi GM$.

Statement - 2

If the direction of field due to point source is radial and its dependence on the distance r from the source is given as $\dfrac{1}{r^2}$, its flux through a closed surface depends only on the strength of the source enclosed by the surface and not on the size or shape of the surface.

Answer	1	(a)	2	(b)	3	(c)	4	(d)	5	(a)	6	(d)
Key	7	(a)	8	(a)	9	(c)	10	(a)	11	(a)		

Mechanics   **Passage & Matrix**   **Exercise 9.4**

PASSAGES

Passage for (Questions 1 & 2) :

Two satellites S_1 and S_2 revolve round a planet in coplanar circular orbits in the same sense. Their periods of revolution are 1 h and 8 h respectively. The radius of the orbit of S_1 is 10^4 km. When S_2 is closest to S_1 find

1. The speed of S_2 relative to S_1
  (a) 2×10^4 km/h   (b) $\pi \times 10^4$ km /h.
  (c) $2\pi \times 10^4$ km/h   (d) 10^4 km/h

2. The angular speed of S_2 as observed by an astronaut in S_1 is
  (a) π rad /h   (b) $2\pi/\,3$ rad/h
  (c) $\pi/4$ rad/h   (d) $\dfrac{\pi}{3}$ rad / h.

Passage for (Questions 3 - 5) :

Two satellites A and B are revolving around the earth in circular orbits of radius r_1 and r_2 respectively with $r_1 < r_2$. Plane of motion of the two are same. At position 1, A is given an impulse in the direction of velocity by firing a rocket so that it follows an elliptical path to meet B at position 2 as shown. Focal lengths of the elliptical path are r_1 and r_2 respectively. At position 2, A is given another impulse so that velocities of A and B at 2 become equal and the two move together.

For any elliptical path of the satellite time period of revolution is given by Kepler's planetary law as $T^2 \propto r^3$ where 'a' is semi major axis of the ellipse which is $\dfrac{r_1 + r_2}{2}$ in this case.

Also angular momentum of any satellite revolving around the Earth will remain a constant about Earth's centre as force of gravity on the satellite which keeps it in elliptical path is along its position vector relative to the earth centre.

3. When A is given its first impulse at that moment :

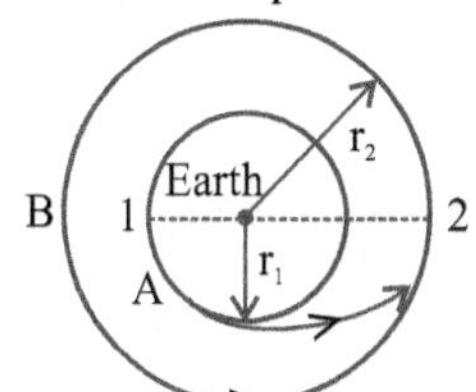

(a) A, B and centre of earth are in same straight line
(b) B is ahead of A angularly
(c) B is behind A angularly
(d) None of these

4. If the two have same mass :
(a) A would have more potential energy than B while on their initial circular paths
(b) A would have less kinetic energy than B while on their initial circular paths
(c) Relative to Earth's centre, angular momentum of A when it is in elliptical path would be less than angular momentum of B
(d) During the whole process angular momentum of B would be more than angular momentum of A

5. If $r_2 = 3\, r_1$ and time period of revolution for B be T then time taken by A in moving from position 1 to position 2 is :

(a) $T\,\dfrac{\sqrt{3}}{\sqrt{2}}$

(b) $T\,\dfrac{\sqrt{3}}{2}$

(c) $\dfrac{T\sqrt{2}}{3\sqrt{3}}$

(d) $\dfrac{T\sqrt{2}}{3}$

6. Column I describes some situations in which a small object moves. Column II describes some characteristics of these motions. Match the situations in column I with the characteristics in column II.   **[IIT-JEE2007]**

Column I	Column II
A. The object moves on the x-axis under a conservative force in such a way that its 'speed' and 'position' satisfy $v = c_1\sqrt{c_2 - x^2}$, where c_1 and c_2 are positive constants.	(p) The object executes a simple harmonic motion.
B. The object moves on the x-axis in such a way that its velocity and its displacement from the origin satisfy $v = -kx$, where k is a positive constant.	(q) The object does not change in direction.
C. The object is attached to one end of a massless spring of a given spring constant. The other end of the spring is attached to the ceiling of an elevator. Initially every thing is at rest. The elevator starts going upwards with a constant acceleration a. The motion of the object is observed from the elevator during the period it maintains this acceleration.	(r) The kinetic energy of the object keeps on decreasing.
D. The object is projected from the earth's surface vertically upwards with a speed $2\sqrt{GM/R}$, where M is the mass of the earth and R is the radius of the earth. Neglect forces from objects other than the earth.	(s) The object can change its direction of motion only once

Answer	1	(b)	2	(d)	3	(b)	4	(c)
Key	5	(c)	6	A. → (p) ; B. → (q), (r) ; C. → (p), (s); D. →(r)				

7. Two concentric spherical shells are as shown in figure. Match the following:

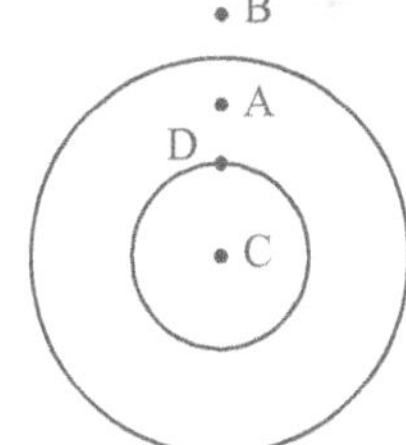

Column I		Column II	
A.	Potential at A	(p)	greater than B
B.	Gravitational field at A	(q)	less than B
C.	As one moves from C to D	(r)	potential remains constant
D.	As one moves from D to A	(s)	gravitational field decreases
		(t)	None

8. A satellite is revolving round the earth in a circular orbit of radius 'a' with velocity v_0. A particle of mass m is projected from the satellite in forward direction with relative velocity $v = \left[\sqrt{\dfrac{5}{4}} - 1\right] v_0$. During subsequent motion of particle, match the following

Column I		Column II	
A.	Total energy of particle	(p)	$-\dfrac{3GM_e m}{8a}$
B.	Minimum distance of particle from the earth	(q)	$\dfrac{5}{8}\dfrac{GM_e m}{a}$
C.	Maximum distance of particle from the earth	(r)	$5a/3$
D.	The kinetic energy	(s)	a

9. Assume v_0 be the velocity of projection of a body from the surface of the earth enables it to become a satellite of the earth close to the earth surface. If R be the radius of the earth then $v_0 = \sqrt{gR}$ where $g = \dfrac{GM}{R^2}$; G – universal gravitational constant and M is the mass of the earth. If v_e be the escape velocity on the earth then $\dfrac{v_0}{v_e} = \dfrac{1}{\sqrt{2}}$. If v be the velocity of projection of body on the surface of earth then, match the following

Column I		Column II	
A.	$v = v_0$	(p)	Path of body is circular
B.	$v < v_0$	(q)	Path of body is elliptical and return to earth
C.	$v_0 < v < v_e$	(r)	Path of body is elliptical but not return to earth
D.	$v = v_e$	(s)	Path of the body is parabolic

Answer	7	A. → (q) : B. → (t) : C. → (r) : D. → (s)	8	A. → (p) : B. → (s) : C. → (r) : D. → (q)
Key	9	A. → (p) : B. → (q) : C. → (r); D. → (s)		

Best of JEE-(Main & Advanced) — Exercise 9.5

JEE- (Main)

1. Imagine a light planet revolving around a very massive star in a circular orbit of radius R with a period of revolution T. If the gravitational force of attraction between the planet and the star proportional to $R^{-5/2}$, then : **[AIEEE 2004]**
   (a) $T^2 \propto R^3$ (b) $T^2 \propto R^{7/2}$
   (c) $T^2 \propto R^{3/2}$ (d) $T^2 \propto R^{3.75}$

2. If the change in the value of 'g' at a height h above the surface of the earth is the same as at a depth x below it, then (both x and h being much smaller than the radius of the earth) **[AIEEE 2005]**
   (a) $x = h$ (b) $x = 2h$
   (c) $x = \dfrac{h}{2}$ (d) $x = h^2$

3. This question contains Statement-1 and Statement-2. Of the four choices given after the statements, choose the one that best describes the two statements. **[AIEEE 2008]**

Statement-1 :
For a mass M kept at the centre of a cube of side 'a', the flux of gravitational field passing through its sides $4\pi GM$.

and

Statement-2:
If the direction of a field due to a point source is radial and its dependence on the distance 'r' from the source is given as $\dfrac{1}{r^2}$, its flux through a closed surface depends only on the strength of the source enclosed by the surface and not on the size or shape of the surface.

   (a) Statement -1 is false, Statement-2 is true
   (b) Statement -1 is true, Statement-2 is true; Statement -2 is a correct explanation for Statement-1
   (c) Statement -1 is true, Statement-2 is true; Statement -2 is not a correct explanation for Statement-1
   (d) Statement -1 is true, Statement-2 is false

4. Two bodies of masses m and $4m$ are placed at a distance r. The gravitational potential at a point on the line joining them where the gravitational field is zero is: **[AIEEE 2011]**

(a) $-\dfrac{4Gm}{r}$ (b) $-\dfrac{6Gm}{r}$

(c) $-\dfrac{9Gm}{r}$ (d) zero

5. Two particles of equal mass 'm' go around a circle of radius R under the action of their mutual gravitational attraction. The speed of each particle with respect to their centre of mass is : **[AIEEE 2011RS]**

(a) $\sqrt{\dfrac{Gm}{4R}}$ (b) $\sqrt{\dfrac{Gm}{3R}}$

(c) $\sqrt{\dfrac{Gm}{2R}}$ (d) $\sqrt{\dfrac{Gm}{R}}$

6. The mass of a spaceship is 1000 kg. It is to be launched from the earth's surface out into free space. The value of g and R (radius of earth) are 10 m/s^2 and 6400 km respectively. The required energy for this work will be : **[AIEEE 2012]**

(a) 6.4×10^{11} Joules   (b) 6.4×10^{8} Joules

(c) 6.4×10^{9} Joules   (d) 6.4×10^{10} Joules

7. What is the minimum energy required to launch a satellite of mass m from the surface of a planet of mass M and radius R in a circular orbit at an altitude of 2R? **[JEE-Main 2013]**

(a) $\dfrac{5GmM}{6R}$ (b) $\dfrac{2GmM}{3R}$

(c) $\dfrac{GmM}{2R}$ (d) $\dfrac{GmM}{2R}$

8. From a solid sphere of mass M and radius R, a spherical portion of radius R, a spherical portion of radius $R/2$ is removed, as shown in the figure. Taking gravitational potential $V = 0$ at $r = \infty$, the potential at the cente of the cavity thus formed is (G = gravitational constant) **[JEE-Main 2015]**

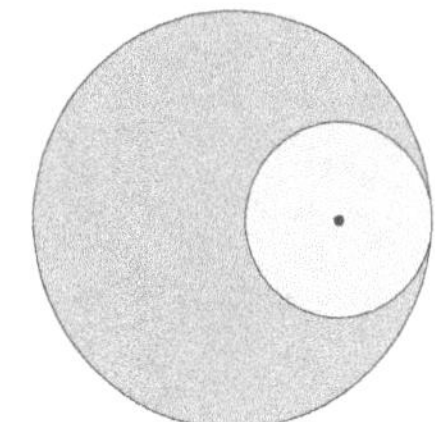

(a) $-\dfrac{GM}{R}$ (b) $-\dfrac{2GM}{3R}$

(c) $-\dfrac{2GM}{R}$ (d) $\dfrac{-GM}{2R}$

JEE- (Advanced)

9. A geostationary satellite orbits around earth in a circular orbit of radius 36000 km. Then the time period of a spy satellite orbiting a few hundred km above the earth's surface (R_{earth} = 6400 km) will approximately be : **[IIT-JEE 2002]**

(a) $\dfrac{1}{2}$ hr   (b) 1 hr

(c) 2 hr   (d) 4 hr

10. A system of binary stars of masses m_A and m_B are moving in circular orbits of radii r_A and r_B respectively. If T_A and T_B are the times periods of masses m_A respectively, then **[IIT-JEE 2006]**

(a) $\dfrac{T_A}{T_B} = \left(\dfrac{r_A}{r_B}\right)^{3/2}$ (b) $T_A > T_B$ (if $r_A > r_B$)

(c) $T_A > T_B$ (if $m_A > m_B$)   (d) $T_A = T_B$

11. A spherically symmetric gravitational system of particles has a mass density $\rho = \begin{cases} \rho_0 & for \ \ r \le R \\ 0 & for \ \ r > R \end{cases}$

where ρ_0 is a constant. A test mass can undergo circular motion under the influence of the gravitational field of particles. Its speed v as a function of distance r ($0 < r < \infty$) from the centre of the system is represented by **[IIT-JEE 2008]**

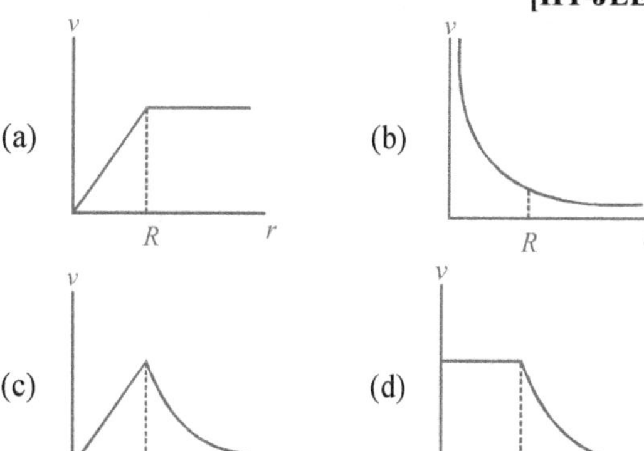

12. A thin uniform annular disc (see figure) of mass M has outer radius $4R$ and inner radius $3R$. The work required to take a unit mass from point P on its axis to infinity is **[IIT-JEE 2010]**

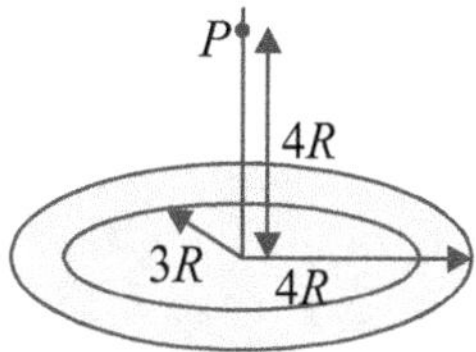

(a) $\dfrac{2GM}{7R}(4\sqrt{2}-5)$ (b) $-\dfrac{2GM}{7R}(4\sqrt{2}-5)$

(c) $\dfrac{GM}{4R}$ (d) $\dfrac{2GM}{5R}(\sqrt{2}-1)$

Answer	1	(b)	2	(b)	3	(b)	4	(c)	5	(a)	6	(d)
Key	7	(a)	8	(a)	9	(c)	10	(a)	11	(c)	12	(a)

13. A satellite is moving with a constant speed 'V' in a circular orbit about the earth. An object of mass 'm' is ejected from the satellite such that it just escapes from the gravitational pull of the earth. At the time of its ejection, the kinetic energy of the object is   **[IIT-JEE 2011]**

(a) $\dfrac{1}{2}mV^2$ (b) mV^2

(c) $\dfrac{3}{2}mV^2$ (d) $2mV^2$

14. Two bodies, each of mass M, are kept fixed with a separation $2L$. A particle of mass m is projected from the midpoint of the line joining their centres, perpendicular to the line. The gravitational constant is G. The correct statement(s) is (are)

[JEE-Adv. 2013]

(a) The minimum initial velocity of the mass m to escape the gravitational field of the two bodies is $4\sqrt{\dfrac{GM}{L}}$

(b) The minimum initial velocity of the mass m to escape the gravitational field of the two bodies is $2\sqrt{\dfrac{GM}{L}}$

(c) The minimum initial velocity of the mass m to escape the gravitational field of the two bodies is $\sqrt{\dfrac{2GM}{L}}$

(d) The energy of the mass m remains constant

Answer Key	13	(b)	14	(b)				

Hints & Solutions

In Chapter Exercise -9.1

1. Gravitational force acting between two point masses $F = \dfrac{Gm_1m_2}{r^2}$, is independent of the nature of medium between them.

   Therefore, gravitational force acting between two point masses will remain unaffected when they are dipped in water.

2. Yes, a body can have inertia (i.e., mass) but no weight. Everyone always have inertia (i.e., mass) but its weight (mg) can be zero, when it is taken at the centre of the earth or during free fall under gravity.

3. Aphelion is the location of the earth where it is at the greatest distance from the sun and perihelion is the location of the earth where it is at the nearest distance from the sun.

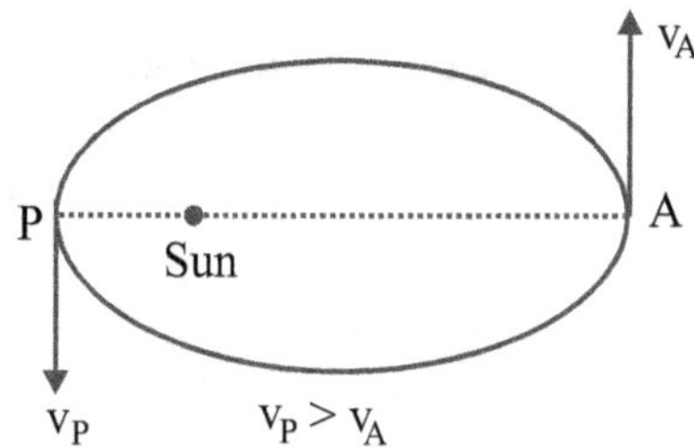

4. Potential energy of an object at the surface of the earth
   $$= -\dfrac{GM_e m}{R}$$

   PE of the object at a height equal to the radius of the earth
   $$= -\dfrac{GMm}{2R}$$

   $\therefore$ Gain in PE of the object $= -\dfrac{GMm}{2R}\left(-\dfrac{GMm}{R}\right)$

   $$= +\dfrac{GMm}{2R}$$

   $$= \dfrac{gR^2 \times m}{2R} \qquad \left(\because GM = gR^2\right)$$

   $$= \dfrac{1}{2}mgR$$

5. Gravitational force acting on an object of mass m, placed at point P at a distance h along the normal through the centre of a circular ring of mass M and radius r is given by

   $$F = \dfrac{GMmh}{\left(r^2 + h^2\right)^{3/2}}$$

   when h = r, then

   $$F = \dfrac{GMm \times r}{\left(r^2 + r^2\right)^{3/2}} = \dfrac{GMm}{2\sqrt{2}\,r^2}$$

   and $\quad F' = \dfrac{2GMmr}{\left(r^2 + 4r^2\right)^{3/2}} = \dfrac{2GMm}{5\sqrt{5}\,r^2}$

$\therefore \qquad \dfrac{F'}{F} = \dfrac{4\sqrt{2}}{5\sqrt{5}}$

or $\qquad F' = \dfrac{4\sqrt{2}}{5\sqrt{5}}F$

In Chapter Exercise -9.2

1. $T_s = 29.5\,T_e$, $R_e = 1.5 \times 10^8$ km;

   From Kepler's 3rd law, $\dfrac{T_s^2}{T_e^2} = \dfrac{R_s^3}{R_e^3}$

   $$\therefore R_s = R_e \left(\dfrac{T_s}{T_e}\right)^{2/3} = 1.5 \times 10^8 \left(\dfrac{29.5 T_e}{T_e}\right)^{2/3} = 1.43 \times 10^9 \text{ km}$$

2. Weight of the body = mg = 63N

   Acceleration due to gravity at a height 'h' $= g' = g\left[\dfrac{R^2}{(R+h)^2}\right]$

   $$= \dfrac{gR^2}{\left(R + \dfrac{R}{2}\right)^2} = \dfrac{4}{9}g$$

   $\therefore$ Gravitational force on the body at a height

   $$h = mg' = m \times \dfrac{4}{9} \times g = \dfrac{4}{9} \times 63 = 28N$$

3. Using law of conservation of energy, $\dfrac{1}{2}mv^2 - \dfrac{GMm}{R} = -\dfrac{GMm}{R+h}$

   $$\dfrac{1}{2}v^2 = GM\left[\dfrac{1}{R} - \dfrac{1}{R+h}\right]$$

   $\Rightarrow \quad \dfrac{1}{2}v^2 = \dfrac{gR^2 \cdot h}{R(R+h)} \quad [\because gR^2 = GM]$

   $\dfrac{1}{2}v^2 = \dfrac{gRh}{R+h} \Rightarrow v^2(R+h) = 2gRh$

   $\Rightarrow v^2R + v^2h = 2gRh$

   $\Rightarrow h(v^2 - 2gR) = -v^2R$

   $\Rightarrow h(2gR - v^2) = v^2R$

   $\Rightarrow h = \left(\dfrac{v^2R}{2gR - v^2}\right) = 1.6 \times 10^6$ m.

4. $v_e = 11.2$ km/s, velocity of projection $= v = 3v_e$

   Let m and v_0 be the mass and the velocity of the projectile far away from the earth, then using law of conservation of energy,

   $$\dfrac{1}{2}mv_o^2 = \dfrac{1}{2}mv^2 - \dfrac{1}{2}mv_e^2$$

   $$v_o = \sqrt{v^2 - v_e^2} = \sqrt{(3v_e)^2 - v_e^2} = \sqrt{8}\,v_e$$

   $$= 2\sqrt{2} \times 11.2 = 2 \times 1.414 \times 11.2 = 31.68 \text{ km/s}$$

5. Since $e = \dfrac{c}{a} \Rightarrow c = ea$

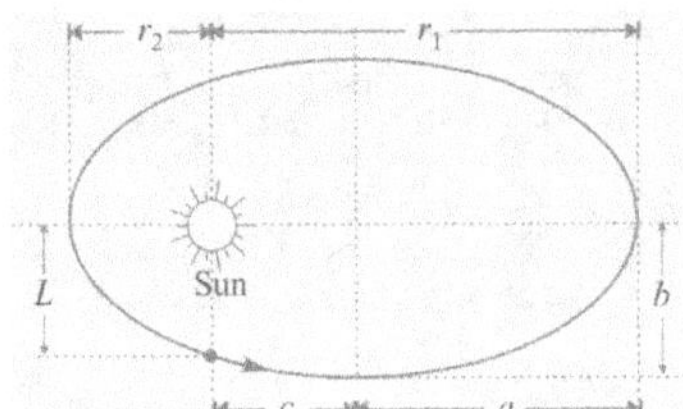

$\therefore$

$$r_1 = a + c = a + ea = a(1 + e)$$
$$r_2 = a - c = a - ea = a(1 - e)$$

Required distance $= \dfrac{1}{2}$ of latus rectum $= \dfrac{b^2}{a}$

$\therefore \qquad\qquad L = \dfrac{b^2}{a}$

We have $\qquad r_1 + r_2 = 2a$

and $\qquad r_1 - r_2 = a(1 + e) - a(1 - e) = 2ae$

$\Rightarrow \qquad\qquad e = \left(\dfrac{r_1 - r_2}{r_1 + r_2}\right).$

Also $\qquad\qquad e = \sqrt{1 - b^2/a^2} \Rightarrow b^2 = a^2(1 - e^2)$

$\therefore \qquad\qquad L = \dfrac{b^2}{a} = \dfrac{a^2}{a}(1 - e^2)$

$$= a(1 - e^2)$$

$$= \left(\dfrac{r_1 + r_2}{2}\right)\left[1 - \left(\dfrac{r_1 - r_2}{r_1 + r_2}\right)^2\right]$$

$$= \left(\dfrac{2 r_1 r_2}{r_1 + r_2}\right). \quad \textbf{\textit{Ans.}}$$

6. The motion of the planet can be approximated to be along a circle of radius $\left(\dfrac{R + r}{2}\right)$.

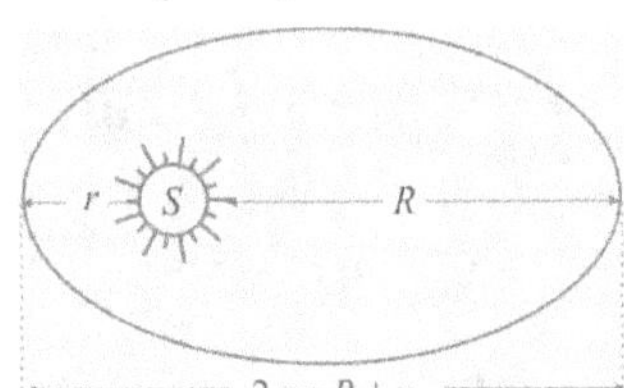

The time period will be given by

$$T = 2\pi\sqrt{\dfrac{\left[\dfrac{R + r}{2}\right]^3}{G(M + m)}}$$

Here m is the mass of the planet and M is the mass of sun. As $m \ll M$

$\therefore \qquad\qquad T = \pi\sqrt{\dfrac{(R + r)^3}{2GM}} \qquad \textbf{\textit{Ans.}}$

7. The energy of the satellite in a orbit of radius r,

$$E = \dfrac{-GMm}{2r}.$$

Here m is the mass of satellite and M is the mass of the moon. If dE/dt is the instantaneous rate of decrease of energy of the satellite, then we have

$$\left(\dfrac{dE}{dt}\right) = Fv$$

Given $\qquad\qquad F = \alpha v^2$

$\therefore \qquad \dfrac{d\left[\dfrac{-GMm}{2r}\right]}{dt} = (\alpha v^2)v$

or $\qquad \dfrac{GMm}{2r^2}dr = -\alpha v^3 dt$

Orbital velocity of satellite,

$$v = \sqrt{\dfrac{GM}{r}} \; .$$

$\therefore \qquad \dfrac{GMm}{2r^2}dr = -\alpha\left[\dfrac{GM}{r}\right]^{3/2}dt$

or $\qquad \dfrac{mr^{-1/2}}{2}dr = -\alpha(GM)^{1/2}dt$

Integrating above expression, we get

$$\dfrac{m}{2}\int_{\eta R}^{R} r^{-1/2}dr = -\alpha(GM)^{1/2}\int_{0}^{t}dt$$

$$m\left|\sqrt{r}\right|_{\eta R}^{R} = -\alpha\sqrt{GM}\, t$$

or $\qquad m[\sqrt{\eta R} - \sqrt{R}] = \alpha\sqrt{GM}\, t$

$\therefore \qquad\qquad t = \dfrac{m}{\alpha}\dfrac{[\sqrt{\eta R} - \sqrt{R}]}{\sqrt{GM}} \qquad \textbf{\textit{Ans.}}$

8. We know that $v = \sqrt{2gR}$

$\therefore \dfrac{v_p}{v} = \sqrt{\dfrac{g_p}{g} \times \dfrac{R_p}{R}} \qquad\qquad \text{...(i)}$

Given $\dfrac{g_p}{g_e} = \dfrac{\sqrt{6}}{11} \qquad\qquad \text{...(ii)}$

Also $\quad g = \dfrac{4}{3}\pi G\rho R \quad \therefore \dfrac{g_p}{g} = \dfrac{\rho_p}{\rho} \times \dfrac{R_p}{R}$

$\therefore \dfrac{\sqrt{6}}{11} = \dfrac{2}{3} \times \dfrac{R_p}{R} \left[\because \dfrac{\rho_p}{\rho} = \dfrac{2}{3}(given)\right]$

$\therefore \dfrac{R_p}{R} = \dfrac{3\sqrt{6}}{22} \qquad\qquad \text{...(iii)}$

From (i), (ii) & (iii) $\dfrac{v_p}{v} = \sqrt{\dfrac{\sqrt{6}}{11} \times \dfrac{3\sqrt{6}}{22}} = \sqrt{\dfrac{3 \times 6}{11 \times 22}} = \dfrac{3}{11}$

$\therefore v_p = \dfrac{3}{11} \times v = \dfrac{3}{11} \times 11\,\text{km/s} = \mathbf{3}\,\textbf{km/s}$

In Chapter Exercise -9.3

1.

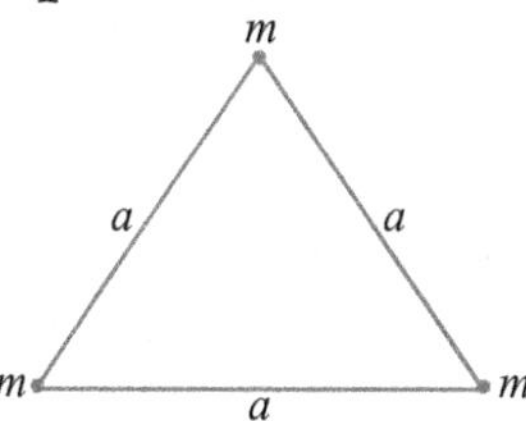

The work done,
$$W = U_f - U_i$$

where
$$U_i = -3 \times \frac{Gmm}{a} = -\frac{3Gm^2}{a}$$

and
$$U_f = -3 \times \frac{Gmm}{2a} = -\frac{3}{2}\frac{Gm^2}{a}$$

Thus
$$W = -\frac{3}{2}\frac{Gm^2}{a} - \left(-\frac{3Gm^2}{a}\right)$$

$$= \frac{3Gm^2}{2a} \qquad \textbf{\textit{Ans.}}$$

2. The velocity of projection of bullet w.r.t. earth,

$$v_A = \sqrt{v_0^2 + \left(\frac{v_0}{2}\right)^2}$$

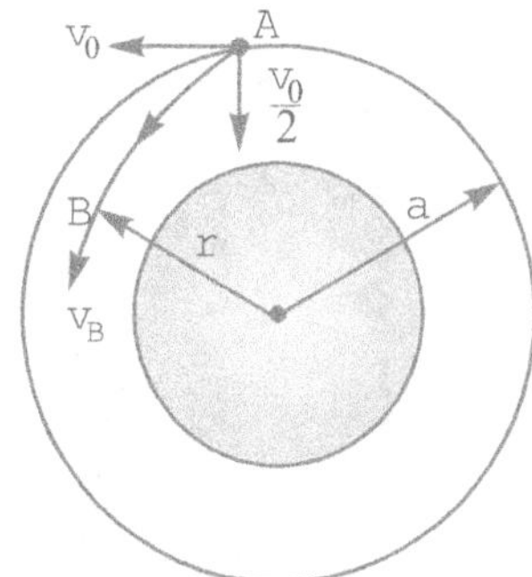

Here
$$v_0 = \sqrt{\frac{GM}{a}}$$

By conservation of angular momentum between A and B, we have
$$mv_0 a = mvr \qquad \dots (i)$$

From conservation of mechanical energy, we have
$$\frac{1}{2}mv_A^2 - \frac{GMm}{a} = \frac{1}{2}mv^2 - \frac{GMm}{r} \qquad \dots (ii)$$

Solving equations for r to get required result.

10. The energy of the satellite in its orbit
$$E_i = -\frac{GM_e M_s}{2R},$$
and close to earth surface
it is
$$E_f = -GM_e M_s / 2R_e.$$
If t is the required time, then
$$-Ct + \left[\frac{-GM_e M_s}{2R}\right] = \frac{-GM_e M_s}{2R_e}$$

$$\therefore \qquad t = \frac{GM_s M_e}{2C}\left[\frac{1}{R_e} - \frac{1}{R}\right]$$

11. The situation is shown in figure. If v_A is the velocity of the object at A, then at A

$$\frac{GMm}{a^2} = \frac{mv_A^2}{a}$$

$$\therefore \quad \frac{1}{2}mv_A^2 = \frac{GMm}{2a}$$

Potential energy at
$$A = -\frac{GMm}{a}$$

Thus total mechanical energy at A
$$= K + U = \frac{GMm}{2a} - \frac{GMm}{a} = -\frac{GMm}{2a}$$

By conservation of mechanical energy, we can write
Mechanical energy at any position = mechanical energy at A

$$\therefore \quad \frac{-GMm}{r} + \frac{1}{2}mv^2 = \frac{-GMm}{2a}$$

After simplifying, we get
$$v^2 = GM\left(\frac{2}{r} - \frac{1}{a}\right)$$

12. The centripetal force acting on each star of mass m
$$F = \left[\frac{GMm}{r^2} + \frac{Gmm}{(2r)^2}\right]$$

By Newton's second law, we have
$$m\omega^2 r = \frac{GMm}{r^2} + \frac{Gm^2}{(2r)^2}$$

$$\therefore \quad \omega = \sqrt{\frac{GM}{r^3} + \frac{Gm}{4r^3}}. \qquad \textbf{\textit{Ans.}}$$

1. **(b)** $\dfrac{d\vec{A}}{dt} = \dfrac{\vec{L}}{2m}$; $\dfrac{d\vec{A}}{dt}$ is constant, if $\vec{L}$ is constant.

2. **(a)** The speed of the planet is faster in region DAB in comparison to the region BCD.

3. **(a)** In elliptical orbit satellite has two forces : centripetal F_n and tangential force (F_t). For small mass satellite $F_t \ll F_n$ and so it always remains towards axis of rotation.

4. **(a)** Gravitational force does not depend on medium between the masses.

5. **(b)** $$F = G\frac{m(M-m)}{r^2}$$

For maximum value of F, $dF/dm = 0$, and so
$$m = M/2.$$

6. **(b)** $$F = \frac{Gm_1 m_2}{(2r)^2 h} = \frac{G(\rho\frac{4}{3}\pi r^3)(\rho\frac{4}{3}\pi r^3)}{(2r)^2}$$
$$= kr^4.$$

7. **(c)**

8. (a) $\vec{g}' = -\dfrac{g\vec{r}}{R}$ for $r \leq R$ and $g' = \dfrac{g}{(1 + r/R)^2}$ for $r \geq R$

    so option (a) is correct.

9. (b) $v_g = -\dfrac{GM}{R}$ for $r \leq R$ and $v_g = -\dfrac{GM}{r}$, for $r > R$, and

    so option (b) is correct.

10. (d) $g = \dfrac{GM}{R^2} = \dfrac{G\rho \dfrac{4}{3}\pi R^3}{R^2} = k\rho R$

    $\therefore \quad \dfrac{g_1}{g_2} = \dfrac{\rho_1 R_1}{\rho_2 R_2}.$

11. (a) $W = 72 = mg$

    At a height $h = R/2$, $g' = \dfrac{g}{\left(1 + \dfrac{R/2}{R}\right)^2} = \dfrac{4g}{9}$

    Thus $W' = mg' = \dfrac{4mg}{9}$

    $\therefore \quad W' = 72 \times \dfrac{4}{9} = 32$ N.

12. (c) $g' = \dfrac{g}{\left(1 + \dfrac{h}{R}\right)^2}$

    or $\dfrac{g}{4} = \dfrac{g}{\left(1 + \dfrac{h}{R}\right)^2} \quad \Rightarrow \quad h = R$

13. (d) $W_{AB} = m(V_B - V_A)$; But $V_A = V_B$ and so $W_{AB} = 0$.

14. (c) $F_{\min} = \dfrac{GMm}{r^2} - \dfrac{GM(2m)}{(2r)^2}$

    $\phantom{F_{\min}} = \dfrac{GMm}{2r^2}$

    and $F_{\max} = \dfrac{GMm}{r^2} + \dfrac{GM(2m)}{(2r)^2}$

    $\phantom{F_{\max}} = \dfrac{3}{2}\dfrac{GMm}{r^2}.$

    $\therefore \quad \dfrac{F_{\min}}{F_{\max}} = \dfrac{1}{3}.$

15. (c) The radiation emitted by sun exerts a radial outwards pressure.

16. (d) $2a = 1100 + 2 \times 6400 + 4100$

    $ = 18000$ km.

17. (b) $\Delta U = \dfrac{mgh}{1 + \dfrac{h}{R}} = \dfrac{mgR}{1 + R/R} = \dfrac{mgR}{2}$

18. (c) The force exerted by shell on any mass inside the shell will be zero.

19. (c) $\dfrac{Gm^2}{(2R)^2} = \dfrac{mv^2}{R} \quad \Rightarrow \quad v = \dfrac{1}{2}\sqrt{\dfrac{Gm}{R}}.$

20. (d) $F = m\omega^2 r = 6 \times 10^{24}(2 \times 10^{-7})^2 \times 1.5 \times 10^{11}$

    $ = 36 \times 10^{21}$ N.

21. (c) $K + U = 0 + 0$

    $K - \dfrac{GMm}{R} = 0$

    $\therefore \quad K = \dfrac{GM}{R^2}mR = mgR.$

22. (d) $\dfrac{Gm_e}{x^2} = \dfrac{Gm_m}{(D - x)^2}$

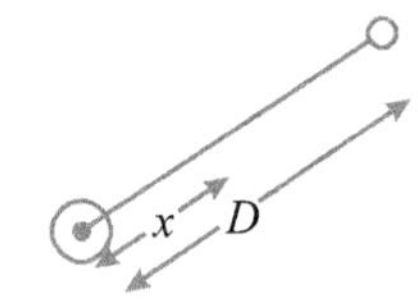

    or $\dfrac{G(81m)}{x^2} = \dfrac{m}{(D - x)^2}$

    $\therefore \quad x = \dfrac{9D}{10}.$

23. (b) $g' = g\left(1 - \dfrac{h}{R}\right)$

    or $\dfrac{g}{n} = g\left(1 - \dfrac{h}{R}\right)$

    $\therefore \quad h = R\left(\dfrac{n-1}{n}\right)$

24. (a) $V = -4\dfrac{GM}{r}$

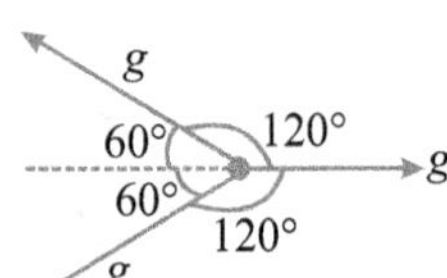

    $ = -4\dfrac{GM}{L/\sqrt{2}} = -\sqrt{32}\dfrac{GM}{L}.$

25. (a) If g be the gravitational field produced by each particle, then

    $g_x = g - 2g\cos 60° = 0$

    and $g_y = g\sin 60° - g\sin 60° = 0$

    $\therefore \quad g = \sqrt{g_x^2 + g_y^2} = 0.$

26. (c) $U = \left[\dfrac{-G \times 1 \times 1}{1}\right] \times 4 + \left[\dfrac{-G \times 1 \times 1}{\sqrt{2}}\right] \times 2$

    $ = -5.4\, G.$

27. (c) As $v_0 = \sqrt{\dfrac{GM}{r}}$, and so with decrease in M, v_0 also decreases.

28. (c) When spoon is dropped gently, its tangential speed is equal to the speed of spaceship, and so it revolves like a satellite.

29. (b) For $r = \infty$, E is positive.

    For $r < \infty$, E is negative.

30. (a) $\dfrac{T_1^2}{T_2^2} = \dfrac{r_1^3}{r_2^3} = \left(\dfrac{7R}{3.5R}\right)^3 = 8$

    $\therefore \qquad T_2 = \dfrac{T_1}{2\sqrt{2}} = \dfrac{24}{2\sqrt{2}} = 6\sqrt{2} \ h$

31. (b) $\dfrac{v_1}{v_2} = \sqrt{\dfrac{r_2}{r_1}} = \sqrt{\dfrac{R}{4R}} = \dfrac{1}{2}$

    $\therefore \qquad v_2 = 2v_1 = 2 \times 3v = 6v.$

32. (b) $\dfrac{GMm}{R} = \dfrac{mv^2}{R}$

    $\therefore \qquad v = \sqrt{GM} \ ; \ v \propto R^0.$

33. (c) $U = 2 \text{ (total energy)} = 2 E_0.$

34. (c) $v = \dfrac{\text{circumference}}{\text{time}} = \dfrac{2\pi R}{T}$ and $a = \dfrac{v^2}{R}.$

35. (b) $v_e = \sqrt{2gR} = 1.414\sqrt{gR} = 1.414 \, v_0.$

    So it 41.4% increase orbital speed to escape.

36. (d) $K = \dfrac{GMm}{2r}$; and $T^2 \propto r^3$

    $\therefore \qquad K \propto T^{-2/3}.$

37. (c) $E = \dfrac{1}{2}mv^2 \implies v = \sqrt{2E/m}$

    and $L = mvr = \dfrac{2mv^2}{2v} r = \dfrac{2Er}{\sqrt{2E/m}}$

    $\qquad = \sqrt{2Emr^2} \cdot$

38. (a) For escape the velocity needed $v = \sqrt{2}v_0$

    So maximum value of $\alpha = \sqrt{2}$

39. (b) $mv_1r_1 = mv_2r_2 \implies \dfrac{v_1}{v_2} = \dfrac{r_2}{r_1}$

40. (a) $K = \dfrac{1}{2}Mv^2.$

    Total energy $= -K = -\dfrac{1}{2}Mv^2$

41. (d) $\dfrac{T_1^2}{T_2^2} = \dfrac{r_1^3}{r_2^3} = \left(\dfrac{1}{4}\right)^3$

    $\therefore \qquad T_2 = 4^{3/2} T_1 = 8 \times 5 = 40 \text{ hr.}$

42. (a) $L = mvr = m\sqrt{\dfrac{GM}{R_0}} R_0$

    $\qquad = m\sqrt{GMR_0} \cdot$

43. (d) Escape speed does not depend on angle of projection.

44. (a) $v_e = \sqrt{\dfrac{2GM}{R}} = \sqrt{\dfrac{2G\rho \times \dfrac{4}{3}\pi R^3}{R}}$

    $\qquad = kR$

    $\therefore \qquad v_e' = 2v_e = 2 \times 11 = 22 \text{ km/s.}$

45. (b) $v_e = \sqrt{2gR}$

    $\therefore \qquad \dfrac{v_1}{v_2} = \sqrt{\dfrac{R_1}{R_2}} = \sqrt{\dfrac{R}{4R}},$

    or $\qquad v_2 = 2v_1 = 2v_e.$

46. (c) If light not to escape from the region (black hole),

    then $\qquad c \leq \sqrt{\dfrac{2Gm}{r}} \cdot$

EXERCISE 9.1 LEVEL -2

1. (c) $g = GMR^{-2}$

    $\therefore \qquad \dfrac{\Delta g}{g} \times 100 = -\dfrac{2\Delta R}{R} \times 100$

    $\qquad\qquad = -2 \, (-1\%) = 2\%.$

2. (b) $g' = g - \omega^2 R \cos^2 \lambda$

    $\therefore \qquad g - g_{30°} = \omega^2 R \cos^2 30° = \dfrac{3}{4}\omega^2 R.$

3. (a) $g_1 = g - \omega^2 R \cos^2 0 = g - \omega^2 R$

    $g_2 = g - \omega^2 R \cos^2 60°$

    $\qquad = g - \dfrac{\omega^2 R}{4}$

    $\dfrac{g_1}{g_2} = f = \dfrac{g - \omega^2 R}{g - \dfrac{\omega^2 R}{4}} \qquad \qquad \dots(i)$

    Also $g = \dfrac{GM}{R^2} = G\rho \dfrac{\left(\dfrac{4}{3}\pi R^3\right)}{R^2} \qquad \dots(ii)$

    On solving above equation, we get

$$\rho = \left(\frac{4-f}{1-f}\right)\frac{3\pi}{4GT^2}$$

4. (a) Mass of the removed sphere

$$M' = \frac{M}{\frac{4}{3}\pi R^3} \times \frac{4}{3}\pi\left(\frac{R}{2}\right)^2 = \frac{M}{8}$$

Thus $F = \dfrac{GMm}{d^2} - \dfrac{GM'm}{(d-R/2)^2}$

5. (b) $$E = \frac{\Delta V}{\Delta r} = \frac{4}{10} = 0.4 \text{ N/kg}.$$

6. (d) $$W_1 = W\left(1 - \frac{2\omega_e v}{g}\right),$$

when train moves along the rotation and

$$W_2 = W\left(1 + \frac{2\omega_e v}{g}\right),$$

when train moves opposite of rotation.

7. (c) Energy required $= E_f - E_i$

$$= -\frac{GMm}{2(3r)} - \left(-\frac{GMm}{2r}\right)$$

$$= \frac{GMm}{3r}.$$

8. (b) $$\frac{v_{\max}}{v_{\min}} = \frac{1+e}{1-e} = \left[\frac{1+0.0167}{1-0.0167}\right] = 1.033.$$

9. (a) $U = mV = kmr.$

Force, $F = -\dfrac{dU}{dr} = -km$

Now $\dfrac{mv^2}{r} = km$, $\therefore\ v \propto r^{1/2}$

$\therefore\ T = \dfrac{2\pi r}{v} = \dfrac{2\pi r}{cr^{1/2}} \Rightarrow T \propto r^{1/2}$

10. (a) $$K = \frac{1}{2}\mu v^2 = \frac{1}{2}\left[\frac{mM}{m+M}\right]v^2.$$

11. (b) $$g' = \frac{g}{\left(1+\dfrac{h}{R}\right)^2} = \frac{gR^2}{(R+h)^2} = \frac{gR^2}{(3R/2)^2} = \frac{4g}{9}$$

$$\therefore W = mg' = 200\times\frac{4g}{9} = 200\times\frac{4\times10}{9} = 889 \text{ N}.$$

12. (d) $$E = E_f - E_i$$

$$= -\frac{GMm}{2(3R)} - \frac{GMm}{2(2R)} = \frac{GMm}{6R}$$

13. (b) $$W = (V_\infty - V)\times m$$

$$= 0 - \left(-\frac{GM}{R}\right)\times m = \frac{GMm}{R}$$

After substituting the values, we get

$$W = 6.67\times10^{-10}\ J.$$

14. (c) $$-\frac{GM_e m}{10\,R_e} + \frac{1}{2}mv_i^2 = -\frac{GM_e m}{R_e} + \frac{1}{2}mv_f^2$$

$$\therefore\quad v_f^2 = v_i^2 + \frac{2GM_e}{R_e}\left(1 - \frac{1}{10}\right).$$

15. (c) $$\frac{1}{2}m(kv_e)^2 - \frac{GMm}{R} = 0 - \frac{GMm}{(R+h)},$$

where $v_e = \sqrt{\dfrac{2GM}{R}}$, after simplifying,

we get $h = \left[\dfrac{R}{1+k^2}\right]$

16. (b) $$\frac{-GMm}{\sqrt{2}\,R} + 0 = -\frac{GMm}{R} + \frac{1}{2}mv^2$$

or $v = \sqrt{\dfrac{2Gm}{R}\left(1 - \dfrac{1}{\sqrt{2}}\right)}.$

17. (c) $$\left(\frac{T'}{T}\right)^2 = \left(\frac{r'}{r}\right)^3 \text{ or } T'^2 = \frac{T^2}{8}$$

The time which planet will take to fall onto the sun

$$t = \frac{T'}{2}.$$

18. (c) $$\frac{1}{2}m(2v_e)^2 - \frac{GMm}{R} = \frac{1}{2}mv^2 + 0$$

or $\dfrac{1}{2}m(2v_e)^2 - \dfrac{1}{2}mv_e^2 = \dfrac{1}{2}mv^2$

$$\therefore\quad v = \sqrt{3}\,v_e.$$

19. (c) $$\frac{-G\,mm'}{r}\times3 + \frac{1}{2}m'v_e^2 = 0$$

or $\dfrac{-3Gm}{(\frac{a}{2}/\cos30°)} + \dfrac{1}{2}v_e^2 = 0$

$$v_e = \sqrt{\frac{6\sqrt{3}\,Gm}{a}}.$$

1. (b)

$$\begin{array}{cccc} \overset{o}{\bullet} & \overset{m}{\bullet} & \overset{m}{\bullet} & \overset{m}{\bullet} \\ x=0 & x=1 & x=2 & x=4 \end{array}$$

$$F_0 = \frac{Gm^2}{1^2} + \frac{Gm^2}{2^2} + \frac{Gm^2}{4^2} + \dots$$

$$F_0 = Gm^2\left[\frac{1}{1^2} + \frac{1}{2^2} + \frac{1}{4^2} + \dots\right]$$

It is a G.P. with common ratio 1/4.

$$\therefore\quad F_0 = Gm^2\left[\frac{1}{1-1/4}\right] \Rightarrow F_0 = \frac{4Gm^2}{3}$$

2. (a,d) Same force acts on both masses.

Hence $a \propto \dfrac{1}{m}$ $(F = ma)$

In absence of external force (remember mutual gravitational force is an internal force for the system) total energy remains constant.

3. (a,c) $M = \dfrac{4}{3}\pi R^3 \rho$ or $R = \left(\dfrac{3M}{4\pi\rho}\right)^{1/3}$

(i) $g = \dfrac{GM}{R^2} = \dfrac{GM}{(3M/4\pi\rho)^{3/2}} = GM\left(\dfrac{4\pi\rho}{3M}\right)^{2/3}$

i.e. $g \propto \rho^{2/3}$ $\therefore \dfrac{g_1}{g_2} = \left(\dfrac{\rho_1}{\rho_2}\right)^{2/3} = \left(\dfrac{1}{8}\right)^{2/3} = \dfrac{1}{4}$

(ii) $v_e = \sqrt{\dfrac{2GM}{R}} = \dfrac{(2GM)^{1/2}}{(3M/4\pi\rho)^{1/6}}$

or $\dfrac{v_1}{v_2} = \left(\dfrac{\rho_1}{\rho_2}\right)^{1/6} = \left(\dfrac{1}{8}\right)^{1/6} = \dfrac{1}{\sqrt{2}}$

4. (b,d) The gravitational field inside shell, $\vec{E}_g = 0$. So if $\vec{E}_1$ and $\vec{E}_2$ are the gravitation field strength at P and Q, then

$\vec{E}_1 + \vec{E}_2 = 0$.

5. (b,d) Satellite experiences force due to the planet. Also satellite is freely moving (falling) object. An object experiences weightlessness inside satellite, because N = 0.

6. (a,c,d) Explained in theory.

7. (a,d) $r_2 = \dfrac{2mr}{m + 2m} = \dfrac{2r}{3}$

$T_2^2 = \dfrac{4\pi^2 r_2^3}{GM}$

$T_2^2 = \dfrac{32\pi^2 r^3}{27GM}$

$T_2 \propto r^{3/2}$; $T_2 \propto m^{-1/2}$

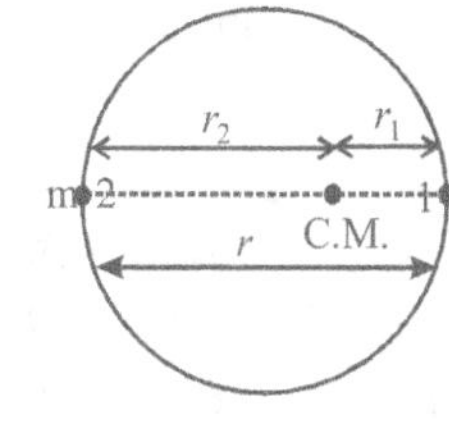

8. (b,c) Net force towards centre of earth $= mg' = \dfrac{mgx}{R}$

Normal force $N = mg'\sin\theta$

Thus pressing force $N = \dfrac{mgx}{R}\dfrac{R}{2x}$

$N = \dfrac{mg}{2}$ constant and independent of x.

Tangential force $F = ma = mg'\cos\theta$

$Q = g'\cos\theta = \dfrac{gx}{R}\dfrac{\sqrt{\dfrac{R^2}{4} - x^2}}{x}$

$a = \dfrac{gx}{R}\sqrt{R^2 - 4x^2}$

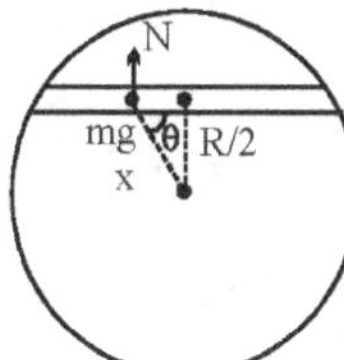

Curve is parabolic and at $x = \dfrac{R}{2}, a = 0$.

9. (a, d) Time period in both the cases comes out to be

$T_1 = T_2 = 2\pi\sqrt{\dfrac{R^2}{GM}} = 84.6\,\text{min}$

But $v_1 > v_2$. Because the difference in potential energy between the extreme position and mean position will be more in the first case.

10. (a, d) At centre, $V = \dfrac{-1.5\,GM}{R}$

and $E = 0$

11. (a,b) For $r_1 < R$, $F = \dfrac{GM}{R^3}r$, $\therefore \dfrac{F_1}{F_2} = \dfrac{r_1}{r_2}$

For $r_1 \geq R$, $F = \dfrac{GM}{r^2}, \therefore \dfrac{F_1}{F_2} = \dfrac{r_2^2}{r_1^2}$.

12. (a,b,c,d) Initially potential and kinetic both energies are zero and from conservation of mechanical energy total enegy of the two objects is zero.

Further, decrease in gravitational potential energy = increase in kinetic energy

or $\dfrac{G(m)(4m)}{r} = \dfrac{1}{2}\mu v_r^2$ ...(1)

Here, μ = reduced mass $= \dfrac{(m)(4m)}{m + 4m} = \dfrac{4m}{5}$

Substituting in eq. (1), we get

v_r = relative velocity of approach

$= \sqrt{\dfrac{10\,Gm}{r}}$

From eq. (1) total kinetic energy

$= \dfrac{G(m)(4m)}{r} = \dfrac{4\,Gm^2}{r}$

Net torque of two equal and opposite forces acting on two objects is zero. Therefore, angular momentum will remain conserved. Initially both the objects were stationary i.e., angular momentum about any point was zero. Hence, angular momentum of both the particles about any point will be zero at all instants.

13. (a,c,d) See example

14. (a, c) From fig.

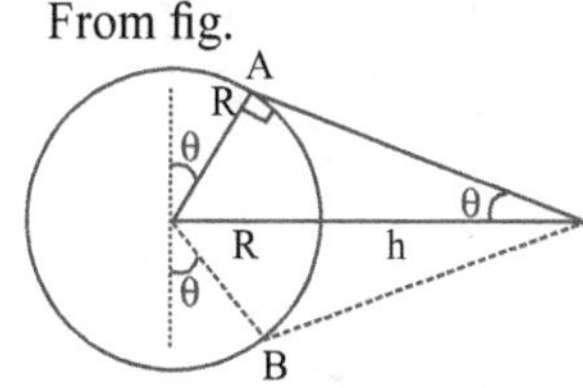

Min. colatitude, $\sin\theta = \dfrac{R}{R + h}$

Curved area AB on earth $= 2\pi R^2(1 - \sin\theta)$

Area on earth escaped from satellite
$= 4\pi R^2 - 2\pi R^2(1 - \sin\theta) = 2\pi R^2(1 + \sin\theta)$

EXERCISE 9.3

1. (a) Statement–2 is the explanation of statement–1.
2. (b) Space rocket are usually launched from west to east to take the advantage of rotation of earth.
   Also $g' = g - \omega^2 R \cos^2 \lambda$, at equator $\lambda = 0$, and so $\cos \lambda = 1$, and g' is least.
3. (c) Gravitational force on the person in satellite is not zero, but normal reaction of the satellite on the person is zero.
4. (d) At the centre of the earth, weight is zero but mass cannot be and never zero.
5. (a) To counter balance the effect of gravity.
6. (d) The tidal effect is due to the gravitation effect of moon and earth both. $g' = \dfrac{g}{\left(1+\dfrac{h}{R}\right)^2}$, for $h = 0$, $g' = g$.

7. (a) An orbit always above Delhi cannot provide required centripetal force.
8. (a) $K = -E = -\dfrac{U}{2}$.
9. (c) Escape velocity for Jupiter is greater than escape velocity for earth.
10. (a) Free fall body experiences weightlessness.
11. (a) $\phi = EA = \dfrac{GM}{r^2} \times 4\pi r^2 = 4\pi GM$.

EXERCISE 9.4

Passage for (Questions 1 & 2)

We have $T^2 \propto r^3$

$\therefore \quad \left(\dfrac{T_1}{T_2}\right)^2 = \left(\dfrac{R_1}{R_2}\right)^3$

or $\left(\dfrac{1}{8}\right)^2 = \left(\dfrac{R_1}{R_2}\right)^3$

$\Rightarrow R_2 = 4R_1 = 4 \times 10^4$ km.

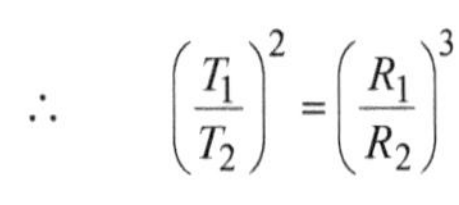
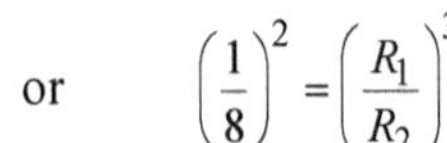

Let v_1 and v_2 be the linear speeds of S_1 and S_2 with respect to the planet. Then

$$v_1 = \frac{2\pi R_1}{T_1} = 2\pi \times 10^4 \, km / h$$

and $v_2 = \dfrac{2\pi R_2}{T_2} = \pi \times 10^4$ km/h.

1. (b) At the closest separation, they are moving in the same direction. Therefore the speed of S_2 with respect to S_1 is
   $|v_2 - v_1| = \pi \times 10^4$ km /h.
   Ans.
2. (d) As seen from S_1 the satellite S_2 is at a distance $r = R_2 - R_1 = 3 \times 10^4$ km. At the closest separation
   $$\omega = \frac{|v_2 - v_1|}{R_2 - R_1} = \frac{\pi \times 10^4}{3 \times 10^4}$$
   $$= \frac{\pi}{3} \text{rad} / h. \qquad\qquad \textbf{Ans.}$$

Passage for (Questions 3 to 5)

3. (b) When A is given its first impulse at that moment B is ahead of A angularly.

4. (c) $U = -\dfrac{GMm}{r}$ and $K.E. = \dfrac{GMm}{2r}$
   for same m, if $r_1 > r_2$, $KE_1 < KE_2$ and $U_1 > U_2$

Also, angular momentum of A before reaching the position 2 (during elliptical path) was less than that of B, Since, some impulse is needed (at position 2) for A in direction of its motion to equal its speed and angular momentum equal to that of B.

5. (c) In the continuation with same comprehension
   $$r = \frac{(r_2 + r_2 / 3)}{2} = 2r_2 / 3$$

   Let time period of A in elliptical path is T_0 .
   $$\therefore \left(\frac{T_0}{T}\right)^2 = \left(\frac{r}{r_2}\right)^3 \quad \therefore T_0 = \frac{T(2\sqrt{2})}{3\sqrt{3}}$$

   $\therefore$ Time taken by A to move from 1 to 2,
   $$t = T_0 / 2 = \frac{T\sqrt{2}}{3\sqrt{3}}$$

6. A.$\rightarrow$ (p) ; B. $\rightarrow$ (q), (r) ; C. $\rightarrow$ (p), (s); D. $\rightarrow$(r)
7. A. $\rightarrow$ (q) ; B. $\rightarrow$ (t) ; C. $\rightarrow$ (r) ; D. $\rightarrow$ (s)
   Inside a shell $V = -\dfrac{GM}{R}$ = constant and $E = 0$

   Outside the shell, $V = -\dfrac{GM}{r}$ and $E = \dfrac{GM}{r^2}$

   As r increases, V increases and E decreases.
8. A. $\rightarrow$ (p) ; B. $\rightarrow$ (s) ; C. $\rightarrow$ (r) ; D. $\rightarrow$ (q)
   Angular momentum of particle
   $$= m \, (v_0 + v) \, a = \sqrt{\frac{5}{4}} m v_0 a \,..... \, v_0 = \sqrt{\frac{GM_e}{a}}$$

   Total energy of particle
   $$= \frac{1}{2} m(v_0 + v)^2 - \frac{GM_e m}{a} = \frac{1}{2} \times \frac{5}{4} m v_0^2 - \frac{GM_e m}{a}$$
   $$= \frac{5}{8}\frac{GM_e m}{a} - \frac{GM_e m}{a} = -\frac{3GM_e m}{8a}$$

   At any distance 'r' T.E. $= \dfrac{1}{2} m u^2 - \dfrac{GM_e m}{r}$

   But angular momentum is conserved,

$$mur = m\sqrt{\frac{5GM_e}{4a}} \cdot a \Rightarrow u = \sqrt{\frac{5}{4}\frac{GM_e a}{r^2}}$$

T.E. at any distance 'r' $= \dfrac{1}{2}m\dfrac{5}{4}\dfrac{GM_e a}{r^2} - \dfrac{GM_e m}{r}$

But through conservation of energy, total energy

$$= \frac{1}{2}m\frac{5}{4}\frac{GM_e a}{r^2} - \frac{GM_e m}{r} = -\frac{3GM_e m}{8a}$$

On solving, $3r^2 - 8ar + 5a^2 = 0 \Rightarrow (r-a)(3r-5a) = 0$

$$\Rightarrow r = a, \ r = 5a/3$$

minimum distance $= a$, maximum distance $= 5a/3$

9. **A.** $\to$ **(p)** ; **B.** $\to$ **(q)** ; **C.** $\to$ **(r)** ; **D.** $\to$ **(s)**

EXERCISE 9.5

1. **(b)** $\dfrac{mv^2}{R} = \dfrac{K}{R^{5/2}}$,

$$\therefore \qquad v = CR^{-3/4}$$

$$T = \frac{2\pi R}{v} = \frac{2\pi R}{CR^{-3/4}}$$

$$\therefore \qquad T^2 \propto R^{7/2}.$$

2. **(b)** $g_{height} \approx g\left(1-\dfrac{2h}{R}\right)$ and $g_{depth} = g\left(1-\dfrac{x}{R}\right)$

Thus $2h = x.$

3. **(b)** Gravitational flux through a closed surface is given by

$$\int \vec{E_g}\, \vec{dS} = -4\pi GM$$

where, $M =$ mass enclosed in the closed surface

This relationship is valid when $|E_g| \propto \dfrac{1}{r^2}$.

4. **(c)** Let the gravitational field at P, distant x from mass m, be zero.

$$\therefore \ \frac{Gm}{x^2} = \frac{4Gm}{(r-x)^2} \Rightarrow \frac{1}{x} = \frac{2}{r-x}$$

$$\therefore \qquad r - x = 2x$$

$$x = \frac{r}{3}$$

Gravitational potential at P, $V = -\dfrac{Gm}{\dfrac{r}{3}} - \dfrac{4Gm}{\dfrac{2r}{3}} = -\dfrac{9Gm}{r}$

5. **(a)** Here, centripetal force will be given by the gravitational force between the two particles.

$$\frac{Gm^2}{(2R)^2} = m\omega^2 R$$

$$\Rightarrow \frac{Gm}{4R^3} = \omega^2$$

$$\Rightarrow \omega = \sqrt{\frac{Gm}{4R^3}}$$

If the velocity of the two particles with respect to the centre of gravity is v then $v = \omega R$

$$v = \sqrt{\frac{Gm}{4R^3}} \times R = \sqrt{\frac{Gm}{4R}}$$

6. **(d)** The work done to launch the space ship

$$W = -\int_R^\infty \vec{F}.\vec{dr} = -\int_R^\infty \frac{GMm}{r^2}dr$$

$$W = +\frac{GMm}{R} \qquad \dots \text{(i)}$$

The force of attraction of the earth on the space ship, when it was on the earth's surface

$$F = \frac{GMm}{R^2}$$

$$\Rightarrow mg = \frac{GMm}{R^2} \Rightarrow g = \frac{GM}{R^2} \qquad \dots \text{(ii)}$$

The required energy for this work is given by

$$= U - W = mgR^2$$

$$= 1000 \times 10 \times 6400 \times 10^3$$

$$= 6.4 \times 10^{10} \text{ Joules}$$

7. **(a)** As we know,

Gravitational potential energy $= \dfrac{-GMm}{r}$

and orbital velocity, $v_0 = \sqrt{GM/R+h}$

$$E_f = \frac{1}{2}mv_0^2 - \frac{GMm}{3R} = \frac{1}{2}m\frac{GM}{3R} - \frac{GMm}{3R}$$

$$= \frac{GMm}{3R}\left(\frac{1}{2}-1\right) = \frac{-GMm}{6R}$$

$$E_i = \frac{-GMm}{R} + K$$

$$E_i = E_f$$

Therefore minimum required energy, $K = \dfrac{5GMm}{6R}$

8. **(a)** $V_{required} = V_M - V_{M/8}$

$$= -\frac{GM}{2R^3}\left[3R^2 - \frac{R^2}{4}\right] + \frac{GM/8}{2(R/2)^3}[3(R/2)^2]$$

$$= \frac{11GM}{8R} + \frac{3GM}{8R} = \frac{GM}{R}$$

9.   (c)   The time period of nearest satellite is 84.6 minute, and so for spy satellite, it should be little higher than this, it may be 2 h

10.   (a) $\dfrac{T_A^2}{T_B^2} = \dfrac{r_A^3}{r_B^3} \Rightarrow \dfrac{T_A}{T_B} = \left(\dfrac{r_A}{r_B}\right)^{3/2}$.

11.   (c)   This is a case of a sphere of uniform mass distribution.

For $r \ge R$, $v \propto \dfrac{1}{\sqrt{r}}$

For $r < R$

When the test mass m is inside the spherically symmetric gravitational system at a distance r from its centre, it will effectively get attracted towards the centre by the mass inside the dotted sphere .

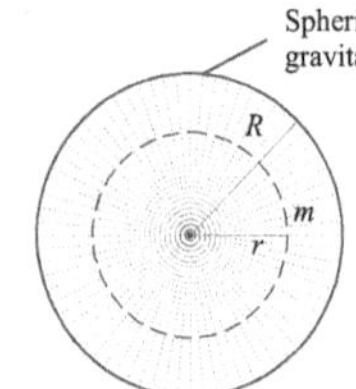

$$\frac{G\left(\rho_0 \times \frac{4}{3}\pi r^3\right) \times m}{r^2} = \frac{mv^2}{r}$$

$\Rightarrow \qquad v \propto r \qquad\qquad$ ...(ii)

equation (i) and (ii) are graphically represented by graph (c).

$\Rightarrow \qquad v \propto r$

12.   (a)   Let us consider a circular elemental area of radius x and thickness dx. The area of the shaded portion = $2\pi x dx$.

Let dm be the mass of the shaded portion.

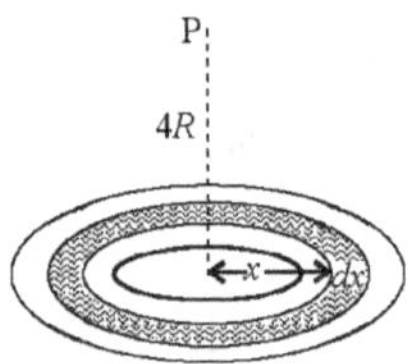

$\therefore \quad \dfrac{\text{Mass}}{\text{area}} = \dfrac{M}{\pi\left(4R^2\right) - \pi\left(3R^2\right)} = \dfrac{dm}{2\pi x dx}$

$\therefore \quad dm = \dfrac{2M}{7R^2} x dx$

The gravitational potential of the mass dm at P is

$$dV = \frac{-G\,dm}{\sqrt{\left(4R\right)^2 + x^2}} = -\frac{G}{\sqrt{16R^2 + x^2}} \times \frac{2M}{7R^2} x dx$$

$$= \frac{-2GM}{7R^2}\frac{x dx}{\sqrt{16R^2 + x^2}} \qquad\qquad (1)$$

Suppose $16R^2 + x^2 = t^2$

$\Rightarrow 2x dx = 2t dt$

$\Rightarrow x dx = t dt$

Also for $x = 3R,\ t = 5R$

and for $x = 4R,\ t = 4\sqrt{2}R$

On integrating equation (1), taking the above limits, we get

$$V = -\int_{5R}^{4\sqrt{2}R} \frac{2GM}{7R^2}\,dt = \frac{-2GM}{7R^2}[t]_{5R}^{4\sqrt{2}R}$$

$$= \frac{-2GM}{7R^2}\left[4\sqrt{2}R - 5R\right] \quad = V = \frac{-2GM}{7R}\left(4\sqrt{2} - 5\right)$$

Now $\dfrac{W_{P\infty}}{1} = V_\infty - V_P = -V_P \qquad \left[\because\ V_\infty = 0\right]$

$\therefore \quad W_{P\infty} = \dfrac{2GM}{7R}\left(4\sqrt{2} - 5\right)$

13.   (b) V is the orbital velocity. If V_C is the escape velocity then $V_e = \sqrt{2}\,V$. The kinetic energy at the time of ejection

$$KE = \frac{1}{2}mV_e^2 = \frac{1}{2}m(\sqrt{2}\,V)^2 = mV^2$$

14.   (b) $\dfrac{1}{2}mv^2 = 2\left[\dfrac{GMm}{L}\right] \Rightarrow v = 2\sqrt{\dfrac{GM}{L}}$

The potential energy is a combined property of the three mass system. The kinetic energy of mass m is only its energy which decreases as it moves.